Market Cultures

Market Cultures

Society and Morality in the New Asian Capitalisms

Robert W. Hefner
Boston University

Westview Press
A Member of Perseus Books, L.L.C.

022 977 030

Copyright © 1998 by Westview Press, A Member of Perseus Books, L.L.C.

Published in 1998 in the United States of America by Westview Press, 5500 Central Avenue, Boulder, Colorado 80301-2877, and in the United Kingdom by Westview Press, 12 Hid's Copse Road, Cumnor Hill, Oxford OX2 9JJ

Library of Congress Cataloging-in-Publication Data
Market cultures : society and morality in the new Asian capitalisms /
    Robert W. Hefner.
        p.   cm.
    Includes bibliographical references and index.
    ISBN 0-8133-3359-8 (hardcover). — ISBN 0-8133-3360-1 (pbk.)
        1. East Asia—Moral conditions.   2. East Asia—Social conditions.
    3. East Asia—Economic conditions.   4. Capitalism—Moral and ethical
    aspects—East Asia.   5. Economic anthropology—East Asia.
    I. Hefner, Robert W., 1952–
    HN720.5.Z9M66   1998
    306'.095—dc21   97-36705
                                                                                                          CIP

The paper used in this publication meets the requirements of the American National Standard for Permanence of Paper for Printed Library Materials Z39.48-1984.

10   9   8   7   6   5   4   3   2

Contents

Acknowledgments

This book is the product of a dialogue that began with a conference at the Fairbanks Center for East Asian Research at Harvard University in October 1994 and then continued in meetings and correspondence for another two years. The 1994 conference was sponsored by the Joint Committees on Southeast Asia and China of the Social Science Research Council (SSRC) and assembled anthropologists, sociologists, political scientists, and historians with firsthand knowledge of markets and society among Chinese and Southeast Asians. I wish to express my gratitude to the SSRC for its support of the initial conference. My co-organizer for the conference was Dr. Hue Tam Ho Tai of the Fairbanks Center and the Department of History at Harvard University. Neither the conference nor this book could have taken place without the tireless organization, insight, and warm collegiality of Dr. Tai.

I also wish to thank Peter Berger at the Institute for the Study of Economic Culture (ISEC), who provided intellectual and logistical support for my participation in this project, and Robert Weller, also at ISEC, for his insightful comments on the volume as a whole. Toby Volkman, now at the Ford Foundation, was the director for the Southeast Asia Program at SSRC and, as always, a wonderfully considerate counselor. My thanks also go to Ruth McVey, formerly of the University of London; Anthony Reid of the Australian National University; and Stanley Tambiah, of Harvard University, all of whom served as informative discussants. Finally, I also want to thank Carol Jones at Westview Press, who spirited this volume along with speed, consideration, and skill.

Robert W. Hefner

Introduction

Society and Morality in
the New Asian Capitalisms

ROBERT W. HEFNER

> But after so many failed prophecies, is it not in the interest of so-
> cial science to embrace complexity, be it at some sacrifice to pre-
> dictive power?
> —**Albert Hirschman (1986:139)**

From an economic historical perspective, the fin de siècle through which we
are now passing is the most remarkable of times. Industrial growth and living
standards once restricted to a handful of Western countries—and regarded by
not a few Westerners as realizable *only* within the framework of Occidental
civilization—have taken hold in numerous non-Western settings. Nowhere is
this development more striking than in the industrializing countries of East
and Southeast Asia. For the better part of twenty years in Southeast Asia and
thirty in East Asia (outside Japan), economies throughout this region have expanded at a rate of 5 to 8 percent per annum; over much the same period manufacturing has grown at two to three times this pace. For a while, some observers dismissed this expansion as a form of dependent development or as
"ersatz" capitalism. In these critics' eyes, the ranks of real capitalist powers
were limited to the industrial West and its honorary exception to the rule,
Japan. Today, however, such a narrow view of modern capitalist growth no
longer seems tenable. Driven at first by export-oriented manufactures, the
scale of growth has now led to the creation of substantial domestic markets
with the heightened standards of living, restless middle classes, labor disputes,
and commercialized culture they inevitably imply. Barring some unexpected
catastrophe, it now seems clear that the ascent of East and Southeast Asia will
figure as one of the defining features of the twenty-first century.

Caught as we are in the midst of this great transformation, we sometimes
attribute to it an inevitability that obscures its complexity and human drama.

1

Unfortunately, several of the intellectual traditions through which we think about economic and cultural change only reinforce this tendency. For example, we sometimes hear that Asia's ascent is first and foremost a demonstration of the wondrous power of the market. Clear the economic field of political obstacles, "get prices right," and the market does what it always does best, sustaining the miracle of modern growth. From this more or less neoclassical economic perspective, the emergence of industrial capitalism in East and Southeast Asia is nothing mysterious but a replica, with a little local color, of something earlier accomplished in the West and little influenced by variations of time or place.

There is little formally wrong with this first kind of account. Moreover, some of the policy issues to which its more sophisticated exponents direct our attention—such as money supply, currency exchange rates, and the costs of inefficient regulation—*do* figure among the requisite terms for understanding the new Asian capitalisms. If these are part of the story, however, they are only one part. As numerous case studies have demonstrated (Haggard and Kaufman 1992; MacIntyre and Jayasuriya 1992; MacIntyre 1994), to say that growth occurs because the market can "get prices right" still does not explain why some societies easily achieve this state of affairs and others fail miserably. Similarly, though the narrative of market magic pretends to be free of social or cultural variables, a number of its key concepts—including the ideas of the "firm" and economic "rationality"—in fact sneak in a good deal of unaccounted and ungeneralizable social baggage. How do firms work? Are they really everywhere the same? What is their internal structure and how are they related to external business networks? Most basic of all, why do people in some societies find it easy to accept the cultural logic of capitalism, whereas others find it morally repugnant? If we are really serious about understanding capitalism and its consequences, we have to open our analysis to such troublingly empirical questions and develop a more culturally and sociologically realistic understanding of market actors and action.

There is, of course, a second, equally familiar narrative on the spread of modern capitalism to Asia, one loosely associated with orthodox variants of Marxism and dependency theory. Though it too comes in several guises, the gist of this story is that Asia's industrialization is but a new chapter in the ongoing saga of a world-conquering and *unitary* capitalism. With its emphasis on labor discipline, capital accumulation, and the extraction of "surplus value" by politically empowered elites, this explanation aims to provide a richer sense of capitalism's sociopolitical reality. To its credit, this approach emphasizes that the construction of markets and industry is not a sui generis process flowing effortlessly from self-sustaining market mechanisms but one deeply shaped by the interests and capacities of states and societal actors. While directing our gaze to important aspects of the capitalist environment, however, this account turns us away from others. For example, whereas it reveals much about elite struggles over state economic policies, this kind of analysis usually has less to say about the nuts and bolts of real business enterprise. "Capital" is often described as if it had an intelligence or agency of its own. In real life, however, investment and enterprise do not work so effortlessly. Like labor, enterprise is deeply social and cultural. It requires a sophisticated assessment of social opportunities and the effective coordination of a complex and invariably truculent array of human and material resources. As with the neoclassical model of economic change, the capitalist-penetration narrative places economic life at too far remove from the social detail and moral poignancy of real economic processes.

Constituting Economy and Culture

The contributors to this volume attempt to analyze market processes in relation to their cultural meanings and human organization. They are especially concerned with two issues. The first is the degree to which there exist moral and organizational precedents for *or against* modern capitalist enterprise in East and Southeast Asia. This effort to examine the relative compatibility of local cultures with modern capitalism is based on the conviction that in their rush to celebrate East and Southeast Asia's achievements, many scholars have overlooked the often uneven nature of popular participation in market growth and the deep ethical arguments it has provoked. In line with this first concern, the authors also seek to examine the relation of such precedents to broader divisions in society, including those based on religion, ethnicity, gender, and class.

This latter focus is related to a broader concern held by a number of contributors to this volume and concerns recent "culturalist" commentaries on Asian politics and economy. Many of these commentaries have been based on simplistic portrayals of Asian culture and, more generally, on a theoretical understanding of culture unfamiliar with recent refinements of the concept in the fields of anthropology and cultural psychology. Though they come from a variety of disciplines and intellectual backgrounds, the contributors to this volume were encouraged to draw on a concept of culture that acknowledges developments in these latter fields. They were asked to think of culture in pluralistic and contingent terms, examining its history and social genesis, its dependency on different social carriers, and its interaction with other forces in Asia's ongoing transformation.

Inasmuch as the authors engage the concept of culture in this manner, they do so in a way that differs significantly from the last community of economic researchers to take the culture concept seriously, that is, the modernization theorists of the 1950s and 1960s. Modernization theory tended to portray culture as a homogeneous thing, equally accessible to everyone and exhaustively determinant of its bearers' worldview and behavior. Though deviants were acknowledged, most people were assumed to share the same modal culture, internalized in a more or less finished fashion from the society around them. Recently this unitary view of culture has been given a new lease on life in writings emphasizing the importance of "civilization" in international conflict (see, e.g., Huntington 1993). These accounts attribute shared passions and interests not merely to members of the same local community but to hundreds of millions of people living across vast expanses of the modern world. Such sweeping generalizations have given the concept of culture a bad name and, not surprisingly, have only confirmed the impressions of mainstream economic researchers that the notion is of little use to them.

Rather than speaking of a uniform Chinese, Malay, or Vietnamese culture, the authors in this book were invited to see culture as heterogeneous and reflect on the way that heterogeneity interacts with political and ethical divides in the society as a whole. Our model of culture is thus a pluralized or "distributional" one. It assumes that culture is not "the undivided property of the whole society" (Bourdieu 1977:73) but is instead subject to contestation and divergent interpretation. As a result, rather than being homogeneous, patterns of cultural meaning tend to vary across society in interesting ways (see Bloch 1989; Lambek 1993; Schwartz 1978).

Just as it has highlighted variation in culture's "lateral" distribution, recent writing in cultural theory has also complicated our understanding of culture's "vertical" penetration into the hearts and minds of social actors. A generation ago, anthropological enthusiasts of the culture concept often compared culture to a computer program or described it as a "template" exhaustively determinant of all levels of human experience.[1] However, recent research in cultural psychology and psychocultural anthropology has invited us to see human subjectivity as constituted by a number of dialectical influences rather than a single, all-powerful cultural "program." Rather than culture writ small, our subjectivity is now seen as constituted by the *interaction* of cultural symbolism, individual biography, biological dispositions, embodied social habits, and deliberative thought. In this revised view, culture is not a finished social fact "internalized" by passive cultural subjects. As it is assimilated by individuals, cultural knowledge is accommodated to an already complex world of emotion, cognition, and previously assimilated social knowledge. Subjectivized in this manner, cultural knowledge acquires a cognitive and affective dynamic more complex than the objectified symbols and meanings of the public world (Kleinman 1988; Obeyesekere 1981:18; Sperber 1975:x). Public culture, therefore, is not the same thing as individual subjectivity and is not the only thing that influences a person's interests, judgment, or dispositions (Hefner 1985:19; Sperber 1996). Even when they come from a similar social background, members of the same society can engage and apply their tradition in varied and even opposing ways.

This pluralized understanding of culture requires some changes in the way we understand cultural tradition in East and Southeast Asia. Rather than speaking of a unitary Confucian or neo-Confucian culture, for example, we can recognize that Chinese tradition has often been interpreted quite differently by, among others, men and women, traders and literati, the wealthy and the poor. Similarly, rather than assuming that, say, Minangkabau Malays in Sumatra responded to nineteenth-century colonial capitalism in an identical manner, we should not be surprised to learn that men's responses differed from women's for reasons related to men's peculiar position in Minangkabau's matrilineal social structure (see Michael Peletz's chapter in this volume).

The problems raised by the chapters in this book require a second adjustment in our concept of culture. Even though highlighting cultural dimensions of economic life, the authors do not assume that culture is invariably more influential than politics or economics in shaping modern market development. Indeed, however varied their views on markets and culture (readers will note different emphases across the chapters), the contributors to this book agree in rejecting "culturalist" explanations that attribute determinative influence to culture and none to institutions, material constraints, or individual creativity. Not all encompassing, our concept of culture is intended to be an interactively "constitutional" one (see Giddens 1984; Hefner 1990; Kleinman 1988). Such an approach assumes that rather than being a sphere apart from economics, politics, and society, culture is a meaning-making medium that interacts with other forces to influence all social spheres, including politics and economics.

From this perspective, then, the culture concept invoked in these chapters is a rather trimmed-down fellow by comparison with the paunchy versions common in some schools of contemporary cultural studies. As such, it should be clear that the goal of this book is not to raise the culturalist banner against the crass infidels of politics or economics. On the contrary, the assumption shared by all of the contributors to this book is that culture and social relations are *intrinsic* to politics and the economy, not free-standing social spheres. Neither a superstructure apart from politics and economics nor a "determinant in the last instance" more decisive than the rest, culture acquires its importance by interacting with other social forces in human action and institutions. As such, it should be clear to readers of this book that these authors aspire to build on, rather than deny, the efforts of scholars in other disciplinary traditions concerned with the nature of markets, politics, and identity in our era.

A Dialogue Renewed

A final goal of this volume is to bring economic issues back into more vigorous dialogue with cultural research in East and Southeast Asia. A generation ago, this kind of interdisciplinary concern inspired lively collaboration between sociocultural researchers and economists. In 1963, for example, no one thought it curious that an up-and-coming cultural anthropologist by the name of Clifford Geertz invoked the work of a leading economic theorist, W.W. Rostow and appealed for "a reconciliation of the economist's and the anthropologist's way of looking at development" (Geertz 1963:6). Shortly thereafter, however, the modernization theory that was to have served as the basis of this joint exercise fell into disrepute. The decline occurred, it must be said, for what were largely good reasons. With its emphasis on market development and liberal democracy, modernization theory had come to be seen as closely linked to U.S. foreign policy interests. A bit more broadly but no less significantly, the approach had also been associated with the developmental optimism of political elites around the world in the early post–World War II era. As the Vietnam War and other conflicts caused fissures in American public opinion and as the developing world was shaken by far-reaching political upheavals, the "orthodox consensus" (Giddens 1984:xv) on which such developmental models had been premised collapsed. Meanwhile, researchers in the human sciences discovered that there were analytic traditions other than modernization theory and structural functionalism through which one might begin to understand the nature of the modern world.

However much modernization theory may have deserved its fate, one lamentable consequence of its decline was that the hoped for collaboration between economists and cultural researchers fell by the wayside. This development was reinforced by trends in the discipline of economics itself. Despite the best efforts of interpretive economists, Austrian marginalists, institutionalists, political economists, and others marginal to the mainstream tradition,[2] the 1970s and 1980s saw a steady decline in mainstream economists' interest in middle-range empirical research, especially that which appealed to the "exogenous variables" of culture, politics, and social organization. Though most of the discipline was not interested one way or another in sociocultural matters, among the few who were there was a growing confidence that the axioms of economics were sufficient unto themselves for understanding human behavior. Everything from the family and divorce to education and racial discrimination, it was claimed, could be explained in terms of a few basic axioms grounded on the bedrock notions of scarcity and rational choice (Becker 1976). Not only did economics not need sociology or anthropology, it seemed, but some in economics were prepared to dissolve these other fields into their discipline.

Meanwhile, among some in the cultural wing of the human sciences, there was an equally significant shift away from interactive models of culture, action, and environment to a purer or more restrictive concern for culture as "text," or a meaning system in itself. In the 1970s, for example, there was growing interest in models of culture based on the ideas of the Swiss linguist Ferdinand de Saussure concerning language *(langue)*. Though de Saussure had recognized that the systematic qualities of language had to be understood in relation to language use *(parole)*, this portion of his message received less attention than his methodological emphasis on language as a internally systematic and self-constitutional system of signs. Even more generally, as the concept of culture diffused from anthropology into the new field of cultural studies, there was a tendency for newcomers unfamiliar with anthropological debates to interpret the concept in sweeping terms, as an all-powerful determinant of human thought, feeling, and action. Recalling the insights of Ludwig Wittgenstein, Gilbert Ryle, and C.S. Peirce, more sophisticated analysts counseled that however vital cultural influences, human subjectivity cannot be reduced to the internalization of prefigured cultural scripts. From Shakespeare to gender studies, however, the culture concept had caught on, and many new users were convinced little more was needed to unlock the mysteries of human experience.

Ironically, this tendency toward abstraction from real actors and complex worlds paralleled developments that had earlier taken place in economics. Reacting against the political and ethical concerns of their predecessors, neoclassical economists in the first decades of the twentieth century had worked hard to bracket their inquiry from the messiness of the empirical world (Black and Goodwin 1973; Shackle 1973). They were interested in "pure" economic phenomena such as prices, which they were convinced could be analyzed without appeal to "externalities." Whereas this methodological narrowing did indeed facilitate certain analytic tasks such as, most famous, the analysis of prices and value, it made others more difficult. Topics once within the purview of economic analysis, such as the questions of what motivates people to work and consume, were suddenly redefined as "non-economic" (McPherson 1980; Hefner 1983). Confronted with cultural researchers' claim that culture was the real determinant of human experience, economists reacted indignantly, confident that their *homo economicus* was preferable to a cultural dummy.

In this way, the collaboration between economists and sociologists that Clifford Geertz and others had envisioned in the early 1960s had, by the late 1970s, more or less collapsed. Despite appeals from respected dissenters (Sen 1978), mainstream economics had given up its earlier flirtation with culture and social relations in favor of a *homo economicus* devoid of cultural influences. Conversely, among some cultural researchers, *homo socius* had come to be portrayed as so thoroughly scripted by culture that he seemed to many analysts like a cultural automaton. The contrast between the two approaches was but an updated version of a long-standing tension in the social sciences between what Dennis Wrong (1961) once referred to as "oversocialized" and "undersocialized" conceptions of social behavior (cf. Granovetter 1985). Though a few lonely voices affirming the need and possibility of a sociocultural economics could still be heard from the wilderness, the methodological polarization that had pushed economics and cultural research in such different directions made renewal of such a collaborative project difficult.

Capitalism's Bedding

As often happens in the human sciences, however, events in the world soon shook researchers to the realization that this existing division of academic labor was not up to the task at hand, and therefore the dialogue between economic and sociocultural research had somehow to be renewed. Several developments influenced this renewal of interest in interdisciplinary inquiry. One was the spectacular growth of capitalist industry and markets in East and Southeast Asia. Another was the collapse of communism in Eastern Europe and the Soviet Union and the rather desperate recognition on the part of policymakers that the effective operation of markets there was not guaranteed by the formal presence of market institutions alone. In the real world of Eastern Europe, "externalities" such as politics, crime, and moral disagreement had a notably annoying habit of intruding right into the heart of market processes.

The development of capitalism in East Asia played the leading role in this revival. It was not just the marvel of extraordinary growth that caught people's attention; the phenomenon was also interesting because it shattered many of the myths that had surrounded capitalism since the nineteenth century. No longer could it be said, as some Western scholars had, that industrial growth was only possible within an Occidental cultural setting. Similarly, the fact that capitalist development in the most successful Asian countries was accompanied by growing national pride and assertive foreign policies served to allay the fears of those who had long believed that the capitalist road inevitably leads to servile dependency. (Surely this same recognition contributed to the change of heart toward capitalist investment on the part of the Chinese Communist leadership.) In addition, the fact that in many Asian countries market growth was accompanied by calls for human rights and constitutional democracy reassured others that market development need not strengthen authoritarianism but might, with a little luck, diminish it. By the mid-1980s, it was not unusual to hear even Marxist or post-Marxist scholars voicing what earlier would have been regarded as liberal sentiments to the effect that the new industrialization could be a democratizing influence.

Others, of course, regarded the collapse of communism and the expansion of capitalism in East and Southeast Asia in simpler terms. In a widely read work, Francis Fukuyama (1989) spoke of a new world era characterized by "the end of history." Its central characteristic was the achievement of a worldwide consensus on liberal democracy and market development. Unfortunately for this prognosis, in many of the former Communist countries of Eastern Europe, programs of economic restructuration for which there had been strong support in 1990 had by 1994 given way to fractious disagreement. Equally seriously, in some of these same countries the collapse of communism gave rise not to an enlightened consensus on the virtues of liberal democracy but to an explosion of religious, ethnic, and national conflict. Both developments seemed to foreshadow not the end of history but, in the words of the English political philosopher John Gray (1993:50), its resumption "on a yet vaster scale." Suddenly history no longer looked as if it were the unfolding of a universal developmental telos but seemed acutely responsive to local society, politics, and culture.

It was in this context, then, that pressures grew to revive research in the relationship of culture and organization to market processes. For many researchers, the analytic key to such a revival was the recognition that rather than being a separate subsystem within society, markets are thoroughly entwined with or, in the sociologist Mark Granovetter's (1985:481) now-famous phrase, "embedded in" culture and social relations (cf. Evans 1992:145; Holton 1992:44).

The language of embeddedness had been around before, of course, in the work of the great economic historian Karl Polanyi (1944) and the "substantivist" school of economic anthropology identified with him (see Dalton 1968, 1971). Though invoking the same idea, Polanyi and the substantivists interpreted embeddedness in a significantly different way than did Granovetter and the new socioeconomics. For Polanyites, embeddedness was a quality especially characteristic of premarket or precapitalist societies. As a society modernizes, Polanyi believed, the economy becomes increasingly autonomous; rather than being an instrument of the society as a whole, it begins to set the terms of its own operation and dominate other spheres in society. Modernization thus brings about the "disembedding" of markets and the subordination of society to impersonal economic powers.

Though it raises an important point concerning the nature of modern economic power, the Polanyite view is marred by the fact that it conflates two issues: the role of the market in mediating the provision of goods and services in modern societies and the question of the meaning, organization, and autonomy of market processes themselves. There can be little doubt that in modern capitalist societies a larger number of goods and services are acquired through market institutions than is the case in most (though not all; cf. Epstein 1968) noncapitalist societies. Such a linkage can create a vulnerability akin to that described by the German social critic Jürgen Habermas as the "colonization of the life world" (Habermas 1984; White 1988:107). That is, by making so much of our ordinary life dependent on the market, the commodification of goods and services can also render our desires and, ultimately, social identities vulnerable to manipulation by the very commercial agencies supposedly servicing our needs. Such a vulnerability will be upsetting to people on all sides of the political spectrum, including environmentalists worried about consumptive waste, religious traditionalists alarmed by sexuality in the media, and civic republicans concerned that the public sphere affirm values more profound than those of private satisfaction alone.

In evaluating our modern dilemma, of course, we must resist the romantic temptation to think of individuals in precapitalist societies as always free of this sort of manipulation or dependency. Western critical theory has a long tradition of this sort of historical romanticism, premised on the idea of "a 'great divide' between monetary and pre-monetary worlds" (Parry and Bloch 1989:29).[3] The appealing polarity of such a divide is problematic in many parts of the world but is especially so in East and Southeast Asia. Though organized in varied manners and subject to different social controls, labor and commodity markets in this part of the world have a long and important history. So too do entrepreneurial minorities, many of whom were active in the region well before the arrival of Europeans.[4] Though in this region and the precapitalist world generally the scope of market forces may have been limited, tastes, values, and identities were often still subject to systematic social controls. Moreover, these controls were not necessarily egalitarian or undivisively communal but often reflected the values and interests of ruling elites, religious authorities, and other social hierarchies.

As Albert Hirschman (1986:42, 1979) has noted, defenders of the market since the age of Adam Smith have pointed to facts like these to argue in favor of free and open markets (cf. Lubasz 1992; Winch 1978). Conceding that there is power and inequality in the market, market advocates assert that it is nonetheless preferable that people should be encouraged to influence others through market suasion rather than direct political coercion. Better the invisible hand—or, today, MTV—than the iron fist. Needless to say, many people will not find such defenses credible, least of all if there is rampant inequality in the distribution of wealth or if they believe that the social order must be grounded on a broader vision of the good arrived at through open and more participatory social avenues than market demand alone.

Polanyites may be right, then, to note that the commodification of exchange in modern capitalism may make human wants vulnerable to heightened dependency on the market. And they may also be right to suggest that where commercial organizations discover ways to manipulate human desires, this can be destructive of human dignity and autonomy. But these issues are different from the claim that the market in capitalist society is thoroughly "disembedded," which is to say that it has become a sui generis power unto itself, independent of culture and social relations and accountable only to itself. In an ironic way, this critique buys rather too much into the neoclassical myth of the market as a self-regulating mechanism.

It is on this point that Granovetter and the new economic sociologists (see Etzioni and Lawrence 1991; Friedland and Robertson 1990) present what they regard as an alternative understanding of the modern market. They argue that modern capitalist development involves not the market's disembedding but its reembedding or recontextualization within a new normative and organizational framework. This framework is still deeply dependent on cultural meaning and pervasively influenced by social and political relationships. Embedded as it is in a different organizational and normative order, Japanese capitalism may be quite different from Chinese, and both in turn from American. Precisely how much they differ, of course, is an empirical question about which I will say more shortly.

Though Granovetter does not concern himself with the question, there is another corollary to the embedded understanding of the economy. Because markets and capitalism vary in their organization and meanings, their impact on politics, popular morality, and social inequality varies as well. The political consequences of capitalism in, say, a society in which there is no free press, few legal protections, and a lopsided concentration of wealth in the hands of a few well-connected families will be quite different from a society in which there is an effective balance of governmental powers, a sound judiciary, and a relatively equitable class structure. Because such variables influence both the operation of the market *and* its impact on politics and culture, it is important to avoid essentialized generalizations based on one historical ideal type when reflecting on capitalism's ethico-political entailments. The image of a monolithic capitalism has to be deconstructed in favor of models that recognize the variable articulation of capitalist institutions with society, politics, and morality.[5]

Granovetter himself was originally trained in the social-organizational wing of contemporary sociology, and his comments on the economy's embeddedness focus less on these large issues than they do on the nitty-gritty relationships involved in business and market transactions. In his early career he published several interesting studies showing that even in modern Western economies, simple economic tasks such as getting a job are heavily dependent on word-of-mouth information, social contacts, and, in a word, "networking" (Granovetter 1974, 1975). Extending this theme, Granovetter's recent work aims to show that there is a higher level of social interaction in the marketplace than economists, with their models of atomized individuals and independent firms, typically acknowledge. Business firms, Granovetter demonstrates, work the way they do not merely because of their management hierarchy or reduction of transaction costs (themes invoked in the economic literature to explain why firms come into existence; cf. Williamson 1975) but because they provide a web of social relations and communication denser than would otherwise develop in the marketplace alone (Granovetter 1985:502). Similarly, Granovetter asserts, the marketplace outside of firms is not the Hobbesian state of nature implied in many economic accounts in which anonymous buyers confront faceless sellers with little other than self-interest and the threat of state sanctions to guarantee fair play. In fact, as Émile Durkheim argued long ago, people regularly transact with one another even in circumstances where conditions for state supervision are weak or nonexistent. They are able to do so because business relations are, to varying degrees according to time and place, regularly mixed up with social ones. When getting a job, hiring a new faculty member, choosing a baby-sitter, or making any number of other economic decisions, people rely not just on price and product information supplied by an impersonal market mechanism but on reports from friends, colleagues, and those around them (including those with whom they identify in the mass media) as to the quality of a particular person, product, or service. All this is to say that, as Granovetter puts it, the economy is "rife with social connections." I might add that it is also rich with cultural meaning and thoroughly dependent on social trust (cf. Fukuyama 1995).

Network Capitalism

If, as Granovetter suggests, networking and information exchange are important even in the lawyer-congested economies of the West, the generalization is true in spades in East and Southeast Asia. It is now widely recognized that in Japan, for example, the networks among businessmen (and most are men), first established at college and continued after they enter the business world in after-hours socializing, play an important role in the affairs of high-level corporate managers. These relationships provide critical information for business decisions and also facilitate government-business cooperation in a manner quite different from the tradition of Anglo-American capitalism (Johnson 1982).

It is among overseas Chinese, however, that the embedding of modern economic life in social relationships assumes what is, from a Western perspective, its most striking form. Indeed, of all the forms capitalist organizations assume, those of the overseas Chinese present the most dramatic contrast with that of Western—and, particularly, American—capitalism. As Gordon Redding (1990) has shown and as Gary Hamilton (see also Hamilton and Biggart 1988), Jamie Mackie, and Robert Weller illustrate in their chapters in this book, Chinese capitalism is first and foremost a *network* capitalism. It is built from the ground up, not on the basis of legal contracts and the supervisory authority of the state but on particularistic relationships of trust. One can hardly think of a more decisive counterexample to Max Weber's faith that the spread of capitalism would everywhere mean the demise of personalistic ties in favor of a faceless bureaucratic machine (cf. Clegg and Redding 1990:2; Hamilton, Zeile, and Kim 1990).

As Gary Hamilton's chapter in this volume illustrates, the networks at the heart of Chinese business life are of two basic types, each characterized by its own norms and ambivalences. The first is the hierarchical relationship of the family, both in its core nucleate and extended patrilineal forms. The second is the system of lateral and reciprocal relationships known as *guanxi*. Though Chinese business is often said to be based on "family firms," in fact the family is a "weak organization," as Gordon Redding (1990) has put it. It is prone to instabilities that *guanxi* is not, and also to more abuses. The effective operation of a family business thus depends as much on the distant and egalitarian ties of *guanxi* as it does on familism.

Family Resources

In its extended form, however, the family does provide the basic building block for Chinese business. Unlike contemporary Western idealizations of the family as a voluntary association of coequals, the Chinese family is patrilineal, patrilocal (marital residence with or near the groom's family), and unambiguously patriarchal; there is no question of an equality of the sexes or generations. Relationships are governed by filial norms with children especially but wives also subject to the patriarchal authority of the father and, more diffusely, the patrilineage as a whole. This authority has very serious economic entailments. The patriarch can lay claim to the labor power and wages of working children. The ideal logic that underlies this expectation is that children are repaying the debt to their parents for their upbringing. In the case of girls, who outmarry and thus, from the patriarch's perspective, are "lost" to the patrilineage, the expectation is that they will hand over a large portion of their pay in work performed prior to marriage.[6]

As Tania Murray Li illustrates in her discussion of Singapore in this volume, on this particular point the contrast between Chinese and Malays (as well as Jennifer Alexander's Javanese, David Szanton's Estancia Filipinos [see their chapters, this volume], and so on) could not be stronger. Quite unlike their Chinese counterparts, Malay and Javanese youths are reluctant to submit to patriarchal authority, at least when it comes to economic affairs. Working adolescents do not readily pool their incomes to meet family goals or contribute unpaid labor to family enterprises. For them, and again quite unlike the Chinese, family enterprise is not a corporate undertaking but the independent responsibility of the parents. There is very little notion of a family or extended-kin "estate." Indeed in some cases, as among the Javanese merchants described by Alexander, even husbands and wives regard their partner's enterprise as a separate concern (see Dewey 1962). The result is that Malays, Javanese, and many other indigenous Southeast Asians cannot, as Li puts it, "rely upon the nuclear family as a business resource." In other words, and quite contrary to certain stereotypes of Asian families as being all alike, Malay and many other Southeast Asian families look more individualistic than their Chinese counterparts. As we shall see, this issue is critical for understanding key differences between Chinese and indigenous Southeast Asian business.

If the family is a source of strength for Chinese business, it is also at times a weakness. Whereas elder patriarchs can depend on the loyalty and unpaid labor of their subordinates, patriarchal authority depends on a father who inevitably grows old and dies. Having established his firm by relying on family labor and loans from family and friends, a successful owner begins by exercising tight control over all important decisions. Gradually, however, he brings his sons (but not daughters) into the business and grooms them for his eventual retirement and death. It is here that the peculiar logic of the Chinese descent system exerts its most decisive influence. By convention sons are expected to be given equal shares in their father's estate. Achieving such equality through the division of an existing business into equal shares is one option. Some families do this, but a problem of coordination arises because no brother can lay claim to the authority the father once enjoyed. Relationships among brothers do not share the quality of selfless duty and consensual hierarchy characteristic of the father's relationship with his sons. Brothers in the same business are prone to jealousy and disagreements that make their relationship unstable.

In the face of these tensions, as Wong Siu-lun (1985; and see Hamilton's chapter in this volume) has demonstrated, the preferred strategy among successful business owners is to assign each son different spheres of influence in the business or, better yet (if one is especially successful), an entirely separate business. The consequences of this inheritance strategy for growth cycles in Chinese business are enormous. Success is marked not by the creation of an ever-larger and vertically integrated corporation, as in South Korea and Japan, but by a mother company's establishment of independent firms loosely tethered in a multifirm business group. These may specialize in the manufacture of a product related to or even identical with that of the mother firm, or they may be in a different line of business entirely. As Hamilton notes, sometimes the result is a hybrid of these two options: a core number of firms specializing in a related product line and characterized by a measure of vertical integration and, alongside them, another set of firms in business networks unrelated to the mother firm's product line. In Hamilton's words, "opportunistic diversification," not vertical integration, is the rule of this game, determined as it is by the logic of patrilineal inheritance.

Though the owner and his partners in the business's inner circle exercise ultimate control over the varied firms composing a business group, day-to-day management of the firms is kept separate, again unlike the pattern of vertically integrated firms in Japan and Korea. It is only recently that the patriarchs of a few large business groups have taken steps to coordinate management across firms in their business groups. Although there is a separation of management hierarchies among firms in the group, key people may hold a range of positions in different firms. This practice is rarely seen in Japan and South Korea, where key personnel hold only one position in one firm in a business group.

Here again, even in the midst of the most modern enterprises, we see the enduring influence of traditional organizational prototypes projected into untraditional economic tasks. In this instance, this split between control and management in family enterprises parallels that between control and management of household and lineage assets. As Hamilton describes it, family-owned business groups follow the same organizational patterns associated with practices in traditional Chinese families. The extension of this traditional structure into a new social field works not because of the irrational commitment of Chinese to some mystically powerful "tradition" but because the organizational prototype is versatile enough to assume new social functions. Tradition has changed even as its basic pattern has been reproduced.

To Western scholars trained in Weberian sociology or conventional management theory, all of this may look like a traditional, "prerationalized" way of doing business, destined to give way over time to a more rational and bureaucratic system of management—characterized above all by a clearer divide between ownership and management. Admittedly, a few Chinese firms have begun to experiment with Western management techniques (one wag having said that the quickest way to ruin a good business is to send a son off to Harvard for an MBA). In general, however, this expectation is premised on a too-narrow sense of the range of cultural variation compatible with modern capitalism. As Hamilton shows, small- and medium-sized firms in Taiwan have responded brilliantly to the new global economy. Today in Taiwan firms with fewer than 300 employees (the threshold below which firms are classified as small-medium) account for 50 percent of manufacture output and 65 percent of all exports. Astoundingly, this proportion changed little during 1966–1986. Although the number of firms in Taiwan increased 315 percent between 1966 and 1986, the average firm size grew by only 15 percent. By contrast, in South Korea, where giant, vertically integrated firms dominate the economic landscape, figures for this same period are almost the inverse: Firm size grew by 300 percent, whereas the total number of firms grew by only 10 percent.

Lateral Passes

One sees a similar pattern of transformation in reproduction among the second category of social relationships critical to Chinese business, those of the lateral and reciprocal ties known as *guanxi*. If family networks among overseas Chinese are hierarchical and characterized by short spans of control, *guanxi* tend to be (relatively) egalitarian, reciprocal, and broad in their reach. Premised as they are on relatively equal relations of reciprocity, *guanxi* appeal not to diffuse, "noneconomic" norms of filial duty but to a trust regularly reevaluated over the course of a relationship. Typically the relationship is also lubricated with gifts, dinners, and other social exchanges. Those active in a *guanxi* network may include distant kin, neighbors, former schoolmates, people with the same surname, and, among overseas Chinese, people from the same part of China or speakers of the same dialect. *Guanxi* are drawn into a variety of economic tasks, including the organization of production and the distribution of finished products. Given the central importance of capital accumulation in modern business, however, the most remarkable of their features is the way they are used to mobilize capital. As in Southeast Asia, in Taiwan it has been only recently that the stock market has come to be used as a source of investment capital. Similarly, although in Korea and Japan in an earlier era the government provided low-interest loans to select business firms, in Taiwan and (to a much less consistent degree) Southeast Asia government finance has played a less important role in the recent economic boom.[7] Far more important have been the reinvestment of profits and the informal money markets that work through *guanxi* networks of family, friends, and associates. In Taiwan still today, these unsecured loans—typically made without formal contract and thus without the sanctioning power of the state—are the dominant source of investment capital. In the competitive world of Taiwanese capitalism, this private capital allows entrepreneurs to respond more quickly to new business opportunities than would be the case were they obliged to apply for bank loans. But the really remarkable feature of the system is the fact that it is based on personalized relationships of trust rather than state enforcement. As Hamilton notes, we are here in the presence of one of the most fundamental differences between modern Western and overseas Chinese capitalism (cf. Fukuyama 1995:65–82; Redding 1990:237).

Guanxi ties also work to counterbalance some of the structural limitations of family-based businesses. Though family members typically exercise ultimate control, most large family firms have at least several nonkin shareholders. These individuals often compose the firm owner's inner circle, a circle that, interestingly, may not include the owner's eldest son. Consisting of kin and nonkin, these larger, overlapping hierarchies are at the heart of Chinese business groups in Taiwan and Southeast Asia, giving their members access to capital, information, and human resources far greater than that of the patrilineal family alone. Again unlike Japan, these clusters of family and nonfamily owners linked by *guanxi* tend to be concentrated in a single business group rather than extending between groups.

Research on *guanxi* and business has helped to correct stereotypes of Chinese society that have filtered into popular and academic media based on bookishly idealized understandings of Confucianism. Premised on official models of family and hierarchy, these stereotypes overlook the fact that the most prosperous portions of Chinese East Asia tended to be at far remove from centers of Confucian orthodoxy (Vogel 1991:84). The stereotypes also prevented us from seeing the extraordinary range of lateral relationships so important in Chinese social and business life and from understanding that even within the family there were alternative ideas as to what constituted Confucian values, most notably on the part of women.

What precisely is the relationship between Chinese business in majority-Chinese societies and in Southeast Asia? The qualities of Chinese business organization discussed previously take on a new and somewhat more ambiguous role when projected into worlds where the Chinese live as minorities in colonial or postcolonial settings. In Taiwan and Hong Kong, we know, *guanxi* networks are used not just for economic affairs but also to mobilize allies for political ends. In non-Chinese Southeast Asian countries, where Chinese constitute as little as 1.5 percent of the population (in the Philippines) or as much as 33 percent (in Malaysia; see Mackie 1992:163), these same networks serve not only to facilitate business but to provide political leverage where official influence is otherwise lacking. Built from the bottom up, *guanxi* in some Southeast Asian countries reach high into the political stratosphere.[8]

Natives and Chinese in Southeast Asia

No aspect of economy and culture in Southeast Asia excites as much controversy as that of the massive domination of private enterprise by ethnic Chinese. Despite numerous government programs to assist native businesses, Chinese dominance in the private sector has held steady or actually increased in most Southeast Asian countries since the 1950s. To take but one example, in Indonesia the Chinese compose just 4 percent of the population. But they are estimated to control 70–75 percent of medium- and large-scale private (nonstate) enterprise. Their hold on firms traded on the recently created Jakarta stock exchange is, by most estimates, even larger (see Hefner, this volume; Robison 1986; Winters 1996:191–194). The only Southeast Asian economies in which the non-Chinese role has recently expanded have been Vietnam, where the government expelled several hundred thousand ethnic Chinese just after the Vietnam War, and Malaysia, where the government has pursued a vigorous and, despite much controversy, credible program of Malay business development (Sieh Lee 1992:104).

The Chinese role in Southeast Asian economic life has long attracted the attention of foreign visitors and fueled speculation as to why the Chinese enjoy the comparative advantage they do. A number of explanations have been presented; interestingly, however, most recent ones have been refreshingly free of idealized references to Confucian culture. Today most areal scholars would agree with Mackie's comment that references to classical "Confucian" values in Southeast Asia are so little helpful they are "best avoided entirely." Such appeals are best avoided not because culture and organization play a minor role in Chinese business but because the traits relevant for business success are more specific and practical than those emphasized in high-Confucian accounts.

There is another issue here as well, one that has to do with the cultural profile of Chinese immigrants to Southeast Asia. In a 1992 essay, for example, a Hong Kong–based scholar of Southeast Asian Chinese, Wang Gungwu (1992), noted that almost all the Chinese who migrated to Southeast Asia came from social classes unlikely to have had any exposure to the high-Confucian tradition of mandarin China. As he and Mackie have noted, echoing themes also presented in Weller's chapter and elsewhere by Peter L. Berger (1988), the popular tradition to which the immigrants were exposed incorporated Taoist, Buddhist, and folk-animist beliefs as well as folk Confucian values.

An Early Start?

Most attempts to explain the Chinese economic role in Southeast Asia have therefore focused on specific institutional and political-economic influences rather than timeless values. For example, building on the work of the China anthropologist Maurice Freedman (1959, 1966), some analysts have presented what might be called, to borrow another phrase from Jamie Mackie's chapter, an "early start" model of Chinese economic success. This explanation emphasizes that Chinese immigrants to Southeast Asia came from a society in which the tools of commerce were already widespread well before the Chinese began their migration. The most notable items in this toolbox were familiarity with the use of money and institutions for managing investment and credit. With this knowledge at hand, it is argued, the Chinese were able to adapt more quickly than native peoples to the commercial opportunities of precolonial and modern Southeast Asia.

The problem with this explanation lies less in what it has to say about the Chinese than in its implicit suggestion that basic commercial skills were not yet widely diffused among Southeast Asians at the time of the Chinese people's arrival. As Denys Lombard's (1990) and Anthony Reid's (1993) studies have demonstrated, such a view represents a serious oversimplification of Southeast Asian economic history. In fact, there was extraordinary commercial activity in maritime Southeast Asia from early on in the postclassical (i.e., post-fifteenth-century) era. During much of what Anthony Reid (1993) has referred to as Southeast Asia's "age of commerce" (from 1450 to 1680 with its apex from 1570 to 1630), the Chinese and the Southeast Asians collaborated in trade ventures, exchanged and refined their marine technologies, and created one of the world's most prosperous trade zones (cf. Kathirithamby-Wells and Villiers 1990).

It is important to recall this history, in part so as not to essentialize native Southeast Asian cultures as uncommercial or "traditional" in a manner inimical to commerce. Even prior to the age of commerce, the use of money was widespread in Southeast Asia (Wicks 1992). By the time the commercial boom was in full gear, local economies relied upon an eclectic mix of Chinese copper coins, Japanese silver, and gold and silver from the Iberian Americas (Reid 1993:25). There was also a lively trade in commercial export crops, including most notably pepper, nutmeg, and cloves. This trade stimulated the expansion of commercial agriculture into previously uncultivated portions of the archipelago and also fueled a demand for luxury goods from India and China. Though Southeast Asia's manufactures were not exported to China and India (Reid 1993:32), its merchants played a dominant role in the finance and organization of the vast trading fleets that transported goods to and from Asian destinations. Seventeenth-century Portuguese reports referred to the Javanese—a people seen by nineteenth-century Europeans as land-loving farmers inept at seafaring—as "men very experienced in the art of navigation" (cited in Reid 1993:36).

There was other evidence of commerce's far-reaching impact on culture and society at this time. There was, for example, sustained urban growth and, with it, a notable shift in power away from inland agrarian states to trade-oriented maritime cities (see Reid 1993:216). By this same period, a growing portion of the region's population was no longer subsistence oriented but actively producing for the world economy. Equally remarkable, as Lombard (1990:155–176) has noted, a new, rationalist, and individualistic concept of the person began to make its way into religion, social structure, and the arts. (However, this new individualism largely excluded women; see Lombard 1990:174–175.) Finally, in the political sphere, one saw pressures in urban centers toward conciliar representation and limits on the authority of kings (Reid 1993:252).

In the end, this commercial boom was brought to a end by the combined efforts of European colonizers and absolutizing native rulers. Unlike their counterparts in northwestern Europe (Hall 1986), native rulers saw little advantage in encouraging safeguards for property or expansive commercial growth. Shaun Malarney and Hy van Luong (in this volume) provide an analysis of a similar policy maintained until the nineteenth century in Vietnam. Threatened by the power of independent merchants, rulers arranged deals whereby the Europeans secured monopoly rights to lucrative trade goods in exchange for payments to the court and military support for the king. There were other factors contributing to Southeast Asia's great commercial decline (Reid 1993:303). However, the most basic facts are that by 1700, lucrative portions of the insular trade were in European hands; the merchant class, once concentrated in Southeast Asian ports, had been destroyed; and the urban population was in decline. The regional revival of an indigenous merchant class would begin only in the late twentieth century.

All this is to say that whatever its merits as regards the Chinese, the early-start theory of the Chinese comparative advantage paints a too simplistic portrait of Southeast Asian economic culture. It fails to emphasize the prior existence of commercial traditions and downplays the significance of their destruction at the hands of absolutizing rulers and colonizing Europeans.

Comprador Capitalism?

More sophisticated variants of the early-start argument acknowledge these historical points and emphasize the additional fact that during the colonial era itself, Western powers utilized Chinese as comprador middlemen. Although barred from owning land or working in government, the Chinese were recruited to collect taxes, manage the colonial state's vast opium trade, and play middle-level roles in state-owned enterprise (Rush 1990; Vitalis 1992). Through these and other arrangements, the Chinese were able to establish a significant hold over industry, finance, and rural commerce in much of Southeast Asia. Though in a few territories (such as the Minang area of West Sumatra, described by Peletz in this volume, or the Red River valley of Vietnam, described by Malarney) native entrepreneurs held their own, no native ethnic group could match the breadth of Chinese economic power across the region as a whole.

In the early independence era, nationalist regimes throughout the region repressed Chinese business and lavished subsidies and contracts on native entrepreneurs. Plagued by corruption and inefficiency, most of these programs proved ineffectual (McVey 1992:11). At the same time, political elites often arranged secret rent-seeking arrangements with a segment of the Chinese community, exchanging government contracts and protection for payments, business shares, or help in starting up their own firms. Though these Chinese partners enjoyed economic success, their opportunities for formal political influence were, and are still today, quite small. Thus, it has been observed that in many Southeast Asian countries, Chinese businesses are vulnerable to manipulation by ruling elites, who siphon off rents without having to worry that their clients will mobilize support from an aggrieved public (Anderson 1983; MacIntyre 1994; Yoshihara 1988).

The Bottoms-Up Advantage

The Chinese may have enjoyed some head-start advantages over their indigenous counterparts. And in the colonial era some among them were most certainly accorded political-economic privileges, some of which have continued with new partners in the independence era. However significant these political-economic advantages—and they are deeply significant—it is nonetheless apparent that these alone do not explain Chinese economic success. Time and time again, and not just in Southeast Asia but in other parts of the Pacific and the Americas, Chinese businesspeople have demonstrated a remarkable capacity to rise from poverty and respond quickly to new opportunities. Sometimes they succeed even in the face of systematic discrimination. Top-down political explanations thus cannot be the whole story; there must also be a bottoms-up organization that ensures Chinese business success. We have already seen some of the organizational precedents Chinese bring to their business activities. The evidence from the chapters in this volume provides two additional clues as to Chinese cultural advantages over indigenous rivals. The first advantage has to do with community organization and the second, with the family.

As Mackie and Li note in their chapters, Chinese immigrants to Southeast Asia were quickly recruited to a variety of organizations, including kinship networks, dialect-group associations, chambers of commerce, and mutual aid organizations. These organizations absorbed immigrants into a multipurpose social network and provided them with access to housing, employment, and, for the well-heeled, business contacts and capital. Though these associations included the *guanxi* ties of lateral reciprocity discussed by Hamilton for Taiwan, they also included relationships of a decidedly hierarchical nature. Among them, for example, were vertical ties of contract or indentured labor whereby a migrant would finance his travel and settlement in Southeast Asia (see Li, this volume). The ties also included clientage within vertical trade structures, such as the vast networks associated in many parts of Southeast Asia with the opium trade (Rush 1990:97).

Whether vertical or horizontal, the web of economic relationships among Chinese immigrants in Southeast Asia stands in marked contrast to the looser texture of economic interdependency among native migrants. Li observes that Malay immigrants to Singapore "had few direct economic linkages among themselves." Relying on non-Malays for employment, Malays interacted among themselves on largely nonmarket terms: the greeting and sociability of everyday life, especially important for affirming Malay identity in the predominantly Chinese city; volunteer assistance during emergencies; and the reciprocal exchange of gifts and labor at weddings, funerals, and other life-passage ceremonies.

We know from contemporary reports on Southeast Asian cities that non-Chinese migrants do often rely on people of the same ethnicity or from the same region to facilitate their adaptation to urban life. Though the segregation of market from intraethnic social life described by Li for Singapore Malays is not fully generalizable to other Southeast Asian settings, then, her and Mackie's more basic point is, namely, that no ethnic group can match the Chinese in the breadth or versatility of their socioeconomic networks. These networks begin at the local level, providing access to basic subsistence resources, and extend to the heights of high finance and, today, international business.

Given the personalistic nature of these ties, it would be a mistake to assume that the majority of Chinese people have access to the full range of these social and material resources. Everything depends upon one's network relationships, not just one's generic identity as Chinese. As Mackie and Li both note, many Chinese are poor laborers and never become anything else. In addition, as Mackie discusses in his chapter, Chinese migrants quite consistently distinguish Hokkien from Hakka, Cantonese from Hainanese, and first-generation immigrants (known in Indonesian as *totok*) from *peranakan* who have lived in the region for several generations.[9] Not all Chinese cooperate equally with others; indeed, most build their ties on social identities more narrowly cast than the category of "Chinese" alone. Nonetheless, the overall effect of Chinese association is significant. Enough people secure access to sufficient resources to ensure a vastly disproportionate representation of Chinese in the ranks of middle- and large-scale enterprise even in the absence of state patronage.

The second advantage enjoyed by the Chinese has to do with their family structure in relation to that of most indigenous Southeast Asians. Though matrilineal or patrilineal kinship is present in some indigenous communities (including Peletz's Minangkabau and Malarney and Luong's Vietnamese), most Southeast Asians have a bilateral or cognatic kinship system. As with kinship in Western Europe and the United States (also cognatic), a key feature of this type of kinship is that it is built around nuclear families linked in grid-like manner to other families. There is no enduring corporate structure or material estate uniting families in a multifamily group like those typically found in societies organized around unilineal descent. In light of these facts, anthropologists emphasize that cognatic kinship is most common in societies where the population is mobile (as the peoples of Western Europe and Southeast Asia have long been) and, for whatever other reasons, multifamily groups do not play a significant role in the management of resources like farmland or in the affairs of government and the military (Buchler and Selby 1968).

By itself, of course, unilineal descent as opposed to cognatic kinship says nothing about any comparative economic advantage. After all, there are many societies with unilineal descent systems that have never used the system to adapt to modern markets; conversely, there are other societies (like most of those in Western Europe) that get by economically quite well without unilineal descent. More critical than unilineal descent alone, then, is the way in which a corporate potentiality within the Chinese patrilineal descent system is harnessed to economic tasks. On this point, there is a world of difference between the Chinese and most indigenous Southeast Asians. As we have seen, Chinese patriarchs are able to draw upon the unpaid labor of their wives and children as a resource in economic affairs. Equally important, as Hamilton's chapter shows so well (cf. Redding 1990), networks resulting from patrilineal relationships are drawn extensively into economic affairs. Kinship and business work well together indeed.

Though some of its details are not fully generalizable, Li's portrait of Singapore Malays rings true for many other indigenous Southeast Asians. Chinese families pool incomes and contribute unpaid labor to the family enterprise because the enterprise is regarded as a corporate affair. By contrast, Malays "do not expect any family member, spouse or child, to work unpaid or pool capital for a family business." Kinship individualists, Malay parents feel that every individual has the right to his or her own labor and income. Hence parents tolerate children's unwillingness to work under paternal authority. Tellingly (and consistent with the situation in Java), Li notes that this unwillingness is especially strong among sons—the same category of kin that, among Chinese, is most systematically drawn into the patriarch's enterprise.

In the end, then, when Malay entrepreneurs do employ family members, they tend to pay market rates or give gifts. Again, "the result is that Malays cannot rely upon the nuclear family as a business resource." The economic consequence of this is seen in turn in Li's image of the Malay food stall at peak hours of the day. Its owner exhausted, the stall simply closes; its Chinese neighbors remain open by utilizing the unpaid labor of children.

Of course, Li's portrait of Singapore Malays does not accord with all details of family life among other Southeast Asians. Populations such as the Khmer and Javanese tend to be more "face" conscious than the average Malay. Consistent with this emphasis, families from these ethnic backgrounds stress respect or even fear of parents (especially the father) as much as they do the idioms of love or affection. Nonetheless, in these cases too, the typical situation as regards kinship and business is like that described by Peletz and Li and provides a telling contrast with the Chinese. Emphasizing patrilineal authority and a corporate kin-mindedness, the Chinese teach sons to see family wealth as an estate in which they have shares. By contrast, the cognatic kinship common among native Southeast Asians reinforces a temporally punctuated and organizationally dispersive pattern of kin-based accumulation. Family wealth is not seen as an estate. Parents are reluctant to draw grown children too directly into explicitly economic tasks; like the Singapore Malays, they provide "gifts" rather than wages to family members. To quote Peletz, "Kinship and business do not—or at least should not—mix." Kinship is insulated from the vicissitudes of the market and the volatile pursuit of self-interest. Numerous researchers in insular Southeast Asia have noted a similar antipathy toward the explicit "economization" of family ties (Banks 1983; Djamour 1959; Swift 1965). The phenomenon is also common in other parts of the world, even in otherwise highly commercial societies (Parry and Bloch 1989:6). Here in Southeast Asia, the trait provides a key point of contrast between native populations and the Chinese.

Women as Entrepreneurs

Though Southeast Asian families typically lack corporate-mindedness in business affairs, they do have one distinctive asset. The (relative to Chinese) slackening of patriarchal authority, the (at least idealized) emphasis on gender complementarity rather than female subordination to the husband (Atkinson and Errington 1990; Peletz 1996:257–308), and the concern for autonomy among mature family members—these and other features of kinship and gender in Southeast Asian have proven conducive to the movement of women out of the home and into economic enterprise. As Hy van Luong shows, even in the Confucian-inflected environment of Vietnam, there has long been a modus vivendus between the official Confucian ideology of female subordination and the practical involvement of women in enterprise. We should add to this list of influences the fact that, as shown by Malarney and Luong in Vietnam, Szanton in Estancia, and Alexander for Central Java, a tightfisted concern with moneymaking tends to be seen as an unflattering trait among males. By contrast, a certain money-mindedness is tolerated or even admired among females. All these qualities provide cultural sanctions for high rates of female labor and enterprise outside the household, a social pattern long characteristic of Southeast Asian society (Reid 1988:146–181).

The regressive story that Luong recounts for Vietnamese women in modern times, however, has its counterpart in other parts of Southeast Asia as well. In the Red River valley, Luong shows, women's role in commerce has changed considerably since the late nineteenth century with significant downward pressures on women's heretofore elevated economic role. The reasons seem varied, but some are generalizable to other parts of Southeast Asia. In colonial times, there was the growing influence of European models of men as breadwinners and women as homemakers (a point Peletz and Alexander note as well). Also significant was the fact that men typically participated in mass education well before large numbers of women did, at a time when middle- and large-scale enterprise was becoming increasingly dependent on literacy skills. Not to be overlooked, finally, is that in this century male involvement in tightfisted moneymaking has lost some of its stigma—though not everywhere, as Szanton's chapter illustrates. At least among the new middle classes, however, business is now where the action is, and men have moved to join the high-status game (McVey 1992:24). All of these factors have pressed down women's participation in enterprise and pushed up that of men. The regression in women's business role tends to be particularly strong in middle- and large-scale enterprise. Not coincidentally, these are also fields where indigenous actors come into extensive contact with Chinese, Japanese, Europeans, and Americans, many of whom have their own ideas as to the proper gender profile for business managers.

Consumption Cultures

As the discussion to this point indicates, the focus of most chapters in this book is on the productive and organizational side of market culture: how economic actors go about their business, how they relate to other people as they do so, who seems well suited to the new market environment and who does not. There is, however, another side to the market transformations sweeping East and Southeast Asia. It concerns not production but the distribution of income and wealth and, more particularly, the uses to which wealth is put as it is consumed as goods and services.

The more general issue here, the distribution of the new wealth, is a topic that lends itself rather well to conventional economic analysis, and it has been the focus of a number of fine studies by economists and political scientists in East and Southeast Asia (see, e.g., Hill 1992). Consumption, however, is another issue entirely, and a few words need be said about it before bringing these introductory remarks to a close.

In mainstream economics, consumption has long been associated with the idea of utility, and utility has been regarded as something that flows more or less directly from the objective properties of a particular good. One eats to satisfy hunger, drinks to sate thirst, and so on. There is nothing mysterious or, from an economist's point of view, particularly interesting here. In the fields of anthropology, sociology, media studies, and management, however, a new and less atomized approach to the study of consumption has developed in the 1980s and 1990s. This new approach emphasizes that the utility of goods is defined not just in terms of material qualities and inner needs but in relation to a particular way of life characterized by its own "socially organized forms of satisfaction" (Leiss 1976:9; see also Appadurai 1986:29; Orlove and Rutz 1989). Consumption, then, is not the economist's inscrutable act of shapeless desire. On the contrary, consumption is implicated in identity and is socially communicative as well as technical or material. Alternately fascinated or repelled by its parade of social difference, people use consumption to "communicate to others their relationships to complex sets of otherwise abstract social attributes (such as status), thus identifying themselves within social structures" (Leiss, Kline, and Jhally 1986:243). Through such processes, consumption marks out social differences in an expressive and public way and helps to recreate the very values to which its actions give visible form (Hefner 1990:159; Douglas and Isherwood 1979:67; Sahlins 1976:178).

In one sense it is surprising that the culture of consumption has yet to become an important field of research in East and Southeast Asia. Among local people themselves, after all, the topic is the object of intense interest. In remote mountain villages in Java (Hefner 1983), in the slums of Manila and Jakarta, and in the affluent suburbs of western Bangkok and Taipei, virtually every grownup is aware of the changes in the way people consume wealth. Some people are quite taken with the new styles, but others are not pleased. The result is that throughout East and Southeast Asia, there is a lively debate over the propriety and fairness of new forms of consumption.

It is beyond the scope of this introduction to map out this aspect of market culture in any detail. But one point should be stressed. Early in this century it was widely forecast that the spread of capitalism to other parts of the world would draw all modern peoples into the same dreary iron cage (as Max Weber put it), characterized by, among other things, rational-bureaucratic organization, secular thought, and individualistic values. The expansion of the market and the commercialization of broad segments of human life have now taken place in much of the world. As we assess their impact, it does indeed seem as if these changes have introduced convergent market pressures, thereby "globalizing" consumption and the status ideals it supports. However, to borrow a phrase from Weller's chapter, the spread of capitalist consumption has not proved to be merely "the triumphant march of the market over everything else." The push of market rationality beyond the borders of traditional economic spheres causes tensions between market-oriented visions of the good and those of traditionalists, moralists, utopians, and others who insist that some domains of social life should remain beyond the market's reach. Whether in the form of antimarket reform movements, romantic longings for past ways of life (real or mythic), or organized movements for the defense of the environment, again and again the expansion of the market unleashes forces unexpected by those who foretold a universal march into the modernist cage. Satellite dishes and blue jeans may be ubiquitous, but so too are debates over the environment, religious values, pornography, and social justice.[10]

Though the spread of a new and more globalized consumption has introduced common fashions, then, it has also spurred complex social currents that can only be understood with reference to local politics, social structures, and ethical traditions. For outsiders, particularly those who rarely make it beyond the local Hilton Hotel or Pizza Hut, it is perhaps easier to take note of the international fashions than it is these local influences and thereby conclude that the globalization of consumption is more of a steamroller than it in fact is. After all, in Taipei, Bangkok, or Jakarta one can more easily observe the spread of blue jeans and American fast food than one can the channeling of new wealth into heightened religiosity. Yet to stay for a moment with the religious example, in virtually all of the societies discussed in this book, market growth has been accompanied by religious revival—indeed, in some countries a revival of historically unprecedented proportions (Keyes, Kendall, and Hardacre 1994). It seems that forecasts of capitalism's secularizing and individualizing impact are, at the very least, premature (cf. Casanova 1994; Martin 1990).

There is a relationship between market growth and religious revival, but it is too complex to summarize in terms of the polar options of co-optation or resistance. Religion is not being everywhere pressed toward individualistic or hedonistic ends, as some might predict in an era of rising affluence and de-traditionalization. Nor is it being uniformly used to mobilize resistance against the individualizing or alienating tendencies of capitalism and urban life. As Weller's, Hefner's, and Malarney's chapters show, there are bits and pieces of both reactions at work in the religious field. As with Weller's enthusiasts of ghost worship, some people *are* turning to religion to help them in the pursuit of private wealth. However, others see religion as a refuge from the individualizing privations of urban isolation and degradation. What the two reactions share is not an identical conclusion on markets and morality but a similar preoccupation with the moral dimensions of a great transformation reshaping people's worlds (cf. Gay 1991).

There is a larger point in all this, and to the logic of this book as a whole. Where it is backed by local authorities, the commodification of "goods" and "services" often creates a precedent not easily confined to one well-bounded social sphere. The logic of consumer choice becomes a model promoted by entrepreneurs in social domains previously regulated by nonmarket norms. Indeed, the idea may even be trumpeted by some libertarians as a prototype for social order as a whole. Thus if there is demand for some good or service, the argument goes, and a supplier is willing to provide what is desired, let the exchange occur. No matter that others in the community may see the service provided as morally objectionable. Here is the elementary core of the libertarian vision, which, often without knowing itself as such, has thrown its weight around ever larger portions of the Western world for over two centuries.

This market ethic is not foreign to Asian societies, least of all those with a history of extensive commercial life. As Lombard (1990:266) has observed, the Chinese in East and Southeast Asia have long abided by a social ethic that encouraged hard work rewarded with intensive distraction:

> Little concerned with asceticism, they were not ashamed of eating well, nor of pursuing distraction. They calculated their laborious efforts in relation to the relaxation or festivals which would follow and compensate that labor. In this they were close to Westerners, who of course quickly appreciated their cuisine, their ceramics, and their fine furnishings.

As Weller's chapter illustrates, however, there were alternative economic ethics even within Chinese societies. There were also ethical alternatives in Southeast Asia, though often they honed in on different concerns. For example, ascetic values—Buddhist and Sufi-Islamic—were historically widespread in Southeast Asian popular cultures. For most people and most periods, these values did not take the form of a generalized rejection of wealth such as one associates with monastic asceticism but worked in a less aggressive, "communitarian" manner, encouraging people to apply a portion of their private wealth to social and, especially, religious ends. Prestige was bestowed on those who used their wealth for something that could be seen as a broader public good. Thus in Islamic and Buddhist portions of Southeast Asia, esteem went to those who built temples or mosques or sponsored religious ceremonies that brought blessing to the community (Sizemore and

Swearer 1990; Hefner 1983). It was not wealth per se that was bad but uses that refused these institutionalized concessions to community interest.

This pressure to make wealth responsive to a broader community had a number of curious expressions. In much of Southeast Asia, for example, eating in public was always regarded as something of an embarrassment. Throughout the region there is a tradition of festival meals at which people come together and food is consumed. Typically, however, it is the coming together and the glorious celebration that is culturally highlighted. The act of consuming food itself is seen as a rather awkward act in the course of the public ceremony. In many countries it was not until this century that a high cuisine developed, and then in part under the influence of Western consumption, tourism, and the development of a more privacy-oriented middle class.

New forms of wealth and the movement of large numbers of East and Southeast Asians into urban settings have undermined this moral economy of consumption. In Jakarta and Bangkok, the new middle class lives in neighborhoods in which local social controls—especially those that may be exercised by people of less privileged class standing—are less important than conformity to lifestyle ideals disseminated in the media. As Ruth McVey (1992:26) has argued, there is emerging in East and Southeast Asia "a common, cosmopolitan, nouveau-riche consumer style." Many of its primary features were first developed in Japan, Taiwan, and Korea, often with strong American influence, and have recently been offered, as McVey puts it, "as the high culture model for modern capitalist Southeast Asia."

As in the West, however, the history of capitalism is not just the story of egoism's unremitting advance. No sooner do the media come to play a central role in the shaping of cosmopolitan lifestyles than—to take the Malaysian and Indonesian examples—Muslim preachers are there as well, warning of the dangers of decadence and urging people to look to a larger good. This effort to remoralize wealth is, of course, not merely a mechanical reflex of affluence; nor, therefore, is its incidence uniform across East and Southeast Asia. As the chapters in this volume illustrate, the form and foci of such efforts vary from country to country depending in large part on the ability of religious and like-minded organizations (including political ones) to respond to the challenges of the new capitalism. Not all religious organizations are created equal on this score. In contemporary China, for example, religious officials among the Muslim Hui, described by Dru Gladney in this volume, enjoy a much greater influence than do their counterparts (to the extent they exist at all) among the Han. Similarly, in Indonesia, Muslim social organizations have been able to respond to the moral challenge of the economy and nation more effectively than, for example, Javanese mystics. As these examples show, the decisive factor in efforts to moralize wealth is not the hold of "traditional" values on society but the ability of religious and ethical movements to develop alternative ideals and organizations viable within the now "globalized" structures of the media and national life.

The culture of modern consumption is powerful and can work to convey global influences. However, as it renders some instruments of consumption uniform, modern consumption also inspires a sometimes desperate search for alternative ideals. At times it helps to generalize notions as to what counts as a minimum standard of living; it may also shape the terms for a heightened debate over the way a people should be. Not the end of history, the expansion of the modern capitalist market will keep these concerns in the public arena for a long time to come.

Conclusion: The Global and the Local

When examined by way of its organizations and meanings, capitalism proves to be a more diverse beast than was once thought. To speak of capitalism's embeddedness is to recognize that market processes are everywhere mediated by a host of facilitative structures. Capitalism not only depends on these moral, legal-political, and organizational arrangements but cannot operate without them. Dependent as capitalism is on these supports, its impact on politics, class, and popular morality also varies from society to society. The state and law play a much smaller role in business life among Taiwanese and overseas Chinese than they do in the United States or Western Europe. Multimillion dollar deals that in the United States are struck only after scrutiny by a small army of lawyers are, among Chinese capitalists, settled with a handshake. Capital that in London is secured from international banks may in Bangkok and Taipei be mobilized through an informal network of trade partners. For those scholars who, following Max Weber, were convinced that the prerequisite for modern capitalism is a well-mannered legal system and impersonal bureaucracy, business arrangements of this sort may be dismissed as "premodern" organizations "in transition" to modern ones. But such a conclusion now seems unduly restrictive, indeed ethnocentric.

This is not to suggest, it must be emphasized, that capitalism in contrasting cultures is an entirely relative, indeterminate thing, its prior commonalities obliterated in our postmodern era. Despite all its changes, modern capitalism has preserved a significant elementary structure throughout its extraordinary evolution. Among other things, it is a system of socioeconomic organization dedicated to the systematic investment of wealth into enterprise productive of additional wealth, where the primary means of production are privately owned and where there is sufficient market competition to create systemic incentives for the owners of the means of production to reinvest a portion of their profits as capital back into productive activities. Much can and will vary as this rather hoary, abstract model is made real. From family firms to corporations, the discretionary authority implied by "private" ownership varies significantly, sometimes even within the same society. Similarly, the degree to which private ownership actually predominates over that of the state also differs across economies we call capitalist. France,

Singapore, and Indonesia differ rather significantly on this score from Great Britain and the United States. And finally, the degree to which the market is actually open to and creative of competitive pressures also varies. The extent of competition may diminish both as a result of extramarket collusion and, equally important, because citizens in most countries insist that the state impose limits on unregulated competition so as to ensure minimum standards of performance in such fields as air transport, water quality, child care, and public morals. Contrary to its often-heard characterization as a wholly self-regulating system or unitary power structure, *not one* among these characteristics of capitalism is determined by the formal logic of the market alone. Each looks to the larger world of which the economy is part. Variation in capitalism's organization is not so much a frill on an otherwise essential whole, then, as it is an intrinsic part of the way in which a generalized system grounds itself in local settings. Whether on Wall Street or in a Surabayan slum, there is no capitalism without local articulation.

Commonalities aside, the global structures within which local capitalisms operate have changed enormously over the past 100 years, and even quite significantly since the mid-1970s. The changes have created new systemic incentives whose impact has affected local capitalisms in convergent, if still significantly varied, ways.[11] A century ago a significant portion of capitalism's expansive dynamic in East and Southeast Asia depended not on self-sustaining free trade or the technological radiance of industrial firms but on a militarily secured alliance between European capitalists and colonial states. Whether this colonial capitalism was the dominant form in the international economy, as some insist, or whether the primary engine was a domestic competition engendering unremitting techno-organizational advance are issues that will continue to be debated for some time. What is clear is that there was no pure market system free of political or cultural influence. Viewed from the social and political structures in which they nested, there were several types of capitalist organization, and there are still today.

For most Asians early in the twentieth century, of course, there was no question as to which form of capitalist organization was dominant. It was not the capitalism of open access and fair play or, least of all, that of individual rights and the rule of law. It was a politically leveraged system of social and economic *apartheid* designed to secure control of the economy's commanding heights for Europeans. This colonial capitalism left a bitter legacy, and it should surprise no one that for some Asians still today this experience provides the prototype for their understanding of modern capitalism. Moreover, all is not just distant cultural memory: There are numerous contemporary examples of the political leveraging of market advantage, now as often with domestic partners as foreign.

Interestingly, however, one of the most significant developments in the international economy since the 1970s has been the outflow of capital from advanced industrial societies (including, in Asia, not merely Japan but Korea, Taiwan, Hong Kong, and Singapore) into lower-wage industrializing ones. The political influence of this investment is sometimes exaggerated, but there can be little doubt that competition among host nations for this foreign investment has introduced significant pressures for the regularization of finance, investment laws, and domestic market structures. In Southeast Asia, the years since the early 1980s have seen a particularly notable increase in the volume of this investment and in the number of nations scrambling to attract it (see Winters 1996:27). This feature of the new world economy seems likely to increase the role of commercial law in business life even in regions of East-Southeast Asia where particularized relationships have long played a primary role in generating market trust.

Whether business growth and a heightened reliance on commercial regulation strengthen the rule of law and will, over the long run, promote democratization are far more complex questions. As is well known, the experience of capitalism in northwestern Europe suggests that the dispersion of economic power out of the hands of a few (whether in government or among an elite social class) and into the hands of many represents an important force for democratization. Unfortunately for this neat generalization, however, business authority in East and Southeast Asia has not everywhere migrated away from the state, and as a result, business's impact on political life has been quite varied. Indeed, even in the European case, Robert D. Putnam's (1993) study of markets and civic traditions in Italy reminds us of how complex the impact of modern capitalism can be. Taking note of the rich associational life of northern Italy, Putnam shows that bureaucracies and markets both work better where they are "undergirded" by horizontal ties of civic associations, as seen in northern Italy's proliferation of "tower societies, guilds, mutual aid societies, cooperatives, unions, and even soccer clubs and literary societies" (Putnam 1993:181). Where, as in southern Italy, these ties are lacking and vertical dependence and lateral isolation are the rule, neither markets nor government functions in an open and inclusive manner.

Putnam provides a sobering reminder of democracy's varied possibilities under modern capitalist growth. Though he does not himself phrase his conclusions in this fashion, the two cases he compares—northern and southern Italy—have long been integrated into an international capitalist economy. The South may not be prosperous, and its patronage and gangsterism are not the sort of things that make market liberals cheer. Yet in this instance it is useful to remind ourselves that we are still dealing with a region long integrated into the modern capitalist world. Capital here is privately owned, there is substantial reinvestment of capital in search of greater profits, and many (but not all) goods and services move about quite labilely in response to supply and demand. But the society in which the market is embedded knows little of the rule of law; and entrepreneurial success is greeted with demands for kickbacks by criminal bosses and patrons. If Putnam's description of southern Italy is at all accurate, it seems that a society can preserve a freedom-denying system of patronal domination despite a long history of involvement with the international capitalist market.

Unfortunately, this model of limited liberalization is by no means unique to southern Italy. It might be suggested, for example, that capitalist Russia resembles southern Italy more than it does the North (Gray 1993). Others might see striking similarities between southern Italy and business practices in some parts of contemporary Southeast Asia (Aden 1992; Bresnan 1993). Southern Italy thus reminds us that modern capitalism can coexist with a wider and less enlightened array of political structures than imagined by some market enthusiasts. A competitive price is paid, of course, for things like cronyist patronage. And in a world where nations are competing for global investment that price may be more readily apparent than would be the case in an era of less mobile capital. But the sad fact is that in some societies ruling elites seem more than willing to pay that price. Market processes depend on more than the logic of the market alone.

It is a truism of contemporary social thought that theories do not develop in a vacuum but emerge from an ongoing and often destabilizing dialogue with the world. The refiguration of our contemporary understanding of capitalism reflects just such a process of dialogical engagement. Events in East and Southeast Asia have revealed an organizational variety to capitalism heretofore unrecognized in accounts of modernity. Though less well understood, that same history has revealed that a varied moral and cultural flora survives within and around capitalist formations. Some among us will predict that it is only a matter of time; the market will take us all into the same radiant future or, alternately, doom all that is solid to melt into dreary air. Thus far, however, the lessons from this portion of the globe suggest a more complex conclusion. Differences in market culture will remain because, human orders that they are, markets work only inasmuch as they embrace the social worlds of which they are irrevocably part.

NOTES

1. Clifford Geertz, one of the most influential cultural anthropologists of the 1970s and 1980s, provides a good example of just such a muscular concept. Culture, he writes, is a system of symbols and meanings that "provide a blueprint or template in terms of which processes external to themselves can be given a definite form. . . . As the order of bases in a strand of DNA forms a coded program . . . , so culture patterns provide such programs for the institution of the social and psychological processes which shape public behavior" (Geertz 1973:92). In other places, especially when invoking the philosophers Gilbert Ryle and Ludwig Wittgenstein, Geertz presents a less deterministic model of culture that recognizes intracultural variation and psychocultural dynamism. In general, however, like many cultural theorists of his generation, he downplays this interactive view of mind, body, and culture in favor of an image of culture as exhaustively determinative of mind and behavior.

2. Two collections that provide especially rich examples of the efforts of nonmainstream economists to expand the horizons of the discipline as a whole are Klamer, McCloskey, and Solow (1988) and Lavoie (1990).

3. See Taussig 1980 for a perspective closer to the conventionally romantic Polanyite view.

4. Among many fine works, the recent studies by Christine Dobbin (1996), Denys Lombard (1990), and Anthony Reid (1993) provide us with particularly insightful portraits of minority entrepreneurs who worked across the East and Southeast Asian region.

5. In an important essay, Maurice Bloch and J. Parry have made a similar argument for the analysis of money. They note that many anthropologists and historians have written as if the use of money is everywhere "an intrinsic revolutionary power" (Parry and Bloch 1989:12). Such a generalization, they observe, impedes recognition of the highly varied—and not always depersonalizing or community-destroying— manner in which money has been integrated into different societies. Rather than gloomy generalizations, Bloch and Parry call for a less romantic and more critical account of money, focusing in particular on the "transactional systems" in which money plays a part (1989:23). A similar sentiment should be applied, I might add, to the study of modern capitalist organization and exchange as a whole.

6. In many Chinese societies, however, a good portion of this wealth is returned to the young woman as dowry when she marries.

7. This generalization would have to be seriously qualified for some contemporary Southeast Asian countries. See the essays on Southeast Asia in Haggard, Lee, and Maxfield (1993).

8. See Ezra Vogel's remark that in traditional China, *guanxi* networks were often and even primarily used "to gain access to leaders to divide the spoils of power" (Vogel 1991:87).

9. This point is discussed in a comparative Southeast Asian perspective in Skinner 1996.

10. Nowhere is this more apparent than in that heartland of modern capitalism, the United States. And nowhere does this debate take on a more unexpectedly intriguing form—unexpected, that is, in light of secularist stereotypes—than among Protestant evangelicals. See Craig M. Gay (1991).

11. That "globalization" has not created a pattern of unqualified cross-national convergence in economic policy and organization is a theme deftly highlighted in a recent collection of essays edited by Suzanne Berger and Ronald Dore (1996).

REFERENCES

Aden, Jean. 1992. "Entrepreneurship and Protection in the Indonesian Oil Service Industry." In Ruth McVey, ed., *Southeast Asian Capitalists*, pp. 89–101. Ithaca: Southeast Asia Program, Cornell University.

Anderson, Benedict. 1983. "Old State, New Society: Indonesia's New Order in Comparative Historical Perspective." *Journal of Asian Studies* 42, 3:477–496.

Appadurai, Arjun. 1986. "Introduction: Commodities and the Politics of Value." In Appadurai, ed., *The Social Life of Things: Commodities in Cultural Perspective*, pp. 3–63. Cambridge: Cambridge University Press.

Atkinson, Jane, and Shelly Errington, eds. 1990. *Power and Difference: Gender in Island Southeast Asia*. Stanford: Stanford University Press.

Banks, David. 1983. *Malay Kinship*. Philadelphia: ISHI.

Becker, Gary. 1976. *The Economic Approach to Human Behavior*. Chicago: University of Chicago Press.

Berger, Peter L. 1988. "An East Asian Development Model?" In Peter L. Berger and Hsin-Huang Michael Hsiao, eds. *In Search of an East Asian Development Model*, pp. 3–11. New Brunswick: Transaction Books.

Berger, Suzanne, and Ronald Dore. 1996. *National Diversity and Global Capitalism*. Ithaca and London: Cornell University Press.

Black, R.D. Collison, and Craufurd D.W. Goodwin, eds. 1973. *The Marginal Revolution in Economics*. Durham, N.C.: Duke University Press.

Bloch, Maurice. 1989. "From Cognition to Ideology." In Bloch, *Ritual, History and Power: Selected Papers in Anthropology*, pp. 106–136. London School of Economics Monographs on Social Anthropology, no. 58. London: Athlone Press.

Bourdieu, Pierre. 1977. *Outline of a Theory of Practice*. Cambridge: Cambridge University Press.

Bresnan, John. 1993. "The Pertamina Crisis." In Bresnan, *Managing Indonesia: The Modern Political Economy*, pp. 164–193. New York: Columbia University Press.

Buchler, I.R., and H.A. Selby. 1968. *Kinship and Social Organization: An Introduction to Theory and Method*. New York: Macmillan.

Casanova, José. 1994. *Public Religions in the Modern World*. Chicago: University of Chicago Press.

Clegg, S.R., and S.G. Redding, eds. 1990. *Capitalism in Contrasting Cultures*. New York: Walter de Gruyter.

Dalton, George. 1968. "Introduction." In Dalton, ed., *Primitive, Archaic and Modern Economies: Essays of Karl Polanyi*, pp. ix–liv. Boston: Beacon Press.

———. 1971. "Introduction: The Subject of Economic Anthropology." In Dalton, ed., *Studies in Economic Anthropology*, pp. 1–15. Washington, D.C.: American Anthropological Association.

Dewey, Alice. 1962. *Peasant Marketing in Java*. Glencoe, Ill.: Free Press.

Djamour, Judith. 1959. *Malay Kinship and Marriage in Singapore*. London: Athlone.

Dobbin, Christine. 1996. *Asian Entrepreneurial Minorities: Conjoint Communities in the Making of the World Economy, 1570–1940*. London: Curzon Press.

Doner, Richard F. 1991. "Approaches to the Politics of Economic Growth in Southeast Asia." *Journal of Asian Studies* 50, 4:818–849.

Douglas, Mary, and Baron Isherwood. 1979. *The World of Goods*. New York: Basic Books.

Epstein, T.S. 1968. *Capitalism, Primitive and Modern: Some Aspects of Tolai Economic Growth*. Canberra: Australian National University Press.

Etzioni, Amitai, and Paul R. Lawrence. 1991. *Socio-Economics: Toward a New Synthesis*. Armonk, N.Y.: M.E. Sharpe.

Evans, Peter. 1992. "The State as Problem and Solution: Predation, Embedded Autonomy, and Structural Change." In Stephan Haggard and Robert R. Kaufman, eds., *The Politics of Economic Adjustment*, pp. 139–181. Princeton: Princeton University Press.

Freedman, Maurice. 1959. "The Handling of Money: A Note on the Background to the Economic Sophistication of Overseas Chinese." *Man* 59:64–65.

_____. 1966. *Chinese Lineage and Society: Fukien and Kwangtung*. London School of Economics Monographs in Social Anthropology, no. 33. London: Athlone Press.

Friedland, Roger, and A.F. Robertson. 1990. *Beyond the Marketplace: Rethinking Economy and Society*. New York: Aldine de Gruyter.

Fukuyama, Francis. 1989. "The End of History?" *National Interest* 26:3–18.

_____. 1995. *Trust: The Social Virtues and the Creation of Prosperity*. New York: Free Press.

Gay, Craig M. 1991. *With Liberty and Justice for Whom? The Recent Evangelical Debate over Capitalism*. Grand Rapids, Mich.: Eerdmans.

Geertz, Clifford. 1963. *Peddlers and Princes: Social Development and Economic Change in Two Indonesian Towns*. Chicago: University of Chicago Press.

_____. 1973. "Religion as a Cultural System." In Geertz, *The Interpretation of Cultures*, pp. 87–125. New York: Basic Books.

Giddens, Anthony. 1984. *The Constitution of Society: Outline of a Theory of Structuration*. Berkeley and Los Angeles: University of California Press.

Granovetter, Mark. 1974. *Getting a Job: A Study of Contacts and Careers*. Cambridge: Harvard University Press.

_____. 1984. "Small Is Bountiful: Labor Markets and Establishment Size." *American Sociological Review* 49, 3:323–334.

_____. 1985. "Economic Action and Social Structure: The Problem of Embeddedness." *American Journal of Sociology* 91:481–510.

Gray, John. 1993. "From Post-Communism to Civil Society: The Reemergence of History and the Decline of the Western Model." In Ellen Frankel Paul, Fred D. Miller, and Jeffrey Paul, eds., *Liberalism and the Economic Order*, pp. 26–50. Cambridge: Cambridge University Press.

Habermas, Jürgen. 1984. *The Theory of Communicative Action*. Vol. 1, *Reason and the Rationalization of Society*. Trans. T. McCarthy. Boston: Beacon Press.

Haggard, Stephan, and Cheng Tun-jen. 1987. "State and Foreign Capital in the East Asian NICs." In F.C. Deyo, ed., *The Political Economy of the New Asian Industrialism*, pp. 84–135. Ithaca and London: Cornell University Press.

Haggard, Stephan, and Robert R. Kaufman, eds. 1992. *The Politics of Economic Adjustment: International Constraints, Distributive Conflicts, and the State*. Princeton: Princeton University Press.

Haggard, Stephan, Chung H. Lee, and Sylvia Maxfield. 1993. *The Politics of Finance in Developing Countries*. Ithaca and London: Cornell University Press.

Hall, John A. 1986. *Powers and Liberties: The Causes and Consequences of the Rise of the West*. Berekeley: University of California Press.

Hamilton, Gary. 1996. "Overseas Chinese Capitalism." In Tu Wei-Ming, *Confucian Traditions in East Asian Modernity: Moral Education and Economic Culture in Japan and the Four Mini-Dragons*, pp. 328–344. Cambridge: Harvard University Press.

Hamilton, Gary, and Nicole Woolsey Biggart. 1988. "Market, Culture, and Authority: A Comparative Analysis of Management and Organization in the Far East." *American Journal of Sociology* 94, Special Supplement:52–94.

Hamilton, Gary, William Zeile, and Wan-Jin Kim. 1990. "The Network Structures of East Asian Economies." In Steward R. Clegg and S. Gordon Redding, eds., *Capitalism in Contrasting Cultures*, pp. 105–129. Berlin: Walter de Gruyter.

Hefner, Robert W. 1983. "The Problem of Preference: Economic and Ritual Change in Highlands Java." *Man* 18:669–689.

————. 1985. *Hindu Javanese: Tengger Tradition and Islam*. Princeton: Princeton University Press.

————. 1990. *The Political Economy of Mountain Java: An Interpretive History*. Berkeley: University of California Press.

————. 1996. "Islamizing Capitalism: On the Founding of Indonesia's First Islamic Bank." In Mark Woodward and James Rush, eds., *Toward a New Paradigm: Recent Developments in Indonesian Islamic Thought*, pp. 291–322. Tempe: Center for Southeast Asian Studies, Arizona State University.

Hill, Hal. 1992. "Manufacturing Industry." In Anne Booth, ed., *The Oil Boom and After: Indonesian Economic Policy and Performance in the Soeharto Era*, pp. 204–257. Singapore: Oxford University Press.

Hirschman, Albert O. 1977. *The Passions and the Interests: Political Arguments for Capitalism Before Its Triumph*. Princeton: Princeton University Press.

————. 1986. *Rival Views of Market Society and Other Recent Essays*. Cambridge: Harvard University Press.

Holton, Robert J. 1992. *Economy and Society*. London: Routledge.

Huntington, Samuel P. 1993. "The Clash of Civilizations?" *Foreign Affairs* 72, 3:22–49.

Johnson, Chalmers. 1982. *MITI and the Japanese Miracle: The Growth of Industrial Policy, 1925–1975*. Stanford: Stanford University Press.

Kathirithamby-Wells, J., and John Villiers. 1990. *The Southeast Asian Port and Polity: Rise and Demise*. Singapore: Singapore University Press.

Keyes, Charles F., Laurel Kendall, and Helen Hardacre. 1994. *Asian Visions of Authority: Religion and the Modern States of East and Southeast Asia*. Honolulu: University of Hawaii Press.

Klamer, Arjo, Donald N. McCloskey, and Robert M. Solow. 1988. *The Consequences of Economic Rhetoric*. Cambridge: Cambridge University Press.

Kleinman, Arthur. 1988. *Rethinking Psychiatry: From Cultural Category to Personal Experience*. New York: Free Press.

Lambek, Michael. 1993. *Knowledge and Practice in Mayotte: Local Discourses of Islam, Sorcery, and Spirit Possession*. Toronto: Anthropological Horizons, University of Toronto Press.

Lavoie, Don. 1990. *Economics and Hermeneutics*. London and New York: Routledge.

Leiss, William. 1976. *The Limits to Satisfaction: An Essay on the Problem of Needs and Commodities*. Toronto: University of Toronto Press.

Leiss, William, Stephen Kline, and Sut Jhally. 1986. *Social Communication in Advertising: Persons, Products, and Images of Well Being*. Toronto: Methuen.

Lombard, Denys. 1990. *Le carrefour javanais: Essai d'histoire globale*. Vol. 2, *Les reseaux asiatique*. Paris: Éditions de l'École des Hautes Études en Sciences Sociales.

Lubasz, Heinz. 1992. "Adam Smith and the Invisible Hand—of the Market?" In Roy Dilley, ed., *Contesting Markets: Analyses of Ideology, Discourse and Practice*, pp. 37–56. Edinburgh: Edinburgh University Press.

MacIntyre, Andrew J. 1990. *Business and Politics in Indonesia*. Sydney: Allen & Unwin.

_____. 1994. "Power, Prosperity, and Patrimonialism: Business and Government in Indonesia." In MacIntyre, ed., *Business and Government in Industrialising Asia*, pp. 244–267. Ithaca: Cornell University Press.

MacIntyre, Andrew J., and Kanishka Jayasuriya, eds. 1992. *The Dynamics of Economic Policy Reform in South-East Asia and the South-West Pacific*. Kuala Lumpur: Oxford University Press.

Mackie, Jamie. 1992. "Changing Patterns of Chinese Big Business in Southeast Asia." In Ruth McVey ed., *Southeast Asian Capitalists*, pp. 161–190. Ithaca: Southeast Asia Program, Cornell University.

Martin, David. 1990. *Tongues of Fire: The Explosion of Protestantism in Latin America*. Oxford: Blackwell.

McPherson, Michael S. 1980. "Want Formation, Morality, and the Interpretive Dimension of Economic Inquiry." Research paper, no. 33. Williamstown, Mass.: Williams College.

McVey, Ruth. 1992. "The Materialization of the Southeast Asian Entrepreneur." In McVey, ed., *Southeast Asian Capitalists*, pp. 7–33. Ithaca: Southeast Asia Program, Cornell University.

Obeyesekere, Gananath. 1981. *Medusa's Hair: An Essay on Personal Symbols and Religious Experience*. Chicago and London: University of Chicago Press.

Orlove, Benjamin S., and Henry J. Rutz. 1989. "Thinking About Consumption: A Social Economy Approach." In Orlove and Rutz, eds., *The Social Economy of Consumption*, pp. 1–57. Monographs in Economic Anthropology, no. 6. Lanham, Md.: University Press of America.

Parry, Jonathon, and Maurice Bloch. 1989. "Introduction" In Parry and Bloch, eds., *Money and the Morality of Exchange*, pp. 1–32. Cambridge: Cambridge University Press.

Peletz, Michael G. 1996. *Reason and Passion: Representations of Gender in a Malay Society*. Berkeley: University of California Press.

Polanyi, Karl. 1944. *The Great Transformation*. New York: Rinehart.

Putnam, Robert D. 1993. *Making Democracy Work: Civic Traditions in Modern Italy*. Princeton: Princeton University Press.

Redding, S. Gordon. 1990. *The Spirit of Chinese Capitalism*. New York: Walter de Gruyter.

Reid, Anthony. 1988. *Southeast Asia in the Age of Commerce, 1450–1680*. Vol. 1, *The Land Below the Winds*. New Haven: Yale University Press.

_____. 1993. *Southeast Asia in the Age of Commerce, 1450–1680*. Vol. 2, *Expansion and Crisis*. New Haven: Yale University Press.

Robison, Richard. 1986. *Indonesia: The Rise of Capital*. Sydney: Allen & Unwin.

Rush, James R. 1990. *Opium to Java: Revenue Farming and Chinese Enterprise in Colonial Indonesia, 1860–1910*. Ithaca: Cornell University Press.

Sahlins, Marshall. 1976. *Culture and Practical Reason*. Chicago: University of Chicago Press.

Schwartz, Theodore. 1978. "Where Is the Culture? Personality as the Distributive Locus of Culture." In George D. Spindler, ed., *The Making of Psychological Anthropology*, pp. 419–441. Berkeley and London: University of California Press.

Sen, Amartya K. 1978. "Rational Fools: A Critique of the Behavioral Foundations of Economic Theory." In H. Harris, ed., *Scientific Models and Men*, pp. 317–344. London: Oxford University Press.

Shackle, G.L.S. 1973. "Marginalism: The Harvest." In R.D. Collison Black and Craufurd D.W. Goodwin, eds., *The Marginal Revolution in Economics*, pp. 321–336. Durham: Duke University Press.

Skinner, G. William. 1996. "Creolized Chinese Societies in Southeast Asia." In Anthony Reid, ed., *Sojourners and Settlers: Histories of Southeast Asia and the Chinese*, pp. 50–93. St. Leonards, Australia: Allen & Unwin.

Sieh Lee Mei Ling. 1992. "The Transformation of Malaysian Business Groups." In Ruth McVey, ed., *Southeast Asian Capitalists*, pp. 103–126. Ithaca: Southeast Asia Program, Cornell University.

Sizemore, Russel F., and Donald K. Swearer. 1990. "Introduction." In Sizemore and Swearer, eds., *Ethics, Wealth, and Salvation: A Study in Buddhist Social Ethics*, pp. 1–24. Columbia: University of South Carolina Press.

Sperber, Dan. 1975. *Rethinking Symbolism*. Cambridge: Cambridge University Press.

_____. 1996. "Modularité mentale et diversité culturelle." In Sperber, *La contagion des idées*, pp. 165–207. Paris: Éditions Odile Jacob.

Swift, Michael G. 1965. *Malay Peasant Socieety in Jelebu*. London: Athlone Press.

Taussig, Michael T. 1980. *The Devil and Commodity Fetishism in South America*. Chapel Hill: University of North Carolina Press.

Vitalis, L. [1851] 1992. "Effects of the Revenue Farming System." In M.R. Fernando and David Bulbeck, eds., *Chinese Economic Activity in Netherlands India: Selected Translations from the Dutch*, pp. 26–42. Sources for the Economic History of Southeast Asia, Data Paper Series, no. 2. Singapore: Institute of Southeast Asian Studies.

Vogel, Ezra F. 1991. *The Four Little Dragons: The Spread of Industrialization in East Asia*. Cambridge: Harvard University Press, 1991.

Wang Gungwu. 1992. *Community and Nation: China, Southeast Asia, and Australia*. 2nd ed. Singapore: Heinemann.

White, Stephen K. 1988. *The Recent Work of Jürgen Habermas: Reason, Justice and Modernity*. Cambridge: Cambridge University Press.

Wicks, Robert S. 1992. *Money, Markets, and Trade in Early Southeast Asia: The Development of Indigenous Monetary Systems to AD 1400*. Ithaca: Southeast Asia Program, Cornell University.

Williamson, Oliver. 1975. *Markets and Hierarchies*. New York: Free Press.

Winch, Donald. 1978. *Adam Smith's Politics: An Essay in Historiographic Revision*. Cambridge: Cambridge University Press.

Winters, Jeffrey A. 1996. *Power in Motion: Capital Mobility and the Indonesian State*. Ithaca: Cornell University Press.

Wong, Siu-lun. 1985. "The Chinese Family Firm: A Model." *British Journal of Sociology* 36:58–72.

Wrong, Dennis. 1961. "The Oversocialized Conception of Man in Modern Sociology." *American Sociological Review* 26, 2:183–193.

Yoshihara Kunio. 1988. *The Rise of Ersatz Capitalism in South-east Asia*. Singapore: Oxford University Press.

Part One
Chinese Capitalisms and Cultural Pluralism

one

Ã

Culture and Organization in Taiwan's Market Economy

GARY G. HAMILTON

Growing at an average of over 7 percent per annum since the 1960s, Taiwan's economy is now one of the most industrialized in Asia. In attempting to explain this extraordinary growth, many writers have argued that, as with other locations in East Asia, Taiwan's industrialization is largely the result of a strong state enacting sound economic policies. Alice Amsden (1985), Thomas Gold (1986), Pang Chien-Kuo (1992), Robert Wade (1990), and Joel Aberbach and his colleagues (1994) have been among those to reach this conclusion.[1] In this chapter, I argue that Taiwan's industrialization can be characterized more accurately as a form of "society-led" development. The driver of Taiwan's economic growth, I maintain, is not the state but rather owners of small- and medium-sized firms operating outside the state's routinized system of control. The organization and economic dynamics of this sector can best be understood by recognizing the owners' connection to Taiwan's social organization—to the normative relationships, networks, organizations, and institutions that constitute Taiwan's society. It is this extra-state social organization that creates Taiwan's "market culture," a symbolically dense, culturally specific environment in which economic decisions and activities are embedded.

The principal thesis of the strong-state theorists of Asian economic development is effectively summarized in the title of Robert Wade's book on Taiwan, *Governing the Market.* The state rules the economy and society and creates the conditions that promote capitalist development. Strong-state theorists have largely derived such interpretations of Asia from Western theories of political economy (Gerschenkron 1962; Moore 1966; Evans et al. 1985) and from several major studies of Latin American economies (Cardoso and Faletto 1979; Evans 1979). In generalizing these theories to Asia, they (e.g., Gold 1986:175; Evans 1987, 1995) have argued that in contrast to other regions of industrializing economies, the state is even stronger in Asia than elsewhere because industrialization has proceeded there more quickly and has gone much further.

In applying their theories to Taiwan in particular, most strong-state theorists (e.g., Aberbach et al. 1994; Amsden 1985; Gold 1988; Pang 1992; Li 1976; Wade 1990) analyze the state's economic policymaking and its role in creating a few exceptionally large businesses. They do not, however, discuss the way the economy is actually organized and works. Instead, drawing on extensive interviews with government elites and prominent industrialists and on government archives, they give what is essentially a view from the center, from Taipei, from the seat of government in its most sophisticated and imposing posture. What they provide, often in a finely framed analysis, is the elites' own views of their roles in promoting industrialization. State leaders and the elite businessmen would like to see themselves cast as the prime movers, *deus ex machina,* creating Taiwan's economic prosperity. This is a view that legitimizes their own positions of power and status in Taiwan's society and, coincidentally, marries nicely with current thinking on the political economy of development.[2] But this is also a view that ignores much of what has actually occurred in the economy, a great deal of which cannot be traced to government policy. In his masterful argument for a strong-state explanation of Taiwan's industrialization, Robert Wade's disarmingly honest assessment of his approach (1990:70) makes this exact point, thus providing a segue to my emphasis on economic organization.

> Taiwan's dualistic industrial structure is densely interconnected, and the export success of the smaller firms cannot be understood independently of the productive performance of the big firms. This being said, I should stress that the organization of firms—their size, the way they grow, their methods of doing business, and the relationships between them—is a major gap in the argument of this book. Any discussion of an economy's development should give a central place to the organization of firms and industries. But since little evidence is available on this subject for Taiwan, and since my primary interest is the uses of public power, I say little more about it.

Disclaimers aside, Wade's generally excellent study of the state's role in Taiwan's industrialization is a little like the sound of one hand clapping: On the one hand, there is the government's effort to shape the economy, and on the other hand, there is the actual shape of the economy. Not knowing the latter, how can we assess the former?

The few researchers in Taiwan who have gotten out in the field to do the necessary observation, interviews, and historical work to interpret how the economy actually works come up with different conclusions than either a strong-state or a free-market interpretation of Taiwan's economic development (Chen 1994, 1995; Fields 1995; Greenhalgh 1988; Kao 1991; Shieh 1992). These researchers observe that Taiwan's economy is densely networked and that these networks themselves have significant independent effects on the economy quite apart from the state or from the global economy.

This is also the conclusion that I have reached. The existing social and economic organizations within a society influence the state's economic planners as much as, and likely more than, the state's planners shape that society's economic organizations. To demonstrate the significance of society's influence on the process of economic development, it is important to understand how Taiwan's economy is organized.

Macroorganizational Features of Taiwan's Economy

Small- and medium-sized firms drive Taiwan's export-oriented economy. To make sense of this fact, it is useful to contrast the organization of Taiwan's economy with that of Japan and South Korea. In both of the latter economies, large business groups—in South Korea the *chaebol* (Amsden 1989; Kim 1997) and in Japan the *keiretsu* and the even larger intermarket groups, the *kigyo shudan* (Fruin 1992; Gerlach 1992; Orrù, Hamilton, and Biggart 1997; Westney 1996)—form the organizational centers of these economies, integrating most other smaller networks of firms into some form of direct or indirect association with these large networks. In both economies, these business networks especially dominate the export sectors in finished consumer goods. By contrast, in Taiwan, networks of small- and medium-sized firms command the export sectors in finished goods and component parts. These networks of firms serve as the integrating center for the Taiwanese economy, an economy that also consists of many large business networks and a substantial sector of government enterprises. The first step in understanding Taiwan's market culture is to understand how the small- and medium-sized firms fit into the overall structure and how they provide the organizational dynamic for the entire economy.

State-Owned Enterprises

In Japan and South Korea, the states' political policies, economic assistance, and at times direct intervention have supported the formation of big business networks. Having a strong role in economic planning and policy implementation, state officials have seen a diminishing need for state ownership or direct state control of key industries. Accordingly, Japanese and South Korean state officials have steadily privatized the state-owned sector. By the 1990s in both societies the state-owned sector contributed less than 5 percent of the total GNP. By contrast, in Taiwan, where state officials have less power to plan and implement economy policy, the state continues to own and to control a substantial piece of the total economy. The state-owned sector during 1970–1990 constituted between 10 and 15 percent of the total value added in manufacturing.[3]

Since 1970 the state-owned sector has played a distinctive role in the overall economy. Most of the state's economic assets, production, and value added has come from only a dozen state-owned enterprises, including Taiwan Power, China Petroleum, China Steel, and China Petrochemical Development.[4] From this list, it is easy to see that Taiwan's state-owned enterprises occupy a position furthermost upstream, supplying the basic raw materials (i.e., the steel and the petroleum) and the electrical power that runs most of the factories. The state-owned enterprises do not export their products; rather these early state ventures in import substitution produced commodities and services for the domestic economy, in effect subsidizing the private sector through maintaining low prices on upstream goods and services. As Taiwan's economy has grown, the demand for these upstream products has increased roughly in proportion to the overall growth, so that, for example, Taiwan Power has had to build more nuclear power generators and China Petroleum has become involved in extensive offshore oil exploration.

In addition to supplying basic commodities and infrastructural services, the state has tried to stimulate specific sectors of the economy by subsidizing upstream manufacturing as well as research and development firms to help establish private firms in targeted sectors (Wade 1990:90–108). These efforts began in the early years of the KMT (Kuomintang) government with direct support for plastic and textile industries and continue today with support for food processing, biotechnology, and semiconductor industries. As in the overall economy, in these targeted sectors, the state supports upstream components of industries, and state-owned enterprises serve the private sector by undertaking those research and development tasks and those capital intensive, economy-of-scale activities that are beyond the capabilities of most private firms. For instance, the charter for the 48.3 percent state-owned Taiwan Semiconductor Manufacturing Company states that the company is "forbidden to make any products of its own." Instead, "partly to prevent it from becoming a rival to the small firms it was set up to serve," the company was created to supply local firms with the semiconductors they needed to make their products (*Far Eastern Economic Review*, August 18, 1988:84).

State-owned enterprises primarily supply infrastructure and basic initial goods and services such as electricity, gasoline, steel, and even technology transfers that in principle all other companies, regardless of size, might use.[5] By removing the production of these essential goods and services from private hands, the government has prevented these sectors from being monopolized by the richest, most powerful, or best-connected firms. In effect, the Taiwan state has blocked the development of Japanese- and South Korean–style business groups in the very areas where some form of monopolization is most likely necessary to achieve the scale and scope of service required by users.

Large Business Groups

To those in the private sector, state-owned enterprises are large and far away, as is the government bureaucracy itself. Ideally, the enterprises exist to preserve economic order by providing infrastructure and essential goods, but they are not intended to interfere or compete with the livelihood of those in the private sector. Within the private sector, competition and mutual interference in pursuit of profit and economic success is the rule. But unlike the strong and sometimes cutthroat competition among business groups in South Korea and to a somewhat lesser extent in Japan, the most intense competition exists not among big business groups but instead among networks of small- and medium-sized firms making similar products for the same export markets. In the midst of this competition, another sort of division of labor emerges, one that divides the big and the little business networks.

If one examines the aggregate statistics on the relative size of business groups (Orrù, Hamilton, and Biggart 1997:151–186, 246–248), it is apparent that Taiwan's business groups are considerably less significant than business groups in Japan or South Korea. That surface appearance now needs to be qualified with a more in-depth look at Taiwan's industrial structure. Such an examination shows that the organization of Taiwan's private sector differs from that of the other two cases not only in degree but, more important, also in kind. The large business groups in Taiwan do not organize the economy but rather are themselves driven by the demand created by the export-oriented sector of the economy, which is in turn dominated by networks of smaller firms.

The clear indication of the qualitative differences between Taiwan and the other two cases is the location of business groups in commodity chains that lead to the production and distribution of export products. With the exception of producing a little over 20 percent of Taiwan's electrical and electronics products, the top business groups predominate in sectors producing intermediate products, goods that are not in final form (Orrù, Hamilton, and Biggart 1997:250). Before the late 1980s, when many of Taiwan's small- and medium-sized export producers in such goods as footwear and garments moved to Southeast Asia and the People's Republic of China in order to reduce their labor costs, the big business groups sold their intermediate products domestically. In the early 1990s the export demand for Taiwan's intermediate goods increased as these overseas Taiwan firms continued buying their inputs from the big business groups. This relationship between the big business networks and the small-firm economy is significant because Taiwan's economy was in the 1980s one of the world's most export-oriented, a trend that continued into the 1990s (World Bank 1988). In 1985, Taiwan's exports as a percentage of GNP were 51 percent as compared with South Korea's 37.5 percent and Japan's 16.4 percent in the same year. South Korea's and Japan's biggest business groups control production and distribution of final export products; they dominate the export sectors of these economies. Yet in Taiwan, a country with one of the world's highest percentage of manufactured export goods to total output, the biggest businesses produced, until recently, intermediate goods sold domestically.

This apparent paradox is easy enough to explain for the large business groups, but the ease of explanation here only adds to the difficulty in explaining how the third sector of the economy, the small- and medium-sized businesses, actually works. The private businesses in Taiwan that have been able to grow large relative to other businesses are upstream producers for the tens of thousands of small- and medium-sized firms that are downstream consumers of their intermediate goods. These intermediate goods are used to produce a final product (Hamilton, Zeile, and Kim 1990; Hamilton and Feenstra 1995). So marked is this tendency that one Taiwanese economist, Chou Tein-Chen (1985), has argued that Taiwan has a dichotomous market structure in the private sector. The smallest firms are those that produce for export, and the largest are those that produce for local use. The Taiwan government calculates that firms having less than 300 employees account for nearly 50 percent of Taiwan's total manufacturing output and 65 percent of all exports, figures that remained steady during the 1970s and 1980s (Wu 1988:6–9; also see Biggs 1988b:3–4). By contrast, large firms with over 500 employees represent a steady, if slightly declining, share of total production. Since the mid-1960s, the share of net value added for these large firms in the total economy went from 46 percent to 37 percent, a figure that would be much less were one counting only exports (Biggs 1988b:3–4).

A second indication of Taiwan's unique industrial structure is that it is not based on a logic of "one-setism," as is the case in Japan and South Korea (Gerlach 1992). Using several standard measures of diversification, measures that assess the relative strength of the main business activity in relation to the entire group of firms, some colleagues and I have found that Taiwanese business groups are considerably less diversified than their counterparts in South Korean and Japan (Hamilton and Feenstra 1995). Whereas South Korean and Japanese business groups attempt to control all links in the commodity chains of the products they produce, from far upstream to far downstream,

Taiwanese business groups tend to control only one upstream link. For that specific link, they may constitute nearly a monopoly in the domestic market. The third indication of Taiwan's unusual business structure is the relative continuity of this tripartite division of labor since 1970 despite a changing composition of groups at the top. The relative percentage of the total output for the state-, big-business, and small- and medium-sized firm sectors remained fairly constant during the 1970s and 1980s, a time when Taiwan's output and per capita income soared. The large-business portion of this output remained fairly constant with perhaps a slight decline in recent years despite considerable variations in the internal mix in the groups listed among the top 100 (Chou 1985:46).

The continuity of the overall division of labor suggests that the export sector of the economy, consisting primarily of the small- and medium-sized firms, creates demands for intermediate goods and services that allow the large business groups and state-owned enterprises to grow at roughly the same rates as the export sector. The changes in the mix of the big business groups on top, however, reflect changes in the demands for intermediate goods and service as the composition of Taiwan's exports change over time. As the demand for specific intermediate goods and services decline, the group or groups supplying those goods decline in importance as well. As one group falls, however, its position among the biggest groups is given over to another group supplying a good whose demand has risen. Business groups of all sizes rise and decline for other reasons as well, but in terms of creating market institutions and controlling economic forces, the data are clear that the largest business groups are not the main organizational force propelling the Taiwan economy, as is the case in both Japanese and South Korean economies. Instead, Taiwan's business groups are themselves the creation of other market forces, in particular the export sector. In short, the small-firm tail of Taiwan's industrial structure wags the entire economy.

Small- and Medium-Sized Firms

How can an economy be propelled into industrialization by the smallest-sized, least vertically integrated segment of its industrial structure? To answer this question, let us start with an analogy. The industrial structure in Taiwan reflects what might be called the "gold-rush effect." In a gold rush, a great many people get caught up in the stampede to find gold, and although a few people strike it rich by discovering gold, those who make the most money are the ones who supply the miners with the goods and services they need. This analogy applies rather directly to Taiwan.

The export segment of the Taiwan economy, composed primarily of a mix of small- and medium-sized firms, represents those who want to strike it rich through manufacturing products for global markets. Entrepreneurs search for products that will hit it big in the export arena, and when one person finds such a product and it becomes known, many other people rush into the same area of production.

One of the clearest demonstrations of this gold-rush effect is the textiles sector, the only manufacturing sector in which business groups produce over 50 percent of the total sales. But business groups account for only 12 percent of the total sales in the garment and apparel sector (Orrù, Hamilton, and Biggart 1997). Business groups produce the fabrics, not the clothes; the next step is done by countless small factories working on consignments from medium-sized clothing firms that in turn produce batch orders for major retail outlets located in the United States, Europe, and Southeast Asia. This same process is repeated in almost every other sector and in almost every large business group.

The explosion of small firms has also occurred around the manufacture of bicycles and such electronic items as TVs and, most recently, laptop computers. So common is this rush into the same area of production that Taiwanese call this sort of competition "a swarm of bees" (i wo feng) (Mark 1972:28). The swarming effect immediately drives down the profits, shortens the product cycle, and limits high returns to the first arrivals. This process—the entrepreneurial discovery of new products to sell in global markets and then the headlong rush into the same area of export production—fuels constant but shifting demands for domestic intermediate inputs and for necessary services to make and deliver those products. Taiwan's economic structure rests on these entrepreneurs, on their search for and their manufacture of new products that will sell well, and the industrial structure itself shifts as these entrepreneurs shift into new areas of production.[6]

In Taiwan, entrepreneurship of individual owners drives the economy as opposed to corporate managerialism, which drives the economies of Japan and South Korea. Although a subject overblown in the local press, entrepreneurialism in Taiwan society is also not a fiction. The desire to be an independent businessperson and to earn one's living and possibly get rich has a basis in reality. Taiwan in the middle 1980s, with a population of around 20 million, had 700,000 registered businesses, all of which had their laoban (manager). There was 1 laoban for every 15 persons, and if we count only adults, then one laoban for every 8 persons (Chang 1988:10).[7] The Taipei businessman that Tyler Biggs (1988a:3) quotes, therefore, was only slightly exaggerating when he said, "If you stood in the middle of this city and tossed a stone in any direction, you'd probably hit a boss."

A contrast with South Korea helps to clarify the nature of entrepreneurship in Taiwan. According to the calculations of Tyler S. Biggs (1988b:3–4, my emphasis), who expanded earlier findings by Scitovsky (1986:146), in Taiwan between 1966 and 1986 "the *number* of reported firms increased by 315 percent . . . and the average firm size expanded 15%." In the same period, the reverse occurred in South Korea, where "average *firm size* jumped by 300 percent and its firms grew in number by only 10 percent." One can make sense of these diametrically opposed developmental trajectories through Brian Levy's case studies contrasting the export production of footwear and computer keyboards in Taiwan and South Korea. "The comparative field research," he concluded (1988:44),

> revealed that Korean producers of footwear tended to be vertically integrated, stitching in-house the uppers for footwear, and manufacturing in-house rubber soles, as well as assembling complete shoes; by contrast, Taiwanese producers specialized in footwear assembly, and subcontracted the task of upper stitching and sole manufacture to independent vendors. Similarly whereas Korean producers of keyboards for personal computers manufactured in-house both plastic key parts and mechanical key-switches, Taiwanese producers tended to procure these components from arms-length suppliers.

Therefore, as economic development in both locations accelerated, South Korean export production grew as the largest businesses further increased their size. In contrast, Taiwan's export production grew through starting new firms and linking these firms to the output of other small- and medium-sized firms. In other words, South Korea grew through management, whereas Taiwan grew through entrepreneurship.

Given the fact that entrepreneurship in a small-firm economy is the source of Taiwan's dynamic form of capitalism, one must ask how rather modest-sized firms in this economy can be so flexible in what, how, and how much they produce. It is somehow understandable that huge business groups in Japan or South Korea, linking sometimes thousands of firms of different sizes and exploiting their internal synergies, could concentrate their research and development efforts and their production expertise to manufacture some of the world's finest products. It is much more difficult to explain—as one walks down dusty streets in central Taiwan and sees family after family working around tables in their storefront homes that are open to everyone's view or as one drives in the countryside and sees small concrete boxes located in the midst of rice fields that are factories employing only handfuls of people—how someone could be producing a piece of a part that will go into a component that is in 50 percent or more of all computers worldwide. Taiwan's business organizations achieve both economies of scale and economies of scope, and they do so because they utilize the resources in Taiwan's densely networked society.

Vertical and Horizontal Controls in Taiwan's Business Networks

Taiwan has been so successful as a small- and medium-sized-firm economy and relatively so unsuccessful as a large-firm economy because of its distinctive patterns of organizing economic networks. Networks within Asian societies should be seen as institutionalized frameworks of control, and in Taiwan these frameworks center on the family. Everyone who has studied Taiwan's business organizations has reached a similar conclusion: Overwhelmingly, Taiwan's privately owned businesses, large and small, are family-owned and family-controlled enterprises. Whereas certainly correct, this conclusion obscures another related and equally important aspect of Taiwan's economic organization. The networks that exist *between* family-owned-enterprises groups are as crucial to Taiwan's economy as are the business networks that exist *within* families, and both provide the structural underpinning of Taiwan's market culture. These two types of networks, the intra- and interfamily networks, represent two distinct types of control structures. The first type of network, the family network, occurs within spheres of strong family control; like family networks in Korea, these networks are hierarchical, but unlike those in Korea, Taiwan family networks have relatively short vertical spans of control. The second type of network, which I call the *guanxi* (relationship of reciprocity; see further on) network, occurs outside spheres of direct family control; these networks are based on norms of reciprocity, are situationally based, and have broad horizontal spans of control.

Family Ownership and Vertical Controls

As in Japan and South Korea, ownership networks provide a first indication of the patterns of interfirm control. All the researchers who have studied ownership patterns among large firms in Taiwan (Mark 1972; Greenhalgh 1988; Hamilton and Biggart 1988; Hamilton and Kao 1990; Numazaki 1986, 1991a, 1991b, 1993) have emphasized the importance of family *(jia)* ownership and family control. An analysis of the 1983 and 1986 data on Taiwan business groups (China Credit Information Service 1983, 1985), as well as interviews with core people in some of the business groups, substantiates this finding. Majority ownership and control of business-group firms are in the hands of core family members and heads of households. My colleagues in Taiwan who are also working on this project have determined, on a group-by-group basis, that 84 of the top 97 business groups in 1983 can be strictly classified as family-owned business groups (Peng 1989:277). Twenty-three of these are primarily owned by a single head of household; the remaining 61 business groups have multiple family members classified as being among the core people in the group, and most of those family members (54 out of the 61) are of three types: fathers and sons, brothers, and brothers and their sons (Peng 1989).

The preponderance of family ownership does not, however, explain the success of Taiwanese firms. Quite the reverse is true. As Wong Siu-lun (1985) has so ably described, the Chinese family firm is inherently short-term and unstable. Gordon Redding (1990) refers to the Chinese family firm as a "weak organization." A large part of this instability arises from institutional sources, from the kinship system in particular.

The Chinese family, the household *(jia)*, or what Fei Xiaotong (1992:81) calls the "small lineage," is the basic unit of the patrilineal, patrilocal kinship system. In principle, a patrilineage traces descent through the male line and, accordingly, joins all males in the same line of descent into an organized network of mutual obligation. It is also patrilocal in that in the normative residential pattern, married sons and their wives live in or near their father's house.

Because the number of males included in a patrilineage grows geometrically across generations and rapidly fills whatever space exists, patrilineages always segment into smaller units that correspond not only to differences in age and generation but also to differences in wealth, power, and residential location (Baker 1979). This quality of segmentation means that every male simultaneously is linked to all other males in his line of descent and is the potential founder of a new lineage segment. In normative terms, males are obligated to their kinsmen, particularly those kinsmen closest to them—uncles, grandfathers, and especially fathers. Males are also obligated to extend their lineage into the future by establishing their own small lineages, their own households with lines of male descendants. This dual obligation to other people in the lineage, on the one hand, and to oneself as a propagator of the lineage in the future, on the other, institutionalizes a conflict over the control of resources within households and among households that reverberates through the entire society and creates institutional patterns that shape the economy.

The first of these institutional patterns is that of ownership and inheritance. In theory as well as in practice, Chinese family firms are the property of the household, "small lineages," and not individuals. In the West, unincorporated firms are the property of an individual owner and can be passed on to one's legal heirs as specified in a will. In the case of corporations, property rights are split among a set of owners, each of whom has a specified number of shares, and inheritance rules apply to the shares held and not to the whole firm. In Chinese societies such as Taiwan, however, firms not only are specifically household property but also are considered to belong, at a more abstract level, to a general pool of resources that lineage members can utilize if the need arises. Therefore, when property is viewed in the short term, the head of household has authoritative control over it. In the long term, however, the head of household is merely the custodian of a past inheritance that will be passed on to future holders, his sons and his sons' sons. At the same time, however, the current head of household is also obligated to the members of his lineage outside of his household. Depending on their distance from him, these relatives have a legitimate moral claim to lineage assets because they are in principle shared assets; the closer the relationship, the stronger the claim on the resources. Conceptually, then, assets, like the lineage itself, are produced and reproduced across time. Individuals may die, property may be sold, but the lineage and its collective assets, though divided and controlled by the many households in the lineage, continue into the future.

Inheritance in this system is necessarily partible: Each son having an obligation to start his own household and each being potentially the head of a lineage segment in the future, all sons receive equal shares of their father's estate. Established inheritance rules specify that at some point after the father dies, the sons will *fen jia*, will divide the household and all its assets on a formal basis. Taking their own shares from the past and being the heads of their own small lineages, the sons will start building their own estates, which will be divided after they die. After *fen jia*, the brothers may jointly cooperate in mutual business activities, but even if they do so, no brother has the authoritative claim to exclusive control over what the father once controlled. Each brother has or will become a father and head of his own household. Subsequently, brothers might cooperate as close colleagues, perhaps formally ranked according to seniority, but this cooperation is unlikely to produce a unified, authoritatively controlled organization, as occurs in the case of Korea.

Based on his studies of Chinese businesses in Hong Kong and Southeast Asia, Wong Siu-lun (1985) has developed a theoretical model of the Chinese family firm that incorporates the institutional dynamics of the patrilineal kinship system. He suggests that firms typically go through a cycle of four stages. In the first phase, the "emergent stage," early in the household's existence, the family, led by the father, accumulates capital through loans from family and friends and sometimes through establishing a partnership with a friend or trusted business acquaintance. In this phase, the head of household has absolute control over the enterprise, and if a system of limited partnership is established, the head of household will claim the "founder's shares," which are typically equivalent in voting power to all other shares combined.

In the second stage, which Wong calls the "centralization stage," the father heavily reinvests the firm's profits and centralizes the control of decision-making over money and strategy. If the business began as a partnership in the first stage, in the second, the founding and dominant family will occupy all the positions of power and responsibility in the firm. Also in this stage, the sons are gradually brought into the business and groomed for various business roles that they will later assume.

In the third stage, the "segmentation stage," the founder retires or dies, and the sons assume control of the firm. If the business is good and sufficient to support the heirs, the surviving sons may decide not to divide the estate at the time of the father's death. If that is the case, the sons involved in the business typically divide the business into spheres of influence over which each son has control. Having served in the firm the longest and having the most managerial experience, the eldest son may take a key managerial role in the overall business. But as this situation continues over time, each son gradually operates more independently of the others and begins to bring his sons into his areas as well.

The fourth stage is the "disintegration stage." The surviving sons of the original founder or their sons decide finally to *fen jia*. By the fourth stage, the points of disagreement and conflict inevitably will have become insurmountable. The sons' sons are dealing with their uncles and with their cousins. Inheritance is further complicated because the sons of the original founder have unequal numbers of sons themselves. In the end, it becomes easier formally to divide the assets of the firm and for each of the surviving households to go its own way, which in turn starts the process of accumulation again.

An analysis of the largest business groups in Taiwan suggests that Wong's model needs to be appended to reflect the fact that successful accumulation results in the creation of a group of independent firms rather than in the enlargement of a single firm. But given that addition, Wong's model is substantially correct. This revision, however, is an important one. Corresponding to what would be the early part of the centralization stage in Wong's model, the founders of successful firms begin to reinvest their profits. At this point, do they expand the size of their successful firm, thereby capturing a greater share of the market in which they are operating, or do they diversify? At this crucial moment of decision, the data show that in case after case, the founders of firms elect to diversify by establishing new independent firms, often in unrelated areas.

Intragroup Diversification. In examining these diversification strategies, however, one quickly recognizes that the strategies themselves are directly shaped by the same kinship dynamics that Wong identified in his model of the Chinese firm. Within business groups, one finds two closely related types of diversification. First, firms in business groups are frequently spread across diverse product lines. There is often a core of vertically integrated firms reflecting the product line of the founding firms, but typically there are also additional sets of firms within business groups in areas completely unrelated to the core product lines. For instance, in the case of one business group of thirteen firms, the first and still most successful firm is in textiles. But the second and third firms are in chemicals. The group started other firms related to textile production but also started a hog farm and a magnet factory. The rationale for starting these factories differed case by case but always revolved around the personal decisions of the owners. In one instance, an old friend asked one of the owners to help him out by investing money in the firm. Later the friend asked him to buy the firm.

Opportunistic diversification seems to be the rule. Business groups usually start with some core firms begun by the founders; these firms are then followed by opportunistic expansion into the same or other lines of endeavor. The strategy of expansion is to start new firms even if they are in the same product line rather than greatly enlarging the size of the original firm. This investment pattern leads to an increasing spread of product lines within groups and results in business groups being largely composed of a series of medium-sized firms. This pattern is particularly relevant when compared with the investment patterns of Korean and Japanese business groups, where strong pressure toward vertical integration exists (Hamilton and Feenstra 1995). By comparison, Taiwan's business groups resemble conglomerates.

According to a survey of the owners of the top business groups in Taiwan in the 1970s (Liu, Huang, and Situ 1981), the eventuality of *fen jia* is one of the main reasons that business leaders choose to diversify. This trend shows up in the analysis of the data on Taiwan business groups as well as in the interviews conducted by Kao Cheng-shu and his research team. Knowing that all household assets will be eventually divided among their sons, founders have an affinity for spreading household assets among independent firms. Sons usually assume top management positions in these firms while the father is still alive, and at the point of *fen jia*, there is no need to take apart a large vertically integrated firm, which would destroy an established business and greatly erode long-term lineage assets. By starting independent firms, the founder has, in effect, already divided the assets. The sons can simply continue as they have done in the past, but now without their father's supervision and control.

Duplicating Hierarchies.   Underlying this diversification among firms is another type of diversification. This is a diversification of the management structure itself, which illustrates the weak, short spans of control achieved in family firms. Firms in a group tend to be organizationally separate from other firms, each having a distinct management structure. Until recently, business groups had no formal unified management organization linking all the firms together, although in some groups there has recently been a move in this direction (China Credit Information Service 1985). Instead, each firm has a person who formally occupies the position of manager *(jingli)*. This person may or may not be a family member and, in fact, often is not. The person is usually a "professional" manager in terms of either education or experience. These firm managers, in turn, are seldom linked to a larger formal management structure beyond the firms. In this way, day-to-day management of firms is separated from the actual control of the group. Management is defined, by comparison, as the lower-level activity and remains distinct from long-term decisions affecting individual firms as well as the group itself. Control of these types of decisions remains in the hands of the owners and of those in the inner circle. Therefore, management tends to be formal and localized to each firm, whereas control tends to be informal and spans the group of family-owned firms.

In theory, this separation of management and control is manifest in the two separate types of positions found in most firms. One type identifies the hierarchy assigned the responsibilities of operational management *(jingli);* the other type identifies the hierarchy associated with control *(dongshi).* In fact, often an owner simultaneously assumes both positions and is known formally as *dongshijang jien zhongjingli* (director of the board and general manager). This split between control and management in family enterprises parallels the split between control and management of household and lineage assets that Myron Cohen (1976:90–91) documents in traditional Taiwanese families: "The general management of family enterprises may be distinguished from the fiscal management and control. The first involves the disposition of family workers and the operation of the family farm or other enterprises, while the second concerns family funds." Cohen shows that control over money is tightly held by the head of household *(chia-chang),* but management responsibilities can be dispersed among family members. It should not be surprising, therefore, that large-scale, family-owned business groups follow the same organizational patterns associated with practices in traditional Chinese families. This research and that of others (Tong 1991) shows that the organizational split between control and management has become an institutionalized feature of large, modern Chinese-owned business groups in Hong Kong and Southeast Asia.

This duplication of hierarchies in firms and the managerial separation of firms in a business group lead to the multiplication of positions that key people in a business group hold. The same people hold a range of positions in different firms. It is not unusual for the same person simultaneously to hold multiple positions in the same firm as well as the same positions in several different firms in the business group. This same pattern holds throughout all the business groups.[8] Moreover, this management pattern further sets Taiwan firms off from their counterparts in Japan and South Korea, where most key personnel have only one position in the business group. In fact, the duplication of an individual's positions commonly results in business cards requiring a full page and sometimes additional pages simply to list all the positions the person holds.

The Inner Circle.   These overlapping hierarchies that form around a handful of key persons in business groups coalesce into an inner circle. The inner circle consists of those few key people with whom the principal owner feels the greatest degree of trust and confidence. This inner circle cannot necessarily be identified by outsiders because it may not contain some individuals, such as an elder son, whom most would expect to be included. However, all informants interviewed by Kao and his team spoke about and felt they could accurately identify the inner circles of their own organizations. Ordinarily, the inner circles of business groups consist of the owners and a few close family members, but they also often include longtime business associates and sometimes other sorts of confidants such as a mistress. In fact, the China Credit Information Service survey lists the same core persons in every business group who are identified by the business groups themselves. This listing can be seen as the core of the inner circle.

The closeness of this core group and the segmentation of firms and managerial positions in the business groups strengthen the control of owners and their confidants and lessen the possibility that their centrality can be challenged successfully. This exclusiveness and concern with control have several practical consequences. In many business groups each member firm keeps separate account books. These separate accounts are not integrated into a central accounting system but rather remain separate, and their contents are fully known only to the members of the inner circle, sometimes only to the key owner himself.[9] Another consequence, said Kao's informants, is that owners are very reluctant to list their companies on the stock exchange for fear of losing exclusive control and of having to divulge financial information about the business group (Kao 1991).[10]

Although control of assets is centralized, the management of people is decentralized, in large part because management involves creating and maintaining identifiable personal relationships between the manager (laoban) and the employees. Many ethnographies of Chinese family firms stress the importance of personal relationships in maintaining the labor force (Shieh 1992). Managers try to employ friends and friends of friends, relatives and relatives of relatives, thereby overlapping an employer-employee relationship with a more personal and accordingly more coercive bond (Cheng and Hsiung 1994). One of the key aspects of management, then, is the maintenance of a double bond composed of firm and family. As most ethnographies show, this double bond often leads to the managers' exploitation of their employees. In Taiwan's highly competitive economy, the needs of business often overwhelm the decorum within families. In the end, the tension between family management and worker exploitation encourages those who are not close family members and those who do not share in the control of assets to escape from the direct control of management, to start their own firms, and to exploit others in turn (Shieh 1992).

Not all firms, of course, are managed this way. A few of the larger firms attempt to "professionalize" their management by utilizing Western management techniques. A few other firms have offered their employees shares of the firms in exchange for their loyalty and continued employment. In all of these firms, however, employee turnover remains high because the desire to start one's own family firm and the opportunities in owning a family firm seem always to outweigh being an employee in someone else's firm.

With the additions mentioned previously, Wong's model shows that Chinese kinship institutions foster a small-firm economy. Even when businesses are very successful, assets, property, even managerial controls are still continually being subdivided. The process of asset accumulation leads to the establishment of new firms and to the formation of diversified business groups instead of large vertically integrated firms or even large vertically integrated networks of firms, as occurs in Japan or South Korea. Firms are primarily asset holders for household and lineage interests, and when firms are not profitable, the assets are shifted to another site. Subdividing, diversifying, and reallocating assets occur within and are accelerated by an institutional environment that makes allowances for the diversification strategies of family ownership. These diversification strategies build upon the entrepreneurial ability to create horizontal linkages and to create interfamily networks that are based on shared resources, or what I call *guanxi* ownership.

Guanxi Ownership and Horizontal Controls

Besides family ownership, most businesses also include a second type of ownership, *guanxi* ownership. *Guanxi* is a Chinese term meaning relationship, but the Chinese do not classify all possible relationships as *guanxi* (Hwang 1984, 1987; King 1991; Chen 1994; Yang 1994). Instead, *guanxi* is a term conventionally reserved for certain sets of ties that are bound by norms of reciprocity *(huibao)* or by what is more commonly called in Chinese human emotion *(renqing* or *ganqing)*. Very close familial ties, such as those between parents and children or husbands and wives, are not based on reciprocity but rather on duty and obedience *(xiao)*, with the subordinate in the hierarchical relationship obligated to obey the superior (Hwang 1987; Hamilton 1990). Although parents and husbands have moral obligations to children and wives, children are normatively required to obey their parents and wives, their husbands regardless of what the other party in the relationship demands. Within the household, therefore, norms of reciprocity do not provide a basis of action. Likewise, many relationships, such as those that occur between people who are formally strangers, as between a clerk and customer in a store, are also not bound by norms of reciprocity. But between the familial and the distant, there are categories of relationships, should individuals choose to activate them, that are bound by norms of reciprocity. These categories include distant kinsmen, neighbors, classmates, coworkers, people of the same surname, and people from the same region.

Most anthropologists and sociologists of Chinese society argue that *guanxi*, which includes relations and relation building, lies at the heart of Chinese society. Ambrose King (1991:79) writes the following:

> *Guanxi* building is based on shared "attributes" such as kinship, locality, surname, and so on, which are the building blocks the individual employs to establish "pluralistic" identifications with multiple individuals and groups. Indeed, network building is used (consciously or unconsciously) by Chinese adults as a

cultural strategy in mobilizing social resources for goal attainment in various spheres of social life. To a significant degree the cultural dynamic of *guanxi* building is a source of vitality in Chinese society.

Probably better than anyone, Fei Xiaotong (1992) has worked out a theory of Chinese society showing that its very structure consists of networks built up from differentially categorized social relationships and *guanxi* ties. Chinese society is not created top-down through encompassing organizations and vertical chains of command but rather, says Fei (1992:78), is created bottom-up from "webs woven out of countless personal relationships." These webs have only small degrees of hierarchy. As Mayfair Yang (1989:40–41, also 1994:109–145) puts it,

> In the art of *guanxi*, this transformation (from the unfamiliar to the familiar) occurs in the process of appealing to shared identities between persons—hence the emphasis on "shared" *(tong)* qualities and experiences. . . . Familiarity, then, is born of the fusion of personal identities. And shared identities establish the basis for the obligation and compulsion to share one's wealth and to help with one's labor.

As these and other writers show, *guanxi* is not merely a cultural practice; it is one of the main organizational principles of Chinese society.

It is therefore not surprising that Taiwan's economic organizations are often products of *guanxi* networks and *guanxi* building (Chen 1994:219–247). For Taiwan's largest business groups, *guanxi* networks are a primary source of investment capital and constitute an important type of ownership. In addition to being family owned, *all firms* within all the top 100 businesses groups are also limited partnerships. Twelve out of the 97 business groups listed in 1983 were actually owned and managed by two or more unrelated individuals (China Credit Information Service 1983). Such partnerships are typically short-term arrangements, for sooner or later one partner or the other assumes control of the group (Wong 1985; Yong 1992). In this sense, limited partnerships in the Chinese context are not equivalent to those found in the West. By long convention, "every Chinese partnership is represented by one individual, who is solely responsible to the outside world for the solvency of his firm" (Anonymous 1887). In many cases, the Chinese practice of creating partnerships is similar to having "silent partners," people who do not participate actively in making business decisions but who earn profits on their capital investments and who may represent the firm or firms to outsiders on behalf of the real owners.

More important in the Chinese context, these silent partners are usually either more distant kinsmen or, just as likely, members of the owners' personal network of acquaintances, his *guanxi* network.[11] In my analysis of Taiwan's largest 96 business groups, which consists of 743 firms, every firm lists a number of such co-owners. Not counting duplications, which are numerous, there are nearly 2,500 names of co-owners listed for the 743 firms, some of whom are close family members; others are friends, coworkers, and distant relatives.

How are the two types of ownership—family and *guanxi*—distributed? The data on the top business groups enumerate only the shareholders and not the actual distribution of shares. Therefore, I cannot quantify the distribution of ownership or, on the basis of names alone, distinguish clearly between the two types of owners. However, based on interviews, on analyses of the few groups and firms whose ownership is known, and on previous studies, it is a general rule of thumb that majority ownership is closely held within the family circle. In the two cases studied by Mark (1972), the family retained over 50 percent of the shares, and among the business-group owners interviewed by Kao Cheng-shu and his research team, family members normally retained majority control (Kao 1991; Peng 1989; Lin 1991; Chen 1994). In one case, however, the founder of a firm who became involved in a joint venture controlled only 25 percent of the shares; later, after a dispute among the other owners, he lost his position entirely. He subsequently started a new firm, proclaiming that he would "never control less than 70% of the shares" of his new firm (Lin 1991:297). As a rule, family control requires majority ownership.

Guanxi investors, however, remain an important feature of ownership. In her survey of firms in Taiwan, Mark (1972:xv) concludes, "Almost all family firms have a large number of non-kin shareholders, while most non-kin enterprises tend to be dominated by several family blocks." "The Taiwan family enterprise," Greenhalgh (1988:234) notes, "relies extensively on networks of kin and friends for strategic resources such as labor, capital, and information." Neither Mark nor Greenhalgh, however, makes the distinction between family and nonfamily networks, but Ichiro Numazaki (1993, 1991a, 1991b) clearly does.

Numazaki argues that partnerships and other types of personal relationships among people from different families constitute a distinctive feature of Taiwan's economy. In an early article entitled "Networks of Taiwanese Big Business: A Preliminary Analysis" (1986), he argues that the relationships among the top business groups are extensively interlocked, and hence Taiwan possesses a cohesive business elite. "The inner circle of the Taiwanese business elite is a distinct and dominant 'class segment' in contemporary Taiwan" (1986:520). His more recent works (1991a, 1991b, 1993) qualify that conclusion somewhat. My own data demonstrate, however, that Taiwan's business elite, unlike in the Japanese case, is by no means unified in terms of mutual shareholding. Nonetheless, Numazaki's main point that a distinction should be made between *guanxi* partners and family owners is very important. On the one hand, he notes (1991a:90), "What these diverse *guanxi* networks share . . . is that all are horizontal networks which allow individuals to expand their contacts beyond the narrow confines of immediate family. This type of personal network enables entrepreneurs to mobilize a wide range of people for investment and political purposes." On the other hand, he argues that family networks "are vertical ones. Father-son relationship stands out as the basic principle of inheritance. . . . In the case of inheritance at least, these vertical networks function as a mechanism for drawing group boundaries" (1991a:90). This distinction between the verticality of family networks and the horizontal nature of *guanxi* networks goes to the heart of Chinese economic organization, as the following examples show.

Investment Networks. As in South Korea, in Taiwan, until quite recently, the stock market was not used as a source of investment capital for business groups' firms. Therefore, until recently, only a few of the 97 business groups had even one listed firm. Unlike in South Korea, however, Taiwan firms are not heavily financed through loans from government-owned banks or from international sources such as the World Bank or multinational corporations. Instead, according to Tyler Biggs (1988b:26–29), capital investments for the manufacturing firms in the private sector come from two main sources. The larger portion, about 45 to 55 percent, comes from accumulated profits that were reinvested to expand existing firms and to start new firms. The smaller the firms, the more likely it is that the owners supplied the capital themselves. The smaller portion, about 30 percent of total investment capital, comes from the unregulated curb market, that is, from family, friends, and personal associates. The smaller the firm, the more likely it is that the owners obtained their investment capital from informal money markets.[12]

Small- and medium-sized firms, as we have seen, constitute the vast majority of Taiwan's firms and the leading segment of export manufacturing. By all accounts, a very large portion of these firms, as well as most large firms, obtain their capital outside of formal channels, and it has been this way throughout the industrializing period (Chen 1995; Fields 1995; Semkow 1994; Winn 1991). "In theory," notes Lee Sheng-Yi (1990:36), "as the money and capital markets become more developed, the informal money market should lose its significance. However, in spite of the falling interest rates [in the formal money markets in 1986 and 1987], the share of the informal money market was no lower." Taiwan's informal money market is, in fact, so large that it accounted, according to Lee's (1990:36–37) analysis of Taiwan's financial system in 1986, for about 20 percent of the money flow for the entire country. And it is also large enough that over time it has become a well-institutionalized source of investment and operating capital. The Central Bank of Taiwan even complies and publishes the prevailing interest rates, including regional differences, for three categories of informal money markets: loans against postdated checks, unsecured loans, and deposits with firms (Lee 1990:34).

The major source of investment capital in the informal market is unsecured loans. These loans are made through various types of savings clubs and mutual aid associations *(hui)*, some of which are organized on a temporary and others on a more permanent basis.[13] "The basic condition for each of these associations," says Lin Pao-an (1991:306), "is its constituted base—a group of people joined by personal trust. The members may be one's relatives, friends, neighbors, or colleagues. For strangers to be included is rather rare. The rights and duties of *hui* members are based on personal trust. There are no formal laws and no administrative agencies to enforce the obligations of *hui* members."

Large businesses use bank loans much more frequently than small businesses, especially for operating expenses (Fields 1995; Semkow 1994; Lin 1991). But even the large business groups, notes Kao Cheng-shu (1991:271), "rely heavily upon the private sector, which includes family members, friends, and business partners." "The private sector," he continues, "is the most important source of funds for businesses. . . . In capital formation or in investment, businessmen always have to build a back-up system that can support them at the right time and in the right place. In [Taiwan] a personal network based upon 'personal trust' is the foundation of this back-up system."

This backup system based on trusted relationships in a personal *guanxi* network is what shows up in the data analysis described previously. This *guanxi* network enables entrepreneurs to accomplish two things: It allows them to achieve flexibility in their use of capital, and it allows them to retain personal control of their majority-owned enterprises. In terms of flexibility, ready access to investment capital allows entrepreneurs rapid entrances into new lines of business. Taiwan's rising productivity comes from the ability of entrepreneurs to make quick investments in new sectors (Pack 1992). Entrepreneurs are able to do this because they can obtain capital quickly from established investment networks rooted in personal relationships of trust. The conservatively oriented, state-owned banks do not make loans quickly or without full collateral, and very few businesses until very recently have used the equity markets at all (Semkow 1994). Therefore, except in the case of the largest firms in the largest business groups, which sometimes enter into joint ventures with multinational corporations, most investment capital for new projects is either from reinvested profits or from one's personal network of family and friends. In most cases, the personal network is probably the more important source.

How do these investment networks normally work? Based on interviews with the owners and managers of some of the top business groups, Kao (1991:268; see also Chen 1994) describes the process of locating partners as follows:

When a firm or enterprise group seeks a partnership with other people or businesses, the same principle applies. Usually, there will be no cooperation without intimate *guanxi*. If they want to make a linkage, it is necessary to find the "right" person first. The cooperative inter-business relationship is primarily based upon the personal trust between the two major *laoban*. If this kind of trust exists, the deal is rather easy to make. . . . Even in those large business groups, the core group is usually constituted by family members, good friends, and old colleagues. . . . From this perspective, it is "personal trust" which makes the network of partnerships actually work. We do not want to overstate the role of "personal trust," but our analysis clearly shows that it is a necessary condition for doing business. Both within and between business organizations, "personal trust" is a basic organizational principle.

One does not normally think of personal trust as an organizational principle, but in Chinese businesses it is. "In Chinese society," continues Kao (1991:269), "trust is inseparable from 'personal intimacy.' Although intimacy is not equivalent to 'trust,' it is a prerequisite." In this context, "personal intimacy" and "intimate *guanxi*" refer to a *guanxi* relationship that two people have activated and in which an intimacy in the form of *renqing* (interpersonal warmth and the willingness to comply with the norms of reciprocity) has been achieved. "Relying upon personal relationships," Kao (1991:272) reminds us, is, however, "not merely a matter of emotionality but of rational calculations" (see also Chen 1994).

The rational calculation rests upon whether the people involved will follow social norms. Through their actions, two people show they are willing to enter into a *guanxi* relationship. This willingness provides a foundation for trust. One's trust in the other arises out of one's recognition that the other has both the power and resources to act and the personal desire to follow norms of the specific *guanxi* relationship that binds the two people together. In this context, trust *(xinyong)* means one's integrity and credibility as a person in relation to not only the other person but also all potential observers. A relationship based upon trust requires that the two people involved will act predictably and in accordance with the appropriate norms of reciprocity.

Embedded in a system of interpersonal relationships, trust in Chinese society has a sociological but not a legalistic foundation. Trust binds people together by obliging them to act according to set rules of social relationships (Fei 1992). "In order to obtain 'trust,'" says Kao (1991:269), "persons have to demonstrate certain qualities according to intersubjective rules. These rules are not objectified, but are usually well recognized by the people involved. Because such informal, rather than formal, rules are used predominantly to regulate business activities, Western contractual relationships do not prevail."

Therefore, to have trust in another is to believe that the other is willing to obey a system of social rules. In the Chinese context, assessments of trustworthiness involve assessments of people. Trust, therefore, is highly personalized even though it is also bound by clear-cut rules of action. To judge another's trustworthiness is to judge, given the rules of interaction, how a specific person will act in relation to another in a specified context. This sort of personal trust rooted in *guanxi* networks is a very different type of trust than that prevailing in Western businesses, where the participants have ultimate faith in the legal system and much less faith in the word of those with whom they do business. The distinction between Chinese and Western trust is not a distinction, as some have argued (Wong 1991; Yong 1992; Menkhoff 1990), between personal trust and system trust.[14] Rather it is a distinction between two different types of system trust: In Chinese society, system trust is based on normative, intersubjective rules that link people who are classified according to relational categories into networks that specify their modes of interaction. In Western society, system trust rests on codified rules that define the jurisdictions of interacting units (e.g., an individual or a firm) and specify the terms and the conditions of that interaction. In Chinese society, system trust is highly personalized; in the West, system trust is more abstract and impersonal. Put more concretely, the backup system for a Chinese businessperson is a *guanxi* network; the backup system for an American businessperson is the courts and lawyers.

Production and Marketing Networks. When used in the context of business, this system of trust can be activated among people linked in horizontally based *guanxi* networks to generate economic organizations.[15] Such *guanxi* networks may have several economic functions; they may be a source of investment capital or a means to organize the production and distribution of commodities. Whatever the economic purpose, the typical organization is the same. People who own or who at some time may own their own firms are linked into a network in which the norms of reciprocity take a concrete form of mutual indebtedness. In other words, doing business is a process of reciprocation with *guanxi* ties being an essential element of that process.

Many previous studies of Chinese businesses, particularly long-distance trading, have documented these horizontal networks (Lim and Gosling 1983; Menkhoff 1990; Yao 1987; Yong 1992). Eddie Kuo (1991), for example, documented a case where the Southeast Asian distribution network for mandarin oranges, which began in South China and through numerous exchanges ended in Malaysia, was able to resist the direct actions of the Malaysian government to intervene in the trade. In this case, the horizontal linkages of trust undermined the attempts to create a vertically controlled, government-sponsored distribution system. The economic power of such horizontal ties is nicely illustrated in a comment by one informant in Yong's study of Chinese rubber businesses in Southeast Asia (1992:94):

We Chinese are always financially tight. We depend a lot on giving credit. For example, rubber from Thailand may be sent here first and then we pay later, or my buyer will give me money first to buy the rubber. Either way, this sort of credit giving, you can basically take and run. So *xinyong* is important. With *xinyong*, I can do business up to a few hundred thousand dollars, even though I have, maybe, only ten thousand dollars.

In Taiwan as well, horizontal *guanxi* networks form the organizational backbone of the manufacturing sectors of the economy. My own data and particularly the interview material collected by Kao Cheng-shu's team in Taiwan show that *guanxi* networks provide small- and medium-sized businesses with the resources by which to organize export-oriented commodity chains (see, e.g., Chen 1994). When used to raise investment capital for manufacturing, personal networks of *guanxi* owners give entrepreneurs many advantages that a formal banking system would not. Such networks give them a ready source of capital that can be used as they wish. Should an area of manufacturing prove successful, these ties give them a potential set of partners in manufacturing and distributing products that can be rapidly increased to the level of the demand. Equally important, the networks give them a low-cost source of information about what to produce, how to improve production, and where and how to sell their products. The data suggest that the denser and more extensive the *guanxi* networks, the more production information, including research and development and product innovations, actually becomes a function of the networks themselves. Without the *guanxi* networks, small- and medium-sized networks could not shift product lines and could not produce the array of products that they do in fact produce. With the assistance of their *guanxi* backup system, entrepreneurs can rationally calculate their speculative investments and, as Kao stated, be "in the right place at the right time."

Satellite Assembly Systems. To explain the numerous ways *guanxi* ties serve as a medium to create economic organizations, it is analytically useful to make a distinction between how entrepreneurs use *guanxi* ties to establish horizontally integrated commodities chains and how they use *guanxi* ties to diversify their assets. In regard to commodities chains, interviews with large- and medium-sized manufacturers of export products reveal that production is usually organized through what is called a "satellite assembly system" (*weixing gongchang*; see Shieh 1992). Satellite assembly systems vary in terms of the relative size of the firms directly involved. In general, a group of small, medium, and sometimes large independently owned firms join together to produce a product that has been ordered by an overseas buyer. Each firm produces one part or one set of parts of the final product. Depending on the size of the order and the complexity of the part, that firm might organize a secondary satellite assembly system to make that part. All the parts are then delivered to an assembly firm that assembles, paints, packages, and ships the final product.

In some satellite assembly systems, the assembly firm is the largest firm in the group and is basically an end producer that subcontracts a portion, sometimes a very large portion, of the final product to small independent firms. For example, a hydraulic jack plant that I visited employed about 200 people and subcontracted as much as two-thirds of the component parts for the jacks to smaller firms in the region. These smaller firms also worked for other local manufacturers. One of the principal owners and the general manager of the firm told me that the company, which sold about U.S.$15 million worth of jacks in 1987, did not sell its products under its own brand name but rather sold exclusively to such Western wholesale and retail companies as Price Club, Wells, K-Mart, and Grand Auto. The company made the jacks to the specifications required by its buyers and painted, labeled, and packaged the product accordingly. He personally arranged for most of the orders by traveling to trade shows and by visiting distributors all over the world. When orders were plentiful, the final assembly plant and the subcontractors worked at full speed, but when the orders slackened, he would reduce his reliance on subcontractors and try to do more production in-house.

In other assembly systems, some of the component parts may be manufactured by firms much larger than the final assembly firm. For example, a large metalworking firm I visited produced metal bicycle wheels as one among a number of component parts it produced. The firm, employing nearly 300 people, also subcontracted with other smaller firms for a portion of the component parts it made. The bicycle wheel that it manufactured, however, went to a number of different satellite assembly systems, all producing different bicycles. The firms in these satellite assembly systems were smaller than the metalworking firm.

This size differential was most pronounced in the case of an automobile-parts maker I interviewed. His firm produced custom-made parts for supply houses and mail-order distributors located primarily in the United States and Europe. He employed four people in his firm, two for quality control and two for processing orders. He, the owner and the fifth person in the firm, traveled to the United States and Europe to arrange for orders from his buyers. His overseas buyers gave him the detailed specifications and sometimes a sample part. He then took the specifications and samples to what he called "his manufacturing group," which consisted of around ten to fifteen independently owned metalworking firms. These firms were all small, around 30 employees each, and 75 percent of his orders, he said, were made by these same firms. The team, led by a mechanical engineer, divided each order into a manufacturing process consisting of smaller component parts and necessary steps. Team members selected the metalworking shops that manufactured each component part or carried out each step in the manufacturing process and then instructed the owners of the shops on how to do the assigned tasks. Sometimes for a large and expensive order, the person we interviewed would lend money for necessary machinery and supplies to the independent owners in the assembly system. Once the process started and the necessary level of quality had been reached, the manufacturing process proceeded without managerial supervision. Each firm carried out its own part of the process and then passed the unfinished part on to the next firm in the manufacturing sequence. When the product was finished and delivered to the exporting firm, the two quality-control persons inspected each part and arranged for its export.

Like all the others we interviewed, the owner of the automobile-parts firm said that to make the manufacturing process work smoothly, human relationships in the group and the personalities of the independent owners were very important. "Business is business," he said, and for business he needed people who "you can trust to do the job." To find these people, he often asked his friends for recommendations. Sometimes he drove around and just talked to small metal-shop owners. When the "feeling" was right, when the "personality" matched, he felt he could do business with the person. Once he located the right person, however, he did not use a contract to seal the deal. Rather, he and his business partner reached an "understanding" that was in turn sealed by reciprocating gifts and banquets. The same lack of contracts, the same equality among independent entrepreneurs, and the same celebratory reciprocation of food and drink and small gifts reoccur in every satellite assembly system I visited.

One other theme found in many cases of establishing subcontracting networks and satellite assembly systems was that some, and often the majority, of the subcontracting firms were initially started by employees in one firm who created their own independent firms and established subcontracting relationships with their former bosses. Employers often encouraged such departures and even invested in firms started by their best and most capable employees in order to develop the subcontracting network. Although it is counterintuitive, such encouragement of and investments in potentially competing firms create a satellite assembly system capable of achieving economies of scale on a temporary basis without enlarging the size of existing firms and without making large capital investments in labor and machines that might not produce at capacity or for very long. Investment capital is put into people who will repay at a premium and who will likely remain morally bound to their former bosses and economically anchored in their satellite assembly systems, at least as long as the business orders hold out.

Diversification of Assets.   *Guanxi* ties are used not only to develop and refine networks of firms to produce export commodities but also to establish entirely new lines of business. Although more research is needed on this topic, it seems that *guanxi* networks provide an information-rich environment that facilitates rapid shifts in capital investment from one sector to another. Business-group data, as I discussed previously, show that many of the large family-owned business groups in Taiwan develop a diversification strategy that is "opportunistic." Entrepreneurial opportunities are nurtured in a highly speculative investment climate where very low overhead is required to establish a reliable production network. Ideas for how to get rich—the gold-rush mentality—come from many sources: from the owners of small firms who travel around the world looking for orders, from big buyers who come to Asia looking for firms that can manufacture the products they want to market, or from local entrepreneurs who hit upon a new way to make an existing product. Wherever the ideas come from, the success of a group of manufacturers stimulates the rapid entry of others into the same product areas.

This ability to diversify rapidly across product lines is nicely illustrated by an owner and manager of an import-export business whom I interviewed. This entrepreneur used the product ideas he obtained from sales trips to organize and supervise many satellite assembly systems for the commodities he exported. He estimated that these commodities, ranging from kitchenware to computers, have a "product life" of around three months. His general strategy was to produce only those products from which he would recoup his full investment in one profit cycle. For the high-end products, primarily computers, he wanted to recover all expenses and gain some profits in the first three months because, he said, a successful product would be mass-produced by firms in other competing countries such as South Korea or the People's Republic of China (PRC). He did not mass-produce products himself. He asserted that his own success in creating a group of firms employing a total of about 110 people and having assets of less than U.S.$2 million and annual sales of around U.S.$60 million was due to the speed with which he could change his product lines to match market demand. He wanted always to enter the market in the early part of a product cycle. What allowed the speed, he said, was the flexible manufacturing system. He owned no factories, he did not directly manage production, his overhead was kept to a minimum, and he never produced a product without having orders in hand for it.

This example is typical. Brian Levy (1988) reports that the number of export traders in Taiwan grew over sevenfold from 2,777 traders in 1973 to 20,597 in 1984. By contrast, at the same time, the number of South Korean export traders grew from 1,200 in 1973 to 5,300 in 1984. Levy concludes, "In Taiwan—but not in Korea—the expansion in the numbers of traders kept pace with the overall expansion of manufacturers." It is likely that most export traders are linked to satellite assembly systems that rapidly and consistently change their product lines. Indeed, as Gary Gereffi and Pan Mei-lin (1994) have shown for Taiwan's garment industry, changing production lines has grown easier since the 1960s because flexibility becomes an expectation that is institutionalized into the production system through the introduction of specialized firms (such as automated machine retoolers) and specialized services (such as rotating credit banks) that allow for ever more speedy transformations of production lines and ever more rapid transfers of capital to areas of opportunity.

The institutionalization of flexibility has had several consequences. First, few manufacturers of export commodities would attempt to develop, and fewer yet would succeed at actually developing, a vertically integrated production facility that aimed for a large market share for the exported product. Indeed, for this reason, Taiwan's large firms are mostly upstream suppliers of intermediate parts or have carved out a service niche for themselves in the domestic economy. In this kind of climate, entrepreneurs do not normally choose to reinvest their profits by enlarging their production capacity to raise their market share, as is the case in Japan and South Korea. Instead, investors typically choose to put their money into areas of expansion, and in recent years that has meant making investments in overseas markets, in production facilities in the PRC, in property in Hong Kong, or in the equity markets in Thailand. Capital rapidly flows where speculators believe the next boom will be. Some capital is, of course, retained and reinvested in existing firms to upgrade production capabilities. But this reinvestment in automation and equipment will likely enhance the flexibility of small- and medium-sized factory owners to participate in a range of satellite assembly systems.

Conclusion:
Guanxi Capitalism and the Taiwan State

What is the state's role in Taiwan's industrialization?[16] We can now answer this question in a somewhat different way than do most students of Asian economic development. Many theorists argue that the strong Asian states—the bureaucratic, authoritarian regimes that have autonomy from society and the administrative capacity to act—create the conditions for rapid economic development. The thesis in this chapter substantially differs from this line of reasoning.

Using the state to explain industrialization is like using a blunt tool to perform a delicate task; everything is pounded into the same shape. More subtle comparisons of the roles of the state in Asian economies are needed. Although state policies and programs certainly enhance an economy's ability to grow and change, the effects of state actions are more limited than the theorists argue. Politicians know their countries. When they act, they act upon a known subject of which they themselves are both product and participant. If politics is the art of the possible, then doing what is possible means to refine what is already present, to cultivate what is already growing. Politicians and state officials build upon existing social patterns, and although they may work to restructure society, they do not start with blank slates. Political actors tacitly accept and take for granted the cultural milieu as well as the organizational features of the societies and economies of which they are a part.

A goal of this chapter is to show that the institutional patterns of Chinese society, particularly the dynamics of relationships among families and friends, shape Taiwan's market culture, which in turn shapes the very organization of the economy itself. Taiwan's economic successes, of course, are not due entirely to the distinctiveness and robustness of its market culture. A globalized economy that has generated wide demand for similar products and that facilitates multiple production strategies to make those products is a key factor in Taiwan's success that is seldom discussed but is very important. Moreover, the market cultures of South Korea, Japan, and Singapore are all quite different from one another and in turn are all different from the market culture of Taiwan. But all these places are economically very successful in this global economy, and they all have about the same rates of growth. Focusing only on state policy and national rates of growth, most analysts neglect to examine either market culture or the organizational patterning and trajectories of these economies. These economies are not similar; they are very different, and they have distinctive trajectories of growth.

During the years of rapid economic growth, the Taiwan state played a very different role in the economy than did the states in South Korea or Japan. Taiwan's state seldom sponsored big businesses in the export sector but continued to control many upstream, largely import-substitution industries, most of which require large economies of scale and upon which small- and medium-sized businesses in the export sectors depend. With these actions, the state established a "public interest" economic sphere for itself, separate in both character and principle from that occupied by private businesses. Moreover, the state's monopolization of such industries as steel, petroleum, and electrical power prevented the growth of huge private businesses that occurred in South Korea and Japan.

This separation of spheres, however, should not lead to the conclusion that the Taiwan state has more concentrated economic power than the Korean or Japanese states, both of which have much smaller state-owned sectors. Quite the contrary is true. Taiwan state enterprises are organizationally decoupled from the rest of the economy and primarily (though not exclusively) respond to the market demand generated by the private economy. They respond to economic development rather than push it forward. Taiwan's huge economic growth has occurred in the export manufacturing sectors, and those sectors are dominated by small- and medium-sized businesses. This economic pattern has changed somewhat because many of Taiwan's small- and medium-sized firms have moved their manufacturing sites overseas, primarily to the Chinese mainland and Southeast Asia. Even in overseas sites, however, the small- and medium-sized firms still continue to order much of their intermediate goods from Taiwan's big business groups. This has caused the big business groups to become important exporters, but the products they export are still intermediate goods. Although no longer defined by Taiwan's borders, the demand structure between big and small enterprises has held firm.

The capitalist states in Asia, along with most states elsewhere, try to control financial institutions, but here again, the "strong state" policies of Taiwan were quite unlike those in Japan and in Korea. The state-owned banking system in Taiwan strongly limited the amount of investment capital it was putting into Taiwan's businesses. At the same time, Japanese city banks and the banks run by the Korean state channeled huge amounts of domestic and foreign capital, in the form of cheap loans, into economic sectors selected for development.[17] In Taiwan, the large business groups and particularly the small- and medium-sized firms got their investment capital from the curb market—from family and friends and from informal money markets. In Korea and Japan, the banking system encouraged large, heavily leveraged firms. For instance, Korea's leverage, expressed as debt-to-equity ratios, was three times Taiwan's ration in the manufacturing sector. This fiscal leverage in Korea also gave the state political leverage; it assumed virtually hegemonic control over the *chaebol* until the early 1980s. The active curb market in Taiwan shows that entrepreneurs could take care of their own financial needs and that the Taiwan state had very little leverage, fiscal or otherwise, over the export sector of the economy.

Robert Wade shows that the Taiwan government had an active role in creating and implementing economic policies that led to rapid growth. But like the banking policy, most of the government's measures build on existing strengths in the economy and thereby encourage the aggressiveness of the export sector. But forever worrying about the small size and the obscure brands of most firms, Taiwan's economic planners have also tried occasionally to "upgrade" some aspects of the economy. For instance, they tried to create large trading companies by emulating the Japanese model. These attempts were unsuccessful because most production networks grew from orders from overseas buyers that originated with or were handled by brokers in Taiwan who had their own, very small trading firms. Accordingly, while these small trading firms proliferated, the government-sponsored trading firms languished (Fields 1995). The state planners also supported the formation of integrated, more or less permanent subcontracting systems, again based on the Japanese model, but these have also failed (Lorch and Biggs 1989). In addition, the state started special banks to increase the size of small- and medium-sized firms through special financing, but the results have been disappointing because businessmen do not want to take loans from state sources. Finally, state planners have tried to build an export-oriented transportation industry so that Taiwan can begin exporting automobiles and trucks. But to date, Taiwan, the country that has one of the highest ratios of manufactured exports to total output and 27 automobile firms (all for the domestic market), exports very few automobiles. All this indicates that state policy does not lead to accomplished fact. The Taiwan state has to contend with and ultimately to accept the established patterns and economic momentum that exist within the society, the very patterns that arise out of Taiwan's horizontal economic networks. Taiwan's capitalism is not state-led capitalism; instead it is *guanxi* capitalism, a capitalism built up and extended out from the networks embedded in Chinese society.

NOTES

This chapter is a condensed version of a paper that was first published in Orrù, Hamilton, and Biggart 1997. I wish to acknowledge the support of the Chiang Ching-Kuo Foundation for support during the preliminary analysis of this material; William Zeile, Lin Holin, and Ho Tuanfan, who served as research assistants during some portion of the research reported here; and Kao Cheng-shu and his research team, who let me come along on many of their interviews with Taiwan businessmen and who have provided a constant source of information and encouragement. Finally, I also wish to acknowledge Nicole Biggart, Robert Hefner, and Marco Orrù, all of whom made comments on an earlier draft.

1. Also see Winckler and Greenhalgh (1988) for an extended discussion of the various types of state interpretation used to explain the political economy of Taiwan.

2. These two views come together most clearly in K.T. Li (1976, 1988). Li, who is known as the chief architect of Taiwan's economic policies, describes the role of the state in laudatory terms. Li's comments are preceded by introductory essays from Gustav Ranis and John Fei, both developmental economists, who use Taiwan as a leading example in the case for a strong-state thesis.

3. In the 1950s, state-owned enterprises accounted for nearly 50 percent of the value added in the manufacturing sectors, but starting in the early 1960s this percentage declined quickly until 1971, when it leveled out at an average for the next 15 years of around 14 percent (Council for Economic Planning and Development 1985:83). Because a great portion of Taiwan's industrialization has occurred since 1970, it therefore stands to reason that during this period the public sector has grown at about the same rate as the private sector. This is only one of a number of "steady-state" ratios in an economy that is in all other respects burgeoning.

4. Ranked by the value of their assets in 1986, the most important state-owned enterprises were Taiwan Power Company, China Petroleum Company, China Steel Company, Taiwan Sugar Company, China Shipbuilding Company, Chunghwa Machinery and Engineering Company, China Petrochemical Development Company, Taiwan Machinery Manufacturing Company, Taiwan Fertilizer Company, Taiwan Aluminum Company, Taiwan Metal Mining Company, and Taiwan Salt Works.

5. Public accounts show that state-owned enterprises are neither efficient nor profit-oriented. Instead, they are reputedly bureaucratic and distant from their customers. This aloof public role of state-owned enterprises in the midst of a surging

and ever-changing private sector composed primarily of modest-sized firms owned by wealthy and very speculative dealmakers helps to explain the continuity of the state-owned sector. Unlike state officials in Japan and South Korea, state officials in Taiwan have shown a great reluctance to privatize state-owned enterprises by turning them into public corporations, thus making their shares available to the public through local equity markets.

6. In this connection, it should be noted that Taiwan has one of the world's largest monetary surpluses and is one of the world's largest importers of gold.

7. This figure is, however, an overstatement because my research shows that many successful entrepreneurs own more than one business.

8. The data for these conclusions are presented in tabular form in a preliminary way in Hamilton and Kao 1990 and in a more complete way in Orrù, Hamilton, and Biggart 1997.

9. See Tong 1991 for a similar conclusion for a Chinese business group in Singapore.

10. This reluctance to open their firms to outside scrutiny does not seem to reduce their willingness to accept investment capital from outsiders, especially from foreign corporations that want to enter into a joint venture. Preliminary analysis has shown that the most tightly held groups, other things being equal, are more likely the ones to have joint ventures.

11. For a more complete discussion of the network structure of Chinese society, see Fei 1992. Also see Hamilton and Wang's introduction to Fei's book.

12. According to Lee (1990:36), "Some small enterprises, which do not yet have a properly audited account and cannot offer adequate collateral to banks, cannot borrow effectively from banks, and therefore have to borrow from the informal money market at a high rate of interest. There are about 70,000 exporting and importing firms, big and small, competing in the market. Moreover, there is a considerable number of small trading and manufacturing firms which are not registered at all, with the convenience of tax-evasion and freedom from all sorts of government regulations with respect to pollution control, fire precaution and other considerations. Naturally, an unregistered firm has to resort to the informal money market." See also Biggs 1988a; Semkow 1994.

13. For a recent explanation of rotating credit associations, see Biggart and Castanias 1994.

14. This distinction was originally made by Luhmann 1979.

15. This is true in a political context as well when factional networks are generated. See Jacobs 1979.

16. The comments in this section draw on Hamilton and Biggart 1991.

17. William Zeile (1993) calculates that the ratio of debt to assets for member firms of the top 50 *chaebol* in 1983 was 453 percent, compared to 158 percent for Taiwan's manufacturing firms. This figure overstates the Taiwan case because it is biased toward larger Taiwan firms that report such financial matters.

REFERENCES

Aberbach, Joel D., David Dollar, and Kenneth L. Sokoloff, eds. 1994. *The Role of the State in Taiwan's Development.* Armonk, N.Y.: M.E. Sharpe.

Amsden, Alice. 1985. "The State and Taiwan's Economic Development." In Peter B. Evans, Dietrich Rueschemeyer, and Theda Skocpol, eds., *Bringing the State Back In*, pp. 78–106. Cambridge: Cambridge University Press.

_____. 1989. *Asia's Next Giant: South Korea and Late Industrialization.* New York: Oxford University Press.

Anonymous. 1887. "Chinese Partnerships: Liability of the Individual Members." *Journal of the China Branch of the Royal Asiatic Society*, New Series 22:41.

Baker, Hugh. 1979. *Chinese Family and Kinship.* New York: Columbia University Press.

Biggart, Nicole, and Richard P. Castanias. 1994. "Collateralized Social Relations." Paper presented at the annual meeting of the Society for the Advancement of Socioeconomics, Paris, July.

Biggs, Tyler S. 1988a. "Financing the Emergence of Small and Medium Enterprise in Taiwan: Heterogeneous Firm Size and Efficient Intermediation." Employment and Enterprise Policy Analysis (EEPA) Project discussion paper, no. 16.

_____. 1988b. "Financing the Emergence of Small and Medium Enterprise in Taiwan: Financial Mobilization and the Flow of Domestic Credit to the Private Sector." Employment and Enterprise Policy Analysis Project. EEPA discussion paper, no. 15.

Chang, Cecilia. 1988. "Everyone Wants to Be the 'Boss.'" *Free China Review* 38, 11:10–12.

Chen Chieh-hsuan. 1994. *Xieli wangluo yu shenghuo jiegou* (Mutual networks and the structure of daily life). Taipei: Lienjing Press.

_____. 1995. *Huobi wangluo yu shenghuo jiegou* (Monetary networks and the structure of daily life). Taipei: Lienjing Press.

Cheng, Lucie, and Hsiung Ping-Chun. 1994. "Women, Export-Oriented Growth, and the State: The Case of Taiwan." In Joel D. Aberback, David Dollar, and Kenneth L. Sokoloff, eds., *The Role of the State in Taiwan's Development*, pp. 321–353. Armonk, N.Y.: M.E. Sharpe.

China Credit Information Service (Zhonghua Zhengxinso), comp. 1983. *Taiwan diqu jitua qiye yanjiu, 1983–1984* (Business groups in Taiwan, 1983–1984). Taipei: China Credit Information Service.

_____. 1985. *Taiwan diqu jitua qiye yanjiu, 1985–1986* (Business groups in Taiwan, 1985–1986). Taipei: China Credit Information Service.

Chou Tein-Chen. 1985. *Industrial Organization in the Process of Economic Development: The Case of Taiwan, 1950–1980.* Louvain-la-Neuve: Ciaco.

Cohen, Myron. 1976. *House United, House Divided: The Chinese Family in Taiwan.* New York: Columbia University Press.

Council for Economic Planning and Development. 1985. *Taiwan Statistical Data Book.* Taipei: Council for Economic Planning and Development.

Evans, Peter B. 1979. *Dependent Development: The Alliance of Multinational, State, and Local Capital in Brazil.* Princeton: Princeton University Press.

_____. 1987. "Class, State, and Dependence in East Asia: Lessons for Latin Americanists." In Frederic C. Deyo, ed., *The Political Economy of the New Asian Industrialism*, pp. 203–226. Ithaca: Cornell University Press.

_____. 1995. *Embedded Autonomy: States and Industrial Transformation.* Princeton: Princeton University Press.

Evans, Peter B., Dietrich Rueschemeyer, and Theda Skocpol, eds. 1985. *Bringing the State Back In.* Cambridge: Cambridge University Press.

Fei Xiaotong. 1992. *From the Soil: The Foundations of Chinese Society.* Berkeley: University of California Press.

Fields, Karl. J. 1995. *Enterprise and the State in Korea and Taiwan.* Ithaca: Cornell University Press.

Fruin, W. Mark. 1992. *The Japanese Enterprise System: Competitive Strategies and Cooperative Structures.* Oxford: Clarendon Press.

Gereffi, Gary, and Pan Mei-Lin. 1994. "The Globalization of Taiwan's Garment Industry." In Edna Bonacich, Lucie Cheng, Norma Chinchilla, Nora Hamilton, and Paul Ong, eds., *Global Production: The Apparel Industry in the Pacific Rim,* pp. 126–146. Philadelphia: Temple University Press.

Gerlach, Michael. 1992. *Alliance Capitalism: The Strategic Organization of Japanese Business.* Berkeley: University of California Press.

Gerschenkron, Alexander. 1962. *Economic Backwardness in Historical Perspective.* Cambridge: Harvard University Press.

Gold, Thomas B. 1986. *State and Society in the Taiwan Miracle.* Armonk, N.Y.: M.E. Sharpe.

Greenhalgh, Susan. 1988. "Families and Networks in Taiwan's Economic Development." In Edwin A. Winckler and Susan Greenhalgh, eds., *Contending Approaches to the Political Economy of Taiwan,* pp. 224–248. Armonk, N.Y.: M.E. Sharpe.

Hamilton, Gary G. 1990. "Partriarchy, Patrimonialism, and Filial Piety: A Comparison of China and Western Europe." *British Journal of Sociology* 41:77–104.

Hamilton, Gary G., ed. 1991. *Business Networks and Economic Development in East and Southeast Asia.* Hong Kong: Centre of Asian Studies, University of Hong Kong.

Hamilton, Gary G., and Nicole Woolsey Biggart. 1988. "Market, Culture, and Authority: A Comparative Analysis of Management and Organization in the Far East." *American Journal of Sociology,* Special Issue on Economic Sociology (July):S52–94.

———. 1991. "The Organization of Business in Taiwan: A Reply to Numazaki." *American Journal of Sociology* 96:999–1006.

Hamilton, Gary G., and Robert Feenstra. 1995. "Varieties of Hierarchies and Markets." *Industrial and Corporate Change* 4, 1: 93–130.

Hamilton, Gary G., and Kao Cheng-shu. 1990. "The Institutional Foundations of Chinese Business: The Family Firm in Taiwan." *Comparative Social Research* 12:95–112.

Hamilton, Gary G., William Zeile, and Kim Wan-Jin. 1990. "The Network Structures of East Asian Economies." In S.R. Clegg and S.G. Redding, eds., *Capitalism in Contrasting Cultures,* pp. 105–129. Berlin: Walter de Gruyter.

Hwang Kwang-kuo. 1984. "Rujia lunli yu qiye zuzhi xingtai" (Confucian theory and types of enterprise organization). In Hwang, ed., *Zhongguo shi guanli* (Chinese-style management), pp. 21–58. Taipei: Gongshang Shibao.

———. 1987. "Face and Favor: The Chinese Power Game." *American Journal of Sociology* 92:944–974.

Jacobs, J. Bruce. 1979. "A Preliminary Model of Particularistic Ties in Chinese Political Alliance: Kan-ch'ing and Kuan-hsi in a Rural Taiwanese Township." *China Quarterly* 78:237–273.

Kao Cheng-shu. 1991. "'Personal Trust' in the Large Businesses in Taiwan: A Traditional Foundation for Contemporary Economic Activities." In Gary Hamilton, ed., *Business Networks and Economic Development in East and Southeast Asia,* pp. 234–273. Hong Kong: Centre of Asian Studies, University of Hong Kong.

Kim Eun Mee. 1997. *Big Business, Strong State: Collusion and Conflict in Korean Development.* Albany: State University of New York Press.

King, Ambrose Yeo-chi. 1991. "Kuan-hsi and Network Building: A Sociological Interpretation." *Daedalus* 120, 2 (Spring):63–84.

Kuo, Eddie C.Y. "Ethnicity, Polity, and Economy: A Case Study of the Mandarin Trade and the Chinese Connection." In Gary G. Hamilton, ed., *Business Networks and Economic Development in East and Southeast Asia,* pp. 274–293. Hong Kong: Centre of Asian Studies, University of Hong Kong.

Lee Sheng-Yi. 1990. *Money and Finance in the Economic Development of Taiwan.* London: Macmillan.

Levy, Brian. 1988. "Korean and Taiwanese Firms as International Competitors: The Challenges Ahead." *Columbia Journal of World Business* (Spring):43–51.

Li, K.T. 1976. *The Experiences of Dynamic Economic Growth in Taiwan.* Taipei: Mei Ya.

_____. 1988. *The Evolution of Policy Behind Taiwan's Development Success.* New Haven: Yale University Press.

Lim, Linda, and Peter Gosling, eds. 1983. *The Chinese in Southeast Asia.* 2 vols. Singapore: Maruzen Asia.

Lin Pao-an. 1991. "The Social Sources of Capital Investment in Taiwan's Industrialization." In Gary G. Hamilton, ed., *Business Networks and Economic Development in East and Southeast Asia,* pp. 294–312. Hong Kong: Centre of Asian Studies, University of Hong Kong.

Liu S.S., Kuo K.M., Huang J.Y., and Situ D.S. 1981. "Taiwan dichu guanxi qiye zhi xingcheng, yingyun yuqi yingxiang" (The formation, operation, and influence of Taiwan's related enterprises). *Qiye Yinhang Jikan* (Enterprise bank quarterly) 4:5–19, and 5:5–23.

Lorch, Klaus, and Tyler Biggs. 1989. "Growing in the Interstices: The Limits of Government Promotion of Small Industries." Paper presented at the annual meeting of the Association for Asian Studies, Washington, D.C.

Luhmann, Niklas. 1979. *Trust and Power.* Chichester: John Wiley.

Mark, Lindy Li. 1972. "Taiwanese Lineage Enterprises: A Study of Familial Entrepreneurship." Ph.D. dissertation, Department of Sociology, University of California–Berkeley.

Menkhoff, Thomas. 1990. "Trade Routes, Trust and Trading Networks: Chinese Family-Based Trading Firms in Singapore and Their External Economic Dealings." Ph.D. dissertation, Department of Sociology, University of Bielefeld.

Moore, Barrington. 1966. *Social Origins of Dictatorship and Democracy: Lord and Peasant in the Making of the Modern World.* Boston: Beacon Press.

Myers, Ramon. 1984. "The Economic Transformation of the Republic of China on Taiwan." *China Quarterly* 99:500–528.

Numazaki, Ichiro. 1986. "Networks of Taiwanese Big Business: A Preliminary Analysis." *Modern China* 12:487–534.

_____. 1991a. "Networks and Partnerships: The Social Organization of the Chinese Business Elite in Taiwan." Ph.D. dissertation, Department of Sociology, Michigan State University.

76   Gary G. Hamilton

_____. 1991b. "The Role of Personal Networks in the Making of Taiwan's *Guan-xiqiye* (Related Enterprises)." In Gary Hamilton, ed., *Business Networks and Economic Development in East and Southeast Asia*, pp. 63–86. Hong Kong: Centre of Asian Studies, University of Hong Kong.

_____. 1993. "The Tainanbang: The Rise and Growth of a Banana-Bunch-Shaped Business Group in Taiwan." *Developing Economies* 31, 4:485–510.

Orrù, Marco, Gary G. Hamilton, and Nicole Biggart. 1997. *The Economic Organization of East Asian Capitalism*. Thousand Hills, Calif.: Sage.

Pack, Howard. 1992. "New Perspectives on Industrial Growth in Taiwan." In Gustav Ranis, ed., *Taiwan: From Developing to Mature Economy*, pp. 73–120. Boulder: Westview Press.

Pang Chien-Kuo. 1992. *The State and Economic Transformation: The Taiwan Case*. New York: Garland Press.

Peng Hwai-jen. 1989. "Taiwan qiye yezhu de 'guanxi' jiqi zhuanbian, yige shehuixue de fenxi" (Relationships among Taiwan business owners and their changes: A sociological analysis). Ph.D. dissertation, Tunghai University.

Redding, S. Gordon. 1990. *The Spirit of Chinese Capitalism*. Berlin: Walter de Gruyter.

Scitovsky, Tibor. 1986. "Economic Development in Taiwan and South Korea: 1965–81." In Lawrence J. Lau, ed., *Models of Development: A Comparative Study of Economic Growth in South Korea and Taiwan*, pp. 178–197. San Francisco: Institute for Contemporary Studies.

Semkow, Brian W. 1994. *Taiwan's Capital-Market Reform: The Financial and Legal Issues*. New York: Oxford University Press.

Shieh, G.S. 1992. *"Boss" Island: The Subcontracting Network and Micro-Entrepreneurship in Taiwan's Development*. New York: Peter Lang.

Tong Chee Kiong. 1991. "Centripetal Authority, Differentiated Networks: The Social Organization of Chinese Firms in Singapore." In Gary Hamilton, ed., *Business Networks and Economic Development in East and Southeast Asia*, pp. 87–105. Hong Kong: Centre of Asian Studies, University of Hong Kong.

Wade, Robert. 1990. *Governing the Market: Economic Theory and the Role of Government in East Asian Industrialization*. Princeton: Princeton University Press.

Westney, Eleanor D. 1996. "The Japanese Business System: Key Features and Prospects for Change." *Journal of Asian Business* 12, 1:21–50.

Winckler, Edwin A., and Susan Greenhalgh, eds. 1988. *Contending Approaches to the Political Economy of Taiwan*. Armonk, N.Y.: M.E. Sharpe.

Winn, Jane Kaufman. 1991. "Banking and Finance in Taiwan: The Prospects for Internationalization in the 1990s." *International Lawyer* 25, 4 (Winter):907–952.

Wong Siu-lun. 1985. "The Chinese Family Firm: A Model." *British Journal of Sociology* 36:58–72.

_____. 1988. "The Applicability of Asian Family Values to Other Socio-cultural Settings." In Peter Berger and Michael Hsiao, eds., *In Search of an East Asian Development Model*, pp. 134–152. New Brunswick, N.J.: Transaction Books.

_____. 1991. "Chinese Entrepreneurs and Business Trust." In Gary G. Hamilton, ed., *Business Networks and Economic Development in East and Southeast Asia*, pp. 13–29. Hong Kong: Centre of Asian Studies, University of Hong Kong.

World Bank. 1988. *World Development Report*. Oxford: Oxford University Press.

Wu Hui-lin. 1988. "A Future for Small and Medium Enterprises?" *Free China Review* 38, 11 (November):6–9.

Yang, Mayfair Mei-hui. 1989. "The Gift Economy and State Power in China." *Comparative Studies in Society and History* 31, 1:40–41.

_____. 1994. *Gifts, Favors, and Banquets: The Art of Social Relationships in China.* Ithaca: Cornell University Press.

Yao Souchou. 1987. "The Fetish of Relationships: Chinese Business Transactions in Singapore." *Sojourn* 2:89–111.

Yong Pit Kee. 1992. "The Social Foundation of Chinese Rubber Businesses in Singapore." Master's thesis, Department of Sociology, National University of Singapore.

Zeile, William J. 1993. "Industrial Targeting, Business Organization, and Industry Productivity Growth in the Republic of Korea, 1972–1985." Ph.D. dissertation, Department of Economics, University of California–Davis.

two

Divided Market Cultures in China

Gender, Enterprise, and Religion

ROBERT P. WELLER

Market economies appear to sap the life from traditional values whenever they begin to dominate social relations. Enthusiasts praise transformation as the rise of motivated individuals, but critics see only calculation and greed. Whatever their view of the consequences, social scientists have been exploring the effects of the rise of market economies at least since Marx wrote on alienation, Durkheim on anomie, and Weber on the iron cage of capitalism and the "unprecedented inner loneliness of the single individual" standing directly beneath the hard gaze of God (Weber 1958:104). All three, in spite of the enormous differences among them, led us to expect a modern market culture of individualism, secularism, and rationality (in Weber's sense of maximizing control and efficiency).

In recent decades, however, an alternative point of view has been developing from several quite disparate sources. This view embraces the market while rejecting individualistic market culture as a peculiarly Western phenomenon that is neither desirable nor necessary in the rest of the world. It is articulated in part through religion, with Islam playing the most important role in the attempt to create an alternative set of market values. At the same time, the economic boom in East Asia has encouraged the idea that "Confucian" culture (vaguely defined) has already provided such an alternative, perhaps even more effective than Western market culture.

Is there in fact one universal market culture or are there many? Are features such as individualism, rationality, and secularism (or selfishness, greed, and godlessness) inherent to capitalist markets? Does a world market imply cultural convergence, or are some earlier systems preadapted to capitalism? Empirically the case is still open, at least for Chinese East Asia. The system continues to transform even as we watch it; family ties, for example, are less important now than they were even a decade ago. The evidence does suggest, however, that capitalist markets exert comparable pressures everywhere in the world but that local systems react differently to those pressures. The result is a complex split with some cultural developments indeed tending toward a kind of global market culture and others countering that trend in context-specific ways. The Chinese cases do not support a simple convergence toward a universal market culture, but neither do they show a clear Confucian riposte. Instead, they reveal an ongoing tension between value and market, community and individual. This tension itself, I will argue, constitutes a shared feature of market modernity. However, the ways in which people resolve this tension, or at least hold it under control, vary widely even within a single society.[1]

In particular, many areas of life outside the economy undergo increasing pressure as market rationality pushes beyond the marketplace itself. Battle lines may be drawn in many places across a society between a utilitarian or rationalist tendency and traditionalist or moralist alternatives. Certainly the history of the West has not been the triumphant march of the market over everything else. The nineteenth-century religious entrenchment against the Enlightenment still echoes today in attacks on secular humanism. In art and literature, the Romantics provided one of the precursors to modern environmentalism. Twentieth-century pressures toward making traditional family functions such as child care or food preparation into commodities have been met by a vigorous defense (or perhaps invention) of traditional family values.

In this chapter I look at two quite different aspects of Chinese society, concentrating on Taiwan, where we have the most evidence, but with frequent reference to the People's Republic of China. First, I take up the use of particularistic ties in business, especially the claim that the Chinese effectively mobilize family and other personal ties to avoid the extreme individualism of the West. I also examine the related attempts to work out a philosophical "post-Confucian" alternative to Western market culture. Second, I take up recent developments in popular religion, which both celebrate and substitute for a perceived amoral market.

The available social and cultural resources influence how tensions between market and social values develop. That means, among other things, that different groups within a single society may react differently. An analysis of such groups could take many lines for Chinese societies; I concentrate on gender differences, finding that variant views of the family and differential access to markets and other social resources have encouraged men and women to react differently. Women have entered the market at all levels in the course of the twentieth century in China and no longer always rely on the mediation of their husbands, fathers, and sons. Yet their opportunities are certainly not identical to men's. The differences between the sexes in some cases have led to unexpected changes, for example, when women lead the way toward less use of particularistic ties in spite of their continuing close association with the family. Differences between men and women in the view of the family pervade gender positions on the use of particularistic ties, within the environmental movement, and in new religious groups.

On Culture and Convergence

The East Asian response to modernization theories of convergence toward Western market culture has centered around claims that Confucianism, broadly interpreted, offered cultural resources that promoted the adoption of market capitalism.[2] Most authors recognize that Confucian ideas alone are not sufficient cause for capitalist development and that contact with the West helped free Chinese culture from an imperial system that impeded market growth. They thus usually talk about post-Confucianism to distinguish current formulations from the millennium-old neo-Confucianism that formed the ideological base of late imperial rule.

Authors vary widely in just what they mean by post-Confucianism, but the list of most important features usually includes an emphasis on human relations and social harmony based on the idea of filial piety, respect for authority and a strong identity with the organization, and a combination of worldly diligence and fatalism.[3] The contrast with Western individualist atomization is implicit throughout. All but the most naive authors, of course, would admit that this post-Confucian model simplifies a great deal of social, geographic, and historical variation. Yet they would also insist (and I would agree) that on the whole, some such set of ideas and practices does in fact usefully differentiate the Chinese and Western cultural spheres. Although it is certainly possible to trace these views, however loosely defined, back to the thought of Confucius himself, they also pervade many aspects of Chinese culture generally even among people who could say nothing about philosophical Confucianism. I will thus refer more simply to Chinese culture and save references to Confucianism and post-Confucianism to the ongoing philosophical effort that I discuss in the following pages.

A general description of Chinese culture based on Confucian tenets has shaped Western ideas about the growth of market economies in the region throughout the twentieth century. Alarmingly, however, the conclusions social scientists now draw from these features are just the opposite of what people concluded from the same observations for the first sixty or seventy years of the century. From Max Weber's original pessimistic predictions through the modernization theorists of the 1950s and 1960s, the standard arguments considered Chinese culture inimical to capitalism. Weber himself had argued that the Confucian "enchanted world" did not create the drive toward change that allowed Protestantism to catalyze the European economic transformation (Weber 1951). Others argued that family-centered particularism blocked rational economic development (e.g., Levy 1949:354–359) or that China had religious impediments to economic growth (e.g., Bellah 1965). Now, however, Weber's Confucian world is offered as the key to East Asian economic success, and Levy's traditional particularism is seen as the key to successful family enterprise.[4]

In retrospect, the problems with the earlier version seem clear. Earlier analyses treated Chinese culture as an abstract, clearly formulated set of propositions and were often based on Chinese elite descriptions of cultural ideals. These analyses specified social and economic consequences based on differences between these ideals and an equally idealized version of Western market culture. Instead of placing actual behavior in real contexts, they assumed an automatic translation of a unitary culture into action. The new version, in part because Chinese scholars have taken the lead in its development, grounds its claims in a far better understanding of Chinese culture and history. It also has the good fortune of coming after the fact and so will not suffer the kind of empirical disproof that awaited the modernization version.

The new version of Chinese culture is thus much deeper than the old one but continues to offer a unitary culture largely out of context. Its post facto origins raise the danger of picking only those bits of traditional China most clearly preadapted to capitalism and ignoring the equally interesting question of how its many ill-adapted features have been overcome. Imperial China, after all, included a number of quite different cultural currents. Neo-Confucianism had the blessing of the state, but other elements also played important roles, even among the elite.

Some of these non-Confucian cultural resources even suggested a kind of individualism, much as one can identify a strong individualistic undercurrent in medieval Europe. Artists, for example, had long identified themselves by name, in contrast to the anonymous art of the Middle Ages. Indeed, the unique individuality of some artists provided the source for their fame, especially for various artists identified as "eccentrics" *(guai)*. Ownership further individualized paintings, as proud possessors would apply their seal (itself considered a work of art) directly to a painting and sometimes add a poem or two. Paintings thus directly commemorated both their individual creators and their specific histories of ownership, recorded permanently on the paper itself.

As I have argued elsewhere, Chinese popular religion has long also included a strong individualistic streak, especially through the worship of ghosts (Weller 1994:130–142). The very definition of ghosts rests on their existence apart from any normal social ties: They are the unincorporated dead, part of no larger social group. Requests to ghosts are uniformly individualistic. One worships for personal gain, not for family or community. Ghosts work on a contract basis with quick and nasty punishment for not paying them back on time and without regard for broader issues of morality. In the ghostly marketplace for miracles cash is exchanged for services and there are no lasting personal ties. Ghosts' individualizing function contrasts with the community base of gods, and their faceless anonymity and insistence on keeping the terms of a bargain recall the market in ways that political petitions and tribute payments to gods do not. Geomancy, the siting of graves and houses to channel good luck to people, showed a similarly individualistic streak; one brother could manipulate the system against another (Freedman 1966:143). In a society that long has had an important market component, it should not surprise us that an individualistic, even selfish, undercurrent ran beneath the niceties of the bureaucratic hierarchy.

Even this individualistic streak did not begin to exhaust the alternatives to Confucian benevolent hierarchy in imperial China. There was, for example, a complex cosmology of interactions and correlations of yin and yang, the five phases, the ten Heavenly Stems and twelve Earthly Branches, the eight trigrams and sixty-four hexagrams, the twenty-four asterisms, and much more. Underneath this lay a view of the universe as unitary and interconnected, not by hierarchy but by shared energy. This view supported a diverse set of practices including Daoist meditation, healing, and fortune-telling. In spite of the clearly ancient roots in China of this alternative set of ideas, the Confucian elite had already begun to attack it by the eighteenth century. It nevertheless continues strongly today in Chinese medicine and the very popular practice of *qigong* exercises.

Even Confucianism itself offered many possibilities; some commentators have suggested differentiating among several Confucianisms. Yu Yingshi, for example, has suggested that a merchant-oriented Confucianism developed in the Ming and Qing dynasties (Yu 1987). Others distinguish between an imperialist and an older, democratic Confucianism (e.g., Huang and Wu 1994). I will not belabor the point further except to add that Confucian hegemony, insofar as it existed, weakened much further with the collapse of the imperial state in 1911. The modernizing regime that replaced it furthered the decline of any kind of institutionalized moral authority because the very attempt to foster "modernity" prevented the new state from building on those older forms of understanding (see Duara 1991; Weller 1994:176–180). As a result, the diverse aspects of identity that coexisted with Confucianism in late imperial China had greater scope in the twentieth century than ever before.

Late imperial China thus offered all kinds of cultural possibilities: Some of these ideologies would indeed thrive under capitalism, but others would prove antithetical. Individualistic ghosts were matched by the imperial metaphor of gods, Confucian this-worldly asceticism was matched by traditional authority, to which it had ties. This diversity suggests that we ask how the various faces of Chinese culture influenced the reception of markets and how expanding market economies in turn selectively encouraged or discouraged various cultural elements by pushing them into unfamiliar terrain. In some ways, diversity itself was the most important preadaptation. A genuinely successful neo-Confucian hegemony that crushed all alternatives in support of the imperial state would have had no hope of making the transition in the twentieth century. This suggests that the most fruitful questions about culture and economic change involve not just identifying the successful roots of modern culture but actively looking at the whole range of resources and at how they change and are in turn changed by the market.

Such an examination requires looking beyond philosophical abstractions of Confucianism and beyond Chinese culture more broadly to place the full range of variation into its social and economic context. The diversity of Chinese culture meant that it was not simply preadapted (or ill-adapted, in older readings) to a new economic system but reacted differentially to historical events. The Chinese have thrived in market economies because they have successfully mined and refined some aspects of their cultural resources and successfully buried others.[5] Out of context, features such as respect for authority might be expected to suffocate entrepreneurial creativity (the old line, still occasionally heard about Japan) as easily as to guarantee labor peace and corporate harmony (the new line). In practice, respect for authority looks less important in Chinese societies than one might have predicted. Employees tend to learn the ropes and then leave to compete with their old employers. As the Taiwanese cliché goes, it is better to be a chicken's beak than a bull's behind. The metaphor of the firm as family thus runs into immediate limits, although managers often make the comparison (Redding 1990).

In much the same way, extensive reliance on particularistic ties opens the door to corruption and graft even as it eases problems of capital formation, marketing, and employee loyalty. Both Hamilton and Mackie (in this volume) show that the Chinese talent for the market comes in part from their ability to draw on horizontal ties and social networks. Yet it is just as important to ask what prevented these networks of particularistic ties from bleeding people dry. Or again, does family loyalty create a high-achievement motivation or encourage disloyalty to others? Over two millennia ago the legalist Han Feizi attacked Confucian family loyalty for implying disloyalty to the state. If children had a duty to preserve their bodies to serve their parents, who would fight the wars? Modernization theorists were not wrong to emphasize the dangers of particularistic ties (as nearly any Chinese entrepreneur will attest); their mistake was to ignore real mechanisms for dealing with those dangers and to assume the inevitability of convergence toward Western market rationality.[6]

In the remainder of this chapter I will take up the use of personal ties in business and the resurgence of popular religion in Chinese societies. In spite of the vast differences between these areas of life, I will argue that each is undergoing comparable transformations rather than evidencing a realization of a fortunate preadaptation or an inevitable convergence. The transformations involve the development of an argument over market culture with one side both celebrating and reflecting the new economy and the other searching for moral alternatives. Both sides of this argument have traditional cultural roots as well as ties beyond China. And within each camp, women and men have partially different cultural resources to offer and thus see the issues differently.

Personal Ties: Utility Versus Morality

Much of the literature arguing for an alternative Chinese market culture centers around the use of personal ties through community and especially family. Two kinds of evidence have made a convincing case for the central role of these ties in Chinese societies: the frequency of discourse about the family as a model for business and about the importance of "connections" *(guanxi)*, and actual behavior.[7] The discursive evidence is especially strong. Managers of large Chinese enterprises (at least outside the People's Republic) claim to act as fathers of large families.[8] They assert the Confucian responsibility the father owes his children and the obedience the children owe their father (see, e.g., Redding 1990:156–169). Managers and entrepreneurs at all levels also speak regularly of the critical importance of interpersonal ties and explicitly emphasize values such as trust *(xinyong)* and human feelings *(renqing)* in doing business (DeGlopper 1972; Silin 1972).

Discourse need not translate into practice, of course, and the situation is more complex when we turn to behavior. Chinese paternalism can contribute to an inflexible corporate structure, and the family model problematizes succession in business just as family disputes can become contentious and angry in Chinese societies. The existence of these problems, however, also provides indirect evidence that people really are applying a family metaphor even when it creates some difficulties. In addition, real, nonmetaphorical family business has been at the heart of the economic boom in Taiwan, Hong Kong, and the People's Republic. This has been especially true for people with limited access to the state and the opportunities it can create. In Taiwan the state promoted large enterprises but left most people to their own devices. Banks, for example, would not make loans to small entrepreneurs, who turned to informal credit arrangements based on their personal connections. In the People's Republic, small entrepreneurs *(geti hu)* also typically have few connections to the vast resources of the state, which its bureaucrats still control. They thus also rely heavily on kinship ties. Larger businesses *(siying qiye)*, which almost invariably have close ties to the state, use family ties much less (McEwen 1994).

Finally, several studies have actually traced the extensive use of kinship networks in the economy. Hamilton, in this volume, shows the use of *guanxi* and trust in Taiwan, and Mackie suggests similar processes among the Chinese in Southeast Asia. Numazaki (1991) has also outlined the wide and amorphous personal networks that unite business groups in Taiwan. At quite another level of Taiwanese society, Ka (1992) has followed in detail the interpersonal ties that shape the subcontracting system for garment construction in a Taipei neighborhood. These various studies leave no doubt that ties of family, marriage, neighborhood, and all the rest play a central role in Chinese business. They imply a clear contrast with an idealized version of rationalized Western market culture, where contractual ties between separate individuals supposedly substitute for personalistic ties of trust.

Two problems, however, prevent us from simply declaring that Chinese societies have established a clear alternative to Western market culture. The first is that the picture of Western business practice on which the contrast relies is itself "occidentalized." Family business, for example, drove early Western capitalism in much the same way as people have recently documented for Chinese society today. Although there has been a gradual (but by no means complete) move away from that model in the West, it may suggest that family-centered capitalism works well during the early development of market economies. If so, then the Chinese evidence may describe an earlier stage of capitalism rather than a true alternative.[9]

The second problem, clearly related to the first, is that these Chinese economies continue to change very rapidly. With the passing of several decades of continuous development, business in Taiwan and Hong Kong is only now beginning to face some of the difficulties that might discourage the family model and the extensive use of personalistic ties: Small family enterprises are becoming large firms, labor-intensive production is moving to the high-technology and service sectors, company founders are searching for successors, and economic growth elsewhere in Asia is creating a more fiercely competitive marketplace. Indeed, some new evidence suggests that people are relying less than ever on traditional interpersonal connections and that the quality of such relations is becoming progressively thinner. Several studies have suggested a dilution of the human feelings *(renqing)* implied in relationships *(guanxi)* in the People's Republic since market-oriented economic reforms began in the early 1980s and the growth of more purely utilitarian ties (Gold 1985; Yan 1993). A recent study of these issues in Taiwan, Hong Kong, and the People's Republic shows that many entrepreneurs now explicitly reject the use of kinship ties as old-fashioned and prefer more "modern" relationships, for instance, with classmates (McEwen 1994). Managers of larger enterprises in the People's Republic particularly like to emphasize their commitment to "scientific" management (McEwen 1994).

The situation remains very much in flux, yet Chinese have clearly drawn on their cultural traditions to address new economic opportunities. Confucian ideas do affect management behavior, and business activity relies heavily on ties established outside the market. The market itself, however, also puts significant pressure on those relationships. Competition strains both real family ties (which threaten to drain business resources) and the family as a metaphor. The result is not yet completely clear, but there is enough evidence to conclude that Chinese *guanxi* do indeed influence market behavior and that they have in turn been changed.

Women's Networks

Much of the literature on Chinese culture and business assumes, in a typically Confucian way, that there are no women, or at best that there are no differences between men and women. If true, this would be surprising indeed. We now have two decades of studies of family and gender clearly showing that women's interests in their families and their views of those fundamental kin relationships at the core of Confucian thought differed significantly from those of their husbands, fathers, and sons. Women's work was in theory confined to the domestic sphere; even when they produced commodities, men mediated access to the market.[10] Wives (who were traditionally called *neiren*, "inside people") had no direct access to their husbands' personal networks, and their own external contacts were confined to their natal families and to other women of their husbands' villages. Women, with their bound feet, did not do agricultural labor; nor did they have any place in the management of corporate properties. They were (and still are in the People's Republic) much more likely to be illiterate than their husbands. Perhaps most important, women had little reason to share their husbands' view of the family as one link in an infinite chain of patrilineal connections. Although most wives dutifully burned incense every morning for their husbands' ancestors, they did not worship their own ancestors. Even if a woman's parents had no other descendants to worship them, her husband's family would probably allow no more than a dusty corner in a back room for their commemorative tablets.[11] Women instead focused on creating a "uterine family" (Wolf 1972:32–41). The birth of a son in particular solidified her place in her husband's house; fostering his continuing loyalty protected her in the years to come.

The idea of a nurturing mother confined to the household does not sound particularly well adapted to capitalism, but women in fact had resources that would become relevant. Although women's spheres of connections were much smaller than men's, they could also be more reliable. Her own natal family had the advantage of being trustworthy but also socially distant enough to prevent it becoming a drain if problems arose. In addition, the close ties uniting village networks of women could make up for the limited scale of the group. Women thus have made extensive use of rotating credit associations. These have been one of the most important ways of raising entrepreneurial capital but rely on high degrees of trust because it is so easy for members to abscond with all the funds. The closeness of women's networks may help them establish the necessary kinds of ties, whereas men may have broader but more utilitarian ties more open to abuse.

Many women have become entrepreneurs in Hong Kong, Taiwan, and the People's Republic. The legislated end of foot-binding (and other legal changes, especially in marriage rights) early in the twentieth century, much greater access to education, opportunities for wage labor, and other changes have helped open the market directly to women. Some estimate that fully half of the petty entrepreneurs in the People's Republic are women (McEwen 1994:340). Men still dominate, however, and very few women run manufacturing businesses.

Family can pose a major problem for women entrepreneurs. They continue to face the responsibility of providing their husbands with sons and of taking care of children and the household. Young women in particular may have to choose between family and career, and preliminary evidence suggests a high divorce rate for young married women (McEwen 1994:162, 254). At the same time, young female entrepreneurs value the new freedoms of their position and its opportunities for self-fulfillment (Gates 1991:25).

As McEwen makes clear for all three of these Chinese societies, many entrepreneurial women feel cut off from the male world of connections (McEwen 1994:148, 239, 341–342). They particularly miss the opportunity to cement ties through the endless banqueting in which men indulge. Some of this takes place in hostess bars, in which the women feel uncomfortable, and most of it involves competitive social drinking, an activity in which women have traditionally not been welcome. Taking part in such events would call the woman's character into question. Yet women also have ways of dealing with this problem. In many cases they go into business with their husbands. More creatively, some women use their sons or brothers as fronts at these events. They remain backstage pulling the strings while their men work the male networks (McEwen 1994:341–342). They thus continue to make use of ties of uterine and natal family, running the business as "inside people" just as they ran the family. Whereas they may have problems meeting traditional family responsibilities, they also draw on traditional family skills in kin management to succeed.

Other women may simply forge their own networks. Some draw on traditional ties to do this, as when they raise capital through a rotating credit association of old friends. Others, however, simply start from scratch by searching out like-minded people. McEwen tells of one informant who needed a business partner in Taiwan. She had no connections at all and no way of manipulating a network to create some. She resorted to looking people up in the phonebook, where she finally found some equally unconnected partners—young people whose study abroad had cut them off from traditional networks—with compatible business interests (McEwen 1994:241). This use of less personalistic kinds of ties does not differ fundamentally from the kinds of changes young men are also advancing. In this case, however, women's relative lack of access to the opportunities that traditional ties create for men has led them to promote something more like a Weberian version of rational market behavior.

There is no simple evolution here. Women draw both on the traditional resources available to them and on innovative kinds of ties. In the process they set loose a series of contradictory processes—affirming the woman's role in the uterine family but making real family life problematic, drawing on traditionally female ties and skills but promoting a more utilitarian kind of relationship network. For women and men, market culture is not just the affirmation of Confucian tradition or just a convergence toward a single (Western-style) market culture inherent to capitalism itself. Instead it creates a new series of tensions around economic life that have ramifications throughout the entire society. These tensions have roots in people's varied cultural resources and in the pressures of the market itself.

Markets, Gender, and Morality

As for all people under capitalism, the necessity of maximizing profits (at least over the long run) may pressure people to loosen other than economic ties. At the same time, areas of life that have never been experienced as part of the economic sphere (child care, religion) increasingly appear as commodities and become open to the rationalizing disciplines of the market. Yet there is nothing inevitable or unstoppable about this process. It is challenged and compromised at all points by people making sense of their changing world. Capitalism thus did not spell the end of religion, as many modernization theorists predicted, but instead is often accompanied by a religious revival (as in nineteenth-century America or late-twentieth-century Iran). Nor has capitalization been the destruction of the family, as Marx and Engels predicted. The challenges to a strict market logic come both from compromises with existing social and cultural resources and from more direct reactions that involve attempting to reconstruct "lost" moral worlds.

In many cases, these direct reactions do not challenge market economics but instead offer alternatives to a perceived moral degradation. This is true of Islam in many countries (see Hefner, this volume) and also true in the Chinese societies of East and Southeast Asia. Taiwan, for example, which has the most vibrant domestic politics in the region, has almost no debate over general business policy and certainly no important voice promoting any noncapitalist economic system. It is, however, filled with moral revivals, most of which extend across the region. The People's Republic of China has itself begun to promote a Confucian moral alternative to Western market culture alongside the older socialist alternative based on equality and self-sacrifice.

Men and women experience this moral dilemma in partially different ways, largely because their relations to earlier moral systems of family and community were not identical, as I have briefly described. For men, business fits neatly into ideas about the infinite extension of a patriline because fathers have a duty to provide for the prosperity of future generations of male heirs. Yet the market has clearly increased the utilitarian aspect of networks of relationships *(guanxi)* in all of these societies, undercutting the Confucian values of loyalty, benevolence, and respect. Even the realities of the firm, for all their use of family metaphors, upset these values. Worker peace in most of these countries, after all, has been maintained by government repression more than by Confucian benevolence. The desire to be a boss, even a little one, also supersedes most feelings of personal loyalty, and turnover is thus high.

The (male-dominated) reaction to these moral dilemmas has been a great rise in debates over the real meaning of Confucianism for modern Chinese society. Many schools of thought compete within this "post-Confucian" movement; social scientists too are trying to assess the relevance of Confucian culture to Chinese economic success. Indeed, Jochim (1992) has argued that rather than competing with post-Confucianism, these scholars' work is best seen as part of a debate about what Confucianism should mean today. Most innovative, however, are the philosophers trying to create (or recreate) a Confucian humanism to serve as a guiding moral system for the modern world. This effort has taken at least two major forms. The first centers in Singapore, where Lee Kwan-yu has become the chief spokesman for a Confucian authoritarianism with deep roots in Chinese culture. Here the family metaphors of paternal benevolence and filial respect are extended to the nation as a whole in a move that recalls both European corporatist ideology (always the champion of the family) and Confucius himself. The second form centers in Taiwan and among some overseas Chinese and advances a more democratic vision of Confucius that it claims cuts through the imperial accretions of the past two millennia. It criticizes the Singapore version as a remnant of the worst in the old tradition and looks back to the original Confucian texts for a truer version of the philosopher. One recent, if rather polemical, version argues for an ecological democracy inherent in classical Confucianism that will "ward off the post-industrial ill of economic technological hegemony, where a person is just a button in a machine, economic or otherwise—easily pushed on and off, easily replaced" (Huang and Wu 1994:82). Adherents to this view believe that

hegemony by technocrats and multi-national corporations—where only money and machines talk—grows in an ideological soil ("Western democracy") where everyone is indifferently equal in a lonely crowd, a mass society. Confucian democracy dissolves this danger. Here everyone is treasured as a social person, that is, not as a faceless individual but as a person in a specific role which is imbued with the special warmth of that particular person (Huang and Wu 1994:83).

This formulation is a clear example of the concern with alternatives to an atomized Western market culture, on the one hand, and to a "feudal" or "imperial" Confucianism, on the other. As with earlier generations of Confucianisms, this one is largely confined to intellectuals. The Singapore version is taking on a broader political significance with some direct influence in the People's Republic and on international debates over human rights. Neither formulation, however, much qualifies as popular culture. Other ideas play comparable roles outside intellectual circles, as I will discuss further on. This rethinking of the teachings of Confucius, however, most represents the developing philosophical alternatives that look to Chinese tradition instead of the West.

Nearly all the major players in these new debates have been men. This is partly a function of male numerical dominance at senior academic levels but is also consistent with male views of the moral crisis of atomization of communal and personal ties in a market culture. A few women, however, have led a kind of anti-Confucian scholarship. Barbara Reed discusses, for example, the Taiwanese legal scholar, political prisoner, and now congresswoman Lü Xiulian's views on Confucian culture, which she blames for women's problems; she looks for "rational" and ethical alternatives. The anthropologist Lin Meirong also rejects Confucianism but looks for new values instead in a more syncretic and uniquely Taiwanese tradition (Reed 1994:227–234). Lin in particular echoes the Confucian literature's search for values appropriate to the modern world, but she finds her answers outside the Confucian tradition.

In spite of these and a few other voices, however, few ascribe to these women's non-Confucian views, and they are less influential than the post-Confucian movement. A more influential but much less thoroughly conceptualized women's alternative has arisen in the context of various philanthropic women's and religious associations. These groups are more interested in improving society than in generating new moral philosophies, but that in itself recalls traditional gender differences.

Market culture poses for women the problem of family above all. Extended families become less viable, especially in crowded cities, and women's own career needs often directly interfere with what they see as their family responsibilities and even their marriage possibilities. At the same time, nonworking wives in wealthy families share a new desire for fulfillment beyond the family. Women have tried to resolve this conflict by reasserting their traditional responsibility for nurturing children and fostering a uterine family but extending this responsibility to society at large.

One of the most important women's organizations is the Homemakers' Union Environmental Protection Foundation in Taiwan.[12] Although this organization began with a commitment to recycling and other environmental issues, members quickly expanded the concept of environment to include moral issues of all kinds, or to the concept of a "spiritual environment" *(xin-ling huanjing)*. They organize popular meetings on child-rearing practices and publish books encouraging children to be more independent, especially as a way of discouraging molestation and abuse.

With a popular base in middle-class housewives, the Homemakers' Union is not willing to take on controversial political issues and is not interested in the more strictly academic lectures and roundtables of other groups. Unlike other national environmental groups, which are mostly male and mostly led by American Ph.D.s, it tries to root its environmentalism in issues of household and motherhood. As Lu Hwei-syin has discussed, the stock Chinese image of the nurturing mother plays a pivotal role in its imagery. The union's introductory brochure thus shows an image of a woman pushing the bandaged earth in a wheelchair with the slogan "Women take care of the wounded earth" (Lu 1991:34).

Comparable Buddhist associations undertake similar activities and often have predominantly female memberships. Taibei's Jinghua Social and Cultural Education Foundation, for example, promotes social education, fights pornography, and runs camps for troubled youths. The spectacularly successful Compassionate Relief Merit Association (which has about 4 million members in Taiwan) undertakes poverty relief and especially medical care for the needy. Its active membership is about 80 percent women. In each case women are extending quite traditional ideas of motherhood to their roles in the general society.

It is simplistic to assume there is a uniform male or female reaction to market culture or uniform male and female adaptations to it. Yet men and women have different vantage points on society and partially different resources for dealing with change. Just as men and women have moved into the expanding market world in slightly different ways, they have reacted to its problems in relation to the particular crises it creates for them. For men, these involve primarily the challenge to community values, and Confucianism provides a possibility to revivify them. Confucianism, however, never offered as much to women, many of whom are now less willing to be told that they serve three masters: their fathers, their husbands, and finally their sons. Women's moral dilemmas concern the family above all, and their reactions thus also center more around quite traditional views of women's appropriate family role—but with the walls of the household itself no longer trapping them inside.

Market Religions

Chinese societies provide strong evidence—if we still need more evidence in light of events around the world—against the claim that modernity propels a necessary secularization. Indeed, religion appears to be thriving more than ever before. Religion in the People's Republic has boomed along with the economic reforms of the 1980s and the accompanying loosening of political controls. Even in Taiwan, whose history of religious discouragement ("repression" is too strong a word) never compared with the mainland, popular religion has made a strong comeback since the 1970s (Qu and Yao 1986). If anything, the data suggest that expanding markets have actively encouraged religious growth.

As with the other areas I have discussed, several recent studies have suggested that Chinese popular religious practice has shown an elective affinity for capitalism. Peter Berger, for example, proposed what he called the "Li Yih-yuan hypothesis," which holds that "vulgar Confucianism" (including popular religion) influenced Taiwanese development more than any of the more institutionalized "great traditions" (1988:8–9). Others have suggested that popular religion supports appropriate market values such as utilitarianism and strengthens the informal social networks critical for raising credit and dealing with related enterprises (Gallin and Gallin 1982:236–237; Li 1992; Yu 1987).

I believe that Chinese popular religion has in fact long included many themes, some apparently preadapted to capitalist development and others apparently antithetical. Chinese societies are developing new religious forms, rooted in the past, that directly address the market and the problem of values in market societies. Once again, these new forms show a rough correlation with gender: Men favor a Confucianist interpretation of texts, and women give stronger support to social action.

Popular Religion, Individualism, and Markets

I have argued elsewhere that the lack of strong interpretive communities that could control religion in China opened a great deal of free space for variation (Weller 1994:53–56). Even so, most people in Chinese societies would quickly agree on a few religious basics. Whatever else ancestor worship may accomplish, for example, nearly everyone who practices it talks about it as a way of energizing values of filial piety. Temples also clearly support community solidarity (but sometimes at the expense of larger solidarities like the nation). Gods, at least sometimes, speak to the naturalness of bureaucratic politics and the prevalence of upright officials.

Much of Chinese popular religion thus valorizes community and family, uniting individuals with these larger social circles. This is the most public face of popular practice and the picture painted by large calendrical rituals. This meshing of the individual into larger webs of social relations is quite different from Weber's Protestantism and quite different from the kind of ideology he expected with capitalism. This is one reason Weber and some later followers felt Chinese religion stood as a major impediment to capitalist development (Weber 1951; Bellah 1965). In retrospect, of course, such pessimism was misplaced. As I have mentioned, such analyses missed the way "traditional" and personalistic ties, which religion helped create, would form a base for entrepreneurs using "relational capital" (Winn 1991) to get started. Gods such as Guan Gong, for example, appear frequently on small-business altars in Taiwan, Hong Kong, and southern China because of an association with loyalty and personalistic ties, especially sworn brotherhoods. These features are critical to survival in the informal economy of small business in all these societies.

Just behind this communal side of religion, however, lurks a far more thoroughly individualistic and competitive religious personality, especially in ghost worship, as I discussed previously. The ghostly side of Chinese religion in Taiwan (the only area for which we so far have extensive data) grew very rapidly in the 1980s, at the point when many Taiwanese for the first time had achieved some significant wealth but when the market economy also appeared particularly threatening and capricious with few productive outlets for capital (see Weller 1994:148–153).

In addition, popular worship in Taiwan has always had a strong utilitarian side. Much worship occurs simply to make concrete requests of deities for cures, for help getting pregnant, or for business advice. Gods who do not really help soon lose their followers, and people can always tell stories of lives saved and enemies vanquished by their major community gods. Useless gods sometimes end up smashed or thrown in rivers.

Spirit-medium cults, the members of which usually worship at private altars, provide similarly utilitarian help and have none of the communal functions of major temples. Such cults have greatly increased recently in Taiwan. At the same time, more and more different gods are appearing on these private altars. Community temples usually feature one primary deity, often captured in many images. Other gods may appear on secondary altars or in minor positions on the main altar. The horde of different gods on private spirit-medium altars—as many as forty or fifty different images in recent years—reinforces the utilitarian functions of such cults (Li 1992:11–13). With each deity having its own specialty, these temples can meet the needs of a wider variety of clients, just like a shop that expands its selection of wares. Not coincidentally, spirit-medium shrines themselves are profit-oriented petty capitalist enterprises.

As for all the areas I have discussed, religion shows less a preadaptation to capitalism than an ability to reproportion itself to the new context. The communal side of religion has easily held its own, reinforcing ties of locality and family that have been important to capitalist development. Yet, at least in Taiwan, ghosts and spirit mediums for (previously) minor gods have taken on a greatly expanded role in a kind of celebration of the individualism and competition of the market.

Sects

Taiwan has also fostered a set of new religions, or sects in the Weberian sense that membership is voluntaristic and individualistic, not given simply by birth or residence.[13] Members of the same sect can be trusted because all are like-minded people, having consciously chosen certain kinds of values (Weber 1946). Churches, in contrast, offer no room for autonomous responsibility and no such guarantees. Taiwanese popular religious practice is not a church in any standard sense but shares with Weber's definition the lack of any individual commitment. Anyone is qualified to worship. The new religions, however, have exactly the sectarian structure that Weber discussed.[14] Membership is entirely voluntary and optional, and individuals take part only on their own account, not on behalf of their family or community. I will briefly discuss two major branches of these new religions: pietistic sects like the Way of Unity (Yiguan Dao), which have organized congregations, an interest in explicit interpretation of texts, and largely male leaderships; and new Buddhist groups, especially the Compassionate Relief Merit Association I mentioned briefly earlier, whose leadership and membership is largely women.

Many of the pietistic sects claim disproportionate business success. The Way of Unity is the most famous, but all share a pietistic tradition with clearly organized congregations, an active concern for evangelization, and an interest in religious texts. They usually also center on a nurturing goddess and rely on spirit writing to produce new sacred texts. Their interpretations tend toward conservative rhapsodies on harmony and Confucian social relations (Jordan and Overmyer 1986). They also often have a general concern with concrete accomplishments in this world. The Way of Unity alone has about a million regular followers, and perhaps 15–20 percent of the adult population may be members of such sects.[15] Many of the sects have strong business support, and anecdotal evidence suggests that a disproportionate number of businessmen are sectarians (Shenmi 1990; Zhao 1992).[16] Membership also appears to have grown rapidly just during the period of Taiwan's most rapid economic growth, but the statistics may be misleading because the Way of Unity was illegal until 1987.

These sects offer codes for individual moral behavior. Each convert is devoted to accumulating enough merit to achieve individual salvation (Bosco 1992); merit accrues to individuals, not families. Even personal spirit-writing revelations usually apply only to the individual involved; there is no attempt to force revelations on others (Jordan and Overmyer 1986:273). This stress on individuals fits easily with the market economy. In contrast, popular worship defines the individual autonomy of ghosts only in negative contrast to the community moralities of most gods and ancestors and defines community in ways that do not control for moral commitment, reliability, loyalty, or other features that might interest an entrepreneur looking for contacts.

Taiwanese sectarians, just like Weber's Protestants, substitute a self-selected group of credit-worthy comrades for the potential problems of ascribed particularistic ties like kinship or residence. Even their vegetarianism marks them as different kinds of individuals, especially at business or religious feasts, which generally feature overflowing platters of meat. Their regular meetings, spirit-writing or spirit-possession sessions, and greater moral discipline distinguish them from the rest of society and offer them a new kind of social resource in business. Many of the sects, including the Way of Unity and the Hall of Compassion, worship a single primary goddess instead of one of the geographically localized gods that typify popular practice. This practice also cuts off the local community associations of sectarian temples and furthers the sectarian separation of members.

These sectarians also heavily emphasize explicit, textually validated values, unlike most popular religious practice. In particular, they consider themselves to be reviving threatened traditional Chinese values as expressed in Confucian and Daoist classics (Jordan and Overmyer 1986:276–280; Zheng 1987). Many spirit-writing sessions produce commentaries on classics, and these may be discussed in regular meetings that resemble a combination of Protestant preaching and Sunday school. Several sects also produce magazines or sponsor inspirational speakers to promote their values. Constant themes include conservative standards in Taiwan such as filial piety, respect for authority, and appropriate relations of hierarchy between men and women, seniors and juniors, parents and children. At the same time, the sects share the utilitarian concerns of popular practice; they stress health, economic success, and similar issues (Zheng 1987; Qu 1989).

Jordan and Overmyer (1986:275–276) argue that the confirmation of "traditional" values and the chance for a respected position in the sect create an alternative route to self-esteem for people cut off from modern routes to success, especially people lacking a modern education. Yet the embrace of "tradition" also constitutes a kind of reaction to modernity that can characterize the educated and successful as well. This reaction is the other side of the celebration of individual autonomy and self-interest in ghost worship and spirit-medium altars; it is an attempt to retrieve communal values in an era that has lost them. Although these sects do embrace a kind of individualism, they embed it firmly in Confucian discourse on broader social relations. They are the spirit-writing equivalent of the philosophers trying to reclaim Confucianism as a moral alternative for the modern world.

Women have sometimes played an important role in these sects, but men dominate the leadership and sometimes the membership. Even the Religion of Compassion (Cihui Tang), with many female members, has few female leaders. In part, the appeal to Confucian tradition itself may discourage women. Jordan and Overmyer document, for instance, how early spirit-writing texts of this genre took a very different tone toward women than the "precious scrolls" *(baojuan)* out of which they evolved. Precious scrolls had often shown great sympathy for the problems of women, but in the new form even the goddess at the core of the sect urged women "to shun arrogance, physical beauty, and cosmetic decoration. Women should be plain, filial, and obedient, must not go out the gate, and are to refrain from talking to outsiders" (Jordan and Overmyer 1986:57). Women active in the modern sects may also reinterpret them. For instance, Jordan and Overmyer document one female sectarian medium who worked revelations into a gender-laden morality of virtuous women and wastrel men (Jordan and Overmyer 1986:206–207; further analyzed in Reed 1994:240).

In contrast to these sects, some of the most important new Buddhist organizations appeal directly to women even though membership is open to all. Like the Homemakers' Union, they also emphasize nurturance. In their case, the key image is not the mother but the bodhisattva, dedicated to helping all beings before achieving nirvana her- or himself. The most spectacularly successful such organization is the Compassionate Relief Merit Association (Ciji Gongdehui). It had almost 4 million members (close to 20 percent of Taiwan's population) and gave out over U.S.$20 million in charitable aid in 1991 (Ciji Gongdehui, n.d.). The charismatic nun who runs the organization, the Venerable Zhengyan, has little concern for fine points of Buddhist philosophy. She emphasizes instead the possibility of creating a "pure land" on earth through humanitarian love, and she preaches that cultivation lies in doing good deeds. Here is a Buddhism for everyone, brought out from the subtleties of the monastery.[17]

Followers are expected to contribute money and time, and Zhengyan's broad following took off with the economic boom of the 1980s. Even token contributions confer membership, but many members contribute as much as NT$1 million (about U.S.$40,000) each year. Women also endure two-year waiting lists to volunteer at the state-of-the-art hospital the group has built. The Compassionate Relief Merit Association now has branches around the world and recently opened a clinic in California.

Medical charity and medical education remain its core activities, but it undertakes a wide range of charity for the poor and moral uplift for its usually wealthy members. The society opposes drinking, which can create a considerable hardship for men in business networks. It also urges a generally ascetic lifestyle, discouraging fancy clothes, makeup, or any form of conspicuous consumption. Members meet frequently to give testimonials about how their lives have changed and to listen to taped lectures by their leader. They often attest to how happy they are now that they have "crossed to the other shore" into the society. Above all they focus on concrete activity. Reading and reciting sutras or a Buddha's name are not core activities, unlike with most other forms of Buddhism. Nor is there any particular concern with establishing doctrinal support for their activities.

Like the pietistic groups, these new-style Buddhists are sects, bringing together a voluntary group of similar people. Both kinds of groups also claim success at adjusting people to the secular world, and both also provide a moral light to lead the way in uncertain times. They thus clearly differ from something like the ghost cult, which thrives on a lack of shared morality. Yet these new religious groups also show major differences. Zhang Rongfa may attribute his tremendous financial success in container shipping to membership in the Yiguan Dao, but the Compassionate Relief Merit Association concentrates its efforts outside the market. In some ways it discourages the market by emphasizing charity and frowning on consumption. In addition, the pietistic sects generally share a concern with interpretation of classical texts and doctrine. They look for abstract moral truth, whereas the women of Compassionate Relief look instead for concrete moral action. The more numerous male groups talk very little of nurturing others, whereas the new Buddhist groups grasp the bodhisattva ideal of saving the world.

Conclusion

Business and religion are quite disparate areas of culture, but both are experiencing closely comparable tensions that recall arguments over the expansion of market culture in the West. On the one hand, they are pushed toward increasing commodification and utilitarian exploitation of resources—human, natural, and divine. On the other hand, people are strongly reacting against what they see as the deterioration of shared community and family moralities.

Although this tension is sometimes phrased as an argument between market and antimarket moralities, it may be better viewed as reflecting a divided market culture. Both sides of the argument have roots in tradition, just as both sides are in some ways reflexes of the market itself. Thus Confucianism offers itself simultaneously as the key to capitalist success and as the answer to the resulting moral vacuum. In religion, ghosts and some spirit mediums had always catered to individuals and private profit, even as gods and bodhisattvas offered instead community and universal moral worlds. At the same time, divided market cultures also borrow directly from the West: from economic theory and its critics and even, to a limited extent, from religion, as when Buddhists borrow Christian ideas of social action.

There is thus no single market culture that simply grew from earlier tradition or from the market itself or from the hegemonic power of the West. The sense of tension over market culture itself—which pervades the Western, "Confucian," and Islamic worlds—largely escapes metaphors of convergence toward a single market culture or adaptation of older resources. If there is any global conclusion about market culture, it lies in this tension itself. The divide between secular humanists and religious fundamentalists, profit and community morality, moderns and postmoderns, is part of the system itself.

The evidence I have discussed also suggests that these market tensions are rooted in the specific experience of different types of people within societies, not just across them. The gender differences that run the entire range of Chinese market cultures are just one example of many possible differences (including those of class, education, ethnicity, political inclusion, and regional variation), most of which have yet to be systematically explored. For gender itself, the variation is more in degree than in kind. Not one of the ideas I have discussed limits itself to one gender or the other, and not one in fact has an entirely male or entirely female following. Yet all clearly also appeal differentially to men and women.

Men have dominated (but not monopolized) the post-Confucian philosophizing that seeks moral principles for the modern world in Chinese tradition, just as they dominate many of the new religious sects in Taiwan. Women tend to be less organized, as one might expect from their social position. When they do speak, however, either in individual interviews or through the few organizations they dominate, they often emphasize different points of view from the men. Women speak most strongly about the contradictions between work and family values, about the ideals of nurturance (through motherhood or through the bodhisattva ideal), and about extending family values to the society at large. Men's family discourse often turns instead to hierarchies of respect and responsibility, to particularistic duties to the ancestral line, and to the creation of a patrimony for descendants. Men also dominate the theoretical arena, only to be challenged by the worldly activism of the women's groups.

Like many reactions to the perceived loss of morality in market culture, much of these women's discourse is simultaneously traditional and innovative. In all versions, it draws on conservative ideas of women's strength as care providers most able to nurture helpless babies into responsible adults. Yet the extension of this idea outside the walls of the home is a crucial innovation, breaking boundaries that have kept women outside the public arena and opening up a new world for them. It reacts against the pro-market strain of market culture but also fits neatly with women's new economic opportunities.

NOTES

1. Tensions owing to the perceived loss of community values through the market are complicated by the historical origins of capitalism in the West and its concomitant ties to colonialism and economic power. Antimarket and anti-Western movements may easily blur.

2. See Jochim (1992) for a useful summary of the Chinese-language literature on this.

3. See Harrell (1985) on the combination of diligence and fatalism. I will not take space here to discuss the combination, which seems counterintuitive but which is also reminiscent of Weber's (1958:98–128) discussion of Calvinism's combination of predestination and a work ethic.

4. See, among many others, Huang (1984), Redding (1990), Yang and Cheng (1987), and Yu (1987). Jochim (1992) summarizes this and much other relevant work. A parallel argument has marked discussion of Chinese immigrants in the United States. Chinese "clannishness," for example, was cited early in the century as a reason Chinese would never assimilate, and Chinese "timidity" as a reason they would never be successful entrepreneurs. These cultural features became arguments to halt immigration. By the late twentieth century, however, these same features were read instead as Chinese family loyalty and respect for authority and cited as reasons for their success in American society (Tan 1986).

5. The adaptation of the Chinese to a market-driven economy owes just as much to their long history of commercialization, familiarity with cash (Freedman 1959), experience with accounting (Gardella 1992), and regular use of corporate management (Sangren 1984). I will, however, continue to concentrate on cultural resources related to family and Confucianism in this chapter.

6. This kind of rationality was never more than an ideal type, after all, even for the West. Business everywhere is socially embedded (Granovetter 1985): It makes use of personal ties and relies on relationships of trust, although the quantity and quality of these ties may vary cross-culturally.

7. See, among many others, Greenhalgh 1989, Hamilton and Kao 1990, Hsieh 1989, Redding 1990, and Wong 1988.

8. This kind of Confucian discourse was long frowned upon in the People's Republic; its recent renewal by the government may enourage its use by managers as well.

9. We know, in addition, that all kinds of personal ties play important roles in Western business, and researchers have not yet attempted a systematic comparison that might reveal just how different the use of connections really is between China and the the West in practice.

10. Early wage-labor opportunities for women in the late nineteenth and early twentieth centuries opened up a few opportunities for women to escape this system, but in general their production continued to remain tied to the household and controlled by men (Topley 1975; Bell 1994).

11. Although the theory of ancestor worship was clear, the practice varied widely. Strong lineages in fact kept affines off the main ancestral altar in all circumstances, but poor areas with weak or no lineages often welcomed any ties they could get, and one could easily find villages where altars with tablets of three or four different surnames were not unusual (Weller 1987:31).

12. See Lu 1991. Information in this section is also based on my interview with Lin Yupei, the general secretary of the foundation, in 1992.

13. It is not yet clear whether we will see comparable developments on the mainland.

14. The following discussion relies especially on Jordan and Overmyer 1986: 274–276.

15. Official statistics in 1991 listed about 1.5 million members of such sects, but they do not include sects officially registered as branches of Buddhism or Taoism

(Cihui Tang is the most important) or people who still deny membership (Yiguan Dao was illegal until 1987).

16. Perhaps 90 percent of Taiwan's vegetarian restaurants, for example, are said to be run by sect members (Zhao 1992). The most prominent business example is Zhang Rongfa, chairman of one of the world's largest container-shipping companies.

17. See Lu (1991) and Huang (1994) for more information.

REFERENCES

Bell, Lynda S. 1994. "For Better, for Worse: Women and the World Market in Rural China." *Modern China* 20, 2:180–210.

Bellah, Robert N. 1965. "Epilogue: Religion and Progress in Modern Asia." In Robert N. Bellah, ed., *Religion and Progress in Modern Asia*, pp. 168–229. New York: Free Press.

Berger, Peter L. 1988. "An East Asian Development Model?" In Peter L. Berger and Hsin-Huang Michael Hsiao, eds., *In Search of an East Asian Development Model*, pp. 3–11. New Brunswick, N.J.: Transaction Books.

Bosco, Joseph. 1992. "Yiguan Dao: 'Heterodoxy' and Popular Religion in Taiwan." In Murray R. Rubenstein, ed., *Taiwan, 1945–1991: Responses to Directed Political and Socio-economic Change*, pp. 423–444. White Plains, N.Y.: M.E. Sharpe.

Ciji Gongdehui. n.d. "Wuyuan daci tongti dabei" (Great beneficence to known and unknown, and boundless compassion for all). Brochure, n.p.

DeGlopper, Donald R. 1972. "Doing Business in Lukang." In W.E. Willmott, ed., *Economic Organization in Chinese Society*, pp. 297–326. Stanford: Stanford University Press.

Duara, Prasenjit. 1991. "Knowledge and Power in the Discourse of Modernity: The Campaigns Against Popular Religion in Early Twentieth-Century China." *Journal of Asian Studies* 50, 1:67–83.

Freedman, Maurice. 1959. "The Handling of Money: A Note on the Background to the Economic Sophistication of Overseas Chinese." *Man* 59:64–65.

————. 1966. *Chinese Lineage and Society: Fukien and Kwangtung*. London School of Economics Monographs in Social Anthropology, no. 33. London: Athlone.

Gallin, Bernard, and Rita Gallin. 1982. "Socioeconomic Life in Rural Taiwan: Twenty Years of Development and Change." *Modern China* 8:205–246.

Gardella, Robert. 1992. "Squaring Accounts: Commercial Bookkeeping Methods and Capitalist Rationalism in Late Qing and Republican China." *Journal of Asian Studies* 51, 2:317–339.

Gates, Hill. 1991. "'Narrow Hearts' and Petty Capitalism: Small Business Women in Chengdu, China." In Alice Littlefield and Hill Gates, eds., *Marxist Approaches in Economic Anthropology*, pp. 13–36. Lanham, Md.: University Press of America.

Gold, Thomas B. 1985. "After Comradeship: Personal Relations in China Since the Cultural Revolution." *China Quarterly* 104 (December):657–675.

Granovetter, Mark. 1985. "Economic Action and Social Structure: The Problem of Embeddedness." *American Journal of Sociology* 91, 3:481–510.

Greenhalgh, Susan. 1989. "Social Causes and Consequences of Taiwan's Post-War Economic Development." In Kwang-chih Chang, Kuang-chou Li, Arthur P. Wolf, and Alexander Chien-chung Yin, eds., *Anthropological Studies of the Taiwan*

Area: Accomplishments and Prospects, pp. 351–390. Taipei: National Taiwan University.

Hamilton, Gary G., and Cheng-shu Kao. 1990. "The Institutional Foundations of Chinese Business: The Family Firm in Taiwan." *Comparative Social Research* 12:95–112.

Harrell, Stevan. 1985. "Why Do the Chinese Work So Hard?" *Modern China* 11, 2:203–226.

_____. 1994. "Playing in the Valley: A Metonym of Modernization in Taiwan." In Stevan Harrell and Huang Chün-chieh, eds., *Cultural Change in Postwar Taiwan*, pp. 161–183. Boulder: Westview Press.

Hsieh Jih-chang. 1989. "The Chinese Family Under the Impact of Modernization." In Kwang-chih Chang, Kuang-chou Li, Arthur P. Wolf, and Alexander Chien-chung Yin, eds., *Anthropological Studies of the Taiwan Area: Accomplishments and Prospects*, pp. 273–284. Taipei: National Taiwan University.

Huang Chün-chieh and Wu Kuang-ming. 1994. "Taiwan and the Confucian Aspiration: Toward the Twenty-First Century." In Stevan Harrell and Huang Chün-chieh, eds., *Cultural Change in Postwar Taiwan*, pp. 69–87. Boulder: Westview Press.

Huang Guangguo. 1984. "Rujia lunli yu qiye zuzhi xingtai" (Confucian theory and types of enterprise organization). In Huang Guangguo, ed., *Zhongguoshi guanli* (Chinese-style management), pp. 21–58. Taipei: Gongshang Shibao.

Huang, Julia. 1994. "In Becoming a Tzu-Chi Mama: The Process of Identity Transformation in a Religious Group." Unpublished manuscript.

Jochim, Christian. 1992. "Confucius and Capitalism: Views of Confucianism in Works on Confucianism and Economic Development." *Journal of Chinese Religions* 20:135–171.

Jordan, David K., and Daniel L. Overmyer. 1986. *The Flying Phoenix: Aspects of Chinese Sectarianism in Taiwan*. Princeton: Princeton University Press.

Ka Chih-ming. 1992. "Chengxiang yimin, xiaoxing qiye yu dushi fei zhengshi jingji zhi xingcheng" (Rural migrants in the city, small enterprises, and the formation of the urban informal economy). Paper presented at the Workshop on Enterprises, Social Relations, and Cultural Practices Studies of Chinese Societies, Taipei.

Levy, Marion J., Jr. 1949. *The Family Revolution in Modern China*. Cambridge: Harvard University Press.

Lianhe Bao (Taiwan newspaper). Various issues.

Li Yih-yuan. 1992. "Taiwan minjian zongjiao de xiandai qushi: Dui Peter Berger jiaoshou dongya fazhan wenhua yinsu lun de huiying" (The modern tendencies of Taiwan's popular religion: A response to Professor Peter Berger's theory of cultural factors in East Asian development). *Wenhua de Tuxiang* (The image of culture) 2:117–138.

Lu Hwei-syin. 1991. "Women's Self-Growth Groups and Empowerment of the 'Uterine Family' in Taiwan." *Bulletin of the Institute of Ethnology, Academia Sinica* 71:29–62.

McEwen, Susan. 1994. "Markets, Modernization, and Individualism in Three Chinese Societies." Ph.D. dissertation, Boston University.

Numazaki, Ichiro. 1991. "The Role of Personal Networks in the Making of Taiwan's *Guanxiqiye* ('Related Enterprises')." In Gary G. Hamilton, ed., *Business Networks and Economic Development in East and Southeast Asia,* pp. 87–103. Hong Kong: Centre of Asian Studies, University of Hong Kong.

Qu Haiyuan. 1989. *Minjian xinyang yu jingji fazhan* (Popular beliefs and economic development). Report to the Taiwan provincial government. Taipei: Taiwan Shengzhengfu Minzhengting.

Qu Haiyuan and Yao Lixiang. 1986. "Taiwan diqu zongjiao bianqian zhi tantao" (Discussion of religious changes in the Taiwan area). *Bulletin of the Institute of Ethnology, Academia Sinica* 75:655–685.

Redding, S. Gordon. 1990. *The Spirit of Chinese Capitalism.* Berlin: Walter de Gruyter.

Reed, Barbara. 1994. "Women and Chinese Religion in Contemporary Taiwan." In Arvind Sharma, ed., *Today's Woman in World Religions,* pp. 225–243. Albany: SUNY Press.

Sangren, P. Steven. 1984. "Traditional Chinese Corporations: Beyond Kinship." *Journal of Asian Studies* 43, 3:391–415.

"Shenmi jiaopai chongshi tianri" (A secret sect sees the light of day again). 1990. *Yazhou Zhoukan,* August 5, 28–39.

Silin, Robert H. 1972. "Marketing and Credit in a Hong Kong Wholesale Market." In W.E. Willmott, ed., *Economic Organization in Chinese Society,* pp. 327–352. Stanford: Stanford University Press.

Tan Hong. 1986. "'Orientalism' and Image-Making: Chinese Americans as 'Sojourner' and 'Model Minority.'" Typescript, Durham, N.C.

Topley, Marjorie. 1975. "Marriage Resistance in Rural Kwangtung." In Margery Wolf and Roxane Witke, eds., *Women in Chinese Society,* pp. 67–88. Stanford: Stanford University Press.

Weber, Max. 1946. "The Protestant Sects and the Spirit of Capitalism." In H.H. Gerth and C. Wright Mills, eds., *From Max Weber: Essays in Sociology,* pp. 302–322. New York: Oxford University Press.

_____. 1951. *The Religion of China: Confucianism and Taoism.* New York: Free Press.

_____. 1958. *The Protestant Ethic and the Spirit of Capitalism.* New York: Scribner's.

Weller, Robert P. 1987. *Unities and Diversities in Chinese Religion.* Seattle: University of Washington.

_____. 1994. *Resistance, Chaos and Control in China: Taiping Rebels, Taiwanese Ghosts and Tiananmen.* London: Macmillan.

Winn, Jane Kaufman. 1991. "Not by Rule of Law: Mediating State-Society Relations in Taiwan Through the Informal Sector." Unpublished manuscript.

Wolf, Margery. 1972. *Women and the Family in Rural Taiwan.* Stanford: Stanford University Press.

Wong, Siu-lun. 1988. "The Applicability of Asian Family Values to Other Sociocultural Settings." In Peter L. Berger and Hsin-Huang Michael Hsiao, eds., *In Search of an East Asian Development Model,* pp. 134–152. New Brunswick, N.J.: Transaction Books.

Yan Yunxiang. 1993. "The Flow of Gifts: Reciprocity and Social Networks in a Chinese Village." Ph.D. dissertation, Harvard University.

Yang Kuo-shu and Cheng Po-shyun. 1987. "Chuantong jiazhiguan, geren xiandaixing ji zuzhi xingwei: Hourujia jiashou de yixiang weiguan yanzheng" (Confucianized values, individual modernity, and organizational behavior: An empirical test of the post-Confucian hypothesis). *Bulletin of the Institute of Ethnology, Academia Sinica* 64:1–49.

Yu Yingshi. 1987. *Zhongguo jinshi zongjiao lunli yu shangren jingshen* (Modern Chinese religious ethics and business spirit). Taipei: Lunjing.

Zhao Dingjun. 1992. "Yiguan dao caili shen bu ke ce" (The immeasurable wealth of the Yiguan Dao). *Wealth Magazine* 121 (April):131.

Zheng Zhiming. 1987. "Youji lei luanshu suo xianshi zhi zongjiao xin qushi" (The new trend in religious worship as seen from biographical travels, memoirs). *Bulletin of the Institute of Ethnology, Academia Sinica* 61:105–127.

three

Getting Rich Is Not So Glorious

Contrasting Perspectives on Prosperity Among Muslims and Han in China

DRU C. GLADNEY

Last Spring, in a solemn ceremony at Beijing's ancient Temple of Heaven, Li Xiaohua the one-time peasant became the first Chinese to own a Ferrari.[1]

When I was on a February 1994 visit to Quanzhou City in southern Fujian Province, Mr. Ding called me from his private car on his cellular phone.[2] I received the call on the beeper (in Chinese a *bi pi ji*) he had lent me (and had to show me how to use, since I had never used one before).[3] When I first met Mr. Ding in 1984, I had just begun to study the collection of villages where the people surnamed Ding, officially recognized as members of the Hui minority nationality in 1979, resided (see Gladney 1996:290–295). The villagers at that time still depended primarily on agriculture and aquaculture for their living and had only just begun to experience the rapid rise in income that would lead to Mr. Ding lending me his beeper just ten years later. In a formal interview, Mr. Liu Zhengqing, the vice-mayor of Chendai Township, told me that the Ding villagers were so wealthy that in one village of 600 households, there were 700 telephones, most of them cellular. When I asked my old friend Ding

Yongwei if he was doing well, he held out his cellular phone and declared: "If I wasn't wealthy, could I be holding this?" *(Bu fu de hua, zheige nade qi ma?).* He later explained that the government's decision to recognize the Ding community as members of the Hui minority in 1979 was primarily responsible not only for their newfound economic prosperity but also for a tremendous subsequent fascination for their ethnic and religious roots—in this case, the Ding claim to be descended from foreign Muslim traders who settled in Quanzhou in the ninth century. When I first began learning about this area in the early 1980s, these Hui were known to be not only among the least developed in southern Fujian but also among the most assimilated into the local Han Chinese culture (Zhuang 1993). Now just ten years later, the members of the Hui nationality in this township had prospered far more quickly than the Han Fujianese, accounting for one-third of the township's income even though their population amounts to only one-seventh of the total.

In this chapter I consider the economic success of the Hui in two communities in China, contrasting "Muslim" entrepreneurialism with recent changes in capitalistic practice among the Han, among whom these Muslims have lived and interacted for nearly 1,200 years. I will argue that whereas the Muslim Chinese may not be more predisposed toward business than any other Chinese, there has been a less ambivalent view toward the market among Muslims than among the Han. This has to do with not only the role of the market in promoting Islam among the Hui but also the role of the state in both encouraging Muslim participation in the market while formerly restricting Han entrepreneurialism as antisocialist. Recent changes in PRC policy toward private business under the late Deng Xiaoping's maxim "To get rich is glorious" has stimulated a profound debate about the market among the Han Chinese in general and a tangible ambivalence, as evidenced by widely publicized corruption cases, growing income discrepancies, and active debates in the public media. This ambivalence does not exist among the Hui. Indeed, entrepreneurial ability has been promoted as their main "national characteristic."

Clashing Civilizations?
"Muslims" and "Confucians" in China

In that it addresses both Hui and Han views about the market, this chapter also seeks to shed light on recent more popular debates about entrepreneurialism and "neo-Confucianism" as well as its role in the so-called clash of civilizations. Samuel P. Huntington's (1993b:22) thesis that "the fault lines between civilizations will be the battle lines of the future" is particularly critical to this chapter in that one of the primary dividing lines Huntington sees is between Muslims and Confucians.

Huntington singles out Confucian and Islamic civilizations as being fundamentally different from each other and as posing the greatest threat to the

West. In all, Huntington (1993b:25) identifies "seven or eight major civilizations" in the contemporary world: Western (including both Europe and
North America), Confucian, Japanese, Islamic, Hindu, Slavic-Orthodox,
Latin American, "and possibly African." It is interesting that in his more recent publications, Huntington has changed Confucian to Sinic, or Chinese,
apparently not regarding the Koreans as Confucian or Sinic enough to be included in this civilizational paradigm. The greatest threat to the West, Huntington predicts, will come from the Islamic and Confucian civilizations, and
the possibility of their forming an anti-Western alliance is Huntington's
greatest fear. This was spelled out most fully in an earlier article, "The Islamic-Confucian Connection" (Huntington 1993a:19–23), in which he argued that the fundamental differences distinguishing European, Confucian,
and Islamic (often glossed as "Arab") civilizations will lead to inevitable
conflict and misunderstanding.

What of the Muslim Chinese, however, who claim descent from intermar-
riages between Arabs (and other Muslims) and Chinese in China over the
course of the past 1,200 years? Some Muslim Chinese go so far as to still
claim "Arab blood" (Pillsbury 1976). This claim, of course, raises the subsequent question of biculturalism and multiculturalism. It also becomes problematic when we consider that many of the most recent clashes in the
post–Cold War period have been *within* cultures and civilizations rather
than *between* them, particularly when we consider Islam.[4]

Standing somewhere between Muslim and Chinese civilizations, the Muslim Chinese Hui are the perfect counterexample to Huntington's thesis that
civilizations are fundamentally different and generally opposed. Interestingly,
it is indeed the market that becomes a site of interaction between Hui and
Han, Muslim and Confucian, civilizations, both physically and discursively. I
have noted elsewhere that during my fieldwork in northwestern China, where
Muslims are more populous and live in more isolated rural enclaves, it was often the case that only in the marketplace did Hui come in contact with Han, in
the trading arena where they maintained distinct competitive exchange and exploitative relationships (see Gladney 1996:315–328). We can also see in recent
debates about the market among the Han a similar point of divergence, where
Han often debate the merits of prosperity (and its concomitant social problems), whereas Hui regard market success as an opportunity for ethnic and religious advancement. Indeed, in his extensive discussion of Hui economic history in China, Lai Cunli (1988:310) has argued that "the commercial capital of
the Hui nationality played an active role in the sprouts of Chinese capitalism."

The flourishing of traditional economic practice among the Hui flies in
the face of a centrally planned Stalinist policy that, as Stark and Nee have argued (1989), originally sought to both limit private enterprise and encourage
national integration. I argue that one of the reasons ethnic nationality has become such an important aspect of one's identity in the People's Republic

(and indeed, in the former and emergent nations of the Soviet Union and Eastern Europe) is the legitimation that Stalinist-Leninist legalization endows on such categories of national identity: Power was available to those who could claim it. Of course, such affiliations could also be detrimental in times of national chauvinism. Rather than any inherent predisposition for trade, I suggest that it was state policy that encouraged and stimulated entrepreneurialism among the Hui—as well as restricted it as antisocialist among the Han. In a recent article I argued that the rise of ethnic consciousness was an unintended consequence of departures from centralized economic planning in China, as well as in the former Soviet Union (see Gladney 1995). In this chapter I argue that economic success in two Hui communities reflects a very different approach with respect to the market among Hui than among Han, one that shifts in Deng's policy have helped to stimulate. These same altered policies have led to profound ambivalences among the Han even as many become enriched through participation in the market.

Muslim Nationality, Chinese State

Having one foot in the Muslim world and another well planted in Chinese civilization, the Hui Muslims (now numbering 8.4 million according to the 1990 census) were traditionally well situated to serve as cultural and economic mediators within Chinese society as well as between the Han Chinese majority and other non-Han minorities. This traditional role was severely limited after the collectivization and religious reform campaigns in the late 1950s and early 1960s. With the relaxation of restrictions on private enterprise and on ethnic and religious expression in the early 1980s, not only did traditional Muslim trading roles reemerge but Muslim communities prospered as well. In this chapter I specifically examine economic and social changes in two Hui communities: a recently recognized Hui lineage community, Quanzhou, on the southeast coast and a Sufi community, Ningxia, in the rural Northwest. Though the state allowed and indeed encouraged economic privatization and ethnic expression in these communities, it was not prepared for the speed and vitality with which Muslims returned to their ethnoreligious identity and exploited opportunities for self- and community advancement.

Hui Muslims were known throughout Chinese history as specialized tradesmen in such areas as transport, the wool trade, jewelry working, and small food stands. Specializations ranged widely in scale and varied regionally according to the socioeconomic position of the Hui in urban or rural settings. Before 1949, the term Hui referred to any person claiming to be Muslim or of Muslim descent. At Yenan and later during the first Chinese census in 1953, it came to designate one "nationality" *(minzu)* that distinguished the Hui from the nine other identified Muslim nationalities in China (Uighur, Kazakh, Kyrgyz, etc.) as well as from the Han majority nationality and fifty-four other minority nationalities. As Walker Connor (1984:25) noted, this policy of nationality recognition in China was in keeping with a *temporary* Leninist-Stalinist policy that sought to enlist minority support for the new nation. It was assumed, however, that national consciousness, like class consciousness, would gradually fade with national unification and the erosion of class differences. In keeping with this policy (perhaps even more faithfully than the Soviets), Chairman Mao and the early Yenan Communists promised only eventual autonomy, not the possibility of secession, for the minority regions that submitted to state authority (see Gladney 1996:87–93).

Hui Muslim traditional specializations were virtually lost after the 1955 collectivization reforms but rapidly returned after the 1978 economic liberalization policy. Not only in the ancient Silk Road maritime port Quanzhou, where this chapter begins, but throughout the villages and towns where Muslims now live, Hui have prospered at an incredible rate through strong participation in small private businesses and industry—in many places far surpassing their Han neighbors. Local Hui say that they are gifted as small businessmen and that new economic policies have allowed them to express that aspect of their ethnic identity. In fact, these policies were originally intended only to raise their standard of living, as well as their consciousness, to that of the Han, never to surpass them!

Many state reforms were originally intended to encourage economic development and the Four Modernizations. In the process, they have allowed freer religious expression of Hui identity. With this resurgence of ethnoreligious identity, socioeconomic development has also improved. Once criticized as "capitalist tails" who thrived on business ventures, the Hui were constantly accused of maintaining feudalist, antisocialist, and exploitative practices. By contrast, in a recent interview, Fei Xiaotong, China's most well known anthropologist and a professor at Beijing University, suggested that socioeconomic development of minority areas would be enhanced if the minorities themselves played a greater role. Minority participation in economic development should be encouraged rather than continuing the former policies of providing government assistance to minority areas and promoting minority customs, such as traditional songs and dances. Professor Fei specifically suggested that Hui entrepreneurial talents should be given more freedom in order to assist the expansion of local market economies, noting that he was "deeply impressed by the fact that the Hui people there are very smart traders. They have been blessed with this talent from their ancestors, who nurtured trading skills during centuries-long commercial dealings between farmers and herdsmen" (Fei 1987:4).

This statement is significant in that it identifies "entrepreneurialism" as one of the main "nationality traits" *(minzu tedian)* that distinguish the Hui and bind them together as a nationality. According to the Stalinist definition of nationality, which has served as the cornerstone of Chinese nationality policy, in order to be recognized as a nationality a group must possess one or more of the "four commons": a common economy, locality, language, or "culture." The Hui have been traditionally difficult to identify according to this scheme because of their vast diversity. They share no common area, customary practice, language, or identity, and the state has been reluctant to allow Islam to serve as the trait binding them together, since not all Hui believe in Islam (some are party members or secularists) and the Chinese Communist state does not wish to encourage its revival (see Gladney 1996:21–36). Nevertheless, it is Islam, or the memory of it, that is the only thing that all Hui have in common, and they are the only minority in China to share a religious identity. Entrepreneurism has no such contemporary salience in Hui culture even though it is a status to which many Hui aspire.

This recognition of the unique contribution Hui entrepreneurial abilities might make to economic development represents a dramatic shift from past criticisms of these characteristics as capitalistic and feudal. Perhaps to seek historical support for this state policy, Lai Cunli, in his 312-page survey *Hui Economic History*—commissioned by the China Minority Nationality Research office of the State Commission for Nationality Affairs—cites extensive historical information to argue that Hui "minority culture" was uniquely entrepreneurial compared to other nationalities in China and that this "business culture" made major contributions to the development of China's economy (Lai 1988:3, 283). "One can see," Lai (276) concludes, "that business activity of the early Hui ancestors was an extremely great influence on the formation of the Hui nationality." The well-known Hui historian Ma Tong (1983:86, 87) has presented similar arguments, observing, "From the very earliest period, the vast majority of Islamic disciples in China were engaged in trade and business activity."

Perhaps as a result of this revisionist cultural history and open state support for Hui traditions of entrepreneurialism, a new Islamic college was recently set up in Xi'an. It advertises courses in small business and "Muslim entrepreneurialism" as well as in Arabic and Persian. Skill in the latter would provide improved travel opportunities to Muslim entrepreneurs.

Ethnoreligious Revitalization in a Northwestern Sufi Community

In one text entitled "Suggestions for Muslims" and inscribed on the entrance of a well-known mosque in Ningxia, northwestern China, I found the following statements:

> You have one hundred [yuan], but want a thousand, you get it and desire ten thousand
> your desire is uncontrollable, without satisfaction, the more you have the more you desire
> Because of contentment you disregard the lessons, committing myriad errors

if you were very wealthy, but you died suddenly, your wealth would be gone
forever
Abounding in grace, extremely wealthy, it looks good for a little while
You enjoy it for this life, but in the afterlife, you certainly will owe a great
deal.[5]

Prosperity has come to Na Homestead with Hui involvement in commercial enterprise since the early 1980s. With prosperity, Hui villagers have had
to be reminded of the purpose of wealth: It is not for personal gain but to
serve the community and the faith; both are vulnerable for Muslims en-
sconced in a society dominated by Chinese Communists. Located near a
bend of the Yellow River just south of Yinchuan City, Na Homestead is a
relatively isolated Hui village in a majority Han area of the Ningxia Hui Autonomous Region. The village is 95 percent Hui in a region that is only 32.1
percent Hui. It is noteworthy that "religious enterprise" has become so
profitable in the village that several of the highest-ranking Communist Party
cadres have left the party to become imam (religious elders) in the mosque.

As an economic indicator, mosque income (sifei) derived from offerings
(nietie) has risen dramatically. According to the mosque's own careful accounting records, in the 1980s it averaged over 20,000 yuan (U.S.$6,700) an-
nual income from offerings. Based on an outside study, over a four-month
period during 1984 and 1985, offerings of grain, goods, or money totaled
8,997.23 yuan (about U.S.$3,000). An economic survey of expenditures of
113 Hui households in Na Homestead revealed that the average household
contribution to the mosque was 47 yuan, or 8.40 yuan per person in 1984
(Wang 1985:7; Gong 1987:38). If this average is applied to the entire Hui
community of the village, then the mosque's total income in 1984 was well
over 32,500 yuan (U.S.$10,833). The money supports the mosque's staff of
seven individuals, including one religious teacher and four students, and is
also used for the daily upkeep of the mosque. Offerings are given during the
three main religious holidays and to individual ahong when they read the
Qur'an at weddings, funerals, and naming ceremonies. Giving at funerals by
the family to guests and to the mosque ranges from 100 to 1,000 yuan. Gifts
as great as 2,500 yuan have been reported for the high-status deceased.

Donations to the mosque come from a village considered fairly poor by
regional standards, with an average annual income of 300 yuan (about
U.S.$100) per household. The 1982 average per capita annual income in
Yongning County was substantially higher, 539 yuan according to the Population Census Office (1987:206). Poor households (pinkun hu) occupy 2 percent of the village. Mosque income, however, does not necessarily reflect total religious giving per household. A study of 17 households from three
different villages belonging to different Islamic orders found that from an
annual average income of 96.67 yuan, 8.96 yuan (9.26 percent) was given to
religious concerns in 1980.

Na Homestead has 5,036 *mu* (805.7 acres) of land under cultivation—growing mainly rice, winter wheat, sorghum, and some fruit in a few orchards. Average land per person is 1.37 mu (.21 acres) and per household, 6.95 mu (1.1 acres), somewhat less than in neighboring Han villages. Average grain yield per mu in Na Homestead is about 200 kilograms, less than the regional average of 238 kilograms. Important shifts in the involvement of the local labor force since the private responsibility system was introduced in 1979, however, reveal significant socioeconomic change. There has been a sharp decline in collective activity and power since the dismantling of the commune, as documented elsewhere in China (see Diamond 1985; Lardy 1986:99–102; and Shue 1984). In 1978, 27.8 percent of the village population was involved in the labor force. However, by 1984 that figure had grown to 49.6 percent of the village, reflecting pre-1950 levels. In the greater Ningxia region, 83.5 percent of the total Hui population engaged in agriculture and husbandry, according to the 1982 census (Ningxia Census Office 1983:74). For the country as a whole, the census reported that 60.7 percent of all Hui and 84 percent of all ethnic groups were engaged in agriculture and husbandry (Population Census Office 1987:xx, 28).

Agriculture and husbandry, industry and construction, and small sideline enterprises (such as cottage industries, private shops and food stands, transportation and service industries) are the three main industries. A significant change in sideline industries has absorbed much of the increased labor. Only 1.6 percent of the labor force was involved in these small enterprises in 1978; participation had increased to 16 percent by 1984, slightly less than the 1950 levels of 17.6 percent. In a study of 113 households, 60 people were engaged in sideline businesses, representing 19 percent of the labor force. In 1978, only one person was involved in food-related small business, and no one from the village was involved in service or transportation. By 1984, however, 85 people were in the food trade, 26 in the service industry, and 24 in transport (Zhu 1985:4). In terms of the small food industry, eight households opened small restaurants in Yanghe Township with several others selling *yang zasui*—a traditional Hui spicy stew made from the internal organs of sheep.

Participation in the market and the private responsibility system has also encouraged Hui in Na Homestead to increase their planting of vegetables and cash crops. Although agricultural income derived from cash crops in 1984 was only half that of 1957, it was more than three times that of 1978. Before 1949, Hui proclivity for growing cash crops in this area was noted by Fan Changjiang. He observed that the opium produced by Han and Hui peasants in the Yanghe area was of a very high quality, but the Han could not make much of a profit from it: They smoked too much of it themselves and were too weak to gain financially from it. However, the Hui did not smoke opium, and their fields were almost twice as productive as Han fields (Fan 1980:312). Hu Yaobang remarked that this area was China's most impoverished region. In 1983, the State Council set up a special committee to encourage economic development in Guyuan District, Ningxia and Longxi and Dingxi Counties, and Gansu.

The Hui from Na Homestead are also playing an important role in the local market economy. The Hui operate 70 percent of the new restaurants, food stands, and private stalls in the nearby Yongning county seat market area even though they constitute only 12.6 percent of the population. They also participate in the central free market in Wuzhong City, thirty kilometers south. There, Hui merchants make up over 90 percent of those doing business in a city that is 95 percent Han. Most of the Hui come into the city to do business from outlying Hui villages such as Dongfeng Township (95 percent Hui). This active entrepreneurial participation is an important aspect of Hui ethnoreligious identity. As one Han peasant from Na Homestead remarked, "The Hui are good at doing business; the Han are too honest and can't turn a profit. Han are good at planting, Hui at trade."

Only 2 percent of households in Na Homestead were *wanyuan hu* (literally, "10,000 yuan per year household," or a very wealthy household or person) at the time of my study, reporting an annual income of over 10,000 yuan. Although this is not a large percentage compared to some areas in China, it is unusual in a fairly poor northwestern region. The prestige and influence of these *wanyuan hu* were significant. Na Jingling, the most successful of Na Homestead's new entrepreneurs, made his original fortune through setting up a popsicle factory in 1982. A former mechanic for the commune, he and his brother have now moved into the transportation and construction business. They have recently entered into a contract with two other investors to build an "Islamic" hotel in Yinchuan City at a cost of 1.4 million yuan. The hotel will feature a restaurant and shopping facilities with "Arabic" architecture.

Recent economic prosperity among rural Hui as a result of favorable government policy and Hui entrepreneurial abilities has led to an unintended and unexpected increase in support for religious affairs. Na Jingling, for example, wants to use his profits to help the Hui in Ningxia, supporting the Mosque and building a "really *qing zhen* (pure and true)" Islamic hotel. Other Hui *wanyuan hu* have told me that because Allah is responsible for their newfound wealth, they should devote some of their profits to promoting Islam and mosque construction. Red posters on the walls in every mosque indicate by name and amount who has given to the construction projects; the names of these *wanyuan hu* and their donations are written larger than the others. More wealthy Hui sometimes complained to me of the pressures brought to bear on them to contribute to the mosque. Local Communist Party cadres complained that they could not stop religious donations without angering local Hui and interrupting economic development.

Hui Economic Prosperity
and Ethnic Reinvention in Fujian

The Fujianese lineage community surnamed Ding has lived in Chendai Township on the southern Fujian coast since the Wanli period of the Ming dynasty (1573–1620). Members of this community supposedly fled at that time from Quanzhou City to avoid persecution for being associated with the former Muslim mayor under the defeated Mongols. Since that time they have been known for their specialized aquacultural economy. Before 1949 they also produced opium and had many small factories that made woven bags and sundry goods. These goods were exported extensively and led to the migration of many Ding Hui to Southeast Asia, Taiwan, and Hong Kong in their business endeavors. After 1955, when private industries were collectivized in China, these small factories were either curtailed or transferred to the larger commune, of which the Ding lineage occupied seven brigades.

I have discussed elsewhere the revitalized Hui national identity among the Ding in Quanzhou and the unintended consequences of departures from centralized state planning in the region (see Gladney 1995, 1996:260–291). Here I will summarize the recent tremendous economic growth in the region for the purposes of this chapter's focus on Muslim prosperity in China. Since 1979 and the implementation of rural economic reforms, the Ding members have been recognized as members of the Hui nationality and have once again become active in private small industry, producing athletic shoes, plastic goods such as sandals, rugs, and other sundries found in Chinese department stores. Of the 3,350 households in Chendai's seven villages (former brigades that are overall 92 percent Hui), over 60 ran small factories in 1991. By 1994, the majority of all households derived their primary incomes from these "sideline" enterprises. Each larger factory employs more than a hundred workers; the smaller ones employ ten or more workers each.

In 1983, the average annual income in Chendai Township was 611 yuan per person, whereas in 1982 the larger Han-dominated Jinjiang County had an average annual income of only 402 yuan (Population Census Office 1987:175). By 1984 Chendai income reached 837 yuan per person for the town; the Hui within Chendai averaged 1,100 yuan. Hui income increased 33 percent in 1985. By 1989, the entire township's average annual per capita income had jumped to 1,000 yuan (Ding 1990:3). This indicates a substantial increase of local Hui income over Han income in the county as well as in the township. It is clear that economic success was not limited to the Hui, as Han in Fujian also prospered during this period.[6]

Income from sideline enterprises in agriculture and small industry has also grown at a rapid rate. In 1984, Chendai was the first town in Fujian Province to become a *yiyuan zhen* (100-million-yuan town). Over half of the Hui in the town have their own two- to four-level homes, paid for with cash from their savings. Many of the multilevel homes that I visited had small piece-work factories in the first level (making a tennis shoe sole here, the lining there, laces elsewhere, and so on); the various family branches lived in the other levels. For example, Ding Yongwei, mentioned at the beginning of this chapter, has two sons. On the first level of his four-story stone-block home, he has a small factory that produces the stretchy fabric that is used to line the inside of athletic shoes. He obtains the materials from a distant relative in the Philippines. His youngest son and wife live on the second floor. His oldest son, wife, and two children live on the third floor (as a Hui, Ding's son is al-lowed to have two children). Ding Yongwei and his wife occupy the top floor.

Income from sideline enterprises has increased eight times over 1979. Prior to 1978 the majority of the labor force (69.9 percent) in Chendai was engaged in agriculture and only 30 percent was involved in industry. By 1992 this had shifted dramatically, with 93 percent of the labor force engaged in industry and sideline enterprises.

The Ding believe that this success is due to their recognition as Hui. After they were recognized as part of the Hui nationality in 1979, they became eli-gible for assistance as members of an underprivileged minority. From 1980 until 1984, the government gave over 200,000 yuan to the seven Hui teams. With the funds they built a running-water system and fish ponds and ex-panded their razor clam industry. The Ministry of Education gave 40,000 yuan to build a middle school and 33,000 yuan for a primary school. The Hui also receive benefits as a minority nationality in the form of preference for high school and college entrance. Under special birth-planning policies for minorities, they are allowed to have one more child than the Han. Hui repre-sentation in the local government is also higher than the Hui's proportion in the population. Two of the ten party committee representatives (*changwei*) were surnamed Ding in 1985, as well as the town's party secretary.

Over 50 percent of the Ding lineage members have overseas relatives—mainly in the Philippines, Indonesia, and Singapore—a higher proportion than among their Han neighbors (see Li 1990:337–346). They have reestab-lished communication with these relatives and have been assisted by fre-quent remittances. This outside income is an important factor in the rapid economic development of the seven Ding villages. All seven Hui villages have elementary schools, thanks to donations from overseas relatives averag-ing 20,000 yuan each. Neighboring Han villages have one elementary school for every three or four villages. The Ding say that their regular contact with overseas relatives results from their strong feelings of ethnic solidarity, which they say surpasses that of neighboring Han lineages. It is remarkable, however, that one conversation with one wealthy village family that main-tained extensive overseas relations revealed that overseas relatives are often reluctant to admit their Islamic heritage!

PRC policy that accords special economic and political privileges to these recently recognized Hui along the southeast coast and that encourages their interaction with foreign Muslim governments has led to a renewed interest in Hui ethnic identity. Fujian provincial and local municipal publications proudly proclaim Quanzhou as the site of the third most important Islamic holy grave and the fifth most important mosque in the world. Religious and government representatives from over thirty Muslim nations were escorted to Muslim sites in Quanzhou as part of a state-sponsored delegation in spring 1986. Foreign Muslim guests are frequently hosted by the local Quanzhou City Islamic Association. The UNESCO-sponsored Silk Roads Expedition arrived in Quanzhou in February 1991 as its main port of entry on China's maritime Silk Road, virtually bypassing the traditional stopping place of Canton. During the four-day conference and Silk Road festivities in which I participated, the foreign guests and Muslim dignitaries were brought to the Chendai Ding village as part of their orientation in order to highlight the recent economic prosperity and government support for the modern descendants of the ancient Muslim maritime traders.

It is, again, important that the reforms and prosperity that have come to Ding villagers have not been restricted to the Muslim Hui Ding; they have benefited the entire township. Not only does Chendai Township have a 10 percent Han population but also among the Ding there are many who do not believe in Islam, including folk religionists and even about 80 households of Christians—who are nevertheless registered as members of the Hui "Muslim" nationality! These Ding converted in the 1930s under the influence of a Western Lutheran missionary, and they too have recently rebuilt their church, possibly because the local government allowed the construction of the Islamic prayer hall. As noted, although the Ding lineage occupies only one-seventh of the town's population, it accounts for more than one-third of the total area's annual income. Economic prosperity has been accompanied by ethnic and even religious revival. Though these lineages have always maintained a Hui identity, it has only recently begun to take on a decidedly Islamic commitment, a development not anticipated by the state when it chose to recognize the Ding as Hui in 1979.

Reflections on Hui Prosperity, North and South

It is clear that Hui in Quanzhou and Ningxia regard their newfound prosperity positively, as an indication of their ethnic solidarity in Quanzhou and as a reward for their religious perseverance in Ningxia. In Quanzhou, material success is attributed to ethnic entrepreneurialism among a lineage that maintains only a distant memory of Islam, but a memory that is now reviving. In Ningxia's Na Homestead, Allah's blessing is frequently invoked and the necessity of tithing is emphasized. It is important to note that in both cases, government policy has played a key role in both restricting ethnic entrepreneurialism prior to the 1980s and encouraging it in the Deng era. The rationalization for material wealth was appropriately summarized in a recent article in a Muslim Chinese newspaper about a prosperous Hui business in Chang Zhou, just south of Quanzhou. The article is published in a new local Muslim-run newspaper, *Qiming Xing*, based in Nanjing, which reports on Hui Muslim and other minority activities throughout China. Similar to the state-sponsored magazine *Zhongguo Musilin* (China's Muslims) and the journal *Ahlabo Shijie* (The Arab World), this state-approved daily reports positively on Muslim affairs inside and outside of China. In an article published on June 15, 1994, entitled "The Concept of Economic Development and Qualified Personnel," the paper juxtaposed a photograph of a Muslim imam, Zhao Huayu, in his new car and one of a recently refurbished mosque. The article reported on his successful company, the Muslim Technique Economy Trade Company in Chang Zhou City:

> As the China Islamic Association in Chang Zhou City has invested in this company and it is located in the mosque, the profits it gains should naturally be used to develop the local nationalities' religious affairs. . . . Imam Zhao Huayu automatically became the president of the company . . . [and he is also] head of the Chang Zhou City Islamic Association and the Standing Committee of the city's People's Political Consultative Committee *[zhengxie]*. All the leaders of the city know about this good-looking, bearded religious leader *[qingzhen jiaozhang]*, so they are willing to give the green light to approve things. . . . After the company was in business for one year, they bought a car. In the old way of thinking *[cong jiu guandian lai kan]*, this was regarded as "extravagant" or "seeking personal pleasure." But according to the new perspective, having a car is beneficial, it saves a great deal of time and allows for more good deeds to be done.

Here, interestingly enough, the imam became the head of the business. As noted for Na Homestead, the party cadres became imams. Undoubtedly, under current government policy, they too have founded their own businesses. In each case, their success is lauded because it allows their people to prosper and the mosque to benefit, as the picture in the paper illustrated. In a controversial but widely circulated 1988 novel about Muslims in Beijing, *Muslim Funeral (Musilin de zangli)*, a Hui woman writer, Huo Da, suggested that the reason Han in Beijing did not negatively stereotype the Manchu as they did the Hui was that the Hui were poor and uneducated. The novel's protagonist suggested that this kind of stigmatized identity should be a thing of the past and that Muslims should overcome this negative characterization through working hard in business and doing well in school (Huo 1992; 1993:162). Economic prosperity and entrepreneurialism are never questioned in the 750-page novel, which describes three generations of a jade-carving Hui family in Beijing. Indeed, the pivotal point of the novel is the decision of the Hui jade carver to give alms and sustenance to an elderly Hui Muslim pilgrim en route to Mecca, an act of kindness that significantly alters the entire course of the succeeding generations.

Han Capitalism in Socialist China

Hui have been officially portrayed as a mercantile nationality and they have sought to capitalize on this stereotype; this has clearly not been the case among the Han Chinese. Indeed, Deng's program of transforming China from a centrally planned economy to a market economy still subject to tight political controls faces three main cultural obstacles. I will briefly describe these as the essentializations of agriculturalism, communism, and Confucianism; all three legacies, I should note, are anticommercial in nature. These legacies have led to clear ambivalences toward the market and economic prosperity at a popular and policy level among the so-called Han.

Although it is difficult, if not somewhat ludicrous, to generalize about the nearly 1 billion Han Chinese, I shall only point out here how the Chinese themselves have attempted to essentialize and explain the fundamental nature of Han identity. Just as Fei Xiaotong theorized that it is entrepreneurialism that is the national characteristic of the Hui, he posited that it is agriculturalism that best defines the essence of Han identity. In a 1988 Tanner lecture in Hong Kong entitled "Plurality and Unity in the Configuration of the Chinese Nationality," Fei (1989:47, 54) traced the rise of the Han people from multiethnic origins prior to the Qin dynasty (300 B.C.) down to the present day. Fei Xiaotong's understanding of ethnic change and national identity is informed by a strong commitment to Stalinist-Leninist nationality policy based on Morgan's theory of stage development evolutionism and Engel's prediction of the withering away of class and national identity with the removal of private property. Although there are many nationalities in China, the Han are defined as being in the cultural and technical vanguard, the manifest destiny of all the minorities. Fei suggests that pastoralists such as the Mongols, Tibetans, and Turks and mercantile peoples like the Hui were fundamentally different from the Han agriculturalists. Fei's ethnic comparison reminds one of some Japanese scholars' arguments that Japanese identity is based on rice growing as opposed to the Ainu and foreigners with whom the Japanese interacted (see Ohnuki-Tierney 1993). If the essence of Han identity is defined in terms of agriculturalism, where is the place for capitalist development?

A second official essentialization that is fundamentally anticommercial is that of the Communist legacy in China. From the idealized representations of the early suffering by the party in Shanghai and Jiangxi, the epic struggles of the Long March, the campaigns against landlords and capitalists during the 1950s, the collectivist extravaganzas of the 1960s, the Cultural Revolution, and early opposition even to Deng Xiaoping, the central Communist legacy has been one of anticommercialism. Whereas private entrepreneurs have been the scourge of the Communists, selfless service on behalf of the masses as immortalized in the figure of Lei Feng has been their essentialized ideal. Whether it be the inability of the state to control the activities of petty entrepreneurs *(getihu)*, as Thomas Gold (1989) has suggested, or the destabilizing nature of the marketplace, as Ann Anagnost (1994) has argued, it is clear that private business has been suspect in the Chinese worldview. Indeed, the recent capitalist fervor in China to get rich quick by any means can easily be seen as evidence of resistance toward and rejection of this long-held anticommercial Communist dogma, both at the official and at the popular level.

Finally, Samuel Huntington notwithstanding, essentialized interpretations of Confucianism in China have consistently supported the devalorization of the merchant. Although Confucianism in general has been criticized as supporting a feudalistic patriarchal hierarchy, the socialist legacy in China has never taken issue with the Confucian subjugation of the merchant. This cuts to the heart of the debate over commercial success and Confucianism, addressed by Robert Weller in this volume. Central to the debate is which Confucianism is to be seen as the real Confucianism, an issue on which even professional scholars have difficulty reaching agreement (see Tu, Hejtmanek, and Wacman 1993). Suffice it to say that regardless of the capitalist success of neo-Confucianism in the Chinese diaspora in Taiwan, Hong Kong, and Southeast Asia, in China itself anti-Confucian Communist policy has also involved anticommercialism. Neither communism nor Confucianism has ever come to terms with economic greed, viewing it and its social carriers negatively.

I would suggest that these three essentialized interpretations of Han identity—agriculturalism, communism, and Confucianism—have contributed to a strong ambivalence toward private market success in contemporary China. This ambivalence is evidenced in debates in the public media over prosperity as well as in highly publicized trials and executions in economic-corruption cases. Though occurring in a very different context, these debates resemble American evangelical Protestant debates about capitalistic success, as outlined by Craig M. Gay (1991). Like the evangelicals, the Chinese have become either *"very* critical or *very* defensive of capitalism and bourgeois culture" (Gay 1991:207; emphasis in the original). This should not be surprising in that for both communities there is more at stake than the nature of the market—in particular, the nature of social and national identity. As Gay (1991:161) notes, "Indeed, it seems clear that capitalism as such is not the only thing at issue in the debate but that the various evangelical factions are contending for entirely different sociocultural visions of American society for which capitalism serves only as a kind of symbol either positively or negatively." This is why in China, ambivalence toward capitalism and economic prosperity reflects fundamental essentialized notions of Han identity, communism, and Confucianism. Peletz (1993) and Weigert (1991) have noted that in general, ambivalence points to a fundamental psychosocial displacement of conflicting values.

A central preoccupation in the Chinese press with economic liberalization is the debate about "moral decay" and "corruption." One source that reveals many of these debates is a series of frank discussions aired and reported in a column entitled "What They Are Saying." The column appears in the English-language newspaper the *China Daily* and contains selections from various local Chinese newspapers around the nation. Since the newspaper is in English and is published for the benefit of China's mainly foreign readership, it is possible that the reporting on local debates over the merits of Deng's policy is a bit more open than that found in *Renmin Ribao* (People's Daily), the official government newspaper. One article cited a recent poll published in the Chinese paper *Legal Daily* (May 12, 1994) by Li Gaungru, Cao Jian, and Li Feng, indicating that though the general public was in support of market reforms, "in market competition, some people seek high profits at the expense of honesty. . . . People should make money on the basis of fair and legal competition. . . . It is essential to regulate market performance with coercive legal measures."[7] In another section entitled "Feudal Remnants," the authors complained, "Remnants of feudal economic relations bring about political and professional privileges and lead to economic monopoly. . . . Graft, malfeasance and bribery are not the by-products of a market economy. Instead, they are unavoidable results of remaining feudal economic relations."[8] Another report by Yan Kalin in the Chinese paper *Economic Daily* revealed that businesses were in the habit of hiring people only on condition of receiving "warranty funds" or other forms of illegal contributions. The article concludes: "Illegal fund-raising should be eliminated through strengthening financial control and extending financial reforms."[9] Finally, in a full-page editorial, Fan Hengshan, an official with the State Commission for Economic Restructuring, complained that the "market economy is misunderstood by too many folk." Revealing again a concern about correct notions of "profit," Fan stated, "A healthy market economy is backed by manufacturing industries, not profiteering. . . . Some people in their thirst for profits, provide false information to mislead the futures and stock markets, produce inferior products, or break contracts."[10]

Uneven economic growth has led to huge migrations of people in search of work and better lives—from villages to cities and from the interior and northern regions to the southern coastal areas. Yet a fundamental problem is that the southern and urban economic boom has been fueled by cheap migrant labor from the interior. These migrant laborers have contributed to a dramatic rise in China's unemployment rate. In one Fujianese tennis shoe factory I visited in Quanzhou in February 1994, of the 89 workers employed, only 5 were local, and they were primarily in managerial positions. The rest worked on piecemeal wages that ranged from 25 to 75 yuan per day (U.S.$3–$7) and were often hired by the day. The village population had swelled to three times its normal size with two-thirds of the population non-local. As in Guangdong, the locals controlled the enterprises; poorer nonlocals were the workers. Since the factory was owned by a Hui minority, I asked the owner if there were problems with anti-Hui sentiment among the poorer workers. He was a bit surprised by my question: "These people are glad to take the money from anybody, they don't even know I'm Hui. What they don't like is the fact that we Fujianese have so much more money than they do." In this region, then, ethnic tension has shifted from Hui versus Han to local versus nonlocal. In this case most of the workers came from Zhejiang, and so there were Fujianese-Zhejiangese tensions in evidence.

When in Beijing in March 1994, I met with one official at the Beijing Foreign Affairs Bureau who noted that the word on the street was that most Chinese leaders feared not another Wuerkaixi, or student leader rising up to challenge their authority, but another Mao Zedong. This indicates that although Deng's supporters may feel the market reforms have not gone far enough, his detractors suggest they may have gone too far.

Han and Hui Market Perspectives: Contrasting Moralities

The debate in China over the social ills concomitant with Deng's market reforms reflects a fundamental ambivalence about prosperity, profit, and the capitalist road on which China has embarked. There are those who fully support newfound market freedoms. But concerns about inflation, income disparities, corruption, crime, and social upheaval as well as a growing nostalgia for the "good old days" of Maoist egalitarianism all highlight the wide range of feeling about Deng's reforms. Moreover, opinions on these matters may be easily manipulated by those on both sides of Deng politically. The essentialized legacies of Han agrarianism with its emphasis on rural simplicity, Confucianism with its well-ordered social hierarchy in which merchants are at the low end of the ladder, and communism with its idealized emphasis on egalitarianism and the common good over personal profit—such varied influences cannot easily be dislodged after forty years of party rule. Dengists can only hope there is not another Chairman Mao unsuccessfully seeking his way into the university.

By contrast, Hui, Uygur, and other Muslim minorities bring to their economic engagements an interest in trade and a desire for maximizing their opportunities of advancement. Whether their motivations be for personal enrichment, religious enhancement, or the strengthening of community solidarity, their marginalized position in Chinese society has put them in a position where trade and mediation are important survival skills. These skills have developed over years of relative isolation within the Chinese majority and in opposition to a non-Muslim state.

What the state has not been able to control or foresee, however, is the important influence Hui ethnoreligious tradition has had on Hui entrepreneurialism and religious practice. Although it is clear that China's early (Stalinist) nationality policy sought to separate nationality and religion and encourage economic development to speed assimilation to a more advanced, namely Han, nationality (see Connor 1984:67–71), events have not worked out as planned. Economic development has brought ethnoreligious revitalization and a growing awareness of Muslim links to the larger Islamic world. Just as the state has courted investment from foreign Muslim governments in China only to find that foreign Muslims have generally preferred to build mosques instead of factories, so among the Hui the state has not been able to divorce national from religious interests or economic development from Islamic awareness.

Standing somewhere between Muslim and Chinese civilizations, the Muslim Chinese Hui become the perfect counterexample to Huntington's thesis that civilizations are fundamentally different and generally opposed. Though sharing differing rationalizations about their participation in capitalist economies, Hui Muslims have much in common with their Han neighbors. Quanzhou Hui venerate Muslim ancestors, raise pigs, and participate fully in southern Min Fujianese political culture; they would object strongly to the dichotomy of East-West, Muslim-Confucian, that Huntington finds so useful. Instead, their daily interactions with Islam, Confucian traditions, local southern Min popular religion, and Southeast Asian business connections have produced a vibrant cultural identity that cannot easily be placed in any category, though they continue to be labeled as Hui by the state. In the Northwest, Na villagers share views of family solidarity, patriarchy, hierarchy, thrift, hard work, perseverance, and honesty that could easily be considered Confucian. Yet their explicit motivations for economic prosperity are often described in terms of religious and ethnic goals. In each case, one finds not predisposition for market success but rather adaptation to government policy and the harsh realities of socioeconomic contexts for personal survival. Prosperity, and even the social ills that may come with it, are never problematic for these Hui; these things are seen as good for the people and, in general, for religion. To some extent, the Hui are essentialized by the state and broader public as entrepreneurs and in turn essentialize themselves this way; this is to their advantage and, eventually, to the advantage of the state as well.

This is not the case for the Han, where market practice is characterized by moral ambivalence. In addition, recent studies have suggested that Han identity, broadly represented as homogeneous and unified, is breaking apart along cultural and regional lines (see Friedman 1994; Gladney 1994a). It is now popular to be Cantonese and Shanghainese in China, and a resurgence of local power bases often drawn along cultural fault lines should give Huntington pause: Not only was he wrong about Muslim homogeneity but he is misinformed about Confucian continuity as well. Hong Kong–based triads are no respector of their fellow Confucians in Beijing if they refuse to cooperate with their expanding operations. Huntington was correct to note the existence of cultural fault lines, as power does often flow along them. He was incorrect to essentialize culture according to general categories of civilizations without regard for culture's redefinition in dialogic interaction in the context of the modern nation-state.

By comparing Muslim and Han economic ideas and practice in Deng's China, I have sought to suggest the need for more contextualized, community-based studies rather than broad generalizations about "Confucianism" and "Islam." Debates about certain market practices within these communities reveal more than do such sweeping generalizations. The Hui, standing somewhere between China and the Middle East, provide an important counterpoint to those who wish to draw broad distinctions between Muslim and Confucian or East and West.

NOTES

This chapter is based on three years of field research between 1982 and 1986 in the People's Republic of China with funding from CSCPRC (Committee on Scholarly Communication with the People's Republic of China), Fulbright, and the Wenner-Gren Foundation and sponsorship from the Central Institute of Nationalities, the Ningxia Academy of Social Sciences, and Xiamen University. My earlier research has also been updated by subsequent research and brief return visits, with the exception of the Ningxia village, to each field site in 1987, 1988, 1989, 1990, and 1994.

1. Reported in "China Is Taking a Great Leap into the Auto Age," *Toronto Globe and Mail*, August 18, 1994.

2. The visit was due to participation in a UNESCO-sponsored conference, Contributions of Islamic Culture on China's Maritime Silk Route, February 21–26, 1994, Quanzhou, Fujian. The conference was hosted by the Fujian Academy of Social Sciences and the Fujian Maritime Museum.

3. On April 17, 1994, a *United Press International* article, "Chinese Mobile Phone Industry Booms," reported that cellular phone users in China increased by 20 percent in the first quarter of 1994 to 784,000 and that pager owners increased 13 percent to more than 6 million.

4. Charles Maier (1994:10) argues that the "Islamic challenge [will] be one that is ultimately fought within the borders of its own civilization." Though reifying "Islamic" civilization, this comment at the very least admits that the potential for conflict between Muslim groups is at least as great as tensions between Muslim and non-Muslim, as the Iran-Iraq War and the Gulf War evidenced. The Malay Muslim scholar Chandra Muzaffar (1994) suggests that reifying "Islamic" civilization as uni-

fied or predominantly Arab also neglects the fact that the largest Muslim populations today are spread across the multinational populations of South and Southeast Asia.

5. For the complete text, see Gladney 1996:157–158.

6. Note that 1989 figures are based on Ding 1991, whereas 1979–1993 records are derived from my field notes and township records.

7. Cited in "Danger to Economy Lies in Moral Decay," *China Daily*, May 18, 1994, p. 3.

8. Cited in "A Call for Quality, Not Quantity," *China Daily*, May 26, 1994, p. 3.

9. Cited in "Proper Financing May Quash Dodgy Levies," *China Daily*, April 29, 1994, p. 3.

10. Cited in "Market Economy Is Misunderstood by Too Many Folk." *China Daily*, May 6, 1994, p. 4.

REFERENCES

Anagnost, Ann. 1994. "The Politics of Ritual Displacement." In Charles Keyes, Laurel Kendal, and Helen Hardacre, eds., *State and Religion in East and Southeast Asia*, pp. 221–254. Honolulu: University of Hawaii Press.

Connor, Walker. 1984. *The National Question in Marxist-Leninist Theory and Strategy*. Princeton: Princeton University Press.

Diamond, Norma. 1985. "Rural Collectivization and Decollectivization in China—A Review Article." *Journal of Asian Studies* 44, 4:785–792.

"Ding Clan Genealogy." 1980. In *Quanzhou wenxian congkan di san zhong* (Quanzhou documents collection), no. 13. Quanzhou: Quanzhou Historical Research Society.

Ding Xiancao. 1990. "Chendai: The Past and the Present." In Chen Guoqiang, ed., *Chendai huizushi yanjiu* (Research on Chendai Hui nationality history), pp. 1–6. Beijing: China Academy of Social Sciences Press.

Fan Changjiang. [1936] 1980. *Zhongguo de xibei jiao* (China's northwest corner). Ed. Chinese Academy of Social Sciences. Beijing: New China Publishing Society.

Fei Xiaotong. 1987. "Minorities Hold Key to Own Prosperity." *China Daily*, April 28, p. 4.

_____. 1989. *"Zhonghua minzu de duoyuan jiti juge"* (Plurality and unity in the configuration of the Chinese nationality). *Beijing Daxue Xuebao* 4:1–19.

Fei Xiaotong, ed. 1981. *Toward a People's Anthropology*. Beijing: New World Press.

Friedman, Edward. 1994. "Reconstructing China's National Identity: A Southern Alternative to Mao-Era Anti-Imperialist Nationalism." *Journal of Asian Studies* 53, 1:67–91.

Gay, Craig M. 1991. *With Liberty and Justice for Whom? The Recent Evangelical Debate over Capitalism*. Grand Rapids, Mich.: Eerdmans.

Gladney, Dru C. 1990. "The Ethnogenesis of the Uighur." *Central Asian Survey* 9, 1:1–28.

_____. 1994a. "Representing Nationality in China: Refiguring Majority/Minority Identities." *Journal of Asian Studies* 53, 1:92–123.

_____. 1994b. "Ethnic Identity in China: The New Politics of Difference." In William A. Joseph, ed., *China Briefing, 1994*, pp. 171–192. Boulder: Westview Press.

_____. 1995. "Economy and Ethnicity: The Revitalization of a Muslim Minority in Southeastern China." In Andrew Walder, ed., *The Waning of the Communist State: Economic Origins of Political Decline in China and Hungary*, pp. 242–266. Berkeley: University of California Press.

_____. [1991] 1996. *Muslim Chinese: Ethnic Nationalism in the People's Republic.* Cambridge: Harvard University Press, Council on East Asian Studies.

Gold, Thomas B. 1989. "Urban Private Business in China." *Studies in Comparative Communism* 22, 2–3:187–202.

Gong Weiduan. 1987. "Yongning xian na jiahu cun shi diaocha." (Yong Ning County Homestead history investigation). *Ningxia Shizhi Yanjiu* 1:34–40.

Huntington, Samuel P. 1993a. "The Islamic-Confucian Connection." *New Perspectives Quarterly* 10, 3 (Summer):19–35.

_____. 1993b. "The Clash of Civilizations?" *Foreign Affairs* 72, 3:22–49.

Huo Da. 1992. *The Jade King—History of a Chinese Muslim Family*. Beijing: Panda Press.

_____. [1988] 1993. *Musilin de zangli* (Muslim funeral). Beijing: Beijing Changpian Xiaoshuo Zhuang Zuo Congshu.

Lai Cunli. 1988. *Huizu shangye shi* (A history of Hui nationality mercantilism). Beijing: Zhongguo Shangye Chubanshe.

Lardy, Nicholas R. 1986. "Agricultural Reforms in China." *Journal of International Affairs* 32, 2:91–104.

Li Tianxi. 1990. "Tradition of Patriotism and Village—Love of the Overseas Chinese of the Ding Clan of Chendai." In Chen Guogjang, ed., *Chendai Huizushi Yanjiu* (Chendai Hui nationality history), pp. 337–346. Beijing: Academy of Social Sciences Press.

Ma Tong. [1981] 1983. *Zhongguo yisilan jiaopai yu menhuan zhidu shilue* (A history of Muslim factions and the Menhuan system in China). Yinchuan: Ningxia People's Publishing Society.

Maier, Charles. 1994. "Will the Fault Lines Between Civilizations Be the Battle Lines of the Future?" *Centerpiece* (Winter-Spring):10.

Muzaffar, Chandra. 1994. Interview in *Third World Network Features*, Penang. Reprinted in "The Clash of Civilizations? Responses from the World." *Centerpiece* (Winter-Spring):8.

Ningxia Hui Autonomous Region Population Census Office. 1983. *Ningxia huizu zizhiqu di san ci renkou pucha* (Ningxia Hui Autonomous Region third population census). Beijing: n.p.

Ohnuki-Tierney, Emiko. 1993. *Rice as Self: Japanese Identities Through Time.* Princeton: Princeton University Press.

Oi, Jean. 1989. "Market Reform and Corruption in Rural China." *Studies in Comparative Communism* 22, 2-3:221–233.

Peletz, Michael. 1993. "Ordinary Muslims and Muslim Resurgents in Contemporary Malaysia: Notes on an Ambivalent Relationship." Paper presented at the conference Islam and the Social Construction of Identities: Comparative Perspectives on Southeast Asian Muslims, cosponsored by the Center for Southeast Asian Studies at the University of Hawaii at Manoa and the East-West Center, August 4–6.

Pillsbury, Barbara L.K. 1976. "Blood Ethnicity: Maintenance of Muslim Identity in Taiwan." Paper presented at the Conference on Anthropology in Taiwan, Portsmouth, New Hampshire, August 19–24.

_____. 1981. "The Muslim Population of China: Clarifying the Question of Size and Ethnicity." *Journal of the Institute for Muslim Minority Affairs* 3, 2:35–58.

Population Census Office of the State Council of the People's Republic of China and the Institute of Geography of the Chinese Academy of Sciences. 1987. *The Population Atlas of China*. Oxford: Oxford University Press.

Shue, Vivienne. 1984. "The Fate of the Commune." *Modern China* 10, 3:250–283.

Stark, David, and Victor Nee. 1989. "Toward an Institutional Analysis of State Socialism." In Victor Nee and David Stark, eds., *Remaking the Economic Institutions of Socialism: China and Eastern Europe*, pp. 1–31. Stanford: Stanford University Press.

Tu Weiming, Milan Hejtmanek, and Allen Wacman, eds. 1993. *The Confucian World Observed: A Contemporary Discussion of Confucian Humanism in East Asia*. Honolulu: East-West Center Press.

Wang Yiping. 1985. "Najiahucun de zongjiao zhuangkuang" (The religious situation in Najiahu village). *Ningxia Shehui Kexue* 9:7–9.

Weigert, Andrew. 1991. *Mixed Emotions: Certain Steps Toward Understanding Ambivalence*. Albany: SUNY Press.

Zhu Yuntao. 1985. "Najiahucun chanye jiegou de diaocha" (Najiahu village industrial production structure research). *Ningxia Shehui Kexue* 9:1–6.

Zhuang Jinghui. 1993. "Chendai dingshi huizuhanhua de yanjiu" (Research on Han assimilation of the Ding lineage in Chendai). *Haijiaoshi Yanjiu* 34, 2:93–107.

Part Two

Indigenes and Chinese in Southeast Asia

four

✦

Business Success Among Southeast Asian Chinese

The Role of Culture, Values, and Social Structures

JAMIE MACKIE

The business success of overseas Chinese throughout much of Southeast Asia provides a good case study from which answers might be sought to the question posed as the central issue in this volume: Are some cultures, and the value systems derived from them, more strongly predisposed than others to accept markets and market outcomes? Or, to reword the question slightly to meet my purposes here: Are the values of the Southeast Asian Chinese more inclined to generate high levels of entrepreneurial drive and dynamism than those of the other societies and cultures in the region? Chinese business success is often invoked in support of such claims, as are the performance records of other East Asian countries with a "Confucian" or "neo-Confucian" cultural heritage. However, "the Confucian values hypothesis," sometimes invoked to explain growth rates and economic dynamism, can be accepted only with strict qualifications. There may be something in it—but, I will suggest, considerably less than many Sinophiles would have us believe.

In the case of the Southeast Asian Chinese it is certainly true that a higher proportion of them have been more entrepreneurial in their business activities than the indigenous populations.[1] Value systems among the latter are less commercially oriented, be they Thai, Javanese, Malay, Burmese, or Vietnamese. Just why indigenous populations might not have been as inclined toward commercial activities as the Chinese is a question too complex to delve into here; my primary concern here is with Chinese commercial success.

Because of the diversity of Southeast Asian Chinese and the varied regional circumstances facing them, many explanatory variables are relevant to the *explicandum* here— social and cultural factors as well as institutional and structural ones.[2] Even the notion of luck or good fortune is one that few Chinese would ignore (many of them are great gamblers), since it has its roots far back in Chinese culture, geomancy, and numerology.[3] Clearly, values and culture are important factors in all this—or, more precisely, values in their sociopolitical context—but structural and institutional elements in Southeast Asian Chinese economic life are also crucial.

Among the latter are the Chinese family and family firm; the legendary networks that crisscross Southeast Asia, binding its economies together; the *bang* (speech group) and lineage or clan associations on which the early migrants depended for mutual support; and the market-integrating capabilities of the modern conglomerates (all highly entrepreneurial versions of the family firm, in essence). Above all, great stress has been put on two factors: the universal reliance on *xinyong* (trust, credit-worthiness) as the glue that holds the edifice of commercial transactions together; and *guanxi* (personal connections) as devices for reducing the transaction costs involved in conducting business in situations where legal safeguards for contract enforcement have often been unreliable.[4] Ultimately, the puzzle facing us is to work out how these various elements have been interrelated in various circumstances with varied outcomes and success.

There is a danger here, however, of creating too muscular a cultural explanation of the business success of Southeast Asian Chinese. Many Chinese, we must remember, are still poor despite their hard work, filial piety, or other "Confucian" virtues. Those characteristics must have played a part in the early success of many small-scale Chinese traders prior to the middle of the twentieth century, but they alone do not provide an adequate explanation for this success and certainly not for their even more remarkable achievements in large-scale businesses since 1945. The problems here are tangled ones with the historical and local context often proving critical. A comparison of Chinese and Southeast Asian traders in the sixteenth and seventeenth centuries, for example, would reveal that the latter played a far more prominent role in the flourishing maritime trade of the region than they did 300 years later. The example should serve to remind us how important yet different social conditions in China and Southeast Asia have been at different times.[5]

The task I have been set in this chapter is to provide a broad overview of the economic roles of the Southeast Asian Chinese and the values associated with them. The question of whether traditional Chinese values and culture have proved conducive or obstructive to the growth of markets in mainland

China (or in Hong Kong or Taiwan) is obviously relevant to our subject here but is only part of the story. In late Qing China such a traditional culture containing market values (if, indeed, it existed in any sense) was not sufficient to guarantee commercial development; nor was it sufficient during the latter years of Mao's rule. Obviously, then, culture and values per se cannot be singled out as the sole, decisive variable, although by focusing on "values in context" we can get closer to an explanation. In Southeast Asia, the success of so many initially impoverished Chinese immigrants from the late nineteenth century until 1941 can hardly be explained solely in terms of their values or behavior patterns, since they did not then differ much from those prevailing among other Chinese in their very poor home provinces in southern China. Yet developments become more explicable if viewed in terms of the interplay between those values and structural and situational factors.

For the purposes of this chapter, then, it will be sufficient to take a theoretically eclectic approach to the matter, drawing on various theories where it suits without becoming enslaved to any one of them. An important part of the explanation can be found in the observation of Benjamin Higgins (1989:33) that when an economy is expanding and business opportunities are abundant, entrepreneurial talents are likely to emerge no matter how unpromising the prevailing value system or cultural framework may be. Much of the fruitless search in the 1950–1960s along neo-Weberian lines into the cultural preconditions and socioeconomic motivations or drives of entrepreneurs ran into quicksand because it focused too much on factors affecting the supply of entrepreneurial qualities without much regard for the demand side of the equation.

Weber's speculations about the links between the Protestant ethic and the rise of European capitalism influenced Clifford Geertz's (1956, 1963) illuminating research into the possibility of an analogous connection in Indonesia between reformist Islam and an emergent entrepreneurial class. Geertz's ideas were immensely stimulating but led into a theoretical blind alley (Castles 1967:90). He gave little attention to the Southeast Asian Chinese, who have since emerged as the dominant capitalists in the five original ASEAN countries. To explain the prominence of the Chinese in business since the 1960s solely along Geertzian or Weberian lines, therefore, is highly problematic, to say the least. But no comprehensive alternative for explaining the business success of the Southeast Asian Chinese has yet been offered, although many writers have touched on the subject peripherally.[6]

Recently, a plethora of what might be called "triumphalist" or even "Han chauvinist" interpretations of Chinese commercial success have appeared in the wake of the economic boom in southern China and throughout the "greater China" arc (Guangdong-Fujian, Hong Kong, and Taiwan). Typically these accounts extol the superiority of Chinese business practices, attributing success to underlying social values and institutions. Although some of these accounts have yielded useful information about the business practices of overseas Chinese, they generally invoke oversimplified assumptions. Some verge on being crudely racist in their theoretical underpinnings. Others are inclined toward a Platonic, essentialist approach toward culture and entrepreneurship, as if a few characteristics of overseas society and culture constitute the crucial ingredient for Chinese business success.

Among the various aspects of this problem (explored further on), two are of special interest. One is the extent to which Southeast Asian Chinese have had an advantage over members of the indigenous societies within which they reside because of what I call their "early start" in the economic race. Another is the benefit they derive from the high degree of mutual trust and civic solidarity derived from their reliance on *guanxi* and *xinyong* as pillars of their commercial culture. These tend to create strong horizontal ties across the community, mitigating against the vertical patronage so characteristic of the region's indigenous societies with their more rigidly hierarchical social relations and behavior patterns. The latter are not conducive to the development of a strong commercial culture or institutions. By contrast, I suggest, there is good reason to believe that the more fluid, competitive characteristics of the Southeast Asian Chinese communities, which have strong horizontal linkages and a vigorous associational life, have helped to develop personal relationships of trust like those vital to commerce in so much of the world.

Homogeneity or Heterogeneity Among Southeast Asian Chinese

The Southeast Asian Chinese are by no means homogeneous. The assumption of uniformity is often made by enthusiasts of the idea of "a Chinese commonwealth" extending across the globe, "a nation without borders" defined in ethnic or cultural terms and of course including Southeast Asian Chinese. Such a view ignores the steadily widening differences between, for example, Sino-Thai, Singaporeans, and Sino-Indonesians, nearly all of whom have taken on local cultural characteristics and loyalties to some degree. It also ignores deep-seated linguistic and occupational differences among the various *bang*—Hokkien, Hakka, Teochiu, Cantonese, and Hainanese. Complicating things even further, for decades there have also been cross-cutting differences between first-generation immigrants (formerly called *totok* in Indonesia and *sinkeh* in Malaya-Singapore) and those who have been settled abroad for several generations *(peranakan* or *baba)*, as well as between rural and urban Chinese and among the various occupational groups, often correlated with *bang* origins. Levels of assimilation or integration into their host communities have also varied greatly, from a high degree in modern Thailand and Cambodia (before Pol Pot) to low degrees in most parts of Malaysia or Indonesia (Skinner 1996; Mackie 1988).

These differences among the Southeast Asian Chinese must be kept in mind as an antidote to any notion of an essential, common Chineseness. Although they share with Chinese elsewhere elements of ethnic and cultural heritage, the historical interaction of the Southeast Asian Chinese with indigenous neighbors has influenced their ethnic and cultural identity in complex ways.[7] Earlier suggestions that the Southeast Asian Chinese have divided loyalties or "double identities" oversimplify the matter. The Southeast Asian Chinese often have *multiple* identities, as do many cosmopolitan sojourners throughout the world these days (Wang 1988, 1996). Few Southeast Asian Chinese retain close family ties or political loyalties to China. Nearly all are becoming increasingly "Southeast Asian" in outlook. More than 85 percent of them were born in Southeast Asia, and most have no wish to go back to China to live, unlike their parents or grandparents sixty years ago.

Culture, Values, and Success: Thrift and Other Virtues

The success of the Southeast Asian Chinese is frequently attributed to legendary qualities of enterprise, hard work, frugality, family solidarity, education, and other "neo-Confucian" or "entrepreneurial" virtues. Raffles noted such qualities among the Chinese miners on Bangka Island in 1815, and a recent account described them as not only diligent and thrifty but "a hardy, self-reliant and risk-taking lot," all good qualifications for becoming modern entrepreneurs of the small-scale kind in developing societies with very imperfect markets and high transaction costs (Bastin 1954:259; Wu 1983:113). There can be little doubt that most overseas Chinese are more lavishly endowed with these and other qualities conducive to entrepreneurial success in the modern world than other ethnic groups in Southeast Asia. But why is that so? Are these qualities derived from their adaptation to harsh experiences as "marginal trading minorities" in the countries to which they have emigrated, compelled by lack of other opportunities to bend every effort toward buying and selling things? Or do these qualities originate from within Chinese society itself? Or finally, have those qualities been deeply ingrained by countless generations of struggle to survive poverty, natural disasters, and a precarious, marginal existence in an overcrowded China?

Surely the answer to these questions has to be "a bit of each." We can rule out, of course, any suggestion that qualities such as hard work, frugality, and the drive for education are genetically inherited rather than culturally or historically determined—although it might be easy to see why some people might imagine they are, since those qualities seem to be distributed among overseas Chinese quite disproportionately. Omohondro has neatly made the point in his fine study *Chinese Merchant Families in Iloilo*, noting that "Chinese are better businessmen than Filipinos because of the advantages in their social structure. . . . Chinese cultural features relating to business success are most likely to be preserved. Thus the merchant niche and Chinese immigrant culture are interacting in several ways" (Omohondro 1981:83, 87). His particular group of Philippine Chinese may not have been entirely typical of Chinese groups in the Philippines, or elsewhere, for it was a small one of only 5,000 people, forming "a closed ethnic community under a tight rein" with powerful sanctions over deviant members. It is unclear that Chinese culture and social structure are as strong and mutually supportive in larger, more fragmented communities like Manila, Singapore, or Jakarta. But Omohondro's account illustrates an important point:

> Many of the mercantile practices used . . . are cultural forms which developed in China and were adapted . . . to colonial and immigrant situations. The banking system, apprenticeship cycle, high reliance on *xin-yong*, certain forms of partnerships, loans and . . . various forms of merchant organizations were social structural features of Chinese society which provide a competitive advantage when doing business among Filipinos, who are without similarly developed institutions. (Omohondro 1981:87)

In short, the culture of the Iloilo Chinese is inextricably entangled with social structures and institutions, shaped by and shaping them. The same is no doubt true elsewhere in the region.

The Legacy of "Confucian" Values

Next, we must turn to the thorny question of whether the commercial success of the Southeast Asian Chinese can be explained wholly or largely in terms of their values and a so-called neo-Confucian cultural heritage. If the answer is yes, even in part, what light does that throw on the other questions confronting us here? When the value systems of the overseas Chinese generally (including those of Taiwan and Hong Kong) are compared with those of the indigenous societies of Southeast Asia, the differences are in many respects striking.

But in fact even the application of terms like "Confucian" and "neo-Confucian" to the culture or values of the Southeast Asian Chinese is so questionable that the terms are best avoided entirely. They are more confusing than illuminating. The Chinese who came to Southeast Asia nearly all derived from social classes unlikely to have been imbued with the "high" Confucian culture of the mandarin class in China (Wang 1992:304–312). Popular forms of "low Confucianism" incorporating Taoist and Buddhist beliefs and practices were more prevalent among them. Wang writes, "Wherever the Overseas Chinese went, far from paying respect to Confucius, they built temples to various deities and to Buddha and sundry Boddhisatvas. . . . Very rarely would there be a reference to Confucius, except when merchants engaged tutors for their children to prepare them for life in China" (312).

The key point about those early Chinese immigrants was that even the merchants who belonged to the *shang* (trader) class, the lowest in the *simin* normative hierarchy of occupational groups, held beliefs and values that "were not so much Confucian as syncretic."[8] They took what suited them from others in order to protect and strengthen themselves as *shang* and to consolidate their respect for trade as a value in itself. But of direct relevance to our concerns here is Wang's observation concerning the social genesis of merchant values:

> Their vocation produced its own autonomous values and that, for commercial success, they had more in common with traders outside China than with the literati in China. . . . It was this commonality, whether in Taiwan, Hong Kong, Singapore or Korea, of the established *shang* merchants adapting to modern capitalist ways and attitudes that distinguishes them and explains their economic success rather than what they had accepted from Confucian values. (Wang 1992:309)

Wang suggests that instead of looking for the mainsprings of their value systems and entrepreneurial drives in their religious beliefs, along crudely Weberian lines, we may be better off to think of the Southeast Asian Chinese as adhering to "the values of trade" many of them shared with the diverse trading populations of the world.

Changing Values

Values change over time in most societies—slowly, of course, but in most circumstances inexorably, as do social structures and the behavior patterns they sustain. So it is dangerous to generalize about any link between "Chinese value systems" and business success as if the former is the decisive variable and the local socioeconomic, political, or cultural context is a matter of no great importance. I would argue, on the contrary, that the local context has nearly always been all important. In Thailand, for example, several leading Sino-Thai families have become highly assimilated to a Thai identity (the Lamsam family most notably), shedding much of their Chineseness in the process; many others have not yet moved nearly as far in that direction. In the Philippines, too, the Sino-mestizo elite was first Hispanicized, then in the eighteenth and nineteenth centuries, Filipinized, to the point that many lost much of their Chinese heritage.

In Java, *peranakan* Chinese have long since differed sharply from first-generation immigrants, the *totok*. The difference is illustrated in the *peranakan* preference for secure employment and salaried jobs or careers in the professions rather than the risks and hassles of commercial life (Willmott 1960:69–70; Skinner 1963:106–107). In preferring the latter, the *totok* may have made a virtue of necessity, since they generally lacked the language skills and education needed to aspire to the former. But there is ample evidence that most choose business careers because their values and experience incline them that way—and because the rewards can be greater. Even today, nearly all the top Chinese businessmen in Indonesia are from *totok* families, with very few *peranakan* reaching the top 20 or even top 200 wealthiest families. It is *totok* Chinese who are said to be hard-driving, risk-taking, and successful.

Economic Roles and "Marginal Trading Minority" Theories

Like marginal trading minorities (MTMs) in other parts of the world, such as the Jews in particular, the Southeast Asian Chinese have gravitated toward commercial, financial, and professional occupations, especially in the twentieth century. However, terms such as "the Jews of the East" and comparisons with Lebanese or Indian trading minorities in Africa are more often misleading than illuminating. Hagen (1962, 1968) elevated a folk observation about such minorities into a much-quoted theory about the psychological drives behind their zeal to achieve business success, linking these traits in good Weberian fashion to his notion of how development comes to be generated. There is no doubt something in this model. If minorities are excluded from landownership, government service, and the armed forces, they have little choice but to make as much success as they can from whatever trading opportunities are open to them. But the MTM theory cannot serve as more than a partial explanation for the success of the Southeast Asian Chinese, for it does not fit well the historical record of how their economic roles and occupations have changed over time.

The vast majority of those who flooded into the region during the half-century before World War II were in fact contract coolies and miners, or farmers or fishermen from rural backgrounds, most of whom stayed only for their contract periods before returning to China with their savings. Of those who stayed on in Southeast Asia, only a small minority became traders, artisans, or small manufacturers at first, although a few of those who did so became quite wealthy. Even in the 1930s, large numbers of the Chinese in the region were still desperately poor and many were little involved in commerce.

Only since World War II have large numbers of Southeast Asian Chinese people moved into urban and commercial pursuits. They have done so at the same time that the economic structures of countries throughout the region have offered wider opportunities for new, more lucrative economic roles. And whereas their status as members of a vulnerable, politically powerless minority ("pariah capitalists" in Fred Riggs's apt term) had earlier inclined them toward commerce rather than industry, partly because of the shorter turnover times required and lower risks of expropriation or extortion, their civic status has improved considerably, if erratically, in most parts of Southeast Asia since the 1960s.[9] The term "pariah capitalists" is no longer appropriate for Chinese people in most parts of the region, although it is still relevant in others. Of the few attempts to apply the MTM theory to Southeast Asia, only Janet Landa's (1983) is very convincing (she uses the clumsy term "ethnically homogeneous Chinese middlemen group"). She too emphasizes the need to reduce transaction costs in situations of contract uncertainty by relying on "personalistic exchange networks based on trust," along lines I shall discuss further on.

The Early-Start Advantage: From Small and Medium Businesses to Large-Scale Enterprises

A crucial reason for the enduring commercial success of the Southeast Asian Chinese in the twentieth century has to do with timing. That is, having achieved greater economic success than indigenous people, the Chinese have proved difficult to displace despite discriminatory regulations at various times in many Southeast Asian countries. This fact raises complex questions about how they got their initial advantage to start with, to which two types of answers are commonly given. One is that the "middleman" or "comprador" roles many Chinese took on in the colonial era as intermediaries between the Western colonial rulers and the indigenous peoples yielded big profits and other advantages, from which a few were able to diversify into more lucrative economic roles well beyond the capabilities of the indigenes. Another explanation has been suggested by Freedman (1979:22–26) to the effect that the Chinese immigrants to Southeast Asia came from societies in southern China in which experience in the handling of money and loans was more widespread than among the indigenous peoples among whom they settled. Hence even the less skilled Chinese immigrants had an initial advantage over the indigenes in their ability to handle commercial transactions and debts that was quite apart from their stronger motivations toward accumulating wealth in order to return home (Hicks 1993, 1995). This advantage may have been important for the many small traders and storekeepers who fanned out across the frontier regions of Thailand, Malaya, and the Netherlands Indies from the late nineteenth century on, although it was only one advantage among many over the local people (Skinner 1957:99–118).

Having gained an initial advantage in small and medium enterprises (SMEs), many Chinese went on to build upon it and transform their businesses into large-scale enterprises (LSEs). The ability of so many Southeast Asian Chinese to make the transition from SME to LSE operations is, in fact, one of the most intriguing features of their entrepreneurial dynamism, to which we shall return. It has not been simply their ability to get started in business that calls for explanation but also the frequency of the rags-to-riches stories of Chinese capitalists whose values, drives, and talents have brought them success at the higher levels of economic life as well as the lower. In the eyes of their indigenous competitors, they have sometimes been stereotyped as "merciless monopsonistic middlemen" and "bloodsuckers," colluding to exclude all rivals. Statistical evidence about their trading margins indicates that this is a gross exaggeration (Gosling 1983).

Trust and Social Solidarity

The reliance on *xinyong* and *guanxi* in Southeast Asian Chinese business circles is so frequently mentioned as one of the key features of Chinese business practice that it is hardly necessary to elaborate on its importance here. Barton (1983:53) has noted that "the Chinese approach to business was based upon personal relationships and word-of-mouth agreements" backed up by informal group sanctions associated with a man's reputation within the network to which he belonged. He quoted the classic explanation for this state of affairs given by Alice Dewey (1962:53) in her pioneering study of rural markets in Java:

> Especially in a society that lacks a well-developed and well enforced civil code, trust, based on non-legal sanctions, is important in trade. If capital is to flow freely, if long-range planning is to be possible, and if merchants are to know what they have bought without constantly supervising others and inspecting goods, there must be mutual assurance that contracts will be fulfilled.

If we ask why the Chinese have relied on personal relationships to guard against cheating and have been uncomfortable with more anonymous, institutionalized arrangements, part of the answer is that the latter simply were not available to them. This is now changing as institutionalized sources of credit and contract enforcement emerge, so a sea change in values and attitudes may be beginning. But the highly personalistic character of so much Southeast Asian Chinese commercial practice will almost certainly persist long after the original need for it has disappeared; it has become deeply ingrained in the culture.

One important consequence of the reliance on *xinyong* is the way in which trust, social solidarity, and a relatively classless, status-free society have combined among the Southeast Asian Chinese to generate civic virtues conducive to successful business dealings inter se. The many brotherhoods and social and economic associations established in the region in the early decades of mass immigration contributed to the creation of a mutually supportive civic culture, strikingly different in several respects from those of the host societies. Latter-day variants of these survive even today in Singapore and the Philippines, although less so elsewhere. The various Southeast Asian Chinese communities have been characterized by high degrees of leadership turnover and social mobility both in their early years and more recently. Wealth has always been linked with philanthropy as a means to win community esteem in highly mobile and relatively egalitarian, competitive societies. Community leaders have usually been drawn from the wealthiest merchants, often men of humble origins who had experienced rags-to-riches careers. One result is that horizontal linkages based on *guanxi* and *xinyong* have predominated in those communities over vertical patronage ties, although instances of the latter are also found among the Chinese.[10] That seems still to be broadly true today even where the wealthiest tycoons are concerned. In that respect Southeast Asian Chinese societies have differed greatly from the indigenous societies with their greater reliance on patron-client relationships and vertically oriented social hierarchies, most notably in the Philippines and Java.

The contrast between the value systems underpinning a hierarchical, authoritarian, and vertically structured society and those of a more horizontal, egalitarian, and competitive society has recently been explored by Robert Putnam (1993) in his account of northern and southern Italy. Putnam examines the social and historical reasons that northern communities in Italy have been able to create a wide range of relatively autonomous cultural and political institutions along with values appropriate to a pluralistic society. The situation he describes for the North differs radically from the clientelistic and essentially authoritarian political culture predominating in the South, symbolized most strikingly by the dominance in that region of the Mafia. The South has developed a combination of vertically organized social relationships, intense dependence on the family (or a fictive family, the *padrone*), and low levels of social trust, since more impersonal social or political institutions could not be relied upon to provide security or protection. There has also been an intense distrust of the state and most other forms of higher authority. Southern communities have had little or no experience of civic solidarity or much inclination to create horizontal alliances or associations to achieve either protection or reform, as in the North. "Vertical social networks, embodying power asymmetries, exploitation, and dependence, contrast with the northern tradition of horizontal associations joining rough equals in mutual solidarity. . . . Patron-client politics in the south was more personalistic, more exploitative, more transitory, less 'civil'" (Putnam 1993:135).

Of special relevance to the parallel I am suggesting with the civic culture of the Southeast Asian Chinese is another of Putnam's (1993:181) observations:

Social trust, norms of reciprocity, networks of civic engagement, and successful cooperation are mutually reinforcing. Effective collaborative institutions require interpersonal skills and trust, but those skills are also inculcated and reinforced by organized collaboration. . . . Norms and networks of civic engagement contribute to economic prosperity and are in turn reinforced by that prosperity.

That conclusion also conforms with what we know about the horizontal linkages among the Southeast Asian Chinese communities and associations.

It also helps to explain why so many of their members have been more successful in business than their indigenous rivals.

Networks and Conglomerates

The legendary networks created by the overseas Chinese can be analyzed as both an extension of their cultural heritage, with its intense reliance on *guanxi* and *xinyong,* and a structural feature of their distinctive forms of business organization (Hamilton 1991). Networks have been important in facilitating commercial activity in situations of poor institutional development and inadequate mechanisms for ensuring that contracts are honored and transaction costs minimized. Once established, these arrangements tend to perpetuate themselves through their impact on the patterns of commercial behavior that become an integral part of the cultural heritage itself. Various networks have developed in Southeast Asia, the commercial and financial perhaps being the most common. Production and marketing networks like those Hamilton describes in this volume are not yet numerous in Southeast Asia, since the need for them has so far not been as great.

Networking is not unique to the Chinese but occurs in most countries in various forms, although rarely as extensively as among overseas Chinese. It is the highly personalized character of so much Chinese business practice that makes this group seem special. A lot of mystification surrounds the working and functions of these networks, for the Chinese tend to stress their importance as a unique phenomenon providing a clue to their economic success. But we should look more closely into their historical and functional significance as well as their cultural underpinnings. Networks have played an important part in the business success of many Southeast Asian Chinese, but not all.

The giant conglomerates that have proliferated in Southeast Asia since the 1970s are often discussed in tandem with the networks as if they were basically the same thing, mainly because twenty or thirty owners of the largest conglomerates have had strong personal and business links with each other in the main cities of Southeast Asia and Hong Kong. But international business networks of this kind are not yet common. They are radically different in structure from both the tight-knit family-controlled conglomerates and the older types of trading and financial networks that were such important features of the business landscape in the past. Analytically, conglomerates should be regarded as a new and quite distinct kind of entity. Ownership and control of a range of firms, usually diversified across various sectors, by a single founder or his family are the key features. Networking with other enterprises belonging to rivals may or may not be common. *Xinyong* and *guanxi* are not such crucial features of today's conglomerates as they were in the older networks (and in modern ones). The core business of all but a handful of conglomerates is confined to domestic markets. International operations (where networking seems most evident) is confined mainly to a few very large firms. The key strategies behind the creation of conglomerates are to spread risks, ensure control of market share, and achieve either horizontal or vertical linkages among the firms controlled. An explanation by Leff (1978) of conglomerates (or business groups, as he calls them) in terms of the benefits of internalizing within the group the high transaction costs of operating in poorly integrated markets seems relevant to at least some of those in Southeast Asia.

In short, we are dealing here with Southeast Asian Chinese institutions that do indeed stem from a common cultural tradition but appear to have had separate functions and histories and quite varied institutional realizations. It is a mistake to bundle all these things together into a single tradition or culture as if they provide a unitary means to understand Chinese success. Here again we must remind ourselves that structural and cultural factors are inextricably intermeshed.

Political Connections

In recent decades, political connections have played such a big part in the success of the wealthiest tycoons in Southeast Asia that some attention must be given to them here. Some individuals have relied heavily on political contacts for commercial favors, Liem Sioe Liong of Indonesia being the outstanding case; others have made far less use of them (e.g., William Soeryadjaya and Tan Kah Kee). Yet outside Singapore, even the richest Southeast Asian Chinese have rarely been prominent in the political life of the region, much less the core of a significant "bourgeoisie" in the conventional Marxist sense because of the political marginality and social vulnerability of the Chinese (Mackie 1988; McVey 1992). Their ability to manipulate political connections in various circumstances depends more on social and economic circumstances than on any nativist political disposition.

Conversely, it is necessary to query the argument put by Yoshihara (1988) that Southeast Asian capitalists, both Chinese and indigenous, are no more than "ersatz capitalists," or rent seekers, depending so heavily on political connections, special privileges, and scarce licenses as well as on imported technology that they are not "real" capitalists at all. Although there is evidence to support such a generalization about some Chinese capitalists, perhaps even many, Yoshihara has weakened his case by overstating it. If the region has been so utterly lacking in true capitalists since the 1960s, it is hard to explain how it has maintained such high growth rates. Capitalists and politicians all over the world grab rent-seeking opportunities when available to them through political connections. The special feature of Southeast Asia is not an ersatz capitalism but the unique position of the Chinese as economically strong and indispensable but politically weak and vulnerable, a situation with complex political and historical roots.

Conclusion: Toward an Explanation

These strands of inquiry must now be pulled together into an explanatory framework that will enable us to relate business success among the Southeast Asian Chinese to its relevant cultural and institutional factors. Let us begin with the fact that the values and business practices brought by Chinese immigrants to Southeast Asia over a century ago gave them a competitive edge over their rivals (including Westerners, in many situations) and enabled them to prosper in varying degrees in the socioeconomic conditions encountered there. That "early start" advantage meant that the communities, family firms, and other commercial institutions they created have continued to prosper more than indigenous businesses, except in the disrupted years between 1930–1950. They were well placed to profit from both the withdrawal of the European and American colonial-era LSEs after World War II and the entry of new multinational corporations seeking capable joint-venture partners soon after. Above all, the rapid growth experienced throughout the region since the 1960s has created unprecedented opportunities that they were better able to seize than others.

We need not assume that *all* Chinese possessed special entrepreneurial talents, although unusually large numbers of them did. But their talents were reinforced by supporting conditions derived from their Chinese associations and commercial institutions (Freedman 1979:61–83). The development of their dialect associations and kinship networks, *siang hwee* (chambers of commerce), and other community arrangements for mutual support have operated to their advantage ever since, creating enduring institutional linkages that local capitalists have been unable to match. Moreover, nearly all Chinese businessmen have had strong motivations to succeed from the earliest years, when poverty was the greatest spur, down to recent times, when insecurity and discrimination have added others. Their frugality and high savings rates coupled with high-turnover, low-margin business practices have made them formidable competitors (Limlingan 1986). Their knowledge of the business skills needed to rise beyond their humble origins into the world of enterprises of great size and complexity has also proved an extraordinary asset.

The distinctive characteristics of the traditional Chinese family firm are of central importance in all this as well (Wong 1985). We are drawn back into questions about the nature of the family, kinship, and socialization in China as well as throughout Southeast Asia (see Freedman 1979:240–254). That socialization process was responsible for instilling the habits of diligence, persistence, and determination to enhance the family patrimony characteristic of so much Chinese entrepreneurial behavior. Chinese families are strongly patrilineal, rooted in principles of filial piety, veneration for ancestors, and maintenance of the family line, and in all these regards they have a big advantage over (most of) their indigenous rivals with their looser social structures and cognatic (bilateral) descent systems. In the pioneering phases of Southeast Asian development, Chinese family firms also benefited from tight control by the father over the labor of all family members and over the assets constituting the family patrimony, a discipline that reinforced the father's economic authority.

In light of these considerations, it is perhaps not surprising that so many Chinese merchants did well in Southeast Asia in the periods before and after World War II, some becoming spectacularly wealthy during boom periods.[11] Although many puzzles arise about the sources of their entrepreneurial talents, the question is not so much why many were so successful in creating small enterprises but how and why so many have gone on to large enterprises, which require such different qualities for success. I leave that question for further study.

NOTES

1. I use the word "entrepreneurial" here to refer to a high frequency of distribution of diverse entrepreneurial qualities (as in Mackie 1992). Not all the overseas Chinese are well endowed with them—many still live in poverty, contrary to the popular stereotype—although the overall frequency is certainly higher than among other Southeast Asian peoples. Of the latter, indigenous groups such as the Buginese, Minangkabau, Mon, and Ilocano have been of a more entrepreneurial disposition than people in the larger agrarian communities, such as the Javanese, Thai, and Malay, although this is changing. The Philippines poses a unique case in Southeast Asia, being the only country with an indigenous propertied class based on landownership (partly Sino-Filipino in ancestry), diversifying since 1946 into commerce and sharpening the entrepreneurial talents of its members.

2. The main theories and writings in English on the factors most relevant to an explanation of the entrepreneurial talents of the Southeast Asian Chinese are summarized in Mackie (1992, 1995).

3. The Chinese love of gambling (Harrell 1987) poses a major analytical problem for any argument that Confucian values played a part in the development of East Asian capitalism analogous to that depicted in Weber's theory of the Protestant ethic in Europe.

4. Useful writings on these matters are Taku (1962), Barton (1983), Limlingan (1986), Harrell (1985), and Redding (1991).

5. Southeast Asian vessels and traders mainly conducted the region's trade with China before the great Ming-dynasty voyages to the Nanyang and beyond; but by the nineteenth century hardly any did (Reid 1996b).

6. Among the best treatments of this question are Castles (1967:1–9, 90–93), Lim (1983:1–22), and McVey (1992:7–32); see also the literature survey on the Southeast Asian Chinese in Mackie (1992).

7. On the changing identities of the Southeast Asian Chinese, see Wang (1988, 1996) and Mackie (1988).

8. Wang goes on to note, however, that "despite their apparent ignorance of Confucian doctrine and their close adherence to Taoist and Buddhist ideas and rituals, it would be hard to say that they were not bearers of Confucian values and did not behave in ways acceptable to the Confucian villages or communities in which they were brought up."

9. For the origins of the term "pariah capitalist" in the 1950–1960s, see Riggs (1966). A good account of how and why Riggs's analysis proved inadequate several decades later is given by McVey (1992).

10. The situation was different in the days of the nineteenth-century Chinese opium kings in Java and elsewhere, who created large subordinate networks of the patrimonialist type with tight control throughout over the flow of funds and key resources. But these networks were all collapsing by 1900–1910 (Rush 1990:96–98).

11. The failure rates among Southeast Asian Chinese merchants were also high, it must be remembered; thousands of them overextended themselves or were caught off guard by the business cycle, including the famous Tan Kah Kee. Few large family firms have survived even the legendary three-generation cycle of creation, consolidation, and collapse (Wong 1985).

REFERENCES

Barton, Clifton. 1983. "Trust and Credit: Some Observations Regarding Business Strategies of Overseas Chinese Traders in South Vietnam." In Linda Y.C. Lim and L.A. Peter Gosling, eds., *The Chinese in Southeast Asia,* vol. 1, pp. 46–64. Singapore and Ann Arbor: Maruzen and University of Michigan, Center for South and Southeast Asian Studies.

Bastin, John. 1954. "Raffles and the Chinese of Indonesia and Singapore." *Indonesie* 10:259–264.

Basu, Ellen Oxfeld. 1991. "Profit, Loss and Fate: The Entrepreneurial Ethic and the Practice of Gambling in an Overseas Chinese Community." *Modern China* 17:227–259.

Castles, Lance. 1967. *Religion, Politics and Economic Behaviour in Java: The Kudus Cigarette Industry.* Southeast Asia Studies Cultural Report, no. 15. New Haven: Southeast Asia Studies Program.

Cushman, Jennifer, and Wang Gungwu, eds. 1988. *Changing Ethnic Identities of the Southeast Asian Chinese Since World War II.* Hong Kong: University of Hong Kong Press.

Dewey, Alice. 1962. *Peasant Marketing in Java.* Glencoe, Ill.: Free Press.

Freedman, Maurice. 1979. *The Study of Chinese Society: Essays by Maurice Freedman.* Stanford: Stanford University Press.

Geertz, Clifford. 1956. "Religious Belief and Economic Behaviour in a Javanese Town." *Economic Development and Cultural Change* 4:34–58.

_____. 1963. *Peddlars and Princes: Social Development and Economic Change in Two Indonesian Towns.* Chicago: University of Chicago Press.

Gosling, L.A. Peter. 1983. "Chinese Crop Dealers in Malaysia and Thailand: The Myth of the Merciless Monopsonistic Middleman." In Linda Y.C. Lim and L.A. Peter Gosling, eds., *The Chinese in Southeast Asia*, vol. 1, pp. 131–170. Singapore and Ann Arbor: Maruzen and University of Michigan, Center for South and Southeast Asian Studies.

Hagen, Everett E. 1962. *On the Theory of Social Change: How Economic Growth Begins*. Homewood, Ill.: Dorsey Press.

_____. 1968. *The Economics of Development*. Homewood, Ill.: Richard Irwin.

Hamilton, Gary, ed. 1991. *Business Networks and Economic Development in East and Southeast Asia*. Hong Kong: Centre for Asian Studies, University of Hong Kong.

Harrell, Stevan. 1985. "Why Do the Chinese Work So Hard?" *Modern China* 11:203–226.

_____. 1987. "The Concept of Fate in Chinese Folk Ideology." *Modern China* 13:90–109.

Hicks, George L., ed. 1993. *Chinese Remittances in Southeast Asia, 1910–1940: Japanese Perspectives*. Singapore: Select Books.

_____. 1995. *With Sweat & Abacus: Economic Roles of Southeast Asian Chinese on the Eve of World War II*. Singapore: Select Books.

Higgins, Benjamin. 1989. *The Road Less Travelled*. Canberra: National Centre for Development Studies, Australian National University.

Landa, Janet. 1983. "The Political Economy of the Ethnically Homogeneous Chinese Middleman Group in Southeast Asia." In Linda Y.C. Lim and L.A. Peter Gosling, eds., *The Chinese in Southeast Asia*, vol. 1, pp. 86–116. Singapore and Ann Arbor: Maruzen and University of Michigan, Center for South and Southeast Asian Studies.

Leff, Nathaniel H. 1978. "Industrial Organization and Entrepreneurship in the Developing Countries: The Economic Groups." *Economic Development and Cultural Change* 26:661–675.

Lim, Linda Y.C. 1983. "Chinese Economic Activity in Southeast Asia: An Introductory Review." In Linda Y.C. Lim and L.A. Peter Gosling, eds., *The Chinese in Southeast Asia*, vol. 1, pp. 1–29. Singapore and Ann Arbor: Maruzen and University of Michigan, Center for South and Southeast Asian Studies.

Lim, Linda Y.C., and Gosling, L.A. Peter, eds. 1983. *The Chinese in Southeast Asia*, vol. 1. Singapore and Ann Arbor: Maruzen and University of Michigan, Center for South and Southeast Asian Studies.

Limlingan, Victor S. 1986. *The Overseas Chinese in ASEAN: Business Strategies and Management Practices*. Manila: Vita Development Corporation.

Mackie, J.A.C. 1988. "Changing Economic Roles and Ethnic Identities of the Southeast Asian Chinese: A Comparison of Indonesia and Thailand." In Jennifer Cushman and Wang Gungwu, eds., *Changing Ethnic Identities of the Southeast Asian Chinese Since World War II*, pp. 217–260. Hong Kong: University of Hong Kong Press.

_____. 1992. "Overseas Chinese Entrepreneurship." *Asia-Pacific Economic Literature* 6:41–64.

_____. 1995. "Economic Systems of the Southeast Asian Chinese." In Leo Suryadinata, ed., *The Ethnic Chinese in the ASEAN States*, pp. 33–65. Singapore: Institute of Southeast Asian Studies.

McVey, Ruth, ed. 1992. *Southeast Asian Capitalists*. Ithaca: Cornell Southeast Asian Program Publications Program.

Omohondro, John T. 1981. *Chinese Merchant Families in Iloilo; Commerce and Kin in a Central Philippines City.* Athens: Ohio University Press.

Putnam, Robert. 1993. *Making Democracy Work: Civic Traditions in Modern Italy.* Princeton: Princeton University Press.

Redding, S. Gordon. 1991. *The Spirit of Chinese Capitalism.* Berlin and New York: Walter de Greuter.

Reid, Anthony, ed. 1996a. *Sojourners and Settlers: Histories of Southeast Asia and the Chinese.* Sydney: Allen and Unwin.

_____. 1996b. "Flows and Seepages in the Long-Term Chinese Interaction with Southeast Asia." In Anthony Reid, ed., *Sojourners and Settlers: Histories of Southeast Asia and the Chinese,* pp. 15–50. Sydney: Allen and Unwin.

Riggs, Fred W. 1966. *Thailand: The Modernization of a Bureaucratic Polity.* Honolulu: East-West Center Press.

Rush, James. 1990. *Opium to Java. Revenue Farming and Chinese Enterprise in Colonial Indonesia, 1860–1910.* Ithaca: Cornell University Press.

Skinner, G. William. 1957. *Chinese Society in Thailand: An Analytical History.* Ithaca: Cornell University Press.

_____. 1963. "The Chinese Minority." In Ruth McVey, ed., *Indonesia,* pp. 97–117. New Haven: Human Relations Area Files.

_____. 1996. "Creolized Chinese Societies in Southeast Asia." In Anthony Reid, ed., *Sojourners and Settlers: Histories of Southeast Asia and the Chinese,* pp. 51–93. Sydney: Allen and Unwin.

Somers Heidhues, Mary F. 1974. *Southeast Asia's Chinese Minorities.* Melbourne: Longman.

Suryadinata, Leo, ed. 1989. *The Ethnic Chinese in the ASEAN States.* Singapore: Institute of Southeast Asian Studies.

_____. 1995. *Southeast Asian Chinese and China: The Politico-Economic Dimension.* Singapore: Times Academic Press.

Taku Suyama. 1962. "Pang Societies and the Economy of Chinese Immigrants in Southeast Asia." In K.G. Tregonnning, ed., *Papers in Malayan History,* pp. 193–213. Singapore: University of Singapore.

Wang Gungwu. 1988. "The Study of Chinese Identities in Southeast Asia." In Jennifer Cushman and Wang Gungwu, eds., *Changing Ethnic Identities of the Southeast Asian Chinese Since World War II,* pp. 1–22. Hong Kong: University of Hong Kong Press.

_____. 1992. *Community and Nation: China, Southeast Asia and Australia.* Sydney: Allen & Unwin for the Asian Studies Association of Australia.

_____. 1996. "Sojourning: The Chinese Experience in Southeast Asia." In Anthony Reid, ed., *Sojourners and Settlers: Histories of Southeast Asia and the Chinese,* pp. 1–14. Sydney: Allen and Unwin.

Willmott, David. 1960. *The Chinese of Semarang.* Ithaca: Cornell University Press.

Wong Siu-lun. 1985. "The Chinese Family Firm: A Model." *British Journal of Sociology* 36:58–72.

Wu Yuan-li, 1983. "Chinese Entrepreneurs in Southeast Asia." *American Economic Review* 73:112–117.

Yoshihara Kunio. 1988. *The Rise of Ersatz Capitalism in South-east Asia.* Singapore: Oxford University Press.

five

Constituting
Capitalist Culture

*The Singapore Malay Problem
and Entrepreneurship Reconsidered*

TANIA MURRAY LI

In the popular imagination, Singapore Chinese are quintessential "economic men," natural entrepreneurs predisposed to seek profit at every opportunity.[1] By contrast, Singapore Malays are imagined to be incapable of, or uninterested in, entrepreneurial endeavors. So pervasive are these views that they form part of the unexamined common knowledge of all Singaporeans. Building upon this popular knowledge base, state officials and community leaders concerned with national unity and progress have asserted that the Chinese have a business culture, whereas the Malays, if they are to compete in the national economy, need to acquire one.[2]

Drawing on the same sources of popular knowledge, an earlier generation of academic studies set out to identify the features that could explain Chinese success and Malay failure in business. The list of traits supposedly characteristic of "the Chinese" included achievement motivation, discipline, family solidarity, and a desire to achieve great wealth both in this world and the next. Contrasting traits were said to adhere in "the Malays" (Betts 1975; Tham 1983). These studies were based on a static view of culture as something given, almost genetic, and inherent in ethnic groups that were, in turn, quite unproblematized. The resulting explanations lacked historical depth, disregarded human agency, and flattened and homogenized culture in ways that served to reinforce existing stereotypes and rationalize inequalities.

In this chapter I propose to reexamine the question of Malay entrepreneurship in the context of the cultural, economic, and ideological processes in which it is embedded. In taking this approach, I (like others in this volume) seek to avoid some of the problems of reification and essentialism that beset earlier studies and examine the relationship between culture and capitalism in broader and more dialectical terms. Presenting an account that emphasizes the constitutional aspect of culture and the interpenetration of structure and agency poses problems of organization, since culture and human agency are simultaneously *explanans* and *explanandum*. The potential for circularity is compounded by the need to problematize the ethnic categories Malay and Chinese and examine the generation and deployment of the identities associated with these labels. The labels must be questioned at the same time as they are *used* to refer to actual groups of people associated with specific sets of cultural practices. Moreover, a contrast between Malays and Chinese, which assumes these to be identifiable and internally homogenous social groups, is the more or less explicit subtext of all popular, academic, and official commentary on matters of entrepreneurship in Singapore. Peletz (this volume) helps to situate Malay entrepreneurship in history by providing a useful intra-Malay contrast, but for Singapore, the Chinese-Malay contrast is unavoidable. Some level of ethnic essentialism is already operating in the social world, and it will reappear in this account, although not without scrutiny. In order to expose various layers of meaning and causation in the relationship between culture and capitalism, the chapter is organized in sections, each of which holds some terms constant while others are explored.

In the first part of the chapter I examine the constitution of capitalism in Singapore as a differentiated social and economic form. I draw upon that tradition in anthropological writing that has argued that the interaction of global capitalist processes with local cultural forms produces diversity rather than homogeneity as people become engaged in reinventing traditions, reimagining community, and renewing or reconstituting ethnic boundaries.[3] In this first section, I ask how Malay and Chinese ethnic identities and cultural practices shaped the form of capitalism in Singapore. In the second section, I examine the cultural practices, at the level of household and community, that have been brought to bear upon people's everyday engagements with capitalism and that have been formed and reformed in that context. I focus on the exigencies of urban wage work, which is the predominant economic activity of both Malays and Chinese, posing common dilemmas to which the two groups have responded rather differently. In the third section, I investigate the opportunities and constraints surrounding Malay entrepreneurship, focusing on the moral dimensions of business as these are negotiated among various subgroups within the Malay community. Far from being a static given internal to "Malay culture," the morality of business is the subject of ongoing struggles over meaning and identity in which the situation of Malays as a minority and stereotypes about the Chinese are major factors. Finally, I address the issue of legitimation, seeking to expose those cultural ideas and practices that render capitalism acceptable as a mode of life and a mechanism of resource distribution. Singapore's version of "Asian capitalism" has taken shape on a differentiated social and cultural terrain, and so too have its characteristic modes of legitimation and management.

The Constitution of Singapore Capitalism as a Differentiated Social and Economic Form

A popular view held by Singaporeans about the Singapore Malays is that they form a predominantly indigenous, rural, unchanging, and perennially impoverished population. This view projects contemporary ethnic differences into the past, treating them as aboriginal facts from which much else follows. It provides an origin myth and charter for inequality. Some historical data, primarily from national censuses, are necessary to set the record straight. It will then be possible to reexamine the constitution of ethnic differences and their association with specific economic niches.

The great majority of Malays, like the Chinese, have been thoroughly integrated into the capitalist economy of Singapore since its inception (Siebel 1961:35). Ethnic stereotypes led colonial city planners to assign Malays to fringe areas in which they could continue to farm or fish and to assign the supposedly entrepreneurial Chinese to the city center. Actual employment patterns, as revealed in census data, diverged significantly from those the stereotypes suggest. In 1931 only about 30 percent of Malays were involved in primary production; there were also Chinese in this sector. By 1957 the figure had dropped to 8–10 percent for both groups and is now insignificant. Similarly, between 1957 and 1980, only about 30 percent of Chinese were entrepreneurs. Since the time of their arrival in Singapore, the majority of both groups have been employees, urban wage workers (Singapore Census 1931, 1957, 1980).[4]

The proportion of the contemporary Singapore Malay population that traces its ancestry to the original inhabitants of Singapore and its offshore islands is small. Most of those who currently identify themselves as Malay moved to Singapore from other areas of the Malay-Indonesian world during the twentieth century in search of urban wage work. Their movement can best be understood in terms of rural-urban migration, beginning before and continuing after the creation of political boundaries dividing the region. These twentieth-century Malay migrants worked in Singapore's uniformed services as gardeners and drivers or as government employees in public works and utilities. Many lived in quarters provided by employers; others lived in Malay residential areas, known as *kampong*. These were settlements built to accommodate incoming workers, mostly on a rental basis, and bore little resemblance to the kin-based fishing settlements of the original inhabitants (Li 1989:93–96).

Prior to 1959, with their established niche as employees of Europeans, the majority of Malays were not generally worse off economically than the majority of the Chinese. In 1953–1954, a social survey noted the discrepancy between favorable Malay economic performance and the already established popular image of Malays as economically backward (Goh 1958:100). True, the Malay elite was small: Only 5 percent of Malays, compared to 16 percent of Chinese, had household incomes of over $400 per month (Goh 1958:19). For the remainder of the population, however, the Malay "average household income is, in fact, larger than that of the immigrant Chinese, who are supposed to be the most successful and enterprising section of Malaya's population" (Goh 1958:100). Although the image of Malay poverty has long been entrenched, and in some parts of the Malay world it accurately reflects economic realities, in Singapore, at least, the relative poverty of Malays is a recent phenomenon.

The pre-1959 elite in Singapore, with per capita incomes of more than $400 per year, was made up of entrepreneurs and professionals. The professional elite was largely restricted to the small group of local-born Chinese, or *peranakan,* who were early settlers in Malaysia and Singapore and who had sent their children to English schools (Roff 1967:110; Nagata 1979:28). Opportunities for Malays and the majority of Chinese to obtain an English education were limited (Roff 1967:28). The general educational standards in the Chinese and Malay vernacular schools were equally low, and the vast majority of Malay and Chinese children before World War II received at best a primary education and went into manual jobs (Turnbull 1977:146).

Constituting Differences in Situ

Although Malays and Chinese were both, in a sense, migrants to Singapore, their patterns of migration were very different. A key feature of Malay migration to Singapore was its individualistic nature. With the exception of some Javanese bonded laborers, few of the migrants to Singapore worked for other Malays. They migrated as individuals, paid off any debts they had incurred for their passage, and set about finding work for themselves. There were few Malay businesses large enough to employ migrant kin. At most, incoming workers expected that kin, neighbors, or other contacts would help them find jobs. Economic independence from kin was often preferred by the migrants themselves: It was the relative freedom and anonymity of the city and the possibility of supporting themselves as independent wage earners that attracted many individuals to Singapore. This was as true for women, often fleeing unhappy marriages and village gossip, as it was for men. Both men and women sought to create their own lives free from some of the constraints of kinship and community in rural settings. Thus in terms of their occupational pattern, Malays were, both by necessity and by choice, thoroughly integrated into multiethnic Singapore, working for non-Malays (Li 1989:93–96).

In contrast, many Chinese migrants came to Singapore under large-scale indenture movements, especially in the late nineteenth century. Others were recruited "voluntarily" but became bound by debts to a labor recruiter, ship captain, or lodging-house keeper in Singapore. The migrant then became a member of a *kongsi,* or group of workers under a contractor. The contractor acted as an intermediary between the Chinese workers and European employers and was able to retain his control in part because constraints of language prevented direct employment (State of Singapore 1960:4).

Other Chinese migrants joined kin or quasi-kin, covillagers, or codialect speakers and worked in their businesses under their paternalistic authority. The migrant's best prospect for mobility lay in starting a business of his own, but this he could not do alone, since particular trades were under the protection of Chinese secret societies and subgroup monopolies. Even as an entrepreneur, the Chinese migrant was necessarily integrated into an entirely Chinese world, which both provided opportunities and engendered abuses (Freedman 1979:65, 73).

It was the combination of Chinese entrepreneurship and the system of labor contracting that placed whole sectors of the economy under the control of particular groups of Chinese and totally excluded non-Chinese. The different economic niches occupied by the two groups thus resulted from a combination of the circumstances of migration and the innovations made by each group in situ as it brought its respective cultural resources to bear upon the new situation taking shape in Singapore.

The Structuring of Economic Opportunities

Two forms of structuring concern us here. First, an emerging income gap between Malays and Chinese led to the association of the two groups not only with different economic niches but with unequal positions in the national order. Second, the cultural and economic dimensions of the ethnic divide—as it relates to entrepreneurship, employment, and negative stereotyping—deepened. In both cases, the structuring has to be seen as a complex outcome of economic and cultural processes in which people contributed to the making of their world at the same time as they were constrained by sets of prestructured opportunities and limitations.

During the period since 1959, a significant income gap has opened up between the Malay and Chinese communities. By 1990, the average Chinese household income was S$3,213, 43 percent higher than the Malay average of S$2,246 (Singapore Census 1990:vol. 2, 7). Even if we treat the income data in the same way as Goh (1958) and exclude the top 17 percent of Chinese and 5 percent of Malays who earned over S$5,000, the Malay median household income was 20 percent less than that for Chinese (Singapore Census 1990:vol. 2, 40). As noted earlier, this gap has not been a permanent feature of the ethnic order in Singapore.

The income gap between Malays and Chinese can be explained by a set of factors, some global and structural in nature and others more clearly generated locally. Malays lost their privileged position in the uniformed services when they were replaced by Chinese after independence. In the 1970s global shifts in power resulted in the closure of British bases, and Malays again lost jobs. At the level of the household, a combination of local and global factors affected the ratio of income earners to dependants. Census data show that Chinese families had the advantage of multiple wage earners throughout the 1960s and 1970s; young women were employed in the Chinese-speaking trade, manufacturing, and service sectors (Cheng 1980:31). It was not until the late 1970s that mass employment opportunities became available to Malay women in the multinational manufacturing sector.[5] The Malay response to these new opportunities was very quick, and by 1980 the female employment rate of the two groups had reached par (Li 1989:104). In the interim, however, a generation of Chinese households had benefited from significantly higher incomes, lower fertility, and lower dependency ratios related to female employment. Education is a third factor in the disparity between Malay and Chinese incomes. By 1990, 16 percent of Chinese adults, compared to 5 percent of Malays, had upper-secondary, technical, or university qualifications that equipped them for jobs in the growth areas of high technology, finance, and communication (Singapore Census 1990:vol. 3, 12). But the majority of Chinese and the majority of Malays have at best completed a primary education and encounter similar problems in obtaining well-paid jobs.

Specifically in relation to the growing income gap between Malays and Chinese in the post-1959 period, differential participation of the two groups in entrepreneurial activities *is* a significant factor. The relative participation rates of the two groups have remained quite constant: Only 4–7 percent of Malay males in the workforce between 1957 and 1990 were either employers or own account workers; the Chinese participation rate in these two categories was in the range of 22–28 percent (Li 1989; Census 1990:vol. 2, 70).[6] Yet as noted earlier, there was no significant income gap prior to 1959.

The key change that occurred in the post-1959 period was the rate of return to entrepreneurship. In Goh's survey of 1953, "own account workers" earned only a few dollars more than employees. For most entrepreneurs (the survey excluded the top 4 percent of income earners), small-scale business did not provide higher incomes (Goh 1958:100). By 1980, the returns for entrepreneurship were significantly higher than those to be gained from employment. This was especially significant for those with a poor education; their prospects for advancement as employees remain limited. In 1980 self-employed men with no education had an average income 36 percent higher than employees with the same education (Li 1989:107). Thus during the 1970s and 1980s, locally oriented small-business activity permitted some Chinese workers to overcome the limitations of their education and achieve higher incomes, whereas Malay incomes stagnated.

Besides the income advantages enjoyed by Chinese entrepreneurs, the involvement of Chinese in small business continues to affect the overall shape of the Singapore economy and the distribution of opportunities for employment. The small-business sector of the Singapore economy grew by 100 percent during the 1970s (*Yearbook of Labour Statistics* 1970, 1980), and it continues to provide a major source of employment. Recruitment of workers is based on family ties, networks, and language affiliation (aspects of the *guanxi* described by Hamilton, this volume) and excludes Malays from this major sector of the economy.

Discrimination based on ethnic stereotypes is a general factor hindering Malay advancement through employment. Whereas the British apparently valued the characteristics of honesty and integrity they ascribed to Malays, among the Chinese the assessment of the Malay population is overwhelmingly negative. There is a widespread conviction among Singapore Chinese that Malays are lazy or, more charitably, that they are interested in spiritual, artistic, or social pursuits but relatively uninterested in material gain (Leong 1978). Malay nonparticipation in entrepreneurship is taken as central proof of this assessment. Although three in four Chinese men are employees, not entrepreneurs, entrepreneurship serves in popular consciousness as an ethnic marker distinguishing Chinese from Malays. Malay noninvolvement supports the view that Malays are indolent and thus deserve their place in the lower strata of Singapore society (cf. Alatas 1977). By cementing ethnic boundaries and negative stereotypes, differential Malay and Chinese participation in entrepreneurship has significant ideological effects. That is, it serves to explain and justify inequalities.

The climate of discrimination forces Malay would-be entrepreneurs to operate in a restricted niche. There are special opportunities for Malays to service their own people in the beauty trades, pilgrim brokerage, the publication of Malay and Muslim texts, and food production. But the possibilities for expansion into more general markets are limited. Before the expansion of government-run training facilities in the 1970s, Malays had little access to the skilled trades requiring apprenticeship in Chinese-owned establishments. Malays had something of a niche in the electrical trades, where training was provided by a major European company, but they were excluded from the building, plumbing, and vehicle-mechanics trades dominated by small Chinese companies (Lim 1960). Malay subcontractors in the ship-building, heavy-engineering, and building-maintenance lines claim to gain contracts mainly from expatriate managers, seldom from local Chinese businesses (Li 1989:139–141).

Malays involved in retail have differing opinions of the possibilities of doing business with the Chinese. Some complain of high prices from Chinese wholesalers; others say wholesalers are primarily interested in regularizing the relationship regardless of race. Some Malay retailers claim that their Chinese competitors cheat on weights and measures to gain clients, putting Malays out of business unless they are willing to "do business in the same way as other races." The assumption that Chinese are involved in cheating makes many Malays reluctant to engage in business partnerships with them. Language is a further constraint, and the lack of familiarity of Malays and Chinese in dealing with each other makes Malay retailers pessimistic about the prospect of gaining Chinese customers.

The perception that Chinese profit through trickery while Malays are constrained by moral and religious scruples is a fundamental part of the ethnic self-image of Malay businessmen. They believe that this difference in morality, which they attribute to ethnicity, gives their Chinese competitors an advantage over them. In contrast, some Malays claim to obtain customers, including Chinese, precisely because of their reputation for honest dealing. For example, an electrical contractor claimed to be recommended to customers by the utilities board

> because they know we think of our name, our mother's and father's name, and God. But after fifty years I am still not rich, unlike some Chinese after one or two years. They are brave, they take on a job beyond their means, and if they fail they go bankrupt, but if they pull through by borrowing here and there, they get very rich. We Malays guard our name first, but we never get so rich.

The practical and supposed moral constraints of doing business with the Chinese force the majority of Malay entrepreneurs to focus on the Malay market. The picture of Malay virtue and Chinese vice becomes more ambivalent, however, as Malay entrepreneurs experience tensions in dealing with their own community. These tensions will be discussed further on.

Many of the structural problems currently faced by first-time entrepreneurs are common to both Malays and Chinese. Urban renewal and government regulations have removed the shelter provided by low-overhead backyard businesses, which formerly enabled small entrepreneurs to accumulate capital and experience. Public-housing flats, owned by the majority of the population, cannot be used as collateral. More Chinese (12%) than Malays (2%) have the advantage of owning private housing (Singapore Census 1990:vol. 3). Their key advantage, however, lies in the *guanxi* networks through which some Chinese are able to secure loans without collateral (Lau 1974:22). Those already well positioned economically and socially have been able to prosper. However, most Malays and the majority of Chinese are not involved in business activities or their attendant social circles.

Whereas this section has emphasized the structuring of the Singapore economy along ethnic lines and the emergent association of Malay ethnicity with lower incomes, it has also noted factors such as poor education and limited opportunities for well-paid employment that affect all Singaporeans. Most Malays and Chinese encounter modern capitalism not as entrepreneurs but as wage workers at lower economic levels. The sets of cultural resources that they bring to bear on their position as wage workers struggling to survive economically and to lead satisfying lives in the context of family and community form the focus of the next section.

Constituting Family and Community Relations in a Capitalist Context

Singapore is a highly commercialized economy in which wages and cash purchases are at the center of daily survival. This section is an examination of the terms upon which relations of family and community are renegotiated in response to market demands, particularly the reliance on wages. Malays and Chinese face similar dilemmas in securing their daily survival and long-term security in a wage-based economy. However, drawing upon rather different sets of cultural ideas and working from their specific locations in the material and ethnic order, they have produced quite distinct practices.

Producing Family Relations

In Singapore, as in other highly commercialized urban centers, every item purchased or service rendered has a known market price. For wage workers, their contribution to the household is immediately obvious, as they hand over a portion of their pay to meet consumption needs. But even women and children who do unpaid work in the home or family business are easily able to calculate the value of their contributions to the household in terms of the wages that they have forgone. This contrasts with situations where families consume what they produce or where household members contribute labor in the productive and reproductive domains without thinking in terms of the individualized cash value of their contribution. On the expenditure side, parents can calculate quite precisely the monetary costs of the education and upbringing of children. Yet parents have few economic mechanisms for securing from their children a portion of their wages. As adult wage workers, their children receive their pay directly as a reward for their own individualized labor and not as an outcome of family investments entailing reciprocal obligations.

Establishing that the *potential* exists for Singapore families, both Malay and Chinese, to calculate the costs and benefits of family engagements does not mean that these calculations will necessarily be made. Even if they are made, this need not imply that they are invested with the same meaning or that they have the same effects. Malays and Chinese differ significantly in their handling of these structural conditions.

The cultural repertoire produced by Singapore Malays to handle the economic exigencies imposed by the market gives major emphasis to the notion of the gift. Women stress that they perform labor services at home and forgo personal income and its corresponding autonomy out of love for their families. Young adults who give money from their wages to their mother stress that they are making gifts from the heart, out of love and concern. The claim that transactions of cash and unpaid labor within the household are gifts is predicated on and takes its meaning from the commoditized context in which these transactions take place. When every item and service has a known price, the gift aspect is enhanced if goods and services are transferred free of charge. More specifically, the claim that cash and unpaid labor are gifts depends on an assertion of individualized claims to labor. It is only possible to make a gift if the item given truly belongs to you and not to your family by virtue of corporate claims.

There are many precedents in the Malay world for an emphasis on individual autonomy and a view of the household as a unit in which emotional bonds rather than corporate property provide the point of coherence.[7] The existing Malay cultural repertoire provides a ready idiom for handling the individualization of labor promoted by the wage form. Gifts are powerful vehicles for "getting and keeping a lasting hold over someone," as Bourdieu has demonstrated (1977:191). It should not therefore surprise us that the notion of the gift becomes especially prominent in a context where the individualizing potential of the wage makes the long-term bonds necessary for the reproduction of households especially hard to maintain.[8] But in stressing the gift element in economic transactions with close kin, Malays are not only responding to exigencies. They are also creating and indeed insisting on forms of interpersonal commitment that they find morally appropriate and personally satisfying.

Part of the satisfaction that Malays derive from their family relationships stems from the comparisons they make between themselves and the Chinese, who have handled the exigencies of urban wage work quite differently. Chinese households in Singapore have been engaged in a renewal or re-creation of family-based patriarchalism, in which corporate family claims over the labor power and wages of working children, especially daughters, are strongly asserted. The stress is not on gifts but on duties and, most significant, the repayment of debts for the (commoditized) costs of upbringing (Li 1989:150–158; Salaff and Wong 1976; Salaff 1981; Chung et al. 1981; Hassan 1977). Cultural idioms promoting filial piety are readily available in the Chinese repertoire (see Hamilton and Weller, this volume). In rural China, the emphasis was on the obligation of sons who would inherit shares of the family property. In Singapore, it is especially girls who are expected to hand over a large proportion of their paychecks. Girls are supposed to make short-run returns on parental investment in their upbringing; sons are expected to advance family fame and fortune over the long term. Sons are nominally expected to care for parents in old age, although as noted earlier, there are few means to hold children to these obligations after they have attained independence. In fact, it is often to daughters that Chinese parents turn for support in old age. At this point, the idiom mediating the relationship between parent and child shifts to one of emotional bonds rather than obligations. Chinese parents, like Malays, find an appeal to emotion to be more powerful than a stress on obligations when their economic leverage is limited (Li 1989:154–158). Malays, however, seem to be more successful at creating emotional bonds that endure. Chinese parents are more often abandoned in old age homes than their Malay counterparts (*ST* March 23, 1981).

The different modes in which Malays and Chinese create family bonds have an impact on the possibility for entrepreneurship. Chinese families more readily pool incomes to meet family goals, submit to patriarchal authority, and contribute long hours of unpaid labor to family enterprises viewed as corporate household concerns (see Hamilton and Mackie, this volume). Malays do not expect any family member, spouse or child, to work unpaid or pool capital for a family business. They recognize that all individuals have the right to their own income and labor, and they tolerate the reluctance of children, especially sons, to work under paternal authority. When entrepreneurs do employ family labor, they endeavor to pay market rates or to compensate with significant gifts that keep their debts of gratitude within bounds. The result is that Malays cannot rely on the nuclear family as a business resource. Any Singaporean knows that Malay food stalls sell out early or are closed even at peak times because of owner exhaustion, whereas Chinese stalls run at all hours, not counting family labor as part of the balance sheet.[9]

Communities: Produced and Imposed

Constructions of community beyond the household likewise reflect creative cultural modes of managing the exigencies of Singapore life. The massive urban renewal programs since the 1960s have eradicated the older, named spaces upon which some Chinese and Malays were able to base a sense of physical community. But even the older kampongs and shophouses included rental units for a shifting population of urban wage workers and new migrants. From early times, then, a sense of community had to be constructed from interpersonal relationships, since it was not a given outcome of spatial arrangements. Chinese, as noted earlier, were largely absorbed into a set of economic relationships based on family, clan, and dialect affiliations that structured their social world. Malays, by contrast, worked for non-Malays and had few direct economic linkages among themselves. This situation is in marked contrast to rural Malay settings, where cooperation among kin and neighbors in rice production has been an important focus of community economic and ritual life (Wong 1987; Peletz 1988).

In the context of increased economic autonomy from one another, the creation of a sense of community among Malays in Singapore has, rather like the household relations discussed earlier, depended on moral commitments and a willingness to make personal investments. A relationship with another person is formed by giving a little of the self. This includes offering assistance and support in crises and attending weddings and funerals. There is little prospect or intention of turning such social contacts to economic advantage. The fact that Malays do not depend on kin, neighbors, or friends and acquaintances for their wages enhances the sense that exchanges of time, goodwill, and material assistance are based on the voluntary spirit of the gift. The debts created are of a generalized sort: People who have led good lives and been active in creating and sustaining relationships with others can expect to gain in public esteem. The evidence is that many people voluntarily attend the weddings of these individuals' children and their eventual funerals. Failure to create and sustain social relations can arise from two sources: excess sociability, which increases exposure to gossip, snubs, and unfulfillable obligations; and exclusiveness, associated with pride when individuals or families act as if they are autonomous from the community.

As well as being developed in interpersonal exchanges, community is, at another level, assumed to exist among Malays in Singapore by virtue of their shared ethnic identity. Non-Malays, as noted earlier, are inclined to impute to Malays a common set of (generally negative) characteristics and predilections. But Malay identity is not only constructed and imposed by others. Malays positively assert a sense of community at the national level, which includes all Malays as part of a single social world. The main external markers of this identity are religion, language, dress, and food. The ethical and moral dimensions associated with Malay identity are the subject of considerable ambivalence and intracommunity variation. There is no monolithic "Singapore Malay culture" but rather a repertoire of identities, practices, and meanings. Malay entrepreneurs draw upon this repertoire as they negotiate the politics and practicalities of business ventures in Singapore. Their dilemmas bring into relief some of the issues faced by the Malay population generally as it seeks to define a sense of community in modern, Chinese-dominated Singapore.

Moral Dilemmas of Malay Entrepreneurship

The central dilemma of Malay entrepreneurship focuses on the extent to which it is possible, desirable, or morally acceptable to conduct profit-oriented business operations among kin, neighbors, and other members of the Malay social world. It is an issue upon which there are varied opinions. A range of arguments and practical strategies have emerged within the Malay community that are loosely associated with gender and class positions. An exploration of these differences highlights the element of cultural creativity and agency that people bring to bear in their engagements with capitalism, this time not as employees but as entrepreneurs.

The moral dilemmas and tensions surrounding Malay entrepreneurship have been noted in numerous other settings. In rural Malaysia, entrepreneurs are described as the subject of hostility (Wilder 1982:112) and bemusement because of their apparent obsession with money and profit (Banks 1983:119). The resulting reluctance to go into business can be stated in positive terms: Malays place such a high value on kin and community relationships that they try to keep them free from calculation and insulate them from naked commercial transactions (McKinley 1975:35; Carsten 1989; Peletz, this volume).[10] Judith Nagata assesses the moral dimension more negatively, at least from the viewpoint of practicalities and profit. Writing about urban Penang, she notes that Malay traders become "entangled in personal and social obligations" to customers and are forced to overextend themselves in credit. Malays exacerbate their difficulties by doing business within the area of residence where they "often fail to observe the cardinal rules of business in separating commercial from private relationships" (1979:112).

Nagata draws a contrast between Malay retailers and their Chinese competitors, who have the advantage of being impervious to "local social custom" (1979:113). In the context of this volume, such a contrast becomes a puzzle. The Chinese in her study are, presumably, impervious to the demands of their Malay customers but fully embedded in *guanxi* relations with fellow Chinese who provide their sources of capital. Among Chinese, according to Hamilton (this volume), it is precisely the personalization of commercial relationships that ensures business success. This must either mean that Chinese have no scruples about profiting from close kin and associates or that they are able to clearly delineate sets of people to whom different sorts of morality apply. Hamilton notes that not all Chinese are *guanxi* to each other: One's partners are a specific and delimited group, and only they receive special treatment. Hamilton says little about the moral tenor of this relationship, whether, for example, there is a tension between the social and business aspects of the relationship or the two are in complete harmony. Finer-grained ethnographic study would be needed to reveal this. Business transactions with fellow Chinese who are not in *guanxi* partnerships are, according to Hamilton's account, socially neutral, creating no reciprocal obligations and apparently no ambivalence. For Malay entrepreneurs, it is more difficult to delimit distinct categories of fellow Malays to whom different moralities apply, and there are fewer occasions in which the rules of pure commerce are appropriate.

The position of Malays as a minority ethnic group in Singapore exaggerates the moral burden born by entrepreneurs when they engage in business transactions within the Malay community. As noted earlier, a sense of community among Malays must be constructed out of personal engagements, since it does not form "naturally" from economic relations or neighborhood ties. As a result, the relationship between individual and community is always potentially a source of tension, readily exacerbated by entrepreneurial activities. To this problem is added the burden of an imposed or assumed sense of community as an ethnic group: In the context of Chinese domination, Malays are forced to recognize a bond with all fellow Malays, whether or not they are personally known to each other. With this bond come some moral commitments.

When Malays claim the qualities of consideration and humanity in relations with others to be part of the definition of Malayness, in contrast to the supposed Chinese characteristic of uncaring, calculated profit seeking, they impose upon themselves a greater level of ethical constraint. An example is provided by a Malay woman factory worker: "I pay $100 to the Malay lady who looks after my child while I'm at work. She would charge $200–300 for a Chinese child, but Malays are considerate, and she knows I don't earn much. If I earned more I could give her more." The imputation of a shared moral code, generalized on an ethnic basis, constrains the Malay baby-sitter from operating as a business concern and attempting to obtain maximum profit by charging market rates or from accepting only Chinese children who can afford to pay more. If she did this she would be accused of greed and she would become socially isolated from her neighbors.

Small-Scale Business Among Lower-Income Women

The assumed social, moral, and ethnic bond that links all Malays and that is held to characterize them *as* Malays makes it difficult for them, especially women working out of their own homes, to conduct pure business transactions within their own community. Petty traders in low-income neighborhoods sell mostly to friends and kin. These traders, who are mostly women, are most vulnerable to slights and alienation from their personally constructed communities as a result of their entrepreneurial activities. A female petty trader gave this account: "I was selling curry puffs and fried bananas from my house, then I got 'condemned,' black magic, so I can't walk. The neighbors did it because I was doing well and they hate to see people better off. They don't see your hard work, only your money."

In this case neighbors denied envy and asserted that the trader was quite healthy. They attributed her unpopularity to her difficult personality. In addition, she had apparently overcharged for goods she had bought in Thailand for resale in Singapore. The criticism of overcharging is made not because profit is illegitimate in principle but because it shows bad faith and insensitivity in interpersonal relations. When selling to friends and neighbors, the trader should not act as if an anonymous deal is being made for as much profit as possible.

Entrepreneurs adopt various strategies to minimize the tensions engendered by their business activities. These include minimizing self-serving motivations and claiming that business is done in order to help others, almost as a public service: "They begged me to start selling noodles because they like my cooking." The extent of business activity may be downplayed by claims that it is only done for fun, as a hobby, part time, or by claims that there are no profits, only a little pocket money for the children. Another option is to avoid setting a price at all. The recipient of the goods or services should voluntarily give a sum appropriate to the time and effort expended by the entrepreneur. This strategy shifts the onus of handling the economic element of the transaction onto the other party and means that the entrepreneur cannot be accused of greed or lack of consideration in charging high prices. The result may be dissatisfaction and resentment. If one side is too calculating or the other side insufficiently generous, the social relationship between the parties can cool. For example, "My mother hires another person's car every morning to take food and utensils down to her food stall. Once she asked the driver to detour to collect something, and the owner charged extra. That caused a cooling of relations with the owner. My mother still uses the car but relations are strained because she feels the owner is calculating and stingy." In this case, the key factors in judging the appropriate price are the state of the social relationship between the parties and the interest either party has in sustaining that relationship.

The risk of strains and tensions when business is done between parties who are neighbors or who are in a close personal relationship prompts some entrepreneurs to make trading at a social and physical distance their main strategy. A woman involved in petty retail stated: "I don't sell my things here in the *kampong*. I have a lot of friends, especially other races, and I sell to them. Round here there are too many stories." Other traders prefer to do business with Malays but avoid their own neighborhood.

Although there are advantages in trading at a social distance, there are also distinct advantages to carrying out entrepreneurial activities such as petty personalized retail among close kin, friends, and neighbors. The existence of a close social relationship between the two parties imposes constraints on both of them. The seller is prevented from aggressively seeking maximum profit, and the purchaser feels under obligation to be generous by purchasing the goods proffered. The seller plays a precarious game: The social relationship will ensure a sale, but if taken too far, too often, or incorrectly played, the social relationship itself could be at risk as the purchaser comes to feel resentful at being forced into an unwanted deal. A shared vision of community enables the transaction to take place, but it is not a vision free from tension and ambivalence.

A development of petty personalized retail is the "party" system, which is extremely successful in Singapore but occurs exclusively among Malays. The party hostess invites friends, relatives, and neighbors to her house, where she provides food and displays the goods she has obtained from an agent. She is given a 10 percent commission on the sales, which often amounts to S$400–$500 for her day's work. The guests feel obliged to make a purchase even if it is the smallest token item, since they accepted the invitation and partook of the food provided. Chinese neighbors or friends are sometimes invited to these parties, but they do not seem to feel the same obligation to buy; if the goods do not interest them, they leave with excuses.

Although the hostess is guaranteed a good profit, there are costs and risks. She should ensure there are enough low-cost items for those who attend out of goodwill but cannot afford to buy much. She cannot hold parties too often, or her guests may become reluctant. She is obliged to attend in turn all the parties held by her guests, and she should attempt to make purchases of equivalent value. To preserve social credit and retain social relations that are valued in themselves and that can be used again in the future, a delicate balance must be maintained. Business profit can be pursued, and everyone knows that this is the real basis of the activity; but it cannot be pursued undisguised or to its fullest potential limits. These social relationships, perhaps like Chinese *guanxi* ties, must remain primarily social, suppressing the economic component or at least rendering it secondary.

Formal Enterprises and Alternative Visions of Community

Class, as it intersects with gender, is the main factor distinguishing the more established entrepreneurs from those discussed earlier. In poorer families, men tend to be wage workers and women undertake petty retail as a way to stretch the household budget and gain some personal cash. This type of entrepreneurship is not expected to provide a major source of livelihood or upward mobility. The few men who are involved in petty trade are subject to the same social constraints as the women. Among more wealthy Malay families, business activities are more likely to be pursued in premises separate from the home and to be the full-time activities of men. Women are not much involved as unpaid helpers, for the reasons discussed earlier. There are only a few established full-time women entrepreneurs.

Some Malays operating formally constituted businesses in premises separate from their own homes experience social tensions similar to those described previously. Competition from another entrepreneur tends to be seen as motivated by envy and spite. In the words of one retailer, "If you have two Malay shops side by side, selling the same product, but one has more customers because he is more friendly, the other will be envious and upset; so he will lower his prices to sell at a loss, until both shops are bankrupt, but he will feel satisfied." Another trader chose to locate his shop far away from areas of intensive Malay settlement because, he said, "there are too many Malays there, they get jealous and try to put a curse on you, or say you are mean and spread stories about you."

Although established traders may prefer to do business at a social distance, the possibility of doing this is constrained by the peculiar configuration of ethnic relations in Singapore. It was noted earlier that the opportunities for Malays to do business with the Chinese are restricted by mutual unfamiliarity, the specialized nature of some foods and other products, and discrimination. This situation forces Malays to look toward their own community for a market. In negotiating the meaning to be given to the notion of "their own community" and in defining the ways that an individual can relate to that community, more established entrepreneurs call upon the expanded range of images and possibilities available to them as citizens of contemporary, multiethnic Singapore.

Class, Islam, ethnicity, and "progress" provide alternative discourses and practices that shape cultural constructions of community for Malay entrepreneurs. By virtue of their class position, established entrepreneurs are removed from the poor neighborhoods, where the pressures to develop a sense of community out of sociability are most intense. With their privatized housing arrangements, men and women in middle- and upper-income apartment blocks pursue neighborhood contacts on the basis of more formal invitations to social or religious occasions and visits prearranged by phone call. Children's activities are closely monitored so that they can concentrate on studies. Yet despite the stress on privacy and the desire to avoid neighborhood gossip and tensions, even these Malays must deal with the requirement to create community out of personal ties.

Islam is frequently cited by established entrepreneurs as legitimation for business activities that fly in face of social pressures. They criticize uneducated Malays for their mistaken belief that Islam constrains business. They note that Islam permits and encourages honest trade, enjoining people to seek wealth so long as they meet their responsibilities for charitable donations. Gladney (this volume) notes a similar rationale among Chinese Muslims. Malay entrepreneurs are especially prominent in community religious activities. Islam also provides entrepreneurs and other professionals with a vehicle through which they can fulfill Malay requirements for sociability but confine them to religiously prescribed contexts. In their privatized neighborhoods, they organize and participate in the groups that meet in the evenings for Koranic study and chanting, but they do not casually visit at other times of the day. Note too that the heightened significance of Islam in daily patterns of interaction in upper-income neighborhoods has reduced the extent of socializing with Chinese and Indian neighbors, with whom common class position might otherwise encourage closer ties.

Ethnicity is a domain of discourse marked by much ambivalence. Malays refer to Chinese discrimination when explaining business failure, and they make the contrast, noted earlier, between Malay virtue and Chinese vice in business ethics. But they also regard the Chinese favorably when commenting on the negative aspects of Malay community life. Chinese are said to support their own, whereas Malays are unwilling to trust or support a Malay entrepreneur, perhaps out of jealousy. Chinese are straightforward, business is business, whereas Malays let their emotions become involved. Though these observations are no doubt stereotypic, the availability of an alternative, Chinese model of entrepreneurial behavior expands the repertoire available to Malay entrepreneurs seeking to renegotiate an identity and set of practices specific to their multiethnic context.

The overwhelming numerical presence of the Chinese defuses the intensity of interaction among Malays—a positive feature noted by the trader cited earlier who seeks to do business in areas where there are some Malays but not too many. His strategy alleviates the problems that he perceives to be generated from within the Malay community. However, he still needs to do business with Malays and to acknowledge some of the obligations imposed by belonging to a Malay community because the ascribed ethnic boundaries that separate him from potential Chinese customers remain in place. In the context of Chinese and Malay shared apartment blocks, workplaces, and class positions, the content of Malayness and Chineseness have been reshaped in ways that reduce some differences but reinforce others, as ethnic boundaries are reconstituted on shifting grounds.

The discourse of progress, modernity, and competition promoted by the Singapore state, the Malay leadership, and, increasingly, by the Malay government in Malaysia provides yet another framework within which to negotiate Malay identity. Singapore and Malaysia share in the new sense of Asian self-confidence as the region experiences an economic boom. Official rhetoric in both countries continuously stresses the need to retain a competitive edge and enjoins people to work harder, seeking out new opportunities. "Asian values" such as diligence, self-reliance, and discipline are touted as the keys to success for the individual and for the nation. Malays in particular are enjoined to be more pragmatic and compete with other races in all sectors of the economy, including business, in order to achieve progress as individuals, as a community, and as contributors to national growth and prosperity.[11] For entrepreneurs who are successful in asserting an identity that relates to this public discourse, pursuing business opportunities can be construed not as selfish ambition but as helping to fulfil the vision of a model, modern Malay community (see *ST* October 6, 1990).

The precise ways in which the new discourse on modernity and Asian values being generated by the state will interact with cultural and ethnic constructions generated in the context of daily life in the homes and workplaces of Malay and Chinese Singaporeans is yet to be seen. Although the discourse of modernity assumes a meritocratic openness, the realities of life for many Singaporeans, Malay and Chinese, indicate that this openness is illusory. Class and ethnic barriers to individual mobility remain entrenched.

The direct effect of culturally constructed and ethnically imposed constraints on Malay entrepreneurship has been that potential avenues of economic mobility are closed off. With low incomes, most Malays are confined to the socially intense neighborhoods where the difficulties of advancement through either education or business activities are most severe. By failing to engage in business, Malays reinforce the Chinese image of them as lazy, incapable, and uninterested in economic gain. This, in turn, contributes to discrimination by Chinese against Malays in employment.

For the Malays, the Chinese represent a powerfully constraining force both culturally and economically. Without the Chinese reputation for entrepreneurship, Malays would not have acquired a reputation for being nonentrepreneurial. Nor would their lack of participation in business have put them at a disadvantage as an ethnic group in the competitive framework of the national economy. The negative images that Chinese produce about Malays have consequences for the lives of the latter on a daily basis. Although, as noted, Malay identity is constructed from a repertoire of shifting terms rather than being imposed monolithically, the politics of identity cannot be reduced to questions of choice. Individually and collectively, Malays negotiate issues of identity within a field of power in which they are materially and numerically weak and in which their capacity to counter the representations produced by others about them is limited.

The "Malay Problem" and the Legitimation of Inequality in Singapore

Over the decades since independence, politicians, academics, the media, Malay community leaders, and the Malay and Chinese public have pondered the cause of "the Malay problem" and have been remarkably consistent in their findings: Malays are less hardworking and ambitious than Chinese and are imbued with cultural and spiritual motivations that equip them poorly for the competitive context of Singapore. Malay lack of involvement in entrepreneurship is taken to be a prime example of this problem.[12] Here, I want to examine the political and ideological consequences of this assessment of "the Malay problem" and its role in legitimizing a particular form of Asian capitalism.

I have already taken issue with the use of static ethnic images as explanations for cultural and economic processes that have complex histories. I have also pointed out that statistics support the image on one count but not on the other two: Malays are definitely much less involved in business than

Chinese, but the majority of Chinese (about 75%) are, like the Malays, employees, not businesspeople. Also, Malays did not fall behind the Chinese economically until the 1960s. Whereas the image of the backward Malay has a long history, the Malay economic "problem" in Singapore is actually a recent creation.

Once Malays did in fact fall behind economically, they became associated with a set of other social problems such as poor educational performance (PR May 30, 1992), large family size, family breakdown, delinquency, and drug addiction (PR July 18, 1992). These problems, which are to a great extent common to all those at lower income levels, affect Malays disproportionately because more of them have low incomes. Yet they appear to be Malay problems because the statistics are always reported on an ethnic basis. The tyranny of race in official statistics and analyses is seldom queried,[13] since it accords with popular perceptions about the centrality of race as an organizing feature of Singapore's social and economic life. The ethnic lens renders invisible many commonalities of experience across ethnic boundaries. Although it was shown earlier that Malays and Chinese handle the exigencies of Singapore life in rather different ways, their predicaments and many of their strategies have much in common. Increasingly, the school system, media, and popular culture provide potential common ground, but ethnic boundaries remain entrenched.

In Singapore, ethnicity has played a key ideological role in explaining the discrepancy between the promise of an open, meritocratic society and the uneven and sometimes disappointing results of capitalist development. When present social and economic conditions are projected back into the distant past and traced to pregiven, supposedly unchanging cultural practices that inhere in bounded ethnic groups, the division of rewards in society is made to appear inevitable, naturally occurring, and therefore just. These ideas were not invented and imposed by the state but form a hegemonic system pervading popular consciousness and are regenerated daily in the course of everyday interactions.[14] The ideological effects of the ethnic lens have been twofold. The systematic inequalities affecting all lower-income Singaporeans have been rendered less visible, and efforts to deal with inequality have been focused on the need for cultural change within ethnic groups.

Few governments are entirely comfortable with capitalism, recognizing the potential political hazards of systematic inequalities. But the Singapore government since independence has steadfastly promoted the central myth that individual enterprise, hard work, and self-discipline are the keys to success in a fundamentally open and meritocratic society (ST February 3, 1991). Factors in the educational system that disadvantage students from lower-income, non-English-speaking homes are seldom acknowledged (Li 1989: 178–182). Nor is it noted that the viability of capitalism is always predicated on the labor of many and the success of a few (Willis 1977).

If we look at inequality in a global context, Singapore's prosperity relies increasingly on state ventures, multinational capital, and the labor power, land, and resources of the Southeast Asian region. It depends less on the self-help efforts of local small-scale entrepreneurs, yet they are still considered to exemplify Singapore, its free-market capitalism, and its promise that any diligent person can prosper. The model citizens are entrepreneurs, they are Chinese, and they rose from rags to riches through their own efforts.

The rendering of inequality in ethnic terms has the further implication that ethnic communities, not the state, have the major responsibility for resolving the problem. During the 1970s and 1980s, emphasis on "the Malay problem" distracted attention from similar problems of poverty and inadequate education in the majority Chinese community and in other minority groups (Li 1989:178–182). The focus was on the cultural failings of the Malays and the changes needed to instill an achievement motivation, thrift, and other values appropriate to competition in multiethnic Singapore. The government argued that it could not bring about the necessary cultural change for the Malays, but it supported programs to accomplish this goal that were organized by Malay community groups and the national foundation Mendaki. Their programs have included tuition schemes, preschools, family counseling centers, a Muslim trust fund, and encouragement for Malays to set up businesses.[15]

In the 1990s, the ethnic model for representing and dealing with inequality has undergone a further evolution. It has become more evident that not everyone is benefiting from Singapore's prosperity and that the gains have been uneven. It has also become obvious that Malays are not the only ones affected by these problems; and Malays have been reminded that "the number of poor Chinese far exceeds the number of poor Malays," so their claims for special treatment should be circumspect.[16] There has emerged a greater willingness to recognize the de facto existence of disadvantage and marginalization but little acknowledgment of institutional processes through which inequality is structured. Individuals and whole ethnic groups are recognized to be disadvantaged by poverty, but this is deemed as resulting from a lack of motivation originating in inappropriate cultural values.

In dealing with the problem of inequality, the government remains determined to avoid direct action on poverty. It promotes a model of Asian capitalism in which the Asian family and community, not the state, provide the "human face" and take on responsibility for the welfare of individuals. In asserting an "Asian" model, the government conveniently homogenizes and blends Malay, Chinese, and Indian family and community life in order to heighten the contrast with the "West," characterized by family breakdown, moral decay, and dependency on state welfare (PR December 23, 1989). The Western alter ego provides the Singapore government with a mandate for a form of governance that is intrusive regarding moral issues, especially in the regulation of family and sexuality, and yet takes no responsibility for the ethical consequences of inequality in a capitalist economic system.

Despite homogenization of ethnic differences in order to assert a common Asian front, ethnic distinctions remain crucial to this form of governance. The idea of an ethnic group as a *community* interjects a necessary distance between the individual and the state. Communities know "their own" members best and can be made responsible for solving "their own" problems (PR June 27, 1992; PR February 7, 1991; *ST* May 17, 1992). They are able to do this by providing various forms of practical assistance (such as school tuition) as well as by identifying the cultural traits that need to be altered among those who are lagging behind. Wealthy people and professionals in each group, those assumed to possess the values required for success, are called upon to assist, reform, and educate others in "their community." Following the Malay community's lead with Mendaki, founded in 1982, the Indian community established its development association, SINDA, in 1990. The Chinese Development Assistance Council (CDAC) was founded in 1992. Each of these organizations enjoys government support in the form of revenue arrangements (voluntary contributions are deducted directly from the payrolls of the requisite ethnic group member), matching government funds, and subsidized space and facilities.

An ethnic framework for dealing with inequality has evolved "naturally" from a politics that sees certain cultural values and the resultant lack of motivation as the main impediments to advancement in a meritocratic society. There is no doubt that leaders in each of the ethnic groups have taken on the task of raising the status of their community with diligence. In the Malay case, leaders have been frustrated that however much improvement is made in, for example, school examination results, other ethnic groups improve even more (PR May 30, 1992; *ST* May 6, 1990). The discrepancy in rates of progress could be interpreted as an outcome of unequal incomes and the resulting disadvantages outlined earlier. Instead, it is seen as evidence of continued weakness in the Malay community and the need for Malays to redouble their efforts.

By reexamining Malay entrepreneurship in the context of the broader cultural, economic, and ideological processes in which it is embedded, I suggest that a socially engineered value change would pose no solution to the "Malay problem." The problem, if indeed there is one, would need to be substantially reposed. Malay nonparticipation in entrepreneurship has complex causes that include the dynamics of family and community life as they have been created and reformed to meet the conditions of life in Singapore. Malay culture and morality are not irrelevant carryovers from the past but contemporary adaptations with fully contemporary meanings and significance. They are subject to ongoing reformation and negotiation in the contexts of everyday life, which Malays encounter from a range of gender and class positions. These contexts include the presence of the Chinese and the presence of the state, each with its own forms of material and discursive power. As this chapter has indicated, Malays are not passive in these encounters. In their endeavors to develop and sustain a moral basis for encounters with modern capitalism, they have expanded the range of human possibilities, demonstrating the diversity of practices upon which "Asian capitalism" actually rests.

NOTES

This chapter draws on interviews with Malay households and entrepreneurs carried out in 1982–1984. The results of this study, additional references, citations, and acknowledgments can be found in Li 1989. The results of the 1990 census and news reports from the early 1990s were used to update the study in 1993, but no new interviews were carried out.

1. As Jennifer Alexander notes (this volume), Chinese profit seeking has not always been regarded as a positive attribute. Colonials often characterized the Chinese as cunning, crooked, and aggressive.

2. See "The Malay Dilemma," *Straits Times or Sunday Times* (hereafter *ST*) September 22, 1990, for comments by Malay and non-Malay businessmen on Malay lack of drive, their satisfaction with the "easy life," and the need for "a total change of attitude and motivation in the Malay community." For government statements, see Singapore government press release (hereafter PR), December 23, 1989; *ST,* October 18, 1989; and numerous references from the early 1980s cited in Li 1989.

3. See O'Brien and Roseberry 1991; Pred and Watts 1992; Gupta and Ferguson 1992.

4. Mackie (this volume) notes that Chinese in the Southeast Asian region have been predominantly employees, often farmers, only some going into business and even fewer with much success. For China, the idea of a generalized, "natural" predilection for business is even more absurd.

5. In the 1990 census 53 percent of working Malay women were in manufacturing compared to 32 percent of Chinese women. Note that these low-wage jobs are especially vulnerable to regional competition.

6. Men's and women's informal-sector activities are not reflected in these figures.

7. See Jay 1969, Djamour 1959, Peletz 1988, Banks 1983, Wong 1987. Aihwa Ong notes that parents hoped to receive "voluntary" cash contributions from their working daughters, but they were often disappointed (1987:71, 130–131).

8. See Bourdieu 1977, Appadurai 1986, Carrier 1992, Parry 1986, and Parry and Bloch 1989 for critiques of the exaggerated and reified opposition between commodities and gifts, household and market, set up by Western cultural assumptions.

9. For religious or spiritual factors that influence the motivation of Chinese and Malay families to accumulate wealth across the generations, see Li 1989:75–88, 161–162. See also Peletz (this volume) on the socially generated motivation to acquire wealth or to "go the extra mile."

10. Carsten (1989:117) citing a study by Lim (1981) notes that the "moral emphasis of Malay fishermen is on mutual help based on kinship, while those of the Chinese

170 _Tania Murray Li_

traders centre on commercial relations and the profit motive." This contrast reflects stereotypes that romanticize Malay life and parody the Chinese. It does not advance our understanding of the ways in which the market is constituted as a moral sphere.

11. Malays in Singapore and Malaysia have adopted a similar rhetoric on progress and stress the need to "instill Islamic values like hard work and team spirit among members of their communities." Singapore Malays have been praised by Malaysians for their openness, drive, and pragmatic willingness to adopt English as the language of education and economic life.

12. See Li 1989 for an extended discussion of this point. See also _ST_ October 18, 1989; _ST_ September 22, 1990.

13. But see Vivian Balakrishnan in _ST_ January 24, 1990.

14. The origin of the myth of Malay backwardness has its own complex history and goes back to the beginnings of the colonial era. It was reworked through the early phases of Malay nationalism. See Alatas 1977; Roff 1967; and Li 1989:166–182.

15. This fund was called Danamis (_ST_ October 4, 1990). The failure of Singapore Malays to develop trade networks with Malaysia, Indonesia, and the Middle East has frustrated the government and led to moves to import Muslim entrepreneurs from elsewhere in the region to fill the gap (PR December 22, 1990; _ST_ September 22, 1990; _ST_ December 23, 1990).

16. See media coverage in PR December 23, 1989; _ST_ May 6, 1990; _ST_ October 8, 1990; PR February 7, 1991; and PR June 27, 1992.

REFERENCES

Alatas, Syed Hussein. 1977. _The Myth of the Lazy Native_. London: Frank Cass.

Appadurai, Arjun. 1986. _The Social Life of Things_. Cambridge: Cambridge University Press.

Banks, David. 1983. _Malay Kinship_. Philadelphia: Institute for the Study of Human Resources.

Betts, Russell. 1975. "Multiracialism, Meritocracy and the Malays of Singapore." Ph.D. dissertation, Department of Political Science, Massachusetts Institute of Technology.

Bourdieu, Pierre. 1977. _Outline of a Theory of Practice_. Cambridge: Cambridge University Press.

Carrier, James. 1992. "Occidentalism: The World Turned Upside Down." _American Ethnologist_ 19, 2:195–212.

Carsten, Janet. 1989. "Cooking Money: Gender and the Symbolic Transformation of Means of Exchange in a Malay Fishing Community." In Jonathan Parry and Maurice Bloch, eds., _Money and the Morality of Exchange_, pp. 117–141. Cambridge: Cambridge University Press.

Cheng Siok Hwa. 1980. "Recent Trends in Female Labour Force Participation in Singapore." _Southeast Asian Journal of Social Science_ 8:20–39.

Chung, Betty Jamie, et al. 1981. _The Dynamics of Child Rearing Decisions: The Singapore Experience_. Singapore: Maruzen Asia.

Djamour, Judith. 1959. _Malay Kinship and Marriage in Singapore_. London: Athlone Press.

Freedman, Maurice. 1979. *The Study of Chinese Society: Selected Essays by Maurice Freedman with Introduction by C. William Skinner.* Stanford: Stanford University Press.

Goh Keng Swee. 1958. *Urban Incomes and Housing: A Report on the Social Survey of Singapore 1953–1954.* Singapore: Government Printer.

Gupta, Akhil, and James Ferguson. 1992. "Beyond 'Culture': Space, Identity and the Politics of Difference." *Cultural Anthropology* 7, 1:6–23.

Hassan, Riaz. 1977. *Families in Flats.* Singapore: Singapore University Press.

Jay, Robert. 1969. *Javanese Villagers: Social Relations in Rural Modjukoto.* Cambridge: Massachusetts Institute of Technology.

Lau Hong Thye. 1974. "The Social Structure of Small Chinese Business Firms in Singapore." Singapore: Academic Exercise in Sociology, University of Singapore.

Leong Choon Cheong. 1978. *Youth in the Army.* Singapore: Federal Publications.

Li, Tania. 1989. *Malays in Singapore: Culture, Economy and Ideology.* Singapore: Oxford University Press.

Lim Kim Huay. 1960. "The Supply of Labour to the Building and Construction Industry in Singapore." Singapore: Academic Exercise in Economics, University of Malaya.

McKinley, Robert. 1975. "A Knife Cutting Water: Child Transfers and Siblingship Among Urban Malays." Ph.D. dissertation, Department of Anthropology, University of Michigan.

Nagata, Judith. 1979. *Malaysian Mosaic.* Vancouver: University of British Columbia Press.

O'Brien, Jay, and William Roseberry. 1991. "Introduction." In Jay O'Brien and William Roseberry, eds., *Golden Ages, Dark Ages,* pp. 1–18. Berkeley: University of California Press.

Ong, Aihwa. 1987. *Spirits of Resistance and Capitalist Discipline.* New York: SUNY Press.

Parry, Jonathan. 1986. "The Gift, the Indian Gift and the 'Indian Gift,'" *Man* N.S. 21:453–473.

Parry, Jonathan, and Maurice Bloch. 1989. "Introduction: Money and the Morality of Exchange." In Jonathan Parry and Maurice Bloch, eds., *Money and the Morality of Exchange,* pp. 1–32. Cambridge: Cambridge University Press.

Peletz, Michael. 1988. *A Share of the Harvest.* Berkeley: University of California Press.

Pred, Allan, and Michael Watts, eds. 1992. *Reworking Modernity.* New Brunswick: Rutgers University Press.

Roff, William. 1967. *The Origins of Malay Nationalism.* New Haven: Yale University Press.

Salaff, Janet. 1981. *Working Daughters of Hong Kong.* Cambridge: Cambridge University Press.

Salaff, Janet, and Aline Wong. 1976. "Women's Work in Singapore: A Handle for Smaller Family Size." Paper presented at Wellesley Conference on Women and Development.

Siebel, Maureen. 1961. "The Changes in the Malaysian Population of Singapore 1819–1959." Academic exercise working paper, University of Singapore.

Singapore Census of Population. 1931, 1957, 1970, 1980, 1990. Singapore: Depart-
    ment of Statistics.
State of Singapore. 1960. *Report of the Commission of Inquiry into the System of
    Contract Labour in Singapore.*
Tham Seong Chee. 1983. *Malays and Modernization.* Rev. ed. Singapore: Singapore
    University Press.
Turnbull, C.M. 1977. *A History of Singapore 1819–1975.* Kuala Lumpur: Oxford
    University Press.
Wilder, William. 1982. *Communication, Social Structure and Development in Rural
    Malaysia.* London: Athlone Press.
Willis, Paul. 1977. *Learning to Labour.* London: Saxon House; reprint 1980, West-
    mead: Grover.
Wong, Diana. 1987. *Peasants in the Making: Malaysia's Green Revolution.* Singapore:
    Institute of Southeast Asian Studies.
Yearbook of Labour Statistics. 1970, 1980. Singapore: Ministry of Labour.

Straits Times (abbreviated in text as ST)

March 23, 1981, "Rahim on Why No Muslim Aged Are in Homes"
October 18, 1989, "Malay S'poreans 'Must Learn to Compete with Everyone
    Else'"
January 24, 1990, "Vital That Minorities Perceive There Is Fair Treatment of All
    Races"
May 6, 1990, "Govt 'Supports Malay Aspirations'"
September 22, 1990, "The Malay Dilemma"
October 4, 1990, "Call for One-Stop Consultation Centre to Help the Commu-
    nity"
October 8, 1990, "Chok Tong Calls for New Mendaki"
December 23, 1990, "Task Force to Woo Malay/Muslim Talent from Abroad"
February 3, 1991, "Why S'pore Won't Change Its Racial Composition"
May 10, 1992, "Chinese Self-Help Group Will Not Split Multi-Racial Singapore:
    Dr. Ow"
May 17, 1992, "20% of Younger Chinese Uncomfortable with English: Mr. Lee"

Singapore Government Press Releases
(abbreviated in the text as PR)

December 23, 1989, Lee Hsien Loong
December 22, 1990, George Yong-Boon Yeo
February 7, 1991, Goh Chock Tong
May 30, 1992, Sidek bin Saniff
June 27, 1992, Lee Hsien Loong
July 18, 1992, Yeo Chow Tong

six

≫ス

The "Great Transformation" Among Negeri Sembilan Malays, with Particular Reference to Chinese and Minangkabau

MICHAEL G. PELETZ

For well over a century now Malays have been involved in the transition to capitalism that is commonly referred to as the Great Transformation. As a transnational and ultimately global phenomenon, the Great Transformation was a central preoccupation of Marx, Weber, and Durkheim and has in fact been *the* major concern of social scientists since the latter part of the 1800s. By all accounts, however, Malay involvement in the Great Transformation is an ongoing process with highly uneven—as well as ironic and unintended—consequences. Partly for this reason and partly because the historical pathways to capitalism both in Malaysia and elsewhere are far less linear, mechanical, and automatic than assumed by extant models, we have relatively little knowledge of the specific variables and combinations of variables that have operated in the Malay case to facilitate the transformation or, alternatively, hinder it. There are also many gaps in our understanding of the precise effects of capitalist forces and institutions—and the discourses they have engendered—in specific locales in Malaysia and other parts of Asia.

This chapter provides historical and comparative perspectives on various aspects of the Great Transformation in a Malay(sian) context; it is organized into three sections. The first examines the ways in which the systems of kinship, gender, and prestige that obtained among Malays in late precolonial Negeri Sembilan predisposed men to take advantage of new opportunities to engage in cash cropping and otherwise provided structural precedents for the economic and social changes associated with state-sponsored capitalism both in the colonial era (1874–1957) and beyond.[1] The second section isolates some of the variables that worked against Negeri Sembilan Malays "taking the extra step" and becoming heavily involved in entrepreneurial activities in the early decades of the twentieth century and in the years that followed. This section of the chapter also includes comparative references to Chinese kinship and entrepreneurial ethics. Most of the comparative discussion, however, is reserved for the third section of the chapter, in which I analyze similarities and differences between Negeri Sembilan Malays and the Minangkabau of Sumatra, from whom Negeri Sembilan Malays trace their descent. The main concern in this part of the chapter is to provide an overview of commonalities between the two populations and to explain why, despite broad similarities of kinship, gender, prestige, and so on, entrepreneurial traditions are far more pronounced among the Minangkabau than among Negeri Sembilan Malays. My explanation of the latter difference focuses on the dissimilar historical experiences of the two societies in relation to largely exogenous forces associated with European mercantilism and colonial rule, many of which were an outgrowth of contrasts in the state policies and interests of the British in Malaya on the one hand and those of the Dutch in Sumatra on the other.

A final introductory comment concerns terminology. I use the term Great Transformation as a shorthand to refer to the social and cultural entailments of the transition to capitalism, which is most definitely a process rather than an event *tout court*. This process is invariably ongoing, which is to say that even in our own "fully capitalist" society there are numerous social and cultural domains that have yet to—and will probably never—be fully "penetrated" by capitalist ethics or social relations, however broadly or narrowly defined. It should be noted as well that although I speak of the Great Transformation in the singular, I do not mean to imply that there is only one pathway to capitalism or that capitalism exists in a single, monolithic form. In light of the "multiheaded hydra that is historical capitalism" (Watts 1992:10), it is clearly more appropriate to speak of great transformations—and capitalisms—in the plural; but for the sake of convenience and style, I go with the singular forms of these terms.

Negeri Sembilan Malays in Historical Perspective

One of the more enduring themes in the social scientific and policy literature on Malaysia is that in terms of economic development, Malays (all of whom are Muslims of the Shafi'i branch of Sunni Islam) "have a problem." The problem is said to derive from profound incompatibilities between Malays' basic values and capitalist ethics of the sort that are presumed to suffuse the thinking and behavior not only of Western economic actors but also of (Han) Chinese both in Malaysia and elsewhere.[2] In particular, Malays are reputed to be both fatalistic and averse to the hard work, long-term planning and accumulation, economic expansion, and overall entrepreneurial spirit for which capitalist actors have long been famous. It is also assumed that Malays invariably strive to avoid immersion or participation in modern market institutions. This avoidance, in turn, is cited to help "explain" why Malays have supposedly been reluctant participants not only in cash cropping and related endeavors but also in the various economic niches (small-scale manufacturing, wholesaling, and retailing activities; the running of roadside stalls, small shops, restaurants, and hotels) in which Malaysia's Chinese predominate.

Most of these stereotypes are spurious, as discussed further on in this chapter and elsewhere (e.g., Li 1989 and this volume). The larger issue is that what might be termed Malay "economic values" are not timeless or unchanging elements of an immutable Malay (let alone ahistorical, essentialized "Islamic") culture but are historically conditioned, even protean, variables that have been informed by state policies, nationalist and transnational discourse, and the ethnic, class, and ecosystemic landscapes to which they have adapted and have in turn helped shape. The same is true of Malay systems of kinship, gender, and prestige, which are clearly linked with Malay economic values as well. This means that in order to understand contemporary Malay discourses on the morality of the market we must not only adopt a historical perspective but must also examine the ways in which state policies, extralocal discourses, and other largely exogenous variables have been refracted through Malay systems of kinship, gender, and prestige and have otherwise been experienced, understood, and represented at the local level.

Let us first briefly consider the ways in which Malay villagers in the state of Negeri Sembilan reacted in the late nineteenth and early twentieth centuries to the possibility of acquiring previously unalienated land that could be planted in cash crops. Moral economists and others who maintain that rural Malays and other peasant villagers invariably strive to keep the market at arms' length would have us believe that local responses to such possibilities are always less than enthusiastic. The reason: The economic and other behaviors of peasant villagers are assumed to be geared toward ensuring the continuity and reproduction of ostensibly redistributive and communitarian institutions that might be undermined by market forces and are otherwise oriented toward minimizing risk and maximizing security (Scott 1976; cf. Taussig 1980). In fact, however, when the British made land suitable for cash cropping available to Negeri Sembilan Malays beginning around the turn of the century, villagers responded with a veritable flood of applications for land and quickly proceeded to plant it in coffee and, more important, rubber trees, the latex from which was enthusiastically sold on the market (*NSGG* 1896:vol. 1, 103, 104; *NSGG* 1897:vol. 2, 83; see also Gullick 1985; Peletz 1988; Kato 1991). There is little evidence that the flood of applications was caused in the main by shortages of rice land or other strategically valued resources on which villagers relied for their livelihood, though in some instances material pressures were central among the factors that motivated villagers' involvement in this domain. Indeed, in most cases the primary determinant seems to have been prestige-driven desires for previously unavailable consumer goods, including perfumes, silk handkerchiefs, and smoking jackets, as well as cash that could be used to help refurbish houses and to sponsor feasts and help finance the pilgrimage to Mecca. It merits note, in any case, that Malay smallholders' demand for such land was so strong, and the efficiency of their production so impressive, that they posed a serious threat to the continued success of large-scale estate enterprises largely controlled by British and Chinese and were, as a consequence, slapped with various oppressive regulations of the sort later enshrined in the Stevenson Restriction Scheme (see Peletz 1988).

Circumstances such as these point up some of the obvious problems with arguments that Malays always try to keep market institutions at arm's length. So, too, of course does the fact that during certain periods of precolonial history, Malay elites and pioneering immigrants hoping to acquire elite status (or at least some measure of wealth and fame) commonly engaged in entrepreneurial activity of both a political and more narrowly economic sort, as did indigenous elites and pioneers elsewhere in Southeast Asia (Graves 1981; Dobbin 1983; Gullick 1985; Reid 1988, 1993; McVey 1992:23). Unfortunately there is not much relevant information bearing on the Malay case, but we do know that in the last few decades of the nineteenth century, and presumably during earlier decades as well, the commercial activities of Malay elites included developing land for letting to tenants, investing in irrigation works and road building, and hiring out fleets of elephants to the Chinese miners and financiers who began taking over the mining industry from Malays in the 1830s (see Gullick 1985).

To understand why Malay villagers in Negeri Sembilan were strongly motivated to engage in cash cropping, we need to consider their nineteenth-century systems of kinship and gender and the encompassing systems of prestige (and stigma) of which they were a part.[3] We also need to bear in mind that most of the new opportunities to engage in cash cropping were made available to men rather than women (hence the focus, further on, on men). One reason for this is that the British saw the local system, characterized as it was by female predominance in the proprietorship and inheritance of houses and land, as both a bizarre anomaly and a wholesale inversion of "natural" gender relations, as defined by the standards of Victorian England. Also, the British wanted to make sure that men had more of a stake in local development and felt that if men were guaranteed title to land in their own names they would participate in greater numbers—and with more enthusiasm—in state-sponsored "progress." As it turned out, Negeri Sembilan men embraced these new opportunities and were motivated to do so by the prevailing structure of prestige.[4] Let me explain.

Upon marriage, a man moved to his wife's village and natal compound. His economic competence and social status and prestige within his wife's community were defined largely in relation to how well he provided for his wife and children. A "good provider" built a house for his wife and children on land that was part of (or adjacent to) his wife's natal compound, and he worked with his wife to expand her agricultural (wet rice) holdings; he also provided his wife and children with cash and commercial items acquired through the rearing and sale of livestock and the collection and sale of forest products. Property rights thus created were defined as "conjugal earnings" *(carian laki-bini, harta sepencarian)*, but the bulk of these rights would pass to the man's wife and children in the event of the dissolution of his marriage through divorce or the husband's death and would become "ancestral property" *(harta pesaka)* defined in relation to the wife's lineage branch, lineage, and localized clan. (They would devolve upon the children and the wife's matrilineal survivors in the event that she died before her husband did.) These features of the system highlight the structurally important role that married men played in the creation and initial transmission of property rights that would ultimately be passed on to only their wives' matrilineal kin. More generally, they illustrate that in-marrying males played a crucial role in the reproduction of the material base of descent units and the larger systems of kinship, political economy, and prestige of which they were a part.

We do not know how affinal relations were experienced by in-marrying men, but if the present is any indication of the past, married men often found that they could not live up to the prestige-driven expectations and demands of their affines and that they otherwise found these situations both rather oppressive and out of keeping with Islamic ideals, which recognize no such political asymmetries or parochial distinctions. One solution to a married man's dilemma would be to divorce or simply abandon his wife, along with any children he might have. This was but a temporary solution, for divorced men (like widowers) would not necessarily be welcome in their mothers' or sisters' homes for extended periods. Nor was living alone (in a local prayer house or in a home by oneself) a viable solution; for socialization and the sexual division of labor left men with little direct knowledge or experience concerning the domestic tasks necessary to maintain themselves, and houses were defined as female property. Avoiding marriage altogether was not an acceptable alternative either, for marriage, along with fathering (or adopting) children, was a sine qua non for adult male personhood.

Another possible and more long-term solution to the predicament faced by in-marrying males was to attain political office or become a healer or shaman. This would enable a married man to establish a separate base of political support and thus partly offset his sociopolitical dependence on and subordination to his affines. It would also provide a separate basis for social identity and self-esteem arguably more in keeping with Islamic ideals emphasizing the seamless brotherhood and equality obtaining among all members of the Muslim community *(umat)*.

This latter solution to the dilemmas experienced by in-marrying males indicates that there was a critically important but largely hidden advantage of political office: Compared to untitled males, political leaders were not nearly as dependent on the cooperation and goodwill of their wives' kin and were relatively autonomous in relation to them. In their roles as in-marrying males, in other words, political leaders were relatively unconstrained by the political and economic entailments of the system of marriage and affinal relations. This was especially true in the case of the *undang* (district chief), who is singled out by Taylor ([1929] 1970) as "the sole exception" to the rule that "a man . . . passe[d] into his wife's clan and . . . [became] subject to her clan chief in all matters effecting her and her family" (cited in Winstedt 1934:78). *Undangs'* relative freedom from the constraints of the system enabled them not only to exert critical leverage toward sociocultural change throughout the colonial era but also to confer legitimacy on myriad departures from tradition.

One should bear in mind, however, that there were not all that many political or ritual offices to go around, and most men were therefore unable to claim roles as political leaders or ritual specialists or otherwise define themselves in occupational or other "positional" terms of the sort associated with the public domain. Rather, most men were characterized simply as kinsmen, that is, as husbands, fathers, brothers. In light of the material presented earlier, it seems reasonable to assume that they were defined first and foremost as in-marrying males and as husbands and fathers in particular.

Nineteenth-century Negeri Sembilan is by no means the only society in which the majority of men, and constructions of masculinity generally, were cast largely in "relational" terms. Such was clearly the case in nineteenth-century Aceh (northern Sumatra), which had systems of kinship, marriage, and prestige that were in many respects similar to those in nineteenth-century Negeri Sembilan. Siegel (1969:68) notes, for instance, that in nineteenth-century Aceh, "[male] villagers were first of all husbands and fathers." This is to say that men's primary identities and senses of self were defined not by their roles or positions in the political economy or in terms of citizenship, nationality, or religion but rather in "relational" terms of the sort that, according to much of the literature on gender (see, e.g., de Beauvoir 1949; Ortner and Whitehead 1981; Chodorow 1989), are ostensibly reserved for women.

Of additional interest, in any case, is that "even when [Acehnese] men lived up to their material obligations, they had little place in their wives' homes. . . . Women . . . allowed men no part in raising children and tolerated them only so long as they paid their own way and contributed money for goods that a woman could not obtain through her own resources" (Siegel 1969:54). Many of these generalizations pertain to nineteenth-century Negeri Sembilan as well as to contemporary Negeri Sembilan (Siegel 1969:183; Peletz 1996).

Having drawn attention to the pressures and difficulties that many, perhaps most, Negeri Sembilan men experienced in their roles as husbands and fathers, I should emphasize that some men did succeed in living up to and gaining prestige from these roles. They did this partly by being "good providers," especially by raising and selling livestock and collecting and selling or trading forest products for commercial items or cash that could be used to supplement the rice and other agricultural products their wives contributed to the household coffers.

Another way in which men gained prestige was by making the pilgrimage to Mecca (the haj). Recall that married men, like the rest of the population, were Muslims and thus bidden to undertake the haj should they be financially able. Making the pilgrimage was not merely a way of meeting one's religious obligations, however; it also brought the pilgrim prestige both as a person of means and as someone who had acquired uncommon and otherwise highly valued religious experience and knowledge. Equally important, the pilgrimage was widely seen as an "outlet for humiliation" (Gullick 1987:233 n. 53, 250; see also Ellen 1983:74) in the sense that its performance enabled individuals to make partial atonement for their social sins and shortcomings.

Not surprisingly, gaining sufficient funds to make the haj was a principal objective of men who engaged in cash cropping in the early years of colonial rule. Even before that time, the sale of forest produce and livestock had been undertaken for this purpose. Thus in 1892 Lister reported that "the money supply for luxuries had always been obtained from the sale of fruit, vegetables, and orchard produce [and] . . . from the sale of buffaloes, goats, and poultry. . . . It was also by this industry that . . . people . . . were able to save up money to accomplish the pilgrimage to Mecca" (quoted in Gullick 1951:48).

We see here the mutual reinforcement of two separate though interrelated criteria for prestige ranking: one based on the cultural construction of affinal obligations, relatedness, and cleavages keyed ultimately to the system of hereditary ranking (see Peletz 1996); the other resting on a more transcendent—and more explicitly religious—ideology according to which all men are equal before God but those among them who journey to Mecca enjoy exalted spiritual and social standing. That men could earn prestige on both accounts through trading activities is, I think, a critical factor in motivating their participation in trade in the first place and in encouraging both the colonial-era acquisition of land by males and their involvement in cash cropping on the whole (see *NSGG* 1896:vol. 1, no. 3; Supplement to *NSGG* 1909:3).

There were, of course, additional variables that motivated men's involvement in new economic opportunities or otherwise facilitated the transition to capitalism, if only by easing the dislocations that the early stages of the transition necessarily entailed. It is beyond the scope of this chapter to discuss these variables in detail, so I will simply list some of the more important ones. They include (1) the conventional sexual division of labor and the relative marginalization of men with respect to the proprietorship and inheritance of (provisional) rights over houses and land, along with the tradition of temporary male out-migration *(merantau)* and the economic ventures and experimentation that the entire nexus of property and social relations at issue here helped animate and sustain; (2) the culturally explicit idea that marriage was a contractual relationship,[5] coupled with the largely implicit convention that marriage payments (especially from the groom's side to the bride's) were drawn from and distributed among a very narrow range of kin; (3) the fact that customs associated with property division at divorce made clear provision for what each spouse brought to the union (albeit not for any increase in the value of either partner's separate estate); (4) the existence of "paternal provisioning" *(tentukan)*, which involved a father's prerogative to convey rights over certain items of (movable) property to his children and which provided a crucial structural precedent not only for the subsequent inclusion of sons in the inheritance of rights over (immovable) property such as land but also for the attendant erosion of the inheritance rights of collateral kin; (5) ideologies of kinship that emphasized equality among members of lineages and clans and that constrained the cultural realization of inequalities engendered by increased dependence on cash cropping and more extensive integration into the global economy (see Peletz 1988; see also Watson 1985 and Bloch 1989); and (6) a panoply of heavily syncretic though largely pre-Islamic beliefs and practices associated with (mystical) poisoning, sorcery, and spirit cults, which served to underscore that much of an individual's fate in this world and the next depended on his or her own actions or inactions (narrowly defined), and on the actions or inactions of one or more highly individualized human or spirit others (also narrowly defined).[6]

Negeri Sembilan Malays and Chinese

Lists of the latter sort could certainly be expanded and refined. More important to bear in mind at this juncture is that although Negeri Sembilan Malays embraced opportunities to engage in cash cropping, they did not usually utilize the fruits of their labor either to acquire more land—let alone bring about long-term improvement of the means of production—or to effect one or another form of lateral expansion. In short, they did not "take the extra step" and get heavily involved in marketing, trading, or other entrepreneurial activities. Even, or perhaps especially, at present, for example, income and wealth tend not to be used for purposes of extending and improving collectively or singularly held capital assets. These resources are expended instead in ways that from a narrow economic perspective might be termed relatively nonproductive: to make houses more comfortable and attractive but not to enhance their resale value or their value in inheritance; to buy land that can be planted in rubber or other cash crops and worked for subsistence purposes but not with an eye to obtaining more land or improving the means of production; and to help underwrite the costs of ceremonial feasts *(kenduri)* and the pilgrimage to Mecca.[7]

To understand why strong entrepreneurial traditions did not develop among twentieth-century Malays in Negeri Sembilan and other areas of the Malay Peninsula, we need to appreciate that beginning in the nineteenth century the British pursued mercantile and colonial policies that effectively discouraged Malays from involvement in trade and business. For example, British policies penalized Malays for not working their *padi* fields, thus undercutting their abilities to move into nonagricultural pursuits and avail themselves of the new economic opportunities associated with tin mining and other European-backed commercial enterprises. British policies also had the effect of enticing large numbers of non-Malay manual laborers into the peninsula. Note here that as early as 1911, the Chinese constituted over 31 percent of Negeri Sembilan's population, and Indians and others made up another 14 percent (*CFMS* 1911). The Chinese, who were mainly from the southern provinces of Fukien and Kwangtung and who in terms of linguistic-group affiliation tended to be either Hokkien, Hakka, or Cantonese (Siow 1983:171), were heavily concentrated in rapidly expanding urban areas and the entrepreneurial niches associated with them, partly because of laws preventing them from settling among Malays and owning land in their own names. These laws worked against their direct involvement in small-scale agriculture of the sort pursued by Malays. They also helped lay the foundation for entrenched patterns of interethnic symbiosis and antagonism that have persisted to the present.

The relative absence of vigorous entrepreneurial orientations among twentieth-century Malays is also usefully viewed in light of four variables that might have been present or pronounced in the Malay case but were (and are) not. One such variable involves the fulfillment of obligations to ancestors and the members of wider kin groups, which is reported to be among the primary determinants of economic activity in some societies with extensive (patrilineal) lineage organizations and vibrant entrepreneurial ethics, such as the southern Chinese discussed by Skinner (1957:92; cited in Madge 1974:185–186). In the Malay case, these obligations seem always to have been either more narrowly construed, less strongly felt, or simply less burdensome in an economic sense. Put differently, such obligations have never provided the incentive for economic accumulation or advancement of the sort commonly associated with corresponding obligations among diverse groups of Chinese both in southern China and beyond.

A second variable has to do with the cultural elaboration of concerns to provide offspring or other descendants with "nest eggs" with which to launch economic and social careers geared toward upward mobility. These interests are highly developed among Chinese in Malaysia, Singapore, Taiwan, and elsewhere, though their actual realization is an altogether separate issue. Among Malays, however, they are not and apparently never have been, perhaps because the opportunities for upward mobility have always been relatively rare. At present, the usual concern among Malays in Negeri Sembilan is to see to it that children, at least daughters, have subsistence guarantees (part of a houseplot, some rice and perhaps rubber acreage, and, in the case of the youngest daughter, a house), however partial and inadequate they may be in contemporary times. The relative lack of interest in ensuring that children have nest eggs with which to improve their lot in life does not actually dampen economic activity on the part of parents but certainly doesn't encourage it in the first place.

A third variable is the presence—and scope and force—of concerns with lineage survival or advancement. Among Chinese, these concerns tend to be highly elaborated, though not uniformly so, and much of what an individual does may come to reflect heavily on his or her localized lineage (see Wong 1985:64). This puts added pressure on Chinese to succeed in culturally appropriate ways, though the pressure is of course highly variable. Malays in Negeri Sembilan also identify with their localized lineages and clans, and their activities and reputations clearly affect the prestige and material standing of these groups or, in the case of married men, of their wives. In present-day Negeri Sembilan, however, Malays do not evince much interest in the actual survival—let alone advancement—of localized lineages or larger kin groups, though the material viability and social reproduction of one's household is of paramount concern (as is true of the Chinese). Thus the added pressure to succeed in culturally meaningful ways that was mentioned earlier in connection with Chinese is largely nonexistent among Negeri Sembilan Malays.

A fourth variable, which I discuss in greater detail, has to do with the absence among Malays of traditions of economic cooperation among all the members of a household or family, such as those associated with the "family firms" of the Chinese, which Redding (1990) aptly dubs "family fortresses." Germane here is the frequently reported observation that among Malays, kinship and business do not—or at least should not—mix (see Djamour 1959:46–47; Swift 1965:171; McKinley 1981:336–337; Banks 1983:163–164; Carsten 1989:126–129; Li 1989 and this volume). Malays do not like to enter joint business ventures with their relatives or cooperate with them in certain other types of economic activities, partly because they seek to insulate and protect kinship ties both from the vagaries of day-to-day economic fortunes and forces and from the self-interest of social actors, all of which are potentially highly destructive *and* recognized as such. Also relevant is the culturally implicit recognition of what might give way in the event that short-term individual and household needs become so pronounced as to jeopardize the morality of kinship, which has long-term political and economic benefit (Bloch 1973). In his incisive study of Malay kinship in the state of Kedah, David Banks (1983:86) reminds us that in the Malay view, conflict, though regrettable, is "a natural state of society." He also points out that ambivalence is an intrinsic and culturally elaborated feature of Malay systems of social relations. More generally, Banks locates numerous variants of tension, discord, and divisiveness *within* Malay kinship systems themselves rather than attributing them to extrinsic material factors or a purportedly universal human nature held to be at odds with local forms of sociability.

Insights along these lines are especially valuable for two reasons. First, they help us avoid the pitfalls of idealizing and reifying kinship—and of otherwise succumbing to misplaced romantic nostalgia. They also caution us against making the dubious assumption that Malays' deeply mixed emotions regarding the moral imperatives of sibling ties, filial bonds, and the like are to be explained primarily in terms of the individualizing and otherwise socially divisive consequences of colonialism, capitalism, and agrarian change.

Malay ambivalence and disdain for entering into economic relations with kin also extends to the domain of tenancy even though, or perhaps especially because, many villagers are involved in tenancy relations mediated by ties of kinship (Peletz 1988; see also Scott 1985). The larger issue is that interests in property, and in money in particular, can "eat" *(makan)* and thus destroy kinship and other social relations. They can nourish and sustain them as well (Carsten 1989) but are in many respects viewed as a "dark, satanic force tearing at the very fabric of society" (Bloch and Parry 1989:6). This is one reason there is profound ambivalence surrounding certain types of financial transactions involving the handing over of money for services rendered, such as those that occur in the context of healing rituals. Cash payments to healers *(dukun)* are often cast in the guise of a charitable or otherwise disinterested "gift" *(sedekah)*, but they are fully enjoined. The fact that there are usually no set schedules or rates for such payments and that their timing and value are left largely to the patient leaves considerable room for resentment and other ill will on the part of *dukun*, who may feel that they have not received adequate compensation for their services. To openly express any such ill will, however, would be highly inappropriate and could well lead to charges that the *dukun* is trying to profit from his or her divinely inspired gifts or is otherwise exploiting patients.

Dilemmas of this general sort sometimes plague local Malay peddlers and undercut their abilities to remain in business, let alone expand their operations. In villages such as Bogang (the site of my fieldwork),[8] local peddlers are mostly men who sell fish or vegetables from the backs of their motorcycles or women who run small provision shops that sell dry goods (kerosene, salt, cigarettes, etc.) and locally prepared food. When peddlers discuss their activities and experiences, they usually downplay the economic aspects of their operations and stress that they are in business primarily to "help" their relatives, especially the female elders among them, and thus to provide a disinterested service to kin and community. But they are also quick to acknowledge some other key points: that kinship cuts both ways; that relatives' requests to purchase goods on credit can be difficult to turn down; and that encouraging kin to make good on past debts is extremely unpleasant, potentially counterproductive, and sometimes fraught with mystical dangers as well. It is of interest here that although factors such as limited access to capital and storage facilities may well be the primary determinants of peddler commercial failure (see Kahn 1980), peddlers themselves commonly conceptualize the major obstacles to their success as the moral entailments of kinship and village citizenship.

In light of the foregoing it should come as no surprise that Malays sometimes prefer to do business with Chinese—this despite the institutionalized antagonism between the two communities and the Malay conviction that Chinese will do anything it takes to get ahead economically. Consider, for instance, the marketing of rubber. In the small town where villagers from Bogang sold their sheets of latex during the period 1978 to 1980, they had a choice of patronizing a Chinese middleman or a Malay. Much to my initial surprise, virtually everyone chose to do business with the Chinese buyer. This was not because the Chinese man offered a better price—the price at which rubber was sold was set by a government board—but rather because he could be trusted more in the weighing of the sheets that villagers delivered to him and, more generally, because everyone claimed to know exactly how he would behave in his dealings with his customers. The relationship was more or less instrumental with no offers of cigarettes or any of the other frills that typically accompany transactions involving the Malay middleman, who, experience suggested, would play down the instrumental aspects of the transaction but would not necessarily deal fairly with his customers.

The more general point I have emphasized here is that Malay ambivalences about (Malay) kinship and "human nature" constrain the development of a tradition of family firms and in this and other ways discourage the emergence of organizational patterns and social instruments that have well served various other groups of people such as Chinese in Malaysia, Singapore, and Taiwan. Having said that, I need also point out that Chinese systems of kinship and social relations are infused with ambivalence as well (see Freedman 1971; Watson 1985; Wong 1985; Yao 1987; Heng 1992; and Hamilton and Weller, both this volume). They are, moreover, characterized by developmental dynamics that not only are conducive to the realization of ambivalences that undermine the long-term viability of family businesses (such businesses cannot claim the longevity of their Japanese counterparts) but encourage the use of nonkin managers in these enterprises (Wong 1985; Hamilton, this volume). Unfortunately, however, there are two problems with exploring such tensions and ambivalences in the Chinese case and comparing them with what one finds among Malays. The first is that the vastly different cultures and historical experiences of the two communities preclude carefully controlled comparison. The second is that, to my knowledge, there are no comprehensive bodies of data focusing squarely on how—and under what specific political, economic, and other conditions—the relevant tensions and ambivalences among Chinese are overcome in the context of, or somehow channeled into, entrepreneurial activities (but see Wong 1985, 1988; Redding 1990, esp. chs. 3 and 7). We obviously need to know much more about how these patterns of mixed emotion are managed in ways conducive to entrepreneurialism in the Chinese case—and how they are keyed to the developmental cycles of families and family firms alike—and why they tend not to be so managed among Malays. More broadly, we need to direct far more analytic attention to the exogenous factors associated with different patterns of market and state organization that enhance, or alternatively, undermine, trust, loyalty, and predictability in the cultures of Chinese and Malay associations alike.

Negeri Sembilan Malays and Minangkabau

Much of the comparison thus far has involved Negeri Sembilan Malays and the culturally dissimilar Chinese. It is arguably far more fruitful to consider some of the correspondences and contrasts between Negeri Sembilan Malays and the Minangkabau of Sumatra, from whom, recall, Negeri Sembilan Malays trace their descent. Of particular interest here is why entrepreneurial traditions appear to be more pronounced among the Minangkabau than among the Malays of Negeri Sembilan. I say "appear to be more pronounced" because we are dealing more with subjective appearances of contrast than with empirically quantified differences. It merits emphasis, however, that the divergent economic ethics at issue have been noted in the literature, the general claims being that, compared to Negeri Sembilan Malays, the Minangkabau are more competitive; have more highly developed orientations toward economic success and upward mobility; and have

distinguished themselves to a greater degree in petty trading and other entrepreneurial activities (and in politics, the arts, etc. [see Swift 1971]). Some of
these distinctions are quite evident to Negeri Sembilan Malays and, presumably, to Minangkabau as well. Interestingly, Negeri Sembilan Malays regard
themselves as both culturally similar and "culturally indebted" to the Minangkabau. But they also express envy and hostility toward them. Indeed,
they commonly remark that the Minangkabau need only "shake a leg"
(goncang kaki saja) to make a living and are far more treacherous than fellow
Malays, being especially given to infusing poisonous gasses into bottles of
"orange crush" earmarked for foreign sale.

A discussion of commonalities between Negeri Sembilan Malays and the
Minangkabau could easily fill an entire volume. Let it suffice to say that they
include many of the basic values of these societies (encapsulated in notions
of *adat, budi, malu*, etc.) as well as their matrilineal descent groups, which
are similar in many respects in terms of both their structure and operation.
Relevant as well is that among the Minangkabau, as in Negeri Sembilan,
women are strongly favored in the proprietorship and inheritance of houses
and most categories of land. Women also manage domestic resources, including the cash incomes of their husbands, and they play important roles in
exchange activities associated with agricultural production and ceremonial
feasting. Minangkabau (like Negeri Sembilan) women do most of the work
in the rice fields (subsistence-oriented rice production provides much of the
economic base, at least in "traditional" Minangkabau villages), though they
also raise cash crops and rear poultry and livestock for sale. Men, for their
part, help their wives and sisters during certain stages of the agricultural cycle but are heavily involved in temporary out-migration *(merantau)*, which
we have seen in Negeri Sembilan as well. It is within this context that they
are most likely to become involved in petty trading, the operation of roadside food stalls and small restaurants, tailoring, and so on. In earlier times,
the yields of men's economic activities were apparently devoted primarily to
their mothers, sisters, and other female kin as opposed to their wives and
affines. These activities, like the clearing of previously unclaimed acreage
suitable for residential or agricultural purposes, were oriented largely toward the creation of property and wealth for their (natal) kin groups, which
could enhance the prestige standing of such groups.

The picture painted thus far is of course highly schematic and "traditional." A good deal has changed in Minangkabau communities. For reasons
that will be apparent in due course, I focus here on changes that closely parallel shifts that occurred in Negeri Sembilan, especially the restructuring of
men's roles as brothers (and mother's brothers) on the one hand and as husbands and fathers on the other.

To convey a clear sense of the transformation of men's roles, we need to
underscore that in earlier times, "a husband did not necessarily have to pro-

vide a living for his wife and children, or send his children to school, or participate in decisions in their home" (Mitchell 1969:126). These were the responsibilities of the head of the wife's group, or *kaum*, that is, her brother or mother's brother. The husband had responsibilities to the *kaum* into which he was born, which included obligations to his sisters and his sisters' children. Note also that a husband "was not necessarily a permanent mate; he might leave his wife over the most minor matter," a fact well captured in the customary saying pertaining to men in their roles as husbands: "Like ashes on a tree trunk, even a soft wind and they will fly away" (Mitchell 1969:128).

Much of this changed over the last 150 years as a result of Dutch colonialism and various economic, political, and religious forces that undermined clans and lineages and key features of the property relations undergirding them (see Benda-Beckmann 1979; Kahn 1980, 1993; Graves 1981). It is important to appreciate, however, that in many respects this process was not as devastating as that which occurred in Negeri Sembilan; in numerous areas of Minangkabau, unlike in Negeri Sembilan, one still finds corporate groups in the form of extended families made up of the children and grandchildren of one woman, all of whom ideally live in one *"adat* house" (a point to which I return further on).

Bear in mind, in any case, Frederick Errington's (1984:68) findings that "the [husband and father] role may have become . . . more demanding in recent years with the change in the relative importance of a man's affinal and matrilineal obligations" (see also Tanner 1982:144). In some communities, the father has become economically central to family life, to the point that, at least in relation to his wife's brothers, "he is now entirely responsible for the support of his wife and children" (Errington 1984:68).

Changes in the distribution of male responsibilities appear to have progressed further in the Minangkabau village of Bayur (the site of Errington's research) than in many other Minangkabau communities. "There is little mention in Bayur of pressures on men from sisters," which are "evidently still a source of marital tension elsewhere in the Minangkabau world" (Errington 1984:68). Worthy of remark, in any event, is that the wife's mother and wife's mother's sisters "judge . . . [the son-in-law] . . . particularly by the amount of his financial contribution to his household" (66). Not surprisingly, "males married to sisters see each other as rivals for the approval of the parents-in-law and feel that their respective economic contributions are always subject to unfavorable comparison" (66). More generally, men feel they are "welcome only as long as [they are] able to make a strong contribution"; but even "their best efforts to provide are often not enough [and] they never win an entirely secure place in their wives' home" (67; see also Tanner 1982:136; Krier 1994).

At this juncture I want to emphasize that the situation outlined here should not be interpreted as yet another peculiar twist on the famed "matrilineal puzzle," as described either in the pioneering work of Audrey Richards (1951) or in the modified version proposed by David Schneider (1961). In Richards's formulation, the matrilineal puzzle turns on how to trace descent through women yet allocate authority to men and on how such authority is to be divided among matrilineally related males on the one hand and in-marrying males on the other. Schneider accepts much of Richards's formulation, but he suggests that the major tension need not focus on the relationship between the in-marrying male and his wife's brother(s), as Richards assumes, but might be realized instead in the relationship between the in-marrying male and other male members of his wife's kin group (who need not be the wife's actual brothers or mother's brothers). What we see in Minangkabau and in Negeri Sembilan, however, is tension arising not so much in connection with contested authority over women and children—women in any case exercise far more authority than all formulations of the puzzle imply (Ng 1987)—but rather from competing claims over the labor power and productivity of in-marrying males. These are very different sets of issues and they have very different theoretical implications, as I have discussed elsewhere (Peletz 1988, 1996).

Consider also that even when competing claims from sisters and other female matrilineal kin do not figure in the picture, as appears to be the case in Bayur, married men are still under tremendous pressure to satisfy the economic expectations and demands of their wives' female kin. These expectations and demands are partly a reflection of the prestige considerations of women who evaluate and rank one another in terms of what their husbands bring home for them. They also index prestige competition among married men themselves; husbands are made to feel insecure and morally inferior by their parents-in-law, who are forever judging and ranking sons-in-laws' economic contributions in relation to those of other married men. Of broader concern here is that status rivalries and concerns with lineage rank are particularly intense among the Minangkabau (see Pak 1986; Krier 1994), far more so than among Negeri Sembilan Malays, perhaps because social stratification is both quite pronounced and more elaborated than in Negeri Sembilan.

The problem for married men, then, is not simply that they are subject to competing claims on their labor power and productivity; indeed, in some cases this is not an issue at all. Rather, it is the economic expectations and demands of their wives' female kin, especially their wives' mothers. But this is only part of the problem. The other salient issue is that the rising social expectations placed on married men occur in postcolonial economic and political contexts in which the realization of men's goals is deeply problematic. Various aspects of this dilemma are highlighted in one observer's remarks that "rising social expectations have not been proportionately paralleled by new channels being created for realizing these aspirations" and that "the desire to accumulate wealth or professional prestige has become an increasing psychological burden on Minangkabau men" (Mitchell 1969:131).

The structure of the desires and "psychological burdens" at issue here provides a powerful incentive for Minangkabau men to engage in temporary out-migration and to distinguish themselves in entrepreneurial activities—the fruits of which can enhance their own material standing and prestige as well as that of wider kin groups. Obviously, not all men are successful, however, and we might consider some of the implications of these facts with respect to divorce and the existence of counterhegemonic views of Minangkabau masculinity.

Data on Minangkabau divorce and its distribution are very much in keeping with the relevant data from Negeri Sembilan (Peletz 1988, esp. ch. 7). Tanner (1982:139) comments that the Minangkabau rate "varies widely" from village to village and that at the time of her research in 1964, divorce "varied from two to forty-four percent." More recent data indicate that the divorce rate among male elders is between 45 and 51 percent and that the rate for female elders is between 32 and 36 percent (Kato 1982:181).

Relatively infrequent divorce, according to Tanner (1982:148, n. 10), is due to "economic prosperity" and "modernist Islam." In light of the existence of similar patterns in Negeri Sembilan, I take the first part of this explanation to mean that divorce is less common among relatively wealthy households because the husbands-fathers in those households are better able to live up to the economic expectations and demands of their wives and female kin than are married men in poor households; the fact that the adult members of such households also have more property and other wealth to lose in the event of divorce may also be relevant. The second part of the explanation, concerning the influence of modernist Islam, may be interpreted to mean that cultural and institutional factors associated with modernist Islam have effectively discouraged divorce (as has happened in Negeri Sembilan and other parts of Malaysia) by impressing upon men and women their marital and parental responsibilities as Muslims or by otherwise contributing to the durability and perhaps the stability of conjugal bonds. Such variables do not operate in a classless vacuum, however, and all things being equal, it is probably harder for poor men and women to honor their familial commitments as Muslims in the context of marriage. This is significant insofar as the alternative discourse on Minangkabau masculinity that depicts men as unreasonable and irresponsible is fueled by perceptions of husbands-fathers at the bottom of the increasingly pronounced class hierarchy; this is clearly the case in Negeri Sembilan as well (Peletz 1994b, 1996).

Given the situation described here, one might reasonably expect to find among the Minangkabau (as in Negeri Sembilan) an alternative discourse on masculinity that is in many respects out of keeping with the official line emphasizing male ascendancy[9] and that is, in addition, highly elaborated. In point of fact, alternative, largely counterhegemonic representations of masculinity concerning male irresponsibility and the ways in which men's "passion" (*nafsu*) dominates their "reason" (*akal*) and renders them morally bankrupt are found in daily discourse and are enshrined in oral and written literature (Whalley 1993; Krier 1994; Blackwood 1995). But unlike in Negeri Sembilan, they do not appear to be highly elaborated. Why this is so is difficult to gauge with any degree of certitude, and it is quite possible that their minimal presence in the ethnographic literature reflects previous observers' narrow focus on official discourse (or on *adat*, matriliny, or women). I think it more likely, however, that the alternative discourse may exist in relatively unelaborated form because Minangkabau masculinity is defined in a much less economically based "performative" fashion than is masculinity in Negeri Sembilan and is thus less easily called into question by the realities of men's economic performances in their roles as husbands and fathers. In other words, because Minangkabau (unlike Negeri Sembilan) constructions of masculinity are informed in significant ways by the notion that men both possess and convey biogenetically and spiritually potent "seed" or "blood" to their wives and their wives' households and lineages (Tanner 1982:137–138; Pak 1986, n.d.; Krier 1994), Minangkabau men are less apt to be defined in negative terms simply because they fall short in a narrow economic sense. The emphasis on men's contributions conveyed through semen and realized in the production of (ideally) "high quality" children belonging to the wife's household and lineage thus constrains the elaboration of negative discourses on masculinity, though it doesn't preclude their (relatively unelaborated) existence in the first place.

One corollary of these arguments is that Minangkabau constructions of masculinity are less vulnerable to the dislocations and other vicissitudes entailed in local communities' heightened integration into state frameworks, global economies, and systems of nationalist and transnational discourse than are constructions of masculinity in Negeri Sembilan. But we still see men being defined and judged in critically important ways in terms of their contributions to their wives and their wives' kin and to reproduction in both the biological and social senses of the term: "While [Minangkabau] women are defined as the source of continuity, [Minangkabau] men are essential to the cycle of continuity; they are the agents who are brought in from the outside or who are sent out to create children; the future reproducers of the women's lineages" (Ng 1987:205).

We are now in a position to address the contrasting economic ethics that exist among the Minangkabau and Negeri Sembilan Malays and to focus on why the entrepreneurial traditions reported for the Minangkabau are so much stronger than those of Negeri Sembilan Malays. The central question is this: In light of the commonalities outlined in the preceding pages, what is it about the Minangkabau case that allowed entrepreneurial activities to flourish to the point where, according to conventional wisdom, the Minangkabau are able to compete successfully with the Chinese? Put differently, why has the development of such activities been hindered among Negeri Sembilan Malays when they share so much with the Minangkabau?

The answers to these questions lie largely in the dissimilar historical experiences of the Minangkabau and the Malays of Negeri Sembilan, particularly their divergent experiences under the mercantile and colonial policies of the Dutch and the British, respectively.[10] Dutch policies (focusing initially on the production and trade of Sumatran pepper, later on coffee and other agricultural commodities) not only drew the Minangkabau into the world market economy long before British policies drew Malays into that same system but also made possible a more expansive range of opportunities for social mobility than did the policies of the British. Beginning in the seventeenth century, Dutch-sponsored economic change in the Minangkabau region increased local trading and other business opportunities. The Minangkabau were already known to have a propensity and knack for commerce and economic experimentation; abundant deposits of gold and iron in the area had helped pave the way for their extensive involvement in the gold trade with Indian merchants as early as the thirteenth and fourteenth centuries (Dobbin 1983:60–62) Neighboring peoples (such as the Batak) apparently lacked these resources. The Dutch presence also created a relatively broad array of new occupational and social positions connected with the development of colonial administration and the attendant spread of state-sanctioned enterprises fueled by Western capital. Due partly to the relatively high population densities among the Minangkabau, the Dutch had no reason to encourage massive Chinese or other immigration into Minangkabau or other regions of Sumatra (but see Stoler 1985).[11] By and large, the Minangkabau were both able and willing to fill these new positions. And because they were "pacified" relatively early on (as compared with, say, the Acehnese), they could avail themselves of certain types of colonial opportunities—including modern education and careers in the civil service—in ways that other local peoples could not.

The British, for their part, also created new economic opportunities, but their policies in Negeri Sembilan and other parts of the Malay Peninsula simultaneously encouraged large-scale immigration into the area. This was due in large measure to the extensive labor requirements of British-backed commercial enterprises (tin mining and the estate cultivation of coffee, gambier, tapioca, etc.) in conjunction with the low population densities of Malay communities and the colonial attitude that "Malay labour is so uncertain . . . that they [Malays] won't do as estate hands" (*RSSU* 1880:2). Compared to the policies of the Dutch in Sumatra, moreover, British policies were apparently more strongly geared toward tying locals (Malays) to the land and otherwise "keeping the natives native." One reason for this is that the British were apprehensive that Malays would embrace something like the Padri Movement, which began among the Minangkabau around 1803 and continued through the 1830s. Padri adherents sought to revitalize Islam and purify and transform rural society, especially in the hill villages where local institutions had been undermined by the dislocating effects of coffee production for the world market (Dobbin 1983). The Padri also had a decidedly anti-colonial bent. This was partly a reaction to Dutch efforts to monopolize trading and attendant opportunities associated with the commercial production of coffee; the Dutch wanted to ensure that the Padri, who relied on profits from the production and trade of coffee to sustain their communities, had no economic base from which to operate.

The upshot of British efforts to "keep the natives native" so as to preclude anticolonial movements cast in Islamic terms (which reoccurred among the Minangkabau in the late 1830s and again in the 1890s and 1908) was that British policies rather quickly arrested the development of the entrepreneurial traditions that had existed prior to colonial rule among Malay elites and other segments of the Malay population. These same policies also helped guarantee that such traditions would not resurface for considerable time to come. Needless to say, once the Chinese became firmly established in large numbers in Negeri Sembilan (recall that as early as 1911 the Chinese composed over 31 percent of the state's population), local Malays with entrepreneurial inclinations found themselves hard pressed to compete economically. The formidable economic odds thus posed by tremendous numbers of largely landless, trade-dependent Chinese never existed among the Minangkabau, the more general point being that by 1991 the Chinese made up around 4 percent of Indonesia's population and about 32 percent of Malaysia's (SarDesai 1994:12).

Similarly, even though not devised with this goal in mind, British policies undercut clans and lineages in Negeri Sembilan to a much greater degree than Dutch policies among the Minangkabau. For these and other reasons, present-day Negeri Sembilan differs from contemporary Minangkabau in that kin groupings such as localized clans are less internally differentiated in a segmentary sense, and kin group identity appears to be less pronounced. Additionally, in Negeri Sembilan one no longer finds corporate groups in the form of extended families composed of the children and grandchildren of one woman, all of whom ideally live in one house. Economic activities among individual males in Negeri Sembilan thus tend not to be undertaken with concerns for the present standing or future security or advancement of larger kin groupings in mind. This constitutes an important contrast with Minangkabau (see Graves 1981:4) and, significantly, with Chinese. In both of the latter cases, such concerns are reported to motivate men's economic activity in important ways or at least to encourage them to "go the extra mile."

The fact that most Minangkabau men are still expected to make economic contributions to their matrilineal kin, especially their sisters and their sisters' children—even though they also assume economic responsibility for their wives and their own children and are enjoined to enhance the economic and prestige standing of their wives' kin groups—also spurs them to economic accumulation. Negeri Sembilan men are not confronted with competing expectations and demands to the same degree and might even be said to experience fewer and less intense demands on their labor power and productivity. The majority of Negeri Sembilan men do not spend much time resting on their haunches, but all things being equal, they can do so if they fulfill the expectations entailed in the roles of husband and father (and of course village citizen and good Muslim), whereas Minangkabau men cannot.

My comparative remarks have focused less explicitly on Islam than is perhaps warranted (see Abdullah 1972; Dobbin 1983), but this is more a function of the constraints of space than anything else. Let it suffice to say that since the eighteenth century, transnational religious impulses such as those realized in the florescence among the Minangkabau of Sufi brotherhoods, or *tarekat* (e.g., the Naksyabandiah, Syattariyah, and Kadiriyah), and subsequently, Wahabi-oriented reformist movements like the Padri, have been of far greater social and cultural centrality among the Minangkabau than among Negeri Sembilan Malays. Some such movements have explicitly encouraged trade and commerce and have in fact been based in prayer houses and larger communities that placed a premium on economic self-sufficiency. Interestingly, the most famous among them, the Padri Movement, not only arose at a time when the Dutch sought to restrict Minangkabau trading activities by monopolizing local and regional commerce but also found its strongest bases of support in hill villages heavily involved in the production of coffee for the world market. The Padri phenomenon had no real counterparts in the Malay Peninsula, and the same is true of Minangkabau reform movements of the 1890s and 1908. This difference may help explain why local mosques and prayer houses have long been more effective in Minangkabau in creating a common identity among in-marrying men and among males as a whole. This strong sense of local, regional, and overall cultural identity forged in part through religious institutions may also provide the basis for economic association and assistance in the context of out-migration (see Graves 1981:19), as has been suggested by various observers of Minangkabau society. Clearly such association occurs among Chinese but not in significant measure among Negeri Sembilan Malays.

The issue of cultural identity and "in-group sentiment" is profitably viewed in the context of nationalist discourse, which in the Indonesian case is Javacentric and somewhat hostile to the Minangkabau. One need not belabor the twofold point that the Minangkabau are an ethnic minority, constituting a mere 3 percent of Indonesia's population and that the maintenance and assertion of their distinctive cultural identity presupposes the reproduction (however much transformed) of various features of matriliny, along with the reconstituted traditions of education, out-migration, and entrepreneurial acumen for which they have long been famous. Nationalist discourse in Malaysia, in contrast, does not represent the Malays of Negeri Sembilan as an ethnic minority or as a minority business community. Rather, it assimilates them to the dominant category "Malay," which is cast in heavily pastoral terms and which—despite but also partly because of the New Economic Policy and Vision 20/20—is increasingly both undifferentiated and defined in sharp opposition to all things Chinese, including the entrepreneurial and attendant values associated with Chinese in Malaysia. To greatly oversimplify, then, locally and regionally defined cultural identities appear to be more pronounced in Minangkabau than among the Malays of Negeri Sembilan and do, in any event, valorize the symbolic and material entailments of entrepreneurial practices and orientations in very different ways. In Minangkabau discourse, these practices and orientations are positively valorized as key features that distinguish Minangkabau from the numerically and culturally dominant Javanese. These practices are, moreover, expressions of the underlying cultural genius that has resulted in their outperforming Javanese and other Indonesian ethnic groups in literary and artistic pursuits and in the fields of education, civil service, and national(ist) politics. In the discourse of Negeri Sembilan Malays, in contrast, entrepreneurial practices and orientations tend to carry negative connotations; such practices are linked with the culturally devalued Chinese, who are widely viewed as "crude and amoral parvenus solely intent on . . . their own private capital accumulation" (Nonini 1983:171).

Conclusion

Comparative exercises of the sort pursued here raise as many questions as they answer, but they do at least have the virtue of helping us delimit some of the topics we need to examine if we are to gain a deeper understanding of the Great Transformation and the variables that have operated in particular historical and political economic contexts to facilitate or, alternatively, to hinder it. A more comprehensive comparison of Negeri Sembilan Malays and Minangkabau would obviously need to focus more carefully on the precolonial experiences of these societies.[12] Key issues to explore further would include the precolonial implications of differences in the two regions' natural resources (especially mineral wealth), agricultural productivity, population densities, land shortages, occupational specialization, socioeconomic stratification, and status rivalries. Most such indices of economic differentiation appear to have been more pronounced in Minangkabau and certainly were so during the era immediately preceding the time when European policies and capital began to have a significant impact on Minangkabau and Negeri Sembilan. It would also be helpful to have a better understanding of the precise effects of the Minangkabau's "greater intercourse with strangers" in the centuries predating contact with Europeans and European capital, as well as the ways these and other variables might have contributed both to the prevalence of pawning and other transactions bearing on the alienation of land and to migration to outlying areas, including the Malay Peninsula.

It is hoped, in any case, that I have made it clear that the economic ethics of the Minangkabau and the Negeri Sembilan Malays are indissolubly linked with their systems of kinship, gender, and prestige and are also usefully viewed in relation to everyday social process and the more encompassing realities of political economy and historical change. This argument is relevant to an understanding of the economic ethics of the Chinese, who, for better or worse, continue to provide the primary point of reference for analytic evaluations of the economic cultures of Malays and other indigenous Southeast Asians. It is, moreover, very much in keeping with the thrust of recent studies indicating that the Chinese do not display entrepreneurial ethics in all economic contexts and that the ethics in question are, among other things, strongly gendered (Harrell 1985; see also Weller, this volume). The position taken in this chapter also resonates deeply with the general orientations of recent scholarship on Southeast Asian entrepreneurs (McVey 1992). A recurrent theme in this literature is that late-twentieth-century economic cultures in Malaysia and elsewhere in and beyond Southeast Asia are heavily informed by patterns of market and state organization in conjunction with the nationalist and transnationalist discourses to which these patterns are keyed. The latter theme is especially striking in the case of the well-capitalized "multiethnic" business and political partnerships that have emerged in Malaysia in the past few decades as a result of interventionist state policies encouraging the combined efforts and resources of Chinese tycoons and their family enterprises, on the one hand, and the well-heeled and increasingly business oriented members of Malay royal families, on the other (Sieh 1992). The rapidly evolving, hybrid, and protean cultures of these partnerships bear close scrutiny, not least for the additional insights they provide on Malaysia's late-twentieth-century experience of the Great Transformation.

NOTES

This chapter draws on fieldwork carried out in the Rembau district of Negeri Sembilan from 1978 to 1980 and 1987 to 1988 and on archival research undertaken in Malaysia and England in 1980. The first period of fieldwork was supported by the National Science Foundation (under grant BNS–7812499) and the University of Michigan (the Center for South and Southeast Asian Studies and the Rackham School of Graduate Studies); the second was supported by the Fulbright Scholars Program, the Wenner-Gren Foundation for Anthropological Research, and the Picker Fellowship Program at Colgate University. I would like to express my gratitude to Robert Hefner, Jennifer Krier, and Hue-Tam Ho Tai for their helpful comments on an earlier draft.

1. The Malays of Negeri Sembilan are known for their matrilineal descent groups and are invariably treated in the literature as a "special class" of Malays that cannot be accommodated by general statements or models that are meant to apply to the bilaterally oriented Malays living in other parts of the peninsula. Elsewhere I argue that the contrasts between Negeri Sembilan and other Malays are greatly overdrawn and that the underlying commonalities merit far more analytic attention than they have received thus far (Peletz 1994a, 1996).

2. For analyses of some of the more important contrasts in the economic ethics of China's dominant Han and the Hui ethnic minority, see Gladney, this volume.

3. The approach developed here builds on anthropological work on gender and prestige (e.g., Ortner and Whitehead 1981; Atkinson and Errington 1990; Kelly 1993) and is elaborated in Peletz (1996). The discussion of nineteenth-century Negeri Sembilan is based on archival and other historical sources cited in my earlier publications (Peletz 1988, 1996). Other recent work on gender and social change in Negeri Sembilan includes Stivens (1985, 1987, 1991) and McAllister (1987). See also Ong (1987, 1990, 1995) and Karim (1992) for analyses of gender and social change elsewhere in Malaysia.

4. For a discussion of some of the ways prestige concerns have figured into economic activity in Vietnam's Red River Delta, see Malarney, this volume.

5. Tania Li provides incisive analyses of the implications of ideas such as these in the context of Malay society in Singapore (Li 1989).

6. Some of these beliefs and practices are described elsewhere (Peletz 1988, 1993, 1996). For insightful discussion of the logic of this point in the context of Taiwanese society, see Weller, this volume.

7. Note also that, in my experience, wealthy Malays are not seen by the village majority as morally superior but as having attained their fortunes through trickery, exploitation of fellow villagers, or "good luck." They are not necessarily viewed as clever or hard working. And they tend to be envied and despised—so much so that the misfortunes that sometimes befall them are often regarded as "their own fault" even though they may also be attributed to envy or other antisocial sentiments on the part of malevolent others (see also Scott 1985).

8. Bogang is a pseudonym for the village in which I did my fieldwork. The village is located in the Rembau district of Negeri Sembilan. Its population in 1980 was 476; by 1988 the population had increased to 503.

9. The extent to which there is an official line emphasizing male ascendancy is actually somewhat in dispute (see Peletz 1996:ch. 7).

10. The first few points noted further on are taken from Swift (1971).

11. The Chinese constituted less than 0.02 percent of Sumatra's west coast population in the mid-nineteenth century and were less than 1 percent even in the 1920s (Graves 1981:44–45).

12. Some of the differences between the two societies (including, perhaps, those bearing on political succession, kinship terminology, and marriage patterns) may reflect the circumstances of the Minangkabau's migration to and settlement in Negeri Sembilan— beginning around the fourteenth century, if not earlier—along with their subsequent interactions (intermarriage, trade, political accommodation, and warfare) with both the non-Muslim aborigines and the (bilateral) Malays inhabiting surrounding areas.

REFERENCES

Official Records (published and unpublished)

(CFMS) *The Census of the Federated Malay States, 1911.* London: 1911.
(NSGG) *Negeri Sembilan Government Gazette,* 1896, 1897, 1909.
(RSSU) *Report on the State of Sungei Ujung, 1880.*

Books, Articles, and Theses

Abdullah, Taufik. 1972. "Modernization in the Minangkabau World: West Sumatra in the Early Decades of the Twentieth Century." In C. Holt, ed., *Culture and Politics in Indonesia*, pp. 179–245. Ithaca: Cornell University Press.

Atkinson, Jane, and Shelly Errington, eds. 1990. *Power and Difference: Gender in Island Southeast Asia*. Stanford: Stanford University Press.

Banks, David. 1983. *Malay Kinship*. Philadelphia: ISHI.

Beauvoir, Simone de. 1949. *The Second Sex*. New York: Random House.

Benda-Beckmann, Franz von. 1979. *Property in Social Continuity: Continuity and Change in the Maintenance of Property Relations Through Time in Minangkabau, West Sumatra*. The Hague: KTLV Press.

Blackwood, Evelyn. 1995. "Senior Women, Model Mothers, and Dutiful Wives: Managing Gender Contradictions in a Minangkabau Village." In A. Ong and M. Peletz, eds., *Bewitching Women, Pious Men: Gender and Body Politics in Southeast Asia*, pp. 124–158. Berkeley: University of California Press.

Bloch, Maurice. 1973. "The Long Term and the Short Term: The Economic and Political Signficance of the Morality of Kinship." In J. Goody, ed., *The Character of Kinship*, pp. 75–87. Cambridge: Cambridge University Press.

_____. 1989. *Ritual, History and Power: Selected Papers in Anthropology*. London: Athlone Press.

Bloch, Maurice, and Jonathan Parry. 1989. "Introduction: Money and the Morality of Exchange." In Parry and Bloch, eds., *Money and the Morality of Exchange*, pp. 1–32. Cambridge: Cambridge University Press.

Carsten, Janet. 1989. "Cooking Money: Gender and the Symbolic Transformation of Means of Exchange in a Malay Fishing Community." In Parry and Bloch, eds., *Money and the Morality of Exchange*, pp. 117–141. Cambridge: Cambridge University Press.

Chodorow, Nancy. 1989. *Feminism and Psychoanalytic Theory*. New Haven: Yale University Press.

Djamour, Judith. 1959. *Malay Kinship and Marriage in Singapore*. London: Athlone Press.

Dobbin, Christine. 1983. *Islamic Revivalism in a Changing Peasant Economy: Central Sumatra, 1784–1847*. Scandanavian Institute of Asian Studies Monograph Series, no. 47. London: Curzon Press.

Ellen, Roy. 1983. "Social Theory, Ethnography, and the Understanding of Practical Islam in Southeast Asia." In M.B. Hooker, ed., *Islam in Southeast Asia*, pp. 50–91. Leiden: E.J. Brill.

Errington, Frederick. 1984. *Manners and Meaning in West Sumatra: The Social Context of Consciousness*. New Haven: Yale University Press.

Freedman, Maurice. 1971. *Chinese Lineage and Society: Fukien and Kwangtung*. London: Athlone Press.

Graves, Elizabeth. 1981. *The Minangkabau Response to Dutch Colonial Rule in the Nineteenth Century*. Modern Indonesia Project, Monograph Series Publication, no. 60. Ithaca: Southeast Asia Program, Cornell University.

Gullick, J.M. 1951. "The Negri Sembilan Economy of the 1890s." *Journal of the Royal Asiatic Society, Malayan Branch* 24, 1:38–55.

_____. 1985. "The Entrepreneur in Late 19th-Century Malay Peasant Society." *Journal of the Royal Asiatic Society, Malaysian Branch* 58, 1:59–70.

_____. 1987. *Malay Society in the Late Nineteenth Century: The Beginnings of Change.* Singapore: Oxford University Press.

Harrell, Steven. 1985. "Why Do the Chinese Work So Hard?" *Modern China* 11, 2:203–226.

Heng, Pek Koon. 1992. "The Chinese Business Elite in Malaysia." In Ruth McVey, ed., *Southeast Asian Capitalists,* pp. 127–144. Ithaca: Cornell Southeast Asia Program.

Kahn, Joel. 1980. *Minangkabau Social Formations: Indonesian Peasants and the World Economy.* Cambridge: Cambridge University Press.

_____. 1993. *Constituting the Minangkabau: Peasants, Culture, and Modernity in Colonial Indonesia.* Providence, R.I.: Berg.

Karim, Wazir Jahan. 1992. *Women and Culture: Between Malay Adat and Islam.* Boulder: Westview Press.

Kato, Tsuyoshi. 1982. *Matriliny and Migration: Evolving Minangkabau Tradition in Indonesia.* Ithaca: Cornell University Press.

_____. 1991. "When Rubber Came: The Negeri Sembilan Experience." *Tonan Ajia Kenkyu* (Southeast Asian studies) 29, 2:109–157.

Kelly, Raymond. 1993. *Constructing Inequality: The Fabrication of a Hierarchy of Virtue Among the Etoro.* Ann Arbor: University of Michigan Press.

Krier, Jennifer. 1994. "Displacing Distinction: Political Processes in a Minangkabau Backcountry." Ph.D. dissertation, Harvard University.

Li, Tania. 1989. *Malays in Singapore: Culture, Economy, and Ideology.* Singapore: Oxford University Press.

Madge, Charles, 1974. "The Relevance of Family Patterns to the Process of Modernization in East Asia." In R.J. Smith, ed., *Social Organization and the Applications of Anthropology: Essays in Honor of Lauriston Sharp,* pp. 161–195. Ithaca: Cornell University Press.

McAllister, Carol. 1987. "Matriliny, Islam and Capitalism: Combined and Uneven Development in the Lives of Negeri Sembilan Women." Ph.D. dissertation, Department of Anthropology, University of Pittsburgh.

McKinley, Robert. 1981. "Cain and Abel on the Malay Peninsula." In M. Marshall, ed., *Siblingship in Oceania: Studies in the Meaning of Kin Relations,* pp. 335–388. Ann Arbor: University of Michigan Press.

McVey, Ruth, ed. 1992. *Southeast Asian Capitalists.* Ithaca: Cornell Southeast Asia Program.

Mitchell, Istutiah Gunawan. 1969. "The Socio-Cultural Environment and Mental Disturbance: Three Minangkabau Case Histories." *Indonesia* 7:123–137.

Ng, Cecilia. 1987. "The Weaving of Prestige: Village Women's Representations of the Social Categories of Minangkabau Society." Ph.D. dissertation, Department of Anthropology, Australian National University.

Nonini, Donald. 1983. "The Chinese Truck Transport 'Industry' of a Peninsular Malaysia Market Town." In L. Lim and L.A.P. Gosling, eds., *The Chinese in Southeast Asia,* vol. 1, pp. 171–206. Singapore: Maruzen Asia.

Ong, Aihwa. 1987. *Spirits of Resistance and Capitalist Discipline: Factory Women in Malaysia.* Albany: SUNY Press.

_____. 1990. "Japanese Factories, Malay Workers: Class and Sexual Metaphors in West Malaysia." In Jane Atkinson and Shelly Errington, eds., *Power and Difference: Gender in Island Southeast Asia*, pp. 385–422. Stanford: Stanford University Press.

_____. 1995. "Malay Families, Women's Bodies, and the Body Politic in Malaysia." In Aihwa Ong and Michael Peletz, eds., *Bewitching Women, Pious Men: Gender and Body Politics in Southeast Asia*, pp. 159–194. Berkeley: University of California Press.

Ortner, Sherry, and Harriet Whitehead. 1981. "Introduction." In Ortner and Whitehead, eds., *Sexual Meanings: The Cultural Construction of Gender and Sexuality*, pp. 1–27. Cambridge: Cambridge University Press.

Pak, Ok-Kyung. 1986. "Lowering the High, Raising the Low: Gender, Alliance, and Property Relations in a Minangkabau Peasant Community of West Sumatra." Ph.D. dissertation, Laval University.

_____. n.d. "Exchange of Men and Ideology of Male Ascendancy Among the Minangkabau of Sumatra." Typescript.

Parry, Jonathan, and Maurice Bloch, eds. 1989. *Money and the Morality of Exchange.* Cambridge: Cambridge University Press.

Peletz, Michael G. 1988. *A Share of the Harvest: Kinship, Property, and Social History Among the Malays of Rembau.* Berkeley: University of California Press.

_____. 1993. "Knowledge, Power, and Personal Misfortune in a Malay Context." In C.W. Watson and R. Ellen, eds., *Understanding Witchcraft and Sorcery in Southeast Asia*, pp. 149–177. Honolulu: University of Hawaii Press.

_____. 1994a. "Comparative Perspectives on Kinship and Cultural Identity in Negeri Sembilan." *Sojourn* 9, 1:1–53.

_____. 1994b. "Neither Reasonable Nor Responsible: Contrasting Representations of Masculinity in a Malay Society." *Cultural Anthropology* 9, 2:135–178.

_____. 1996. *Reason and Passion: Representations of Gender in a Malay Society.* Berkeley: University of California Press.

Redding, S. Gordon. 1990. *The Spirit of Chinese Capitalism.* Berlin: Walter de Gruyter.

Reid, Anthony. 1988. *Southeast Asia in the Age of Commerce, 1450–1680.* Vol. 1, *The Lands Below the Winds.* New Haven: Yale University Press.

_____. 1993. *Southeast Asia in the Age of Commerce, 1450–1680.* Vol. 2, *Expansion and Crisis.* New Haven: Yale University Press.

Richards, Audrey. 1951. "Some Types of Family Structures Amongst the Central Bantu." In A.R. Radcliffe-Brown and D. Forde, eds., *African Systems of Kinship and Marriage*, pp. 207–251. London: Oxford University Press.

SarDesai, D.R. 1994. *Southeast Asia: Past and Present.* 3rd ed. Boulder: Westview Press.

Schneider, David. 1961. "The Distinctive Features of Matrilineal Descent Groups." In D. Schneider and K. Gough, eds., *Matrilineal Kinship*, pp. 1–29. Berkeley: University of California Press.

Scott, James. 1976. *The Moral Economy of the Peasant: Subsistence and Rebellion in Southeast Asia.* New Haven: Yale University Press.

_____. 1985. *Weapons of the Weak: Everyday Forms of Peasant Resistance.* New Haven: Yale University Press.

Siegel, James. 1969. *The Rope of God.* Berkeley: University of California Press.

Sieh, Lee Mei Ling. 1992. "The Transformation of Malaysian Business Groups." In Ruth McVey, ed., *Southeast Asian Capitalists*, pp. 103–126. Ithaca: Cornell Southeast Asia Program.

Siow, Moli. 1983. "The Problems of Ethnic Cohesion Among the Chinese in Peninsular Malaysia: Intraethnic Divisions and Interethnic Accommodation." In L. Lim and L.A.P. Gosling, eds., *The Chinese in Southeast Asia,* vol. 2, pp. 170–188. Singapore: Maruzen Asia.

Skinner, G. William. 1957. *Chinese Society in Thailand: An Analytical History.* Ithaca: Cornell University Press.

Stivens, Maila. 1985. "The Fate of Women's Land Rights: Gender, Matriliny, and Capitalism in Rembau, Negeri Sembilan, Malaysia." In H. Afshar, ed., *Women, Work, and Ideology in the Third World,* pp. 3–36. London: Tavistock.

_____. 1987. "Family and State in Malaysian Industrialization: The Case of Rembau, Negeri Sembilan, Malaysia." In H. Afshar, ed., *Women, State, and Ideology,* pp. 89–110. Albany: SUNY Press.

_____. 1991. "The Evolution of Kinship Relations in Rembau, Negeri Sembilan, Malaysia." In J. Kemp and F. Husken, eds., *Cognation and Social Organization in Southeast Asia,* pp. 71–88. Leiden: Koninklijk Instituut voor Taal-, Land-, en Volkenkunde.

Stoler, Ann. 1985. *Capitalism and Confrontation in Sumatra's Plantation Belt, 1870–1979.* New Haven: Yale University Press.

Swift, Michael G. 1965. *Malay Peasant Society in Jelebu.* London: Athlone Press.

_____. 1971. "Minangkabau and Modernization." In L. Hiatt and C. Jaywardena, eds., *Anthropology in Oceania,* pp. 255–267. Sydney: Augus and Robertson.

Tanner, Nancy M. 1982. "The Nuclear Family in Minangkabau Matriliny: The Mirror of Disputes." *Bijdragen to de Taal-, Land-, en Volkenkunde* 138, 1:129–151.

Taussig, Michael. 1980. *The Devil and Commodity Fetishism in South America.* Chapel Hill: University of North Carolina Press.

Taylor, E.N. [1929] 1970. "The Customary Law of Rembau." In M.B. Hooker, ed., *Readings in Malay Adat Laws,* pp. 109–151. Singapore: Singapore University Press.

Watson, Rubie. 1985. *Inequality Among Brothers: Class and Kinship in South China.* Cambridge: Cambridge University Press.

Watts, Michael. 1992. "Capitalisms, Crises, and Cultures I." In A. Pred and M. Watts, *Reworking Modernity: Capitalisms and Symbolic Discontent,* pp. 1–20. New Brunswick, N.J.: Rutgers University Press.

Whalley, Lucy. 1993. "Virtuous Women, Productive Citizens: Negotiating Tradition, Islam, and Modernity in Minangkabau, Indonesia." Ph.D. dissertation, University of Illinois.

Winstedt, Richard O. 1934. "Negri Sembilan: The History, Polity, and Beliefs of the Nine States." *Journal of the Royal Asiatic Society, Malayan Branch* 12, 3:35–114.

Wong, Siu-lun. 1985. "The Chinese Family Firm: A Model." *British Journal of Sociology* 36, 1:58–72.

_____. 1988. "The Applicability of Asian Family Values to Other Sociocultural Settings." In P. Berger and M. Hsiao, eds., *In Search of an East Asian Development Model,* pp. 134–152. New Brunswick, N.J.: Transaction Books.

Yao, Souchou. 1987. "The Fetish of Relationships: Chinese Business Transactions in Singapore." *Sojourn* 2, 1:89–111.

Part Three
Southeast Asian Capitalisms

seven

ᕯ

Women Traders in Javanese Marketplaces

Ethnicity, Gender, and the Entrepreneurial Spirit

JENNIFER ALEXANDER

Analyses of the relationship between economic behavior and culture have often been centered on accounts of the economic abilities of particular ethnic groups. In the literature on Java the overarching context for such discussions is the implicit assumption that the apparent absence of Javanese entrepreneurs, both now and during the colonial period, does not require a specific explanation beyond reference to values inherent in Javanese culture that, however admirable, are ill adapted to commercial life. Scholarly attention has therefore focused on the apparent anomalies: small groups of Javanese—subcommunities—that either are unusually wealthy or dominate particular trades and industries. Given the initial assumption, the research problem is framed as a demonstration of intracultural difference, that is, how these successful communities differ from proper Javanese.

The same groups of Javanese market traders are repeatedly singled out for mention in the colonial reports. Prominent among them are the dried-fish merchants of Semarang, the goldsmiths of Kotagede, the batik traders of Solo, and the tobacco traders of Magelang and Madura. Other communities are identified with services, for example, the money-lending Kalang, the "traveling salesmen" from Tasikmalaya, and the shopkeepers of Bawean. Some members of many of these communities are still in the same businesses. Some were, and are, reputed to be staunch Muslims. The historical associations among Islam, trade, and north coast communities and the fact that many wealthy Javanese have been on the haj are also frequently noted, albeit with different levels of esteem. For some writers hostile to Islam, such persons were alienated by both their religious and their economic practices from the authentic Javanese community. Other perceptive scholars from van Deventer (1904) to Geertz (1963), although agreeing that the desire to accumulate sufficient wealth to participate in the pilgrimage to Mecca set such Javanese apart to some extent from the mass of society, argued that their religion both encouraged and legitimated their taking a more economically rational approach to business dealings. They also pointed to the role of the experience gained from international travel in modernizing the home communities and alerting them to economic possibilities, although Geertz (1963) put more weight on membership of reformist Islamic organizations, especially the first indigenous trade association, which was formed in 1911 to challenge Chinese domination of the batik cloth industry (Noer 1973).

Although not always explicit, the key analytical point is that members of the entrepreneurial communities are thought to have acquired through their religious practices values that differentiate them from other Javanese. The notion that entrepreneurs owe their success, at least in part, to the internalization of "economic" values such as thrift, diligence, and rational calculation is evidently seductive (not least to the entrepreneurs themselves), and several detailed studies of specific, relatively wealthy communities whose inhabitants are reputed to be especially pious have uncovered attitudes about economic calculation, accumulation, and social relations that appear conducive to, or at least congruent with, economic success. Dobbin's (1991) careful study of the famous traders of Bawean, for example, points out that by the 1850s this small island produced more pilgrims than any other district. Although she does not regard them as "a group of Muslim Puritans of religiously inspired entrepreneurial temper," she suggests that "the care with savings exhibited by those making the *haj* and the frugality with which they conducted their daily lives was an important contributory factor to later commercial success on Java" and attributes their "pre-adaptation" to commerce to their early interactions with Chinese smugglers, their extensive land market, and their export-orientated local industry of matmaking (1991:123). The extent to which these set the Bawean apart from other Javanese might be debated; certainly the three social institutions that are central to Bawean commercial operations (the *pondok* [the Qur'anic boarding school], supplier credit, and partners in other regions who are often siblings) are not unique to them. But despite these caveats, it must be acknowledged that claims concerning the salience of particular values in the economic success of specific Javanese subcommunities are grounded in a considerable body of empirical material.

There are, however, some equally considerable empirical difficulties. In the first place, the claimed correlation between entrepreneurship and Islamic piety is not compelling for the colonial period, let alone contemporary Java. That the vast majority of *haji* are relatively wealthy is true by definition, but this need not imply that most of the wealthy are *haji* or that religiosity preceded wealth rather than the reverse. Especially in some cases, colonial writers evidently inferred piety from economic practices. Nakamura (1983:11) claims that the Kalang from Kotagede, "moneychangers" eschewing direct interest charges by making loans in one currency and taking payment in another and usually termed "pious Muslim Kalang," were not particularly devout. As with the Hui in China (see Gladney, this volume), entrepreneurial ability was evidently seen by others as a defining ethnic characteristic. Nor is there compelling evidence that trade and small industry—supposedly the "entrepreneurial" sectors—were more certain paths to wealth than, say, renting out land or lending money (Hüsken 1989). Indeed, there are strong grounds for thinking that it was precisely the profits that the village elites derived from renting out land and lending money that financed much of the rural industry and trade (White 1991).

Not only is there some danger in inferring specific "economic" values from membership in particular cultural communities, it is also unlikely that most successful indigenous traders and small industrialists belonged to such groups. The subcommunities repeatedly noted in the colonial reports were probably singled out precisely because they were small but very visible minorities in the rural marketplaces. They were visible both because they were men and because they traded in commodities produced by or destined for sale to non-Javanese. As is demonstrated elsewhere (Alexander and Alexander 1991), the colonial authorities were simply not interested in the much larger sector of the rural economy comprising commodities produced by Javanese for consumption by Javanese, in part because most of the participants in this sector were women.

The widespread participation of Javanese in land, finance, and labor markets, as well as the very large numbers of Javanese traders, some of whom operated substantial businesses (Fernando and Bulbeck 1992:254–259), makes it unreasonable to assume that values compatible with economic success were not also present among the Javanese population at large, especially among the numerically largest group of women traders. More generally, it suggests that trawling for values that might be congruent with economic success among members of particular ethnic groups is unlikely to be a fruitful line of inquiry. It is difficult to establish the significance of any particular value, say, thrift or honesty, for the creation of wealth, and although general cultural ties are often critical in maintaining group identity and the commercial benefits that follow, the specificity of the cultural content seems much less important. In most cultures,[1] including the Javanese, the connection between cultural identity and economic success is inevitably rather tenuous.

This is not to deny the importance of shared cultural associations—be they ethnic, kinship, regional, religious, or based on "old school ties"—in fostering group identity or to deny that this shared identity may have economic consequences. For example, extreme specialization of production to the extent that single villages produce single products seems as common in contemporary Java as it was in the nineteenth century, when many (but again not all) of the renowned groups of Javanese traders were from such communities. The often subtle subcultural distinctions that accompany an emphasis on subcultural identity are clearly important in "localizing" the production of a specific commodity in a particular village or region. But it is also becoming increasingly clear (see, e.g., Goodman 1989; see Luong, this volume) that localization of production, far from reflecting an unreflexive attachment to tradition, has considerable advantages in an innovating economy: Among other things, it facilitates the acquisition of skills and new techniques; it promotes an efficient division and subdivision of tasks between subcontractors; it makes effective use of scarce finance while distributing risk; and it provides an orientation point for potential buyers. This in turn provides both the opportunity and the need for interregional trade.

The general difficulties of functionalist arguments—partial descriptions masquerading as explanations—are now widely appreciated, but an additional major problem, which might be termed the "strong" cultural argument, is that such arguments continue a long scholarly tradition of treating the economy as separate from, and in some senses opposed to, society and culture. One alternative is to recognize that in all societies the economy is no more (or less) a "brute fact" than kinship or religion: All three are culturally constituted. From this point of view, practices such as the gendered division of labor, the relationships linking traders, the use of bargaining to set prices, and the typical trajectory of commodities are all aspects of the "economic culture" that constitutes the Javanese economy as Javanese. But they are also, simultaneously, aspects of general Javanese culture. Rather than simply attributing aspects of the economy to aspects of the culture—many traders in Java are women because Javanese culture is matrifocal—we need to investigate the economy as a cultural system (Gudeman 1986).[2]

The *Pasar* System

One indication of the historical significance of commerce in the Javanese rural economy is the continuity of trading practices. All the Javanese terms that are used today for types of traders and forms of trading relationships can be found in the nineteenth-century official reports. Although there are obviously important historical and regional variations, it is thus possible to sketch the rudiments of a "Javanese" economic culture that constitutes a range of social practices such as the "*pasar* system." I should emphasize that transactions in what I term the *pasar* system take place in numerous sites other than the *pasar* (marketplace) proper, including vast numbers of "stores" *(warung)* in villages and small towns.[3] Similar trading practices are also used in rural labor and finance markets and are by no means confined to "traditional" commodities (Alexander 1987:86–110; Hart 1986).

My approach to understanding the commodity markets of Central Java is based on their conceptualization as three analytically distinct systems, which I gloss as "trade," "traders," and "trading" (Alexander 1987). The trade conceptualization treats the market as a system of material exchanges, examining the geographical distribution of marketplaces and the production and circulation of commodities. The salient problems of this perspective concern the relationships between the spatial distribution of marketplaces and their economic functions (e.g., Skinner 1985). In the traders perspective, the approach usually adopted by anthropologists (e.g., Gerke 1992), the market is a social system, and the emphasis is on describing the types of traders, their careers, and the social institutions that link them into complex webs of social relationships. The variables are types of traders—retailers, wholesalers, brokers—linked by institutionalized relationships that are simultaneously economic and social: economic because they channel supplies of commodities and finance; social because they link kinsmen, patrons and clients, or members of the same ethnic group. Much of the theoretical discussion within this perspective has been concerned with a perceived contradiction between the social and the economic aspects of such relationships on the grounds that the long-term goal of maintaining the relationship is incompatible with short-term profit maximization (Plattner 1985). The trading perspective, one that is too often ignored, conceptualizes the market as a structured flow of culturally grounded information and examines the ways in which traders make their living by acquiring information and concealing it from others (Geertz 1978; Alexander 1992). This last perspective focuses our attention on the processes of buying and selling through an analysis of trading practices ranging from the "localization" of vendors of similar commodities in one place and the prevalence of stable trading partnerships to the use of bargaining as a price-setting mechanism.

When commodity markets are considered from the perspective of trade— investigated as a system of commodity exchanges or, better, as "the trajectory or flow of a single item, thing, service and so on as it passes from hand to hand, from place to place" (Dilley 1992:9)—the most important features of Javanese rural commodity markets are the wide variety of unstandardized commodities, the great range in the value of individual transactions, the large number of selling points, and the enormous numbers of traders, three-quarters of them women. These factors combine to produce highly segmented markets. The *pasar* system might well be seen less as a single market for commodities than as an amalgamation of numerous, widely different, small commodity markets. Differences among these "submarkets" range from the scale of the typical transaction and of the enterprises involved through entry conditions to trading conventions including the gender of the participants. The major ordering principle of this diversity is spatial: Particular submarkets are localized.

Switching to the perspective of traders highlights the social aspects of the marketing system: the types of traders and the relationships that link them into complex trading networks. Although there are scores of terms differentiating particular types of traders (in itself evidence of highly segmented markets), Javanese distinguish two main categories: *juragan* and *bakul*. *Juragan* are "wholesalers" and are often men or Indonesian Chinese, although there are large numbers of women *juragan,* and most *juragan* are Javanese. *Bakul* are predominantly women, dealing with varying success with a wide range of agricultural and manufactured commodities. It is unusual for *bakul* to cooperate to run a single enterprise; even when both spouses are *bakul* trading in the same commodities, they normally operate independent businesses. But *bakul* often cooperate for such tasks as arranging transport, combine to purchase a large quantity of produce, or "lend" particular items of stock to one another. *Juragan,* however, often combine into partnerships. These sometimes take the form of a single business using common funds, in which case the owners are usually related women, but more commonly involve the relatively permanent trading relationships with *juragan* in other regions, which I discuss further on.

In the 1980s a reasonably successful *juragan* buying vegetables locally for sale elsewhere had at least 5 million rupiah[4] in trading finance and a daily turnover of five times this amount. Such *juragan* had three or four agents buying on commission and perhaps a dozen *bakul* as regular suppliers but bought from a large number of producer-vendors as well. *Juragan* have numerous avenues for the disposal of their purchases, but the bulk is shipped by truck to *juragan* in other regions. Often such *juragan* visit to make their purchases (and to check on supply conditions), but it is common for goods to be sent first and prices negotiated later. It is also common for large-scale buyers to pay a considerable advance *(persekot)* at the beginning of the season. At the other end of the marketing system, *juragan* enterprises serve a bulk-breaking function for all commodities except manufactured goods. Although a successful *bakul* might have stock worth several million rupiah, as much as a small *juragan,* her finance is unlikely to exceed a million rupiah. Most *bakul* operate with less than Rp30,000 in stock and many with less than Rp5,000. *Bakul* operating in the marketplace are "middlemen" in the (more or less) strict sense of the term: They buy all of the goods they sell.

Even such a brief description indicates that many apparently discrete and transitory transactions take place between established trading partners. These relationships combine several levels of traders or producers into a complex financial system in which the debtor at one level becomes the creditor of other, smaller traders. This system serves a critical economic function of cheaply and efficiently distributing scarce finance through the marketing and production system as a whole.[5]

There are two main forms of institutionalized trading relationships: *langganan tetep* and *ngalap-nyaur*. In a strict sense, the *ngalap-nyaur* relationship, characteristic of much petty trade, involves the provision of very short-term credit: Goods are distributed in the morning and paid for about noon after the marketplace closes. All or some of the goods may be returned in lieu of payment. Stripped to its essentials, the more important *langganan tetep* ("regular customer") relationship is a set line of interest-free credit. The creditor advances goods up to the fixed limit, the debt must be repaid in full after the Fasting Month, and the credit line is reextended. The trader normally pays cash for her fortnightly or monthly purchases (although often in arrears) so that the debt does not exceed the limit, but further short-term credit might be granted. For the debtor, who is usually a *bakul*, the greatest advantage is the opportunity to obtain far more stock than her own finance permits, but she can also replenish stock at "discount" rates and gets accurate knowledge of benchmark prices. For the supplier, both *juragan* and *bakul*, *langganan tetep* are advantageous because they ensure regular cash flow while reducing the risk of reneging.

These trading relationships are gradually established over a considerable period, so successful traders require not only the bargaining and general market skills that produce reasonable returns but also the personal skills to establish and maintain cordial social relationships. From the point of view of *bakul*, the critical difference between *ngalap-nyaur* and *langganan tetep* is the constraint imposed on the scale of their businesses. *Langganan tetep* are essential to maintain a high turnover, and traders unable to establish such relationships must work far harder and far longer for a far lower income.

Trading, the third and least common perspective, conceptualizes the market both as a structured flow of information and as a contested, culturally grounded system of meanings.[6] As in other "bazaar" economies (Geertz 1978), accurate information, particularly price information, is the scarcest commodity in Javanese marketplaces. Because commodities are not standardized and are variable in supply, because prices are seldom marked on the product or stall, and because soft-voiced bargaining is the usual means of negotiating a deal, prices vary considerably from transaction to transaction. This is not a form of "market failure" (Plattner 1985); Javanese traders see this unequal distribution of accurate price information as an opportunity to profit from their superior knowledge. The reason trading as a *juragan* is more profitable than trading as a *bakul* is not only the greater turnover but also the superior price information obtained from occupying a strategic point in the marketing system. *Juragan* can anticipate price changes about a day before most *bakul,* and they acknowledge that it is the "windfall profits" derived from the use of this information rather than the average markups that provide the largest rewards.

Another way to make this point is to emphasize that for most traders earning a reasonable living in the *pasar* system is not a matter of redistributing goods after adding a markup. Such methods require both extensive finance and a strategic position in the marketing structure: becoming a large *juragan* or moving outside the *pasar* system to become a shopowner in town. Consequently, most successful *bakul* employ a much more active strategy, attempting to maximize the return on each transaction by buying as cheaply as possible and selling for as much as the market will bear. This style of trading involves long periods of waiting broken by brief flurries of intensely concentrated activity: They often have only one or two genuine customers an hour. Although Javanese are generally regarded (and, more important, regard themselves) as reserved and restrained in their manner, the *pasar* itself is positively valued as *rame* (noisy, crowded) and for that reason is often thronged with people, many of whom have no intention of making a purchase.

The success of a *bakul* dealing in potentially profitable commodities depends on two commercial skills: her ability to negotiate prices when buying and selling and her ability to maintain the reputation of being able to pay on demand. As the latter depends in large degree on the former, it is not surprising that *bakul* emphasize bargaining skills (including the ability to judge quality) as the key to success. Buyers aim in the bargaining process to obtain a price toward the bottom of the current price range. Sellers describe such prices as *bak-bok,* implying (usually falsely) that they themselves have bought at that price, and their aim is to obtain a "good addition" *(bati apik),* preferably selling above the current price range. When *bakul* speak of their occupation as mainly requiring the virtues of patience *(kesabaran)* and a willingness to take pains *(terlaten),* they are putting themselves in the position of a buyer. A clever buyer must be persistent, almost passive, repeating her bids over and over again and raising them by only very small amounts at very long intervals. Her intention is to convince the seller that she knows the current price range and will pay no more. When *bakul* stress that the ideal *bakul* is also vivacious and friendly *(grapyak sumeh),* they switch the focus to the seller. Talking continuously, *bakul* try to strike up a friendly conversation with every potential customer, attracting customers to their stall, answering their questions, and fueling their desire for a particular item. A *bakul* might well ostentatiously demonstrate her generosity if one of the numerous beggars approaches her stall at this time. In both cases the virtues of a good trader are more likely to be attributed by Javanese to women rather than men.

But watching a skillful trader strew her stall with swathes of cloth and— chattering nonstop and sometimes nonsensically—first steer a customer toward a particular length and then entice, cajole, or even bully her into paying as much as possible for it suggests that other, less culturally valued, qualities are equally important for success. Whereas each completed transaction is usually followed by a gracious exchange of compliments and the seller tries to convince her customer that she has bought cleverly, protracted bargaining often becomes noisy, assertive, and rambunctious, even acrimonious and aggressive. I was frequently told that pious Muslims charged reasonable prices and were more circumspect in their claims (and almost as frequently told just the opposite) but seldom saw my informants act on these precepts. And although *bakul* frequently assert their honesty, it is commonly recognized that both buyer and seller will make unreliable assertions as they bluff and counterbluff. Indeed, Javanese asked by strangers how much they paid for the new goods they are carrying seem automatically to quote a lower price, apparently for fear of being thought foolish for paying too much.

So although the marketplace is positively valued for its bustle, it also has a number of negative characteristics. Much of the behavior of a successful trader would be regarded as vulgar *(kasar)* if repeated in other contexts, and it is easy for customers to pay far too much. Both characteristics make the *pasar* unpleasant for many men as well as wealthier women who are not themselves traders. Higher-status persons, both men and women, certainly fear getting into a shouting match with an aggressive *bakul*, which would compromise their dignity, but can easily avoid it by offering an ample price on a "take it or leave it" basis. Contrary to general belief, my experience is that although the wealthy do not bargain to the last rupiah, and some give generously to the unfortunate, they do not pay significantly more than anyone else. For buyers of lower status with less wealth, the market can be a source of anxiety simply because of the considerable stress of having to buy things they need but can barely afford. Even *bakul*, although generally positive about their occupation compared to the others open to them, acknowledge that theirs can be a very stressful and exhausting way to earn an income.

Does Gender Make a Difference?

The prominent economic roles of women and, in this particular case, the high percentage of female traders and the "feminine" characteristics of some of their trading practices raise the interesting possibility that Javanese market cultures are gendered; that is, in terms of the approaches described in the introduction to this volume, gender roles in *kejawaan*[7] Javanese society may have been "preadapted" to authorize substantial participation in market relationships by women.

Certainly from a comparative perspective, *kejawaan* Javanese society has few of the features that restrict and constrain the economic activities of women elsewhere. Indeed (and rather ironically given the frequent attribution of entrepreneurship to pious Islamic communities), the restrictions appear to be far stronger in the *santri* (orthodox Muslim) variant of Javanese culture (Mather 1983).[8] In rural society there is little direct economic discrimination against women. For example, although daughters usually inherit a smaller share of their parent's meager land than sons, women hold property (including land) in their own right before and after marriage and on divorce are entitled to their own property as well as a share of the household's wealth. Women, including married women, are not overly restricted in their movements as long as they return home each evening, work well into pregnancy, and normally resume work very soon after childbirth. As cooking and other routine household tasks are not highly valued in Javanese culture and children are often cared for by others, household responsibilities do not much inhibit a commercial career. Women are barred from very few jobs, and agricultural tasks conventionally performed by females mesh with the time requirements of the marketplace. Contrary to a tendency to see the high proportion of young women in factory labor forces as a recent development (e.g., Wolf 1992), very large numbers of women worked in nineteenth-century factories (Knight 1982; Saptari 1991). Then as now, women wage laborers were paid at considerably lower rates than men. The majority of women have more than one job, and this pattern of female employment is part of a rather unusual rural occupational structure in which most households as well as a high proportion of individual household members have multiple sources of income (White 1991).

Typical family and household relationships also facilitate female entry into commerce. In her definitive study Hildred Geertz (1961) described the Javanese family as matrifocal, contrasting the warm emotional links between mother and children (especially daughters) with the formal, almost avoidance, relationships between father and sons. Although fathers are treated with respect, sons often try to avoid interaction with their fathers and seldom work with them for long. The perpetuation of family relationships thus centers on the mother. For example, daughters, but not sons, often return to the household after divorce (which was formerly very common); girls often learn commercial skills from their mothers or mother's sisters; and absent children channel financial contributions to the household through their mother. The absence of clearly demarcated lines of power and the emphasis on individual autonomy might seem more striking to a contemporary observer than the matrifocal elements; the Javanese family certainly lacks the patriarchal and patrilineal emphasis that apparently facilitates the lifelong subordination of sons to fathers in some other Asian societies (see Hamilton, this volume). In common with other Austronesian societies, gender differences are not strongly marked and power is not identified with economic control (Errington 1990:5).

The barriers to female participation are, however, much stronger in other areas of social life; although women have considerable economic autonomy, they are politically and socially subordinate to men. Hierarchical social relationships appear to be more culturally marked among the elites (Hatley 1990:181), but village women also are expected to defer to men in language and demeanor, publicly and privately, and most women most of the time meet this expectation. Not only are women's formal political and religious activities severely restricted but they are also subject to legal sanctions. For example, men are the official heads of households, official male wage rates are 50 percent higher, and women find it more difficult to initiate divorce. It is important not to underestimate these restrictions, and they certainly caution against inferring social status from economic autonomy. But these social constraints do not impinge strongly on the economic activities of women within the *pasar* system; traders often told me how much they valued the freedom from social restrictions made possible by their occupation.

But the relationship between Javanese notions of appropriate feminine behavior and female economic participation has been cast more strongly than the previous discussion implies. It has often been argued that there are features of *kejawaan* Javanese culture that positively advantage women over men in pursuing a commercial career. Most of these "advantages" are seen to turn on the hierarchical nature of Javanese culture, in which the superior status of males is predicated on their ability to maintain control of their emotions and desires. For example, Siegel (1986:163–202), in his comprehensive account of what he calls "the domestication of money," argues that although money is a potential threat to hierarchy it can be assimilated to hierarchy by treating it as a token of respect from subordinate to superior—as a gift or even "a sacrifice." A proper "man's authority installs sufficient respect/fear in his wife to keep her attentive to his wants, which he need never express" (Keeler 1987:55). Commercial monetary transactions are potentially stressful for men because they place them in situations in which their claims to status might be questioned and because their use of money for purchases signals that they have not conquered desire. They are therefore content not only to "hand over their money to their wives" (Siegel 1986:200) but to assign all commercial transactions to them. This is appropriate because "a woman makes fewer claims to ascetic detachment from material concerns, and she need not feel shame at being the center of a scene" (Keeler 1987:54). For men conscious of their dignity, female success in commercial activities, far from being a threat to male authority, simply confirms their weaknesses. Other men, less status conscious perhaps, have put it to me more positively: *Sing wadon nek golek duwit ulet*—"the wife's good at making money."

As most of the largest Javanese commercial enterprises are in fact owned and run by men, this argument is implausible. It places too much weight on the views of a small elite and on, moreover, a rather simplified version of these views, as is indicated by Brenner's (1991:78–82) account of the differing roles of women in the merchant and the noble families of Solo. In any case, we need to pay rather more attention to the consequences of such cultural notions for social action in specific contexts. One female manager, for example, told me that she preferred to negotiate with men because women aggressively used their emotional and bargaining skills to gain the upper hand. But she thought women office staff were too often languid *(lamban)*, whereas males were full of enthusiasm. There is little doubt, however, that a view of commerce (and not only petty commerce) as an appropriate domain for women is widely held by Javanese men and women, and this, at least, legitimates female commercial activities in ways not possible in societies where commerce is seen as man's work.[9]

This argument might be pushed a little further by looking briefly at changes introduced in the 1980s and 1990s by the New Order government. There seems little doubt that the development policies of the postcolonial state in combination with general economic growth have rapidly increased well-paid employment for many women. There appear to be few barriers to the employment of women university and upper-high-school graduates in government and private firms, and women are not restricted to lower-level positions. Although I am not aware of any figures, I suspect that compared to in the United States, a considerably higher proportion of middle- and upper-level managers in Indonesia are women. Certainly a significant proportion (12%) of the very richest indigenous businessmen are in fact businesswomen (Raillon 1991:108–109).

In contrast to the elites, the relative economic position of the majority of women, and particularly their ability to act independently in economic matters, is probably deteriorating. The most important reasons are structural changes in the economy that are eliminating the *pasar* system in favor of a "modern" structure of wholesalers and retailers of manufactured commodities; however, female economic autonomy also seems increasingly at odds with the cultural values epitomized by state policies. Whether the values are more appropriately termed "traditional" or "reinvented" is, as in many other societies (see Luong, this volume), open to debate, but the policies ostensibly based on these values do appear to "reinforce patriarchal stereotypes by circumscribing women's social and political roles more rigidly along gender-specific lines" (Gouda 1993:22). Although contemporary social developments are herding the middle ranks of Javanese society toward nuclear families with "modern" family roles, the economic consequences are by no means obvious and do not always run in the expected direction. There seems to be more obvious and direct economic cooperation between spouses than was common earlier: Households where one or both spouses are civil servants often establish a joint business to use the subsidized credit that is a major benefit of such employment.

Are Javanese Traders Entrepreneurs?

This ethnographic material demonstrates that Javanese culture is not inimical to commerce: As soon as a new opportunity arises, dozens of enterprises spring up to produce, process, and market the commodity. It is true that established market traders deny that their main goal is either to increase their capital or to maximize their profits; they say their primary aim through a series of transactions is to maintain their *modal* (stock) at the optimum level while extracting sufficient sums of money each day for household expenses as well as saving for larger purchases. But such statements should be read as a realistic appraisal of the opportunities open to them, not construed as an aversion to risk or to capital accumulation. In the multioccupation economy of rural Java, both now and during the colonial period, trading enterprises are not the best avenue open to their owners for capital accumulation. And because they provide a less "lumpy" income than agriculture, such businesses are the main source of money needed for day-to-day expenditures, which at times leads traders to sacrifice profit for turnover. But in contrast to the Filipino and Malay traders (See Szanton and Peletz, this volume), some of whom are Javanese migrants (see Li, this volume), Javanese traders seldom speak of a need to quarantine kin relationships from economic transactions. One reason may be that in heavily populated Java only a minuscule proportion of potential customers (even for a village shopkeeper) are kin; another is that kinship is a less salient mode of social classification, and there is no sharp distinction between kin and other persons, especially neighbors. But given their long familiarity with the market, it is not surprising that Javanese traders easily differentiate social exchanges from economic transactions. In sum, traders use finance in creative ways and are certainly not adverse to risks or to profits; unlike most firms in industrialized economies, they are very sensitive to supply and demand conditions in their attempt to obtain the highest possible price in each individual transaction.

If we accept the claim that Javanese traders operate in markets in a "disembedded," entrepreneurial fashion, it might be argued that they are not entrepreneurs because their businesses do not expand and seldom survive over generations. In other words, Javanese are engaged in commerce but not in capital accumulation; they are entrepreneurs, perhaps, but not capitalists. Although this argument is technically correct, in my view it misses the mark: The main reason Javanese, by and large, remained mired in petty commerce until very recently was not a lack of desire or ability but the practical difficulties in effectively appropriating the finance and labor of others. In other words, the markets within which they operated were not structured to facilitate capitalist accumulation; their subordinate position in the colonial and immediate postcolonial economy made it difficult for them to construct "modern" forms of economic organization, and their social organization lacked templates for hierarchical, extractive, economic relationships.

In any useful comparative sense, Javanese commercial enterprises are not "family firms"; neither term in the couplet is applicable. It is not simply that the corporate basis of such enterprises is very weakly developed, although even substantial businesses operate with little legal foundation other than a simple government license, pay no income taxes, and keep very few records. More significantly—and in sharp contrast to both the specific Chinese pattern, where family firms are the property of the household or an even larger kinship group (see Hamilton, this volume), and a general tendency in China to see peasant households as corporate units—Javanese enterprises are typically owned by individuals. Unlike Indonesian Chinese (Cator 1936; Vleming 1926), even in situations where some form of collective household enterprise might appear economically efficient, Javanese make considerable efforts to ensure that individual contributions are calculated and paid for separately. Thus a household producing and selling small implements may divide the production tasks among the husband and two adult children, each of whom is paid piece rates, and then sell the product to the wife, who keeps whatever she makes on resale. Although the household does act collectively with reference to consumption and members do contribute freely to household expenses without an obvious toting up of debts, each individual retains considerable control of his or her own finance and labor.

This inability to use "the nuclear family as a [cost-free] business resource" (see Li, this volume), let alone draw on the resources of a larger kinship group, is one constraint on the growth of Javanese enterprises. In the initial stages, for example, there is little possibility of pooling assets to provide start-up finance, although individuals commonly borrow from relatives to begin a business. Although some household-based enterprises may use family labor, particularly children and women, without payment for a short period, there is no equivalent of the lifelong appropriation of female labor characteristic of Chinese "petty capitalist" production (Gates 1989). And whereas the hierarchical relationship between father and sons is often used as a mechanism for expanding a Chinese firm without the family losing control (see Hamilton, this volume), Javanese "family heads" have little de facto economic authority over their wives or adult children.

Chinese family firms have been described as weak organizations that are inherently short term and unstable on the grounds that the process of accumulation and expansion cannot be sustained in the face of the disagreements that emerge among the founder's adult sons or grandsons (Redding 1990). Javanese enterprises appear several magnitudes weaker still: Not only is there little obvious capital accumulation within the business but it seldom survives the withdrawal of its owner. Both of these points, however, should be contextualized. First, for reasons discussed in more detail further on, it would not be sensible for successful traders to expand their enterprises by reinvesting profits. Most traders have what they see as more productive avenues for using any finance they can accumulate, and so business profits are continually being siphoned off and invested in other areas. Buying agricultural land and renting it out, for example, is both considerably more profitable and less risky than investing a similar sum in trading and also produces considerable capital gains. Another long-term investment possibility is education: A very high percentage of household wealth is spent on education in the hope that the children will obtain well-paid jobs. Of course, landowning and higher education are both highly valued in "traditional" Javanese culture, but there is not a lot of evidence that "status" as opposed to "profit" is the major motive for such investments. Second, although usually businesses perish with their owners, there is, as in agriculture, a fair degree of "prepartum" inheritance. Children learn skills from their parents and parent's siblings, are introduced to suppliers, are provided with initial finance, and may well also take over their parent's stock. Given the weak corporate base of these businesses, that is about as far as inheritance can go.

The question of business expansion and capital accumulation is more complex. There are strong parallels between the Javanese, and more broadly Malay (see Li and Peletz, this volume), constitution of household economic roles as reciprocal and the ways in which Javanese expand their enterprises. As the account of trading practices demonstrates, successful trading enterprises—whether *bakul* or *juragan*—are essentially one-woman affairs. Success depends heavily on individual entrepreneurial skills, and this in turn severely inhibits the possibilities for expanding such businesses. Although the vast majority of small businesses in industrialized economies also remain small, and apparently for the same reasons (Curran, Stanworth, and Watkins 1986), those that expand usually do so either by employing more people or by obtaining and utilizing more financing. Both of these options are tightly constrained for Javanese trading and small industrial enterprises within the *pasar* system.

One of the more striking features of such businesses in Java is that whereas there is plenty of labor (including well-educated staff), wages are low, and though there is little cultural opposition to working for wages, relatively little wage labor is utilized. Most work not carried out by the owner—mainly menial tasks concerned with transport or security—is paid on a fee-for-service basis, and even persons working more or less full time are paid piece rates. Although this widespread use of "contracts" seems particularly compatible with Javanese culture, conventional economic reasons for the lack of delegated tasks are by no means obscure and essentially turn on the problems of supervising staff. For example, even if prices were fixed, the absence of books, let alone cash registers, would make it difficult to allow an employee to control transactions and still ensure that all receipts end up with the owners. But when prices vary between identical transactions, even owners confident of the bargaining skills of their staff would face considerable difficulties in controlling the cash.

Despite these problems, Javanese businesses do expand by delegating tasks to others and have developed institutions for ameliorating the problems. One arrangement—if far less common than anthropological accounts of other peasant societies might suggest—is the cultivation of trust. Most often this simply involves a relative or neighbor working with the owner in a village shop, but occasionally such a person is given the responsibility for operating a separate section of the business and trusted to remit the proceeds. This is, however, a high-risk option, and expansion is further limited to the number of suitable acquaintances. A more common technique is also used in similar circumstances in industrialized economies: Someone, often a relative or friend, runs a branch of the enterprise, remitting a set (or even a negotiable) amount rather than the proceeds or a proportion of them. Most rural transport—trucks and buses as well as bicycle rickshas—and agricultural equipment is operated in this way. This alternative has two major drawbacks: The equipment can be overused, and the good operators start up on their own. A third method, by far the most common among *juragan*, is to allow an employee to negotiate prices within an agreed limit but to record the amount owing on a slip of paper and always pay, usually personally, at least a day in arrears. One advantage of this simple form of bookkeeping is that unless agent and seller combine, fraud is difficult; it also reduces the need for cash by balancing sales against purchases.

In arguing that problems of supervision and the potential for fraud limit the possibilities of expanding a business by employing more staff, I do not mean to imply that Javanese are especially untrustworthy or, for that matter, unusually suspicious. Fraud is certainly common enough in Java (although, as in the West, "modern" financial markets seem the major locus) to make the most trusting businesswoman chary of economic arrangements that deprive her of financial control. But the difficulties are essentially problems of economic structure, not character or ethics.

The discrete and relatively immediate limits on the possibility of expanding an enterprise by productively using more financing can be illustrated by a brief look at marketplace retailers. Despite the prevalence of bargaining, *bakul* recognize a positive relationship between turnover and "profit" and also recognize that turnover is positively related to the size of their stock and thus is the reason traders involved in *langganan* relationships gain higher incomes than others. But the upper size of a trading enterprise is limited by the amount of stock the owner can deal with, which in turn is a function of the commodity and the size of the usual transaction. Cloth traders, for example, can comfortably control a far greater value of stock than, say, meat sellers. Successful *bakul* quickly reach the economic limits on the expansion of their businesses. At the bottom of the scale, for example, a village egg-buyer is limited to the eggs laid in her hamlet, and she cannot combine buying eggs with, say, buying spinach because the two items sell to different customers in different places. So although such women have very little financing and make a miserable living, it is not their lack of financing that keeps their egg-buying businesses small. At the top end of the scale, a successful cloth trader has stock financed almost solely by her suppliers. Far from being short of financing, such *bakul* are often pushed by their suppliers to take even more goods on interest-free credit, but their ability to do so is limited by the capacities of their stalls and the number of subsidiary credit relationships they can effectively control.

Although financing is not an important constraint on the expansion of an established business—and this is one of the reasons small- and medium-sized enterprises have been slow to take credit from government schemes—it is a major barrier to entry into the more rewarding occupations. *Bakul* do change occupations in an attempt to improve their economic position, but in these exceptionally segmented markets the chances of a successful upward move are not good. Newcomers have to cultivate new supplier relationships and create a clientele as well as learn new skills of valuing commodities and finance themselves for the initial period. A more likely possibility is to move from *bakul* to *juragan* status, but this is where external financing is needed. In Java, as in industrialized societies, most new small businesses quickly become *bankrup*.

Successful traders lift their incomes less by expanding their own businesses than by increasing the quality of their economic relationships with other traders. Very successful *bakul*, for example, retail only a small proportion of the commodities they buy on credit from their suppliers. The rest they sell to smaller *bakul*, again on credit. As commodities move down the chain, the amount of financing and goods gets smaller, and the credit period shortens. From one point of view, such a *bakul* is making most of her income from "wholesaling"; from another, she is "employing" the smaller trader. Whatever the term, this is a very efficient economic system in which there are precise economies of scale at each level, "the market" determines prices, and credit is based on cash flow rather than assets. However, such *bakul* are successful only because they can balance their retailing and wholesaling functions. If they did not retail themselves, they would not obtain the accurate market information they need to negotiate prices, but this retailing limits the number of credit relationships they can sustain.

Juragan expand through similar processes: They increase their turnover by extending their relationships both downward toward production and upward toward the marketing end. This provides even more creative ways of using money—ways so creative that it is very difficult for an outside investigator to find exactly where the funds enter the system. When the opportunity arises, *juragan* bypass marketing levels, but they seem to have little interest in vertical integration within a single business. Large-scale furniture exporters, for example, may set up warehouses for storing and finishing furniture but seldom get directly involved in manufacturing. Instead they cultivate relationships with hundreds of small workshops. It is worth emphasizing that many *langganan* relationships link Indonesian Chinese and Javanese businesses, and although the former are usually the larger, such relationships do not appear significantly different from those in which both parties are Javanese. *Langganan* relationships obviously have much in common with the notion of *guanxi* in Chinese societies, although they have attracted nowhere near as much scholarly attention, perhaps because most empirical accounts have concentrated on the smaller rural enterprises. The relationships are used for similar economic purposes. Hamilton's summary (this volume) of the ways in which Taiwanese small- and medium-sized "entrepreneurs use *guanxi* ties to establish horizontally integrated commodity chains" would serve as well for Java. But the differences are equally important: *Guanxi* relationships are culturally constituted as reciprocal in opposition to the hierarchical relationships appropriate among kinsmen, whereas in Javanese culture (at least outside the royal court centers) both types of relationships involve reciprocal economic obligations. Consequently, because *langganan* link individuals, not firms, they cannot be used to create networks of ownership. Whereas reciprocal *guanxi* ties link strongly corporate families into tightly intralinked groups, reciprocal *langganan* ties link individuals into much looser, relatively unbounded systems of dyadic relationships.

NOTES

The research on which this chapter is based was supported by a number of grants from the Australian Research Council. I have drawn freely without citation on work done jointly with Paul Alexander.

1. This is not simply scholarly caution; there clearly are cases where cultural identity is grounded in a specific attitude toward the economic (see, e.g., Hefner 1990; Alexander and Alexander 1995).

2. Although space precludes a fuller discussion, this analysis depends heavily on the work of earlier scholars, especially Alice Dewey and Clifford Geertz.

3. The trading practices and economic logic of the *pasar* differ in several significant ways from the shops (*toko*) selling urban manufactured products in rural Java.

4. This was equivalent to about U.S.$5,000 at that time. A more useful indication is that it was about fifty years' income for an agricultural laborer.

5. This is a major topic in my current research on the export furniture industry in Jepara, Central Java. I have found that cash advances from banks are often distributed through five levels of enterprise before being used to pay wages or to pay for raw materials. The notion that there can be no credit without an overt or covert interest charge is not true of these complex financial systems.

6. My own analysis (1987) gave too little attention to the latter aspect.

7. *Kejawaan* (Javanist), seems a less perjorative term than *abangan* ("red" or "peasant").

8. West Javanese women factory workers, like their counterparts in Malaysia, have been portrayed as subservient to their bosses, their fathers, and their religious leaders and as apt to react to stress with outbreaks of hysteria. I share Stivens's (1994) unease

with the notion that protest by women inevitably takes the form of gossiping or passive resistance.

9. Compare, for example, South India, where "women who must work outside their homes still face extensive sexual harassment and possible rape" (Lessinger 1986:588), or the difficulties faced by modern Chinese women who are cut off from the male world of business connections (see Weller, this volume).

REFERENCES

Alexander, Jennifer. 1987. *Trade, Traders and Trading in Rural Java*. Singapore: Oxford University Press.

Alexander, Jennifer, and Paul Alexander. 1991. "Protecting Peasants from Capitalism: The Subordination of Javanese Traders by the Colonial State." *Comparative Studies in Society and History* 33, 2:370–394.

_____. 1995. "Commodification and Consumption in a Central Borneo Society." *Bijdragen tot de Taal-, Land- en Volkenkunde* 151, 2:179–193:

Alexander, Paul. 1992. "What's in a Price? Trading Practices in Peasant (and other) Markets." In R. Dilley, ed., *Contesting Markets*, pp. 79–96. Edinburgh: Edinburgh University Press.

Brenner, Suzanne A. 1991. "Competing Hierarchies: Javanese Merchants and the Priyayi Elite in Solo, Central Java." *Indonesia* 52:55–84.

Cator, W.J. 1936. *The Economic Position of the Chinese in Netherlands Indies*. Oxford: Basil Blackwell.

Curran, James, John Stanworth, and David Watkins. 1986. *The Survival of the Small Firm*. London: Gower.

Dewey, Alice G. 1962. *Peasant Marketing in Java*. Glencoe, Ill.: Free Press.

Dilley, Roy, ed. 1992. *Contesting Markets*. Edinburgh: Edinburgh University Press.

Dobbin, Christine. 1991. "The Importance of Minority Characteristics in the Formation of Business Elites on Java: The Baweanese Example, c. 1870–c. 1940." *Archipel* 40:117–127.

Errington, Shelly. 1990. "Recasting Sex, Gender and Power: A Theoretical and Regional Overview." In J.M. Atkinson and S. Errington, eds., *Power and Difference: Gender in Island Southeast Asia*, pp. 1–58. Stanford: Stanford University Press.

Fernando, M.R., and David Bulbeck. 1992. *Chinese Economic Activities in Netherlands India: Selected Translations from the Dutch*. Singapore: Institute of Southeast Asian Studies.

Gates, Hill. 1989. "The Commoditization of Chinese Women." *Signs* 14:799–832.

Geertz, Clifford. 1963. *Peddlers and Princes: Social Change and Economic Modernization in Two Indonesian Towns*. Chicago: University of Chicago Press.

_____. 1978. "The Bazaar Economy: Information and Search in Peasant Marketing." *American Economic Review* 74:1089–1095.

Geertz, Hildred. 1961. *The Javanese Family: A Study of Kinship and Socialization*. Glencoe, Ill.: Free Press.

Gerke, Solvay. 1992. *Social Change and Life Planning of Rural Javanese Women*. Bielefeld Studies in Development Sociology, no. 51. Saarbrücken and Fort Lauderdale: Breitenbach.

Goodman, Edward, ed. 1989. *Small Firms and Industrial Districts in Italy*. London: Routledge.

Gouda, Frances. 1993. "The Gendered Rhetoric of Colonialism and Anti-Colonialism in Twentieth-Century Indonesia." *Indonesia* 55:1–22.

Gudeman, Stephen. 1986. *Economics as Culture: Models and Metaphors of Livelihood*. London: Routledge and Kegan Paul.

Hart, Gillian. 1986. "Exclusionary Labour Arrangements." *Journal of Development Studies* 22:681–696.

Hatley, Barbara. 1990. "Theatrical Imagery and Gender Ideology in Java." In J.M. Atkinson and S.S. Errington, eds., *Power and Difference: Gender in Island Southeast Asia*, pp. 177–207. Stanford: Stanford University Press.

Hefner, Robert W. 1990. *The Political Economy of Mountain Java*. Berkeley: University of California Press.

Hüsken, Frans. 1989. "Cycles of Commercialization and Accumulation in a Central Javanese Village." In G. Hart, A. Turton, and B. White, eds., *Agrarian Transformations: Local Processes and the State in Southeast Asia*, pp. 303–331. Berkeley: University of California Press.

Keeler, Ward. 1987. *Javanese Shadow Plays, Javanese Selves*. Princeton: Princeton University Press.

Knight, G.R. 1982. "Capitalism and Commodity Production in Java." In H. Alavi et al., eds., *Capitalism and Colonial Production*, pp. 119–158. London: Croom Helm.

Lessinger, Johanna. 1986. "Women, Work, and Modesty: The Dilemma of Women Market Traders in South India." *Feminist Studies* 12:581–600.

Mather, Celia E. 1983. "Industrialization in the Tangerang Regency of West Java: Women Workers and the Islamic Patriarchy." *Bulletin of Concerned Asian Scholars* 15, 2:2–17.

Nakamura, Mitsuo. 1983. *The Crescent Arises over the Banyan Tree*. Yogyakarta: University of Gadjah Mada Press.

Noer, Deliar. 1973. *The Modernist Muslim Movement in Indonesia, 1900–1942*. Singapore: Oxford University Press.

Plattner, Stuart. 1985. "Equilibrating Market Relationships." In S. Plattner, ed., *Markets and Marketing*, pp. 133–152. Lanham, Md.: University Press of America.

Raillon, François. 1991. "How to Become a National Entrepreneur: The Rise of Indonesian Capitalists." *Archipel* 41:89–119.

Redding, S. Gordon. 1990. *The Spirit of Chinese Capitalism*. Berlin: Walter de Gruyter.

Saptari, Ratna. 1991. "The Differentiation of a Rural Industrial Labour Force." In P. Alexander, P. Boomgaard, and B. White, eds., *In the Shadow of Agriculture*, pp. 127–150. Amsterdam: Royal Tropical Institute.

Siegel, James. T. 1986. *Solo in the New Order*. Princeton: Princeton University Press.

Skinner, G. William. 1985. "Rural Marketing in China: Revival and Reappraisal." In S. Plattner, ed., *Markets and Marketing*, pp. 7–48. Lanham, Md.: University Press of America.

Stivens, Maila. 1994. "Gender and Modernity in Malaysia." In A. Gomes, ed., *Modernity and Identity: Asian Illustrations*, pp. 66–95. Melbourne: Latrobe University Press.

van Deventer, C. Th. 1904. *Overzicht van den Economischen toestand der Inlandsche Bevolking van Java en Madoera.* The Hague: Nijhoff.

Vleming, J.L., ed. 1926. *Het Chineesche Zakenleven in Nederlandsch-Indië.* Weltevreden: Landsdrukkerij.

White, Benjamin. 1991. "Economic Diversification and Agrarian Change in Rural Java, 1900–1990." In P. Alexander, P. Boomgaard, and B. White, eds., *In the Shadow of Agriculture,* pp. 41–69. Amsterdam: Royal Tropical Institute.

Wolf, Diane. L. 1992. *Factory Daughters: Gender, Household Dynamics and Rural Industrialization in Java.* Berkeley: University of California Press.

eight

✦

Markets and Justice for Muslim Indonesians

ROBERT W. HEFNER

Contrary to its conventional portrayal, capitalism has coevolved with a variety of social structures and moral traditions over its past two centuries. Not singular but many, the new Asian capitalisms illustrate this complexity with particular clarity. Whether with *guanxi* networks for capital accumulation in Taiwan or Communist sponsorship of private enterprise in Vietnam, capitalism works by articulating with local polities, organizations, and cultures (see Redding 1990; Clegg and Redding 1990). Inevitably, as this local embrace deepens, enterprise redirects local resources and relationships toward new ends, adjusting or even obliterating their prior form and meaning. Sometimes, as with the family and *guanxi* among Chinese, this harnessing of old structures and sentiments to new social ends provides capitalism with exceptional local vigor and, no less significant, ethical legitimacy. In such instances, capitalist enterprise will appear not alien or intrusive but a novel application of existing relationships to new social projects. Other times, the old ways may prove incompatible with the new economy and will be quarantined or marginalized as the market system prevails. A dual economy of morality may develop in which market behavior violates values and sentiments central to other sectors of social life. A society can learn to live with such moral segmentation and the political inequality on which it is typically premised. For such an accommodation to be reached, however, the local tradition now subordinate to the economy must renounce its claim to an overarching social vision. Where the junior partner to this unhappy union continues to insist on a more expansive ethical project—such as, say, subordinating the market to religious norms—the capitalist order may be experienced as alien, immoral, and illegitimate.

In either case, capitalism's ongoing redeployment of personnel, energies, and values invariably affects the broader balance of power *and* morality in society. Though recent sociological discussions (and much of the argument of this book) have rightly emphasized the role of local organizations in coordinating capitalist production and distribution, politics and social ethics are also parts of the economy's "embedding." Indeed, when nineteenth-century social thinkers grappled with capitalism's relationship to society, it was these issues of power and ethics, not resource coordination, they typically had in mind. However, their understanding of this relationship was premised on a rather unilinear view of capitalism's cultural trajectory. Marx, and not a few liberal theorists, believed that capitalism's triumph spelled the end of a moral imagination based on religion, ethnicity, or language ties. Faced with capitalist modernity, these antiquated allegiances would give way to impersonal ties of market and class. Though destructive of the old ethics, this economization of social values was a necessary prelude, Marx believed, to the demystified recognition of that category of concern he regarded as most real—class interest. Without such a clarified economic consciousness, which is to say without the demystification of the old solidarities of religion, region, and status, the social order could not be made right (see Parkin 1979:3–42).

If there is any element in Marx's analysis that missed the surging rhythm of its time, however, it is this one. The nineteenth and twentieth centuries have provided regular reminders that however much capitalism might reshape "non-economic" solidarities, it has not succeeded in pushing them fully to the side. Modern capitalism's history is not merely a matter of the rise of narrow self-interest; it is also a history of the revival and reinvention of religion, ethnicity, gender, and nation. Reshaped by the economy, these entities are not its passive dependents but agencies that sometimes return to contest that which has altered them.

It is against this dialectical understanding of capitalism's pluralism, politics, and social "embeddedness" (Granovetter 1985; Hamilton and Biggart 1988) that I want to examine the situation of Muslims in contemporary Indonesia's economic transformation. What I propose to do is, first, provide a brief overview of the Indonesian economy, focusing on its linkages of state and society, especially as these affect the Muslim community. Against this background, I then examine Muslim ideas and initiatives on business and ethics. Rather than pretending to summarize the diverse views of this vast population (officially, 88% of Indonesia's 200 million citizens), I provide a brief sketch of a few recent Muslim economic initiatives and the ideological context against which they have taken place. I conclude with a general reflection on the political and ethical dilemmas faced by the Muslim community in attempting to gain a toehold in the "New Order" economy.

This example illustrates two points of general relevance for a comparative understanding of capitalist ethics and organization. The first is that the social impact of capitalist development is deeply affected by the values and interests of its political carriers, especially the developmental coalitions that initially establish capitalism's institutional nest. The second point to emphasize is that once erected, this institutional framework does not become invisible but invariably becomes the object of political and ethical contestation. Contrary to Marx's vision, the groupings drawn into this contest are animated by interests and solidarities more varied than those of income or production alone. Indeed, as in Indonesia, rather than being consigned to the dustbin of history, class inequalities may interact with nonclass identities to give new life to "old" ethnic and religious divides. The endless refiguration of identities and commitments that follows from this illustrates that whether in Indonesia or elsewhere, global capitalism is not likely to eliminate local cultural variation any time soon.

Participation and Justice in a Patronal Capitalism

Since the early 1970s Indonesia has moved from the ranks of the world's poorest countries to the threshold of Southeast Asia's industrializing giants. Of course, by comparison with its prosperous neighbors, Thailand and Malaysia, Indonesia remains a poor country. Per capita GDP is just U.S.$600, less than one-half the figure for Thailand and just one-fourth of Malaysia's. Statistics on per capita wealth, however, obscure the depth of recent changes in the Indonesian economy. During the 1970s, for example, the average annual rate of growth was a healthy 7.9 percent, compared to a mere 2.0 percent for the period from 1960 to 1965 (Booth and McCawley 1981:4). Even during the economic downturn of the early 1980s, the GDP growth rate remained a vigorous 5.3 percent—somewhat less than Thailand's but stronger than Malaysia's (World Bank 1990:206–207).

However, the full breadth of Indonesia's economic achievement is not apparent even in these already impressive figures on GDP growth. Until the early 1980s, Indonesia differed from most of its neighbors in that oil and gas production, not export manufacturing, dominated industrial expansion. So thorough was this dominance that between 1975 and 1984 the share of nonpetroleum industries in Indonesian manufacturing actually declined. Relative to its East and Southeast Asian rivals, then, Indonesia was slow to take advantage of its potential advantage in labor-intensive manufactures (Hill 1992:209). Beginning in 1982–1983, however, in response to a sharp decline in oil prices (which worsened in 1986) and state revenues, the government implemented an array of economic reforms. Most of these measures were designed to stimulate export-oriented manufacture and make up for the decline in oil revenues (Sjahrir 1992a, 1992b; MacIntyre 1992; Winters 1996:142–191). For the most part, the reforms had the desired effect, stimulating growth in private manufacturing and pushing industrial exports to unprecedented heights.

Initially spurred by declining state revenues, the reforms were also prompted by broad policy changes in international investment and lending. The late 1980s saw an enormous inflow of capital from Western and East Asian nations into Southeast Asia. Among international donors—who to this day continue to provide a hefty annual aid package to Indonesia—there was also a new consensus on the importance of basic structural reforms as a precondition for aid. Typically these reforms focused on stabilizing the exchange rate, reducing protective tariffs, deregulating domestic industries, and related measures designed to enhance the competitive advantage of late-industrializing countries (Haggard and Kaufman 1992:5; MacIntyre and Jayasuriya 1992:3). In a broad survey of countries undergoing structural reforms in the early 1980s, Haggard and Cheng (1987) noted that where the reforms entailed a shift from import-substitution industrialization (as had been practiced in Indonesia throughout the 1970s) to export-oriented industrialization, they frequently encountered opposition from entrenched beneficiaries of state protection. Under such circumstances, the reforms succeeded only when and where some larger economic crisis made preservation of the status quo unattractive to ruling elites. In Indonesia, the collapse in world oil prices and the resulting crisis in state revenues provided just such a push for export-oriented reform. Not insignificantly, however, several important sectors escaped the deregulatory drive, most notably in fields dominated by firms with patronage ties to Indonesia's political elite (Aden 1992; Sjahrir 1992b:136; MacIntyre 1992:155).

Despite the unevenness in their implementation, the reforms of the 1980s had immediate and far-reaching consequences. In the last half of the decade, the manufacturing sector grew at a pace of 15–20 percent per year; the value of manufactured exports grew at an annual rate of almost twice that amount (Hill 1988). Between 1980 and 1987, the total value of manufactured exports rose from U.S.$500 million to $4 billion. Having earlier depended on oil and gas for three-quarters of its export earnings and two-thirds of government revenue, Indonesia in the late 1980s pulled itself into the ranks of Asia's new industrial powers. A mere 11 percent in the mid-1960s, industry by the early 1990s contributed more than 40 percent to the gross domestic product (Hill 1996:5). Equally important for the politics of growth, for the first time in Indonesian history, the late 1980s saw the proportion of private fixed investment overtake state investment in the national economy (World Bank 1989:34). That share continued to grow steadily in the 1990s.

None of this is to say that Indonesia's turn down the capitalist road has been without jitters or bumps. An estimated 35 percent of nonagricultural enterprise remains in state hands, and a significant portion of the political elite maintains a lively interest in state-subsidized enterprise. Interest in the latter is prompted by, among other things, the desire of some politicians to provide economic opportunities for non-Chinese or *pribumi* (indigenous) Indonesians, viewed as disadvantaged relative to the Chinese. Overall, however, the scale and endurance of the economic boom have convinced even skeptics that the standard of living of most ordinary Indonesians is improving, though not as rapidly as economic growth for the nation as a whole (an impression that most objective economic indicators seem to confirm; see Hill 1996:191–213).

Equally important for a political system as centrally controlled as Indonesia, since the late 1980s the idea of private enterprise has shed many of its pejorative connotations among members of the political elite. Indonesia, one must remember, is a country where as late as the mid-1960s even Muslim economic discourse showed the strong imprint of Marxist and socialist ideas. Support for state subsidies and protective tariffs remained strong even after official support for Indonesian socialism declined. The recent shift in attitude is thus significant, all the more in that it has been especially apparent among offspring of the political elite. For the children of army generals and high-ranking bureaucrats, private enterprise has acquired a brilliant luster, whereas state employment, the traditional vehicle of indigenous mobility, has gone gray (see MacIntyre 1992:151; McVey 1992).

Though attitudes toward the market and capitalism have changed greatly, there remains one obstinate problem in public perceptions of the new capitalism: the widely shared conviction that Muslims do not enjoy a fair share of Indonesia's economic pie. Though recent economic growth has expanded the ranks of the Muslim middle class, a sizable proportion of the Muslim community remains poor. Equally important—and of greater political volatility—the gap between Muslims and Chinese in modern enterprise remains enormous. Again, Muslims constitute almost 88 percent of Indonesia's population. In precolonial times, they were the proud bearers of one of the world's greatest mercantile traditions (Castles 1967; Lombard 1990; Reid 1993:62–131). This tradition of Southeast Asian mercantilism was destroyed in the seventeenth and eighteenth centuries under the combined influence of European colonialism and absolutizing rulers. From that point on, Europeans controlled the commanding heights of the economy, and with only a few exceptions, Chinese predominated in its middle sectors. With the infrastructure of economic colonialism in place, there was a small revival of Muslim enterprise in the late nineteenth and early twentieth centuries. During the first years of Indonesian independence, Muslim leaders and Western social scientists alike looked to this native business class with the hope that it might provide the nucleus for an Indonesian equivalent to Max Weber's Calvinist capitalists (Geertz 1963). However, the political instability of the

1950s and early 1960s wreaked havoc with the fortunes of this business community. After the New Order's ascent, hopes for its revival were rekindled, but the Muslim business community only continued to decline.

Recent figures on ethnic shares in Indonesian business are notoriously imprecise, but what data we have confirm the severity of this imbalance between Muslims and Chinese. In the mid-1980s, it was estimated that 70–75 percent of domestic private capital was owned by Sino-Indonesians (Robison 1986:276; cf. Hill 1992:234; Yoshihara 1988:37–67). This ethnic concentration is all the more remarkable in light of the fact that as a group, the Chinese compose just under 4 percent of the population. Equally significant, the high rate of Chinese ownership obtains despite a series of government affirmative action programs that in the 1950s and early 1960s ostensibly discriminated against Chinese business in favor of an indigenous business class (MacIntyre 1993:130; Mackie 1992:178; McVey 1992:11; Robison 1986:272).

To make matters worse, this ethnic concentration is accompanied by what is, in comparative terms, a high degree of market concentration in industrial manufacturing, where Chinese-owned conglomerates dominate the field. Indeed, in general, Indonesia's modern private sector differs from those elsewhere in Southeast Asia, Hong Kong, and Taiwan in that it is dominated not by mid-sized family firms (see Hamilton, this volume; Redding 1990) but by giant, vertically integrated conglomerates. Most of these multifirm enterprises are owned and operated by Chinese entrepreneurs with close ties to Indonesia's political elite (Booth 1992:32). The economist Hal Hill has summarized the general situation aptly: "Indonesia's modern corporate economy is increasingly dominated by a number of large conglomerates with widely dispersed activities in industry and commerce. . . . The owners of most of these huge conglomerates have close personal ties with the President and senior figures in the New Order" (Hill 1992:233–234; cf. Robison 1992:71).

The structural reforms of the 1980s seem only to have enhanced the market dominance of these massive, multisector firms and renewed fears that as the Indonesian economy liberalizes, the role of Muslims and *pribumi* will further decline. The rather complex way in which religious, class, and ethnic tensions intermingle in postliberalization discussions was illustrated in events surrounding the banking industry, one of the first sectors to be significantly deregulated in the late 1980s. Though government officials hoped otherwise, the great majority of private commercial banks founded in the aftermath of deregulation were Chinese owned. Equally important, contrary to the pattern of the 1960s and 1970s (when state banks provided the bulk of commercial credit), these private banks quickly came to provide a significant portion of the total credit in the economy (Hefner 1996; MacIntyre 1993:145). Although this change has had the beneficial effect of increasing competition in the financial sector and ensuring that the allocation of credit is based less on political than commercial considerations, the consequence of bank deregulation has been, once again, that Sino-Indonesians have only extended their control over yet another vital sector in the national economy. This has spurred some Muslims to call for an entirely separate "Islamic" banking system (see further on).

Tainted by the charge that the initial Sino-Indonesian advantage is due to "connections" *(koneksi)* rather than business acumen, the market's legitimacy remains uncertain in Muslim eyes (see *Prospek* 1991). In the early 1990s, this issue of *transparensi* in the market and in politics moved center stage in both Muslim and reformist critiques of the New Order political economy (Kwik and Marbun 1991; Sjahrir 1992b:72–76). For Muslims, a central issue in this debate has been the question of whether the failure of Muslim and *pribumi* firms was the result of their inability to compete in the marketplace or of deliberate policy decisions by the government. Familiar as they were with the analyses of Western scholars (e.g., Anderson 1983; Mackie 1992:177; Robison 1986:271), those who gave credence to the latter view argue that New Order officials gave special privileges to Chinese capital because, as an entrepreneurial minority, Sino-Indonesians were unlikely to protest against the rent-seeking depredations of government officials.

In private discussions these days, high-ranking government officials do not deny this charge entirely but insist that it was economic emergency, not political expediency, that drove them into the arms of Sino-Indonesian business. One cabinet officer with whom I spoke in 1993 put the matter this way:

> When we took over in 1966 the economy was in shambles. We knew how to run the army, but what did we know about managing an economy? There were no foreign investors. We had no funds for development. So yes, we turned to the Chinese. They had the skills, and they had business contacts outside the country that they could use for investment. But it is absurd to say we were against Muslims. Most of us *are* Muslim.

As this minister's comments indicate, the Chinese business community was made a partner in national development and during the first years of the New Order provided capital, entrepreneurial skills, and access to financial networks in East and Southeast Asia (Robison 1986:272). In fact, this collaboration was not new. It continued a pattern that had begun with the nationalization of foreign properties in the late 1950s. At that time, much of the nationalized property had been handed over to the military, and it in turn forged ties with Chinese to facilitate its management (Crouch 1978:273–303).

Whether initially motivated by political expediency or market necessity, this collaboration between Sino-Indonesian entrepreneurs and high-ranking government officials has not proved short lived. Had the state's reliance on Chinese capital been temporary and had there been a concerted campaign to provide equal opportunities for other business groupings, the ethnic problem in Indonesian capitalism would today have a less explosive moral charge.

Unfortunately, developments after the early New Order did little to help in this regard. Even after the reforms of the late 1980s, a small segment of the Chinese business community (the so-called *cukong*) continues to benefit from trade monopolies, protectionism, access to state credit, and state contracts. A few years ago, Richard Robison reported that in the 1970s, 80 percent of all state credit allocations were said to have gone to Chinese. It is difficult to assess the accuracy of such figures, but a high-ranking government official in the Ministry of Finance with whom I spoke in 1992 suggested that almost twenty years after the period on which Robison's figures were based, 70–75 percent of all state credit still went to Sino-Indonesian firms. In return for cozy deals, a select elite among these business leaders provide their *pribumi* partners with compensation in the form of direct payments, dummy partnerships, or joint ventures (see Crouch 1978; Robison 1986:272–277).

This perception of backstage dealmaking and ethical impropriety is, of course, not merely an issue of concern to Muslims and other *pribumi*. Many Sino-Indonesian businesspeople also resent the privileges enjoyed by their better-connected compatriots. For example, in the late 1980s and early 1990s, Chinese and *pribumi* businesspeople alike were adamant in their criticisms of the Indonesian Chamber of Commerce and Industry (KADIN). In 1987, KADIN had won formal recognition as the sole organization entitled to represent the business community before the government. It did so over the bitter objections of many in the business community, including both Muslim *pribumi* and Chinese (cf. MacIntyre 1990:43–50; Robison 1992: 83–85). The organization's critics claim it neglects the interests of the business community as a whole while promoting its leaders' personal interests. During interviews in 1992 and 1993, I was repeatedly told by Chinese and Muslims alike that KADIN is too closely linked to the government to be an effective representative of the business community.

As this example suggests, problems of patrimonialism and insider dealing are of as much concern to politically unconnected Chinese as they are to *pribumi*. Moreover, from a narrowly neoclassical market perspective, the fact that it is Chinese who control much of the private sector is not particularly important. Were it clear, for example, that this domination is the product of open competition rather than backstage cronyism, Chinese dominance might be seen merely as a consequence of market efficiency. Indeed, thought experiments aside, it is empirically evident that Chinese-owned conglomerates *do* provide economies of scales in finance, marketing, and technology that allow Indonesian firms to compete with other big players in the international market.

Here again, however, we are reminded that markets are everywhere embedded in a political and ethical context, in addition to a productive-organizational one. Though it may violate neoclassical credos, it is a familiar occurrence in modern times that social groupings marginalized from the market

don't always accept the rules of the game and resign themselves to competing more vigorously in the marketplace; sometimes they look to political institutions to correct for their economic displacement. (As in Indonesia, of
course, their elite rivals are often fond of manipulating the same nonmarket
levers—and wield them with greater effect!) The history of modern capitalism has shown repeatedly that public perceptions of inequality and im-
morality can engender political tensions capable of undermining the economic system as a whole. Capitalism's loss of legitimacy and the collapse of
its institutional nest are prospects not typically factored into neoclassical
evaluations of market efficiency. Capable as they are of disrupting the economy, however, they are issues that must be accorded central importance in
any sociological assessment of long-term market growth.

Divergent Strategies

The reaction of Muslim Indonesians to their economic marginalization has
been highly varied. A few Muslim leaders have engaged in fierce anti-Chi-
nese polemics; others have sought to draw Chinese businesspeople into joint
ventures. Whereas some have called for a strict application of Islamic law
(shariah) to all sectors of the economy, others have insisted that there is no
such thing as Islamic economics and Muslims must learn modern management techniques. Finally, a few have advocated massive programs of state industrialization, and others have insisted that independent enterprise is the
only way to revitalize Muslim fortunes.

To make sense of these reactions, it is important to remember that economic marginalization was but one part of a broader exclusion of Muslim
organizations during the first two decades of the New Order. Muslim economic strategies have been influenced not merely by their perception of
market justice but—the moral embedding issue once again—by their perception of the logic and legitimacy of the political-economic system as a whole.

Though Muslim organizations actively supported the New Order's rise to
power during 1965–1966 (and participated in the decimation of the Communist Party; see Cribb 1990; Hefner 1990), they were excluded from positions
of influence once the new government was in place. Like other national parties, Muslim political organizations saw their independence severely restricted in the late 1960s; in the early 1970s, they lost their independence entirely when they were forced into a government-imposed coalition of
Islamic parties (Ward 1974). There were other initiatives during the 1970s
and early 1980s restricting Muslim organizational autonomy (Emmerson
1976; Syamsuddin 1991). All these were in keeping with the New Order's
strategy of demobilizing the populace and enhancing social control through
the superimposition of vertical command structures on mass organizations
(Reeve 1985).

I have discussed elsewhere the varied Muslim responses to these government controls (Hefner 1993, 1997) and here want to emphasize just two points. First, reacting to the government restrictions on politics, some in the Muslim community withdrew from party politics and dedicated themselves to programs of mass religious education and social welfare. In part, this was a strategic move, since the government barred Muslims and everyone else from engaging in independent political activity, particularly in the countryside. However, the shift in strategy also reflected a deep disaffection among some liberal Muslims with the politicization of religion during the Sukarno era. Many felt that in the end, this had only hurt their cause and marginalized Muslims from mainstream society.

From the beginning, the religious and educational campaign of these moderate Muslims enjoyed the quiet support of some segments of the government, especially mid-level officials in the Department of Religion. Privately, many government officials were unhappy with the continuing isolation of Muslims and quietly supported the social and educational efforts of the Muslim leadership even while pressing it toward cultural rather than explicitly political ends. With the quiet assistance of the department, mosques and religious schools were constructed at a pace faster than at any time in modern Indonesian history, almost doubling their number in a decade; religious education was made mandatory from elementary school to university; and a small army of Muslim preachers fanned out across the countryside, devoting special attention to territories regarded as lax in the profession of the faith (Labrousse and Soemargono 1985).

The fruits of these efforts became apparent in the 1980s, as Indonesia experienced an Islamic revival on a scale never before seen. In the mid-1980s, areas of rural Java long regarded as bastions of a heterodox, "Javanist" Islam began to show evidence of far-reaching Islamization (Hefner 1987, 1990; Pranowo 1991). The revitalization had an equally important effect on the Muslim middle class. Whereas prior to the decade, many in this group affected the lifestyles and consumption habits of East Asia and the West, in the 1980s many in the new middle class turned to Islam for ethical inspiration. (Outside university campuses, however, most remained notably uninterested in Islam as an instrument for political action.) As government officials caught wind of this change, they began to make concessions to Muslim interests unthinkable a decade earlier. The government courted rural Muslims by providing financial support to Qur'anic schools, mosques, and cooperatives. The government also sponsored new legislation tightening requirements for religious instruction, strengthened the position of Islamic courts, sponsored a national Islamic cultural festival (Festival Istiqlal), reversed a policy prohibiting Islamic head coverings for high school girls, abolished the national sports lottery, and sponsored a new compilation of Islamic law (Effendy 1994; Hefner 1993).

Perhaps the most significant of the government's gestures was its sponsorship of a national association of Muslim intellectuals, known by its acronym, ICMI (Ikatan Cendekiawan Muslim Se-Indonesia). In a pattern of corporatist organization employed by the government in other spheres (Anderson 1983; Reeve 1985), ICMI was intended to group all of the Muslim community's leaders and intellectuals into a single organizational structure. In principle, the resulting corporatist organization would allow the conveyance of Muslim aspirations upward to the government; in practice, the organization could also be used to relay state directives and controls downward into the Muslim community. Earlier, in the mid-1980s, prominent Muslims had made several efforts to organize an independent association of Muslim intellectuals, but these had always been suppressed by security officials. The government's change of heart in 1990 was widely seen as an effort on the part of President Suharto to court Muslim support in advance of the 1993 elections. Whatever his motives, the president indicated the seriousness with which he took the new organization by appointing one of his most trusted advisers, B.J. Habibie, the minister of research and technology, to lead the new organization.

The creation of ICMI and the appointment of Habibie had a dramatic effect on Muslim debates on economic policy. Over the next few years, three primary streams of Muslim economic thought emerged from this discussion. The first stream was a statist-nationalist one, closely identified with Minister Habibie himself. An energetic and intelligent man who had worked as an executive engineer in the West German aircraft industry, Habibie is a well-known advocate of what in Indonesia is called the "technological" development strategy. This is an elite-nationalist strategy that emphasizes state-sponsored enterprise as the engine of economic growth. In this respect, it is similar to the elitist economic nationalism popular in the early 1970s among large segments of the political bureaucracy (Chalmers and Hadiz 1997:71–90). However, Habibie's "technologism" adds several new twists to the old economic nationalism. It emphasizes that Indonesia must not confine its national development to the labor-intensive industries in which it has a comparative advantage (and in which, therefore, foreign investors are willing to sink their funds). Rather, Habibie argues, the state should intervene to sponsor capital-intensive, high-technology industries so that when foreign investors shift their funds to some even lower-wage nation, Indonesia will not be left technologically backward (see Chalmers and Hadiz 1997:176–181). Less prominently emphasized but equally important in Habibie's formula is that the state should utilize the awarding of business contracts to promote the development of a Muslim business class.

The statist-nationalist model of development is most commonly contrasted with a more or less liberal economic policy, which in contemporary Indonesia has come to be called "technocratic." The technocratic model emphasizes the need for government deregulation, foreign investment, exports, and labor-intensive industries in which Indonesia has a strong comparative advantage. Headquartered for most of the New Order in the Ministry of Finance and the National Planning Agency (Bappenas), "technocrats" have been plagued by their inability to rally mass support for their programs. A generation ago some among them were associated with the Indonesian Socialist Party, a small, social-democratic party banned in 1960 by President Sukarno (Liddle 1973; MacDougall 1975). Today, the ranks of technocratic advocates have expanded to include a few reform-minded progressives who feel that economic reform can be used to promote political liberalization and the rule of law. Though elements of such a social liberalism—especially the idea of regularizing the rule of law—have broad appeal among the Indonesian public, support for the full policy package is handicapped by Muslims' fear that a free and fair market will do little to address the structural imbalance between them and Sino-Indonesians.

As minister of research and technology and director of the state's "strategic" industries (including arms manufacture, shipbuilding, and airplane production), Habibie has demonstrated how he might put some of his ideas into practice. During the late 1980s, when statist economic nationalism was otherwise on the defensive, the industries under his direction enjoyed state subsidies of approximately U.S.$2 billion each year. Precise figures for different industries are unknown because budgets for Habibie's industries are not subject to public disclosure, a fact that has only added fuel to the fire of his liberal critics. Some of these enterprises, such as the shipbuilding industry, have been described as white elephants that, although inefficient, still manage to produce an item that can be used by domestic firms. However, others, such as Minister Habibie's airplane- and helicopter-building companies, are regarded as serious drains on the national budget, producing an item of questionable quality at a high cost in subsidies and, given their capital intensity, very few employment benefits. Market efficiencies aside, Habibie has used these industries to sponsor the development of Muslim-owned enterprise, the directorship of which is usually linked to him through ICMI.

Even within ICMI, however, Habibie's is not the only voice on economic matters. A second stream of opinion is widespread among the more independent membership and represents what can be called a populist-Islamic economics. Though proponents of this economic strategy agree with Habibie on the need to develop an Islamic business class, they disagree with many of his ideas on how to do so. Populist Muslims tend to be uneasy with the image of state dependency and elitist patronage that hangs over many of Habibie's undertakings. Many note that a few Muslims have always benefited from sweetheart deals during the New Order but insist that such patronage has little to do with improving the welfare of the Muslim community as a whole. As one high-ranking ICMI officer unsympathetic to Habibie explained to me in 1994,

"Yes, there are rich Muslims, but so what? If you have corrupt business owned by Muslims, is that Islamic?" As this gentleman's comments hint, the populist-economic perspective favors government intervention to support Muslim enterprise but insists that it be distributed in a fairer and more open fashion. Though a generation ago proponents of this position might have advocated an Islamic socialism, most today embrace market-oriented policies even while insisting that government intervention be used to address social inequalities. In private, many of the populists cite Malaysia's New Economic Policy as a model for the combination of market-growth and government intervention they have in mind (see Crouch 1996:211–217).

A second feature distinguishing the populist-Islamic perspective from Habibie's elitist nationalism is the populists' greater enthusiasm for Islamic economics. Habibie supporters see themselves as promoting Islamic institutions and values and played a crucial role in the political intrigues that led to the formation of Indonesia's first Islamic bank (see further on). In general, however, they tend to be lukewarm or even hostile to the technical detail of "Islamic economics." For them, the key to Islamic revitalization lies in Muslim progress in the fields of education, scientific technology, and modern management—in conjunction, of course, with affirmative action in the awarding of business contracts. Again, the populists have little difficulty with most of these things, but they also believe that there is something to the idea that Islam can provide an alternative to some of the excesses of Western-style capitalism. Among other things, this has meant that the populists have sought to extend Islamic banking out of the affluent heights of the economy and down into grassroots credit programs. Originally promoted by Sri Bintang Pamungkas—an outspoken member of parliament and ICMI convicted in 1995 of slandering the president—these small-scale Islamic banks have shown an impressive ability to get credit at low cost to small businesses. Populists have promoted other ideas, such as management training for petty entrepreneurs, and the channeling of religious alms *(zakat)* into cooperative enterprises for the poor, but most of their ideas have yet to receive sufficient official support to have any impact.

The third stream in contemporary Islamic economic thought insists that aside from a spirit of honesty and social justice, there is no such thing as an Islamic alternative to market economics. This view is actually rather widespread in the Muslim business community even among many of the people who, for strategic reasons, have been associated with Minister Habibie or the Islamic populists. The person most widely identified with this view, however, is Abdurrahman Wahid, the chairman of Nahdlatul Ulama (NU), the largest of Indonesia's Muslim social organizations with an estimated following of some 30 million people (see Feillard 1995). Since ICMI's founding, Wahid has refused to have anything to do with the organization, claiming it is sectarian, antinationalist, and likely to encourage Islamic fundamentalism.

Wahid has also been a fierce personal critic of Habibie, arguing that ICMI was a clumsy attempt to control the independent wing of the Muslim community and split the democratic opposition along religious lines. This opinion is shared by many activists in nongovernmental organizations and the human rights community.

In economic matters, Wahid has shown an equally iconoclastic spirit. Not opposed to government assistance, he has pressed for credit and educational programs targeted at small- and mid-level business enterprise. He has at the same time insisted that rather than being awarded in a backstage manner, government contracts should be subject to open and competitive bidding so as to avoid the patronage pressures of off-stage deals. Equally important, if more controversial, Wahid has argued that rather than stigmatizing wealthy Sino-Indonesians, Muslims should collaborate with them in joint ventures, management training, and banking. As he explained in an interview with me during 1993, Wahid feels there is no such thing as an explicitly Islamic economics. What should be Islamic, he insists, is the spirit of fairness and justice that one brings to enterprise. To think otherwise or, in particular, to argue that *shariah* (Islamic law) contains systematic instructions on economic affairs is, Wahid argues, "an exercise in self-delusion."

Whatever one's assessment of these three rival perspectives, there is a larger sociological context to their disagreement. With the decline of old Muslim businesses and the rise of the new Muslim professionals, the center of economic gravity for the Muslim community has moved from trade and small industry into government and the professions. Marginalized from hands-on business operations, the new Muslim middle class is poorly positioned to reshape relations of production in any concrete manner. In interviews over a five-year period, I have been struck by, on one hand, the political and intellectual sophistication (not to mention decency) of middle-class leaders and, on the other, their surprising lack of business expertise. In almost all respects the new Muslim middle class is less prepared to compete in the marketplace than its forebears. Unlike their Sino-Indonesian rivals or, for that matter, the Minangkabau entrepreneurs Peletz has described in this volume, much of this new middle class lacks the kinship and civic resources with which to build enterprise "from the bottom up." Under these circumstances, it is not surprising that some might be tempted to believe that business can be built from the top down.

Indeed, if this new middle class lacks many of the ground-level skills and organizations with which to run businesses, they are nonetheless well positioned to play a role in the production and distribution of political ideas. It is here that the new Muslim middle class is leaving its mark. Recent years have seen a host of speeches, books, and university seminars on Islamic economics. Consistent with this, much of the Muslim struggle for economic justice has moved out of the market and into publications and academic seminars in the well-meaning but rather desperate hope that abstract moral critiques might transform economic policies.

The only really powerful exception to this last pattern, of course, is Habibie's programs for state industry and a state-subsidized business class. Whatever their long-term benefits, Habibie's enterprises present immediate opportunities for profit, at least for a well-connected few. Trained as an aircraft engineer in West Germany, Minister Habibie is no ideologue. His passion is high-technology industry, not state enterprise or Islamic economics itself. Were a stronger private sector already in place, it seems likely that he would promote his ideas on technology and "value-added industry" (the buzzword among Habibie supporters) there. Similarly, were the Muslim community not at such a disadvantage relative to Chinese business, it seems doubtful that there would be much enthusiasm for statist schemes, especially ones with as few likely benefits for the Muslim populace as Habibie's industrial projects. For the time being, however, the rise of the "de-enterpreneurized" Muslim middle class and the persisting gap between Muslims and Sino-Indonesians have sustained the conviction among Muslims that some kind of government intervention is desperately needed. In the absence of more concrete opportunities, Habibie's enterprises thus have an inevitable allure, but not enough to convince many observers that they will make a really significant difference.

From Ideal to Practice

In 1991–1992, an issue emerged that illustrated the tensions among these three visions of Islamic economics. The issue concerned the efforts by some in the Muslim community to organize Indonesia's first legally sanctioned Islamic bank, the Bank Muamalat Indonesia.

As in many majority-Muslim countries, in Indonesia the idea of Islamic banking has always been controversial. Even respected Muslim scholars disagree on whether the Qur'anic prohibition on *riba* (lit., "increase"; see the Qur'an, Sura Al Baqarah 275) forbids all interest on loans or, as many liberal commentators insist, merely those so high as to be usurious. Indonesian religious scholars have never reached a consensus on this issue, with different scholars issuing contradictory opinions (Hefner 1996). For example, in 1950, the largest of Indonesia's Muslim organizations, the Nahdlatul Ulama, established two conventional, interest-charging banks in Jakarta; a third was established in 1960 in Semarang. Though all three enterprises eventually failed, they provided a clear precedent for the NU's establishment of interest-charging people's credit banks (BPR, or Bank Perkreditan Rakyat) in 1990. The latter was an entirely private initiative. Indeed, it was established despite a notable lack of support from the government. At that time, the government was unhappy with NU's leader, Abdurrahman Wahid, as a result of his public statements on democratization and opposition to the government-sponsored Association of Indonesian Muslim Intellectuals. Though the initial plan was for NU to establish 2,000 people's credit banks over a twenty-year period, only nine eventually came on line.

What was most remarkable about the bank was not just that it charged interest on loans but that it welcomed cooperation with Chinese bankers. In my interviews as well as in public statements, Wahid stressed that it made good economic sense to draw on Chinese experience and capital; but he also insisted that it was in the best interest of Indonesian democracy and pluralism. Thus in its first months, NU worked with the Chinese-owned Bank Susila Bhakti; sometime later it shifted its partnership to the much larger SUMMA bank. At that time, the SUMMA bank was owned by the Soeryadjaya family, one of Indonesia's wealthiest Chinese families (Mackie 1992:161,187). Later this choice would prove to be an unfortunate one because in 1992–1993, the SUMMA bank collapsed under the weight of losses in Jakarta's real estate market (see *Tempo* 1992). By 1993, NU had to shelve its plans for long-term bank expansion, and only a handful of its banks survived.

From the beginning, others in the Muslim community, including some influential *ulama* in NU itself, condemned NU's banking initiative. In the most infamous exchange in 1990, Misbach Nustofa, the elderly director of the Al Balal Qur'anic school in Rembang, Central Java, published a book in which he condemned the BPR banks as contrary to Islamic law. In uncompromisingly hostile language, he implied that Abdurrahman Wahid was, in effect, acting as an agent of Chinese capital (*Prospek* 1990:84–87). Though other critics were more temperate in their statements, many agreed with Nustofa's charge that interest-bearing loans are contrary to Islamic law. Indeed, what information we have indicates that a significant portion of the urban Muslim populace shares these reservations. For example, a press survey in 1990 of 479 Jakartan Muslims found that only 34 percent of those interviewed approved of bank interest. A full 25.9 percent were "inclined to disapprove" *(kurang setuju)*, and almost 40 percent either "disagreed" *(tidak setuju)* or "strongly disagreed" *(sangat tidak setuju)* (Rachbini 1990).

It was in this context of the Islamic revival and widespread disagreement among Muslims concerning the propriety of conventional banks that efforts were made by others in the Muslim community to win government approval for the formation of a no-interest Islamic bank. The idea for such a bank had been discussed as early as the 1970s but had been consistently rejected by officials in the National Planning Board (Bappenas) and the Ministry of Finance as well as by leading figures in the armed forces. These officials feared that government approval of such a bank would imply that conventional banks were contrary to Islamic law. This would in turn wreak havoc with Indonesian banking at a time when the government was trying to educate the public as to the practical benefits of bank finance. Consistent with these concerns, the government maintained a statute prohibiting the depositing of funds in banks that did not pay interest on deposits. Hence until the statute's repeal in 1991, Islamic banking was technically illegal.

International developments and the Islamic revival of the 1980s, however, served to keep the topic of Islamic banking in the air. Earlier, in 1973, the Saudi government had put its considerable influence behind the establishment of no-interest Islamic banks with the founding of the Islamic Development Bank (IDB). Though the Indonesian government was a signatory to the IDB's founding charter, it declined to sponsor the opening of even a single branch of the IDB in Indonesia, instead requiring that applications for bank capital proceed through the Indonesian Department of Finance. As the Islamic revival swept across Indonesian campuses in the late 1970s and 1980s, however, pressures grew for a reversal of the prohibition so as to allow for the establishment of banks conforming to the anti-interest interpretation of Islamic law.

As in so many other aspects of the university revival, students, faculty, and alumni associated with the Salman Mosque at the Institut Teknologi Bandung (ITB) pioneered these efforts to develop an alternative Islamic bank. Barred by government regulations from doing so, the Salman leadership created a "cooperative," taking care to ensure that its operation was in strict compliance with government regulations. In practice, the cooperative, which came to be known as the Baitut Tamwil Teknosa, or simply the Teknosa cooperative, worked like a small Islamic bank. It took in savings deposits and paid depositors a share of the cooperative's profits according to the amount and duration of their deposit. The bank used its funds to provide capital for joint-venture *(musyarakah)* and equity partnerships *(mudharabah)* as well as to finance credit-purchase arrangements *(murobahah* and *al-bai'u bithaman ajil)* for businesses procuring capital goods. Under the terms of all these contracts, no interest is paid on capital advanced to a bank partner. Instead, both the joint ventures and equity partnerships work on the basis of profit and loss sharing (Hefner 1996).

Ultimately the Teknosa cooperative collapsed under the weight of several bad investments. At its height, however, it had a membership of 500 people and demonstrated that such a bank could provide investment capital for small businesses. It thus served to keep the idea of Islamic banking in the air. In part in response to the Teknosa effort, the government-sponsored Council of Muslim Indonesian Religious Scholars (Majelis Ulama Indonesia, MUI) began to discuss the feasibility of Islamic banking during these same years, probing to determine whether the government's policy on the matter might be revised. After several unsuccessful discussions with government ministers, in 1989 the MUI was given the green light to hold a workshop the following year on Islamic banking. The seminar was attended by high-ranking officials from the Bank Indonesia, the Monetary Council, and the Department of Finance. From this, it was clear that some in government were now willing to approve the formation of an Islamic bank.

There was a flurry of activity in the weeks that followed, much of it designed to consolidate ministerial support before opponents of the idea, especially in the military and Ministry of Finance, mobilized against it. The charismatic minister of research and technology and eventual chairman of ICMI, B.J. Habibie, played an especially important role in securing the president's support. Around this same time, efforts were under way to establish ICMI. The president's eventual approval of both initiatives—over the objections of influential military and technocratic advisers—appears to have been related to his effort to expand his base of support in the face of tensions with the military and to his recognition of the political significance of the Islamic revival.

There were other obstacles to be overcome before the bank was officially approved. Among the most daunting was the Department of Finance's requirement that bank operators accumulate Rp10 billion (approximately U.S.$4.6 million) for working capital. Here again, the president's intervention proved decisive. Having approved the founding of the bank, he provided a small cash contribution from his own funds and a much larger donation from his Pancasila Foundation for Islamic Good Works (Yayasan Amal Bhakti Muslim Pancasila), a religious foundation established by the president in the 1980s. The president also ordered his assistants to organize a meeting to appeal to the Muslim public to purchase shares in the bank.

Details of these presidential initiatives later proved controversial and indicate the way in which the president's actions were linked to broader political concerns. For example, a portion of the funding the president provided was actually drawn from profits of the national sports lottery (SDSB), a state-sponsored gambling operation bitterly opposed by most of the Muslim community and abolished in 1994. Ten days after receiving the lottery contribution, bank officers returned it, a gesture that by the standards of Indonesian politics represented a surprisingly bold assertion of Muslim ethics against the president.

Another controversy complicating efforts to organize the bank was the fact that when founding shares were sold to wealthy entrepreneurs at the swank Hotel Sahid the night of November 3, the largest buyer proved to be none other than Mohammad "Bob" Hasan. Though a close confidant of the president and a convert to Islam, Bob Hasan is Sino-Indonesian. His wealth is primarily derived from vast forestry concessions secured in part through his ties to the president. As word of his purchase of shares was broadcast in the press, observers openly lamented the fact that the largest portion of a bank intended to promote Muslim interests ended up being owned by a Sino-Indonesian of questionable ethical standing. Though in public bank supporters defended Hasan's right to purchase shares, in private many expressed dismay at his participation. "After all," one Muslim politician told me in an interview, "the

whole purpose of the bank is to allow Muslims to regain control of our economy. And there's Bob Hasan right in the middle of things!" Muslim initiatives
had again bumped heads with the problem of social justice.

Conclusion: Politics and Justice
in the Scaling of Social Capital

Recent literature on the conditions of market growth has emphasized that
economic dynamism depends not only on the formal presence of capital and
markets but on organizations and values dispersed throughout society as a
whole. Free markets are not free in the sense that they can operate without a
supportive social environment. They depend on a wider infrastructure of
civil ties through which skills are socialized, capital accumulated, and trust
maintained. As Robert Putnam has noted (Putnam 1993:167), "Features of
social organization, such as trust, norms, and networks . . . can improve
the efficiency of society by facilitating coordinated action." They represent a
"social capital" as vital to economic life as physical capital itself (cf.
Fukuyama 1995; Granovetter 1985).

The literature on social capital is a useful addition to our understanding of
markets and society. Among other things, it correctly emphasizes that where
it takes hold, "global" capitalism often draws on the energy of local organizations, including ones not originally designed for market purposes (as in, for
example, the Chinese kinship system). Equally important, as the chapters in
this book show, the variety of organizations and ethical traditions compatible
with such an economic dynamism is wider than scholars trained in European
and American economic history have recognized. Not all capitalisms need
highlight the possessive individualism of the Atlantic liberal tradition.

One shortcoming in the literature on social capital, however, has been its
tendency to ignore problems of scale and assume that if market precedents
exist, their generalization to the whole of economic society in modern times
is an unproblematic task. In reality the existence of such economic endowments is no guarantee of their easy expansion upward into a full-blown market economy. As Peter Evans (1996:1124) has noted, one of the most serious
challenges of modern economic development is "'scaling up' micro-level social capital to generate solidary ties and social action on a scale that is politically and economically efficacious." As illustrated by the chapters in this
volume, many societies in premodern times had bits and pieces of market organization, but the scope of their operation was limited. Transferring these
institutions upward into a modern economy may present daunting problems, in part because such organizations were never designed to coordinate
large numbers of people over vast social expanses.

Peter Evans draws our attention to the problem of scaling so as to encourage us to investigate the processes whereby different societies develop the

networks, trust, and social organization on which a modern economy depends. These are deeply important issues, but the Indonesian example reminds us that they touch on matters of politics and morality as much as social organization. As markets are scaled up into encompassing social institutions, they inevitably confront alternative discourses on social order and the public good. As the social carriers of a market ethic see their fortunes grow, citizens marginalized from the expanding economic order may question its justice. Others may feel that although market principles were fine in certain circumscribed social fields, their extension to vast areas of social life is dehumanizing or immoral. As in the contemporary West, debates may rage as to whether such things as medicine, fresh air, sexuality, education, or child care should be treated as ordinary commodities, regulated by no more than the principles of supply and demand. Finally, questions may also be raised as to whether considerations of social justice not acknowledged in the formal market—such as a fair representation of ethnic, religious, or other social groups in the ranks of economic winners—should not also figure in public economic policy. In these and other instances, the modern market is subjected to the demands of a moral economy (Hefner 1990).

Over the past generation, Sino-Indonesian entrepreneurs have demonstrated great skill at scaling up their economic organizations. In doing so, however, they have unwittingly reinforced the marginalization of Muslim entrepreneurs and raised doubts in Muslim minds about the legitimacy of the market system as a whole. Muslim Indonesians have reacted to these developments by promoting their own strategies for scaling up enterprise. Lacking an organizational precedent as concrete and effective as that of the Chinese, however, they have shown little agreement on just what such initiatives should involve. Minister Habibie has advocated the utilization of state-owned strategic industries for technological development and, through it, government sponsorship of an elite Muslim business class. Muslim populists have insisted that greater emphasis be given to programs of benefit to the mass of poor Muslims. The third option, associated most directly with Abdurrahman Wahid, has sought to work with Sino-Indonesians, promoting business collaboration rather than confrontation and downplaying the idea that, aside from issues of honesty and justice (important in their own right), there is such a thing as Islamic economics.

Viewed from afar, these disputes touch on two general questions as to how Muslims should scale up to a modern market system. The first has to do with how much Muslims should and can draw on preexisting religious precedents, especially those enshrined in the *shariah*, as the grounds for such a reorganization. For many Muslim and Western observers of Islam, of course, this question is the most impassioning one. Is Islam incompatible with modern forms of capitalist organization, as Max Weber implied? Or, as Maxime Rodinson (1974) and most Muslim modernists argue, is Islam entirely compatible with modern economic arrangements? Alternatively, as some Islamists insist, must Muslims create an economic system all their own?

Like their counterparts in other parts of the Muslim world, most pious Indonesian Muslims are committed to the idea that their religion is an all-encompassing way of life. However, they disagree, sometimes rather seriously, as to exactly what this conviction entails. Does it mean that the institutions of modern life can be precisely regulated through precedents taken from the Qur'an, Hadith, and *shariah*? Or does it mean, as liberal Muslims insist, that Islam should encourage concern for dignity and justice but allow for flexibility and modern change?

The interesting thing about Muslim thinkers in Indonesia is that although a few hardheads insist that there can be only one answer to these questions, the majority have concluded that the best strategy is to encourage an array of initiatives and see which prove most effective at improving Muslim circumstances. Though some of the defenders of no-interest banking thought it immoral that any Muslim could countenance conventional banking, many do not. Most cite pragmatic rather than transcendental arguments to support the idea of Islamic banking (Hefner 1996). Similarly, the great majority of defenders of Nahdlatul Ulama's bank initiative or of other joint enterprise with Chinese showed a practical "let's see what works" attitude. Such a spirit of pluralistic experimentation is well suited to the demands of a fast-changing marketplace.

If, over the long term, the question of what part of modern capitalism is compatible with Islam proves to be relatively tractable, there is a related issue on which consensus may prove less manageable. This is the question of the market's ability to deliver social justice and whether market processes need to be complemented with state intervention. Though at first sight this may look like a prosaic issue, it may well prove more decisive for Indonesia's future.

No significant faction in the Muslim community believes that laissez-faire policies are enough to correct market imbalances and improve Muslim fortunes; all believe some measure of government intervention is required. But just what form that intervention should take is a matter of intense disagreement. As the ICMI example illustrates, some Muslims are convinced that the way to improve their circumstances is through top-down patronage. Others, however—including some nongovernmental activists within ICMI—agree more with such figures as Abdurrahman Wahid, Dawam Rahardjo, and Nurcholish Madjid that if Indonesia is to create a dynamic Muslim business class and a nonauthoritarian polity, it must develop institutions that, though supported by the state, ultimately reside beyond its reach.

Clearly there is a political as well as an economic problem here. The latter model of economic development, a "civil" one, goes against the grain of official policy in contemporary Indonesia. Though Indonesia's rate of economic growth has been impressive, its dominant mode of political organization remains corporatist. Where organizations have been allowed to operate, their leadership has been subject to strong pressures and patronage. By centralizing organizational life in this fashion, the New Order government has preserved many of the heavy-handed features of Sukarno's Guided Democracy even as it has repudiated its economic policies. The result has been an institutional structure in which social power flows out from and back to the state. People that aspire to public influence come to understand that they must work through the corridors of state power.

Of course, even a state with aspirations as encompassing as the New Order has limits to its power. However much the Muslim and business communities have been subjected to controls, they have nonetheless managed to establish spheres of limited independence. In the case of business, the government recognized early on that it had to allow more latitude than business had enjoyed under Sukarno's Guided Economy. Equally important, in recent years as Indonesia has sought to court foreign investment, the government came to understand that it was in its interest to regularize vast portions of the economy and allow a freer play of investment. Though for the moment the drive toward further liberalization has stalled because it threatens the interests of certain protected elites, deregulatory pressures seem likely to increase.

In the Muslim community itself, the verdict on just what balance should be struck among government, the economy, and civil society is as yet unclear. It is useful to remember that, as Marshall Hodgson (1974) and Ellis Goldberg (1993) have argued, there was a lively civil tradition in medieval Islam, exemplified in the work of the great writer Ibn Taymiyya. Like the social-contract tradition of the Scottish Enlightenment, this tradition recognized that without proper safeguards, humans—sultans and kings as well as commoners—are prone to a dangerous egoism. As a result, even as they affirmed that the state must work to promote Islamic law and ideals of the good, writers like Ibn Taymiyya emphasized an "essentially contractarian view of life" (Goldberg 1993:256) in which obedience to rulers was premised on their fulfillment of social responsibilities. In addition, much like Anglo-Scottish Enlightenment thinkers, these Muslim writers affirmed the importance of private property, seeing personal wealth as an essential safeguard against royal power. "The rights of individuals to their goods were both the representation of and the instantiation of their autonomy, and thus of their liberty in civil society" (Goldberg 1993:261). We know from historical accounts that in the sixteenth and seventeenth centuries, a not dissimilar precedent for civil politics and economics existed in Muslim Southeast Asia. But its efflorescence was ultimately extinguished by an unholy alliance of European colonialism and native absolutism (Reid 1993).

This understanding of premodern Islam's civil potentialities runs contrary, of course, to Western stereotypes of Islam as absolutist or theocratic. Equally important, it contradicts radical Islamist claims that in Islam, unlike in the West, there is a necessary and totalizing union of religion and politics. Certainly one is hard pressed to find in Islamic tradition a precedent for a separation of religion and state as austere as that of postrevolutionary France or that of extreme secularist discourse in today's United States. But there is much in the Islamic tradition that warns of the dangers of idolizing rulers, which is to say confusing the spirit of the law with the law's self-appointed guardians (Al-Azmeh 1993:12; cf. Eickelman and Piscatori 1996:155–164).

Is this history relevant to the problem of markets and justice for Muslim Indonesians? The New Order's constraints on civic organization have had the unfortunate effect of reinforcing the conviction among some that the only way to promote effective economic change is through top-down, patronal intervention. Historically, Indonesian Muslims have been no more prone to such a corporatist vision than others in the political arena. Indeed, in most respects they have been much less so. They are the ones, after all, who maintained an independent tradition of schools, mosques, and welfare associations not only throughout the New Order period but during the degradations of the colonial era.

When all politics is forced to the center, however, when the state suppresses organizations that show too much independence, a precedent is set and norms established. The danger in this for Indonesia as a whole is that this tendency to suppress civil autonomy may leave citizens with little choice but to play by what seem to be the rules of the game and see the end toward which all public initiative must aim as being fusion with whoever happens to be in power. The danger in this for Muslim Indonesians, in particular, is that it will diminish what remains of their once considerable entrepreneurial endowments and reinforce the mistaken belief that effective economic organization can be created from above.

In a modern economy, where even the most liberalized markets depend upon a vast array of state-supplied services, government *is* important (cf. Evans 1992). However, whether in Indonesia, Taiwan, Singapore, or Thailand, economic success also depends upon family- and community-based organizations for socializing expertise, coordinating labor, accumulating capital, and building trust. Unless state programs work *with* rather than *against* initiatives in civil society, government efforts to assist Muslims are unlikely to have any profound impact. As Indonesia moves into the post-Suharto era, the belief that all must be coordinated by a corporatist state may be as great an impediment to Muslim economic dynamism as any putative deficit in entrepreneurial skills.

REFERENCES

Aden, Jean. 1992. "Entrepreneurship and Protection in the Indonesian Oil Service Industry." In Ruth McVey, ed., *Southeast Asian Capitalists,* pp. 89–101. Ithaca: Southeast Asia Program, Cornell University.

Al-Azmeh, Aziz. 1993. "Muslim 'Culture' and the European Tribe." In Al-Azmeh, *Islams and Modernities,* pp. 1–17. London: Verso.

Anderson, Benedict. 1983. "Old State, New Society: Indonesia's New Order in Comparative Historical Perspective." *Journal of Asian Studies* 42, 3:477–496.

Booth, Anne. 1992. "Introduction." In Booth, ed., *The Oil Boom and After: Indonesian Economic Policy and Performance in the Soeharto Era*, pp. 1–38. Singapore: Oxford University Press.

Booth, Anne, and Peter McCawley, eds. 1981. *The Indonesian Economy During the Soeharto Era*. Kuala Lumpur: Oxford University Press.

Castles, Lance. 1967. *Religion, Politics, and Economic Behavior in Java: The Kudus Cigarette Industry*. Cultural Report Series, no. 15. New Haven: Southeast Asian Studies, Yale University.

Chalmers, Ian, and Vedi R. Hadiz. 1997. *The Politics of Economic Development in Indonesia: Contending Perspectives*. Routledge Studies in the Growth Economies of Asia. London and New York: Routledge.

Clegg, S.R., and S.G. Redding, eds. 1990. *Capitalism in Contrasting Cultures*. Berlin and New York: Walter de Gruyter.

Cribb, Robert, ed. 1990. *The Indonesian Killings, 1965–1966: Studies from Java and Bali*. Clayton, Australia: Centre of Southeast Asian Studies, Monash University.

Crouch, Harold. 1978. *The Army and Politics in Indonesia*. Ithaca: Cornell University Press.

———. 1996. *Government and Society in Malaysia*. Ithaca: Cornell University Press.

Editor. 1991. "Ganjalan Pada 110 Miliar" (110 billion in support). 5, 9 (November 16):75–76.

Effendy, Bahtiar. 1994. "Islam and the State: The Transformation of Islamic Political Ideas and Practices in Indonesia." Ph.D. dissertation, Department of Political Science, Ohio State University.

Eickelman, Dale F., and James Piscatori. 1996. *Muslim Politics*. Princeton: Princeton University Press.

Emmerson, Donald. 1976. *Indonesia's Elite: Political Culture and Cultural Politics*. Ithaca: Cornell University Press.

Evans, Peter. 1992. "The State as Problem and Solution: Predation, Embedded Autonomy, and Structural Change." In Stephan Haggard and Robert R. Kaufman, eds., *The Politics of Economic Adjustment*, pp. 139–181. Princeton: Princeton University Press.

———. 1996. "Government Action, Social Capital and Development: Reviewing the Evidence on Synergy." *World Development* 24, 6:1119–1132.

Feillard, Andrée. 1995. *Islam et armée dans l'Indonésie contemporaine*. Paris: l'Harmattan.

Fukuyama, Francis. 1995. *Trust: The Social Virtues and the Creation of Prosperity*. New York: Free Press.

Geertz, Clifford. 1963. *Peddlers and Princes: Social Development and Economic Change in Two Indonesian Towns*. Chicago: University of Chicago Press.

Goldberg, Ellis. 1993. "Private Goods, Public Wrongs, and Civil Society in Some Medieval Arab Theory and Practice." In Ellis Goldberg, Resat Kasaba, and Joel S. Migdal, eds., *Rules and Rights in the Middle East: Democracy, Law, and Society*, pp. 248–271. Seattle: University of Washington Press.

Granovetter, Mark. 1985. "Economic Action and Social Structure: The Problem of Embeddedness." *American Journal of Sociology* 91:481–510.

Haggard, Stephan, and Cheng Tun-jen. 1987. "State and Foreign Capital in the East Asian NICs." In F.C. Deyo, ed., *The Political Economy of the New Asian Industrialism*, pp. 84–135. Ithaca: Cornell University Press.

Haggard, S., and K. Jayasuriya. 1992. "The Politics and Economics of Economic Policy Reform in South-East Asia and the South-West Pacific." In A. MacIntyre and K. Jayasuriya, eds., *The Dynamics of Economic Policy Reform in South-East Asia and the South-West Pacific*, pp. 1–9. Singapore: Oxford University Press.

Haggard, Stephan, and Robert R. Kaufman. 1992. "Introduction: Institutions and Economic Adjustment." In Haggard and Kaufman, eds., *The Politics of Economic Adjustment*, pp. 3–37. Princeton: Princeton University Press.

Hall, John A. 1986. *Powers and Liberties: The Causes and Consequences of the Rise of the West*. Berkeley: University of California Press.

Hamilton, Gary G., and Nicole Woolsey Biggart. 1988. "Market, Culture, and Authority: A Comparative Analysis of Management and Organization in the Far East." *American Journal of Sociology* 94, Special Supplement:52–94.

Hefner, Robert W. 1987. "Islamizing Java? Religion and Politics in Rural East Java." *Journal of Asian Studies* 46, 3:533–554.

———. 1990. *The Political Economy of Mountain Java: An Interpretive History*. Berkeley: University of California Press.

———. 1993. "Islam, State, and Civil Society: ICMI and the Struggle for the Indonesian Middle Class." *Indonesia* 56:1–35.

———. 1996. "Islamizing Capitalism: On the Founding of Indonesia's First Islamic Bank." In Mark Woodward and James Rush, eds., *Toward a New Paradigm: Recent Developments in Indonesian Islamic Thought*, pp. 291–322. Tempe: Center for Southeast Asian Studies, Arizona State University.

———. 1997. "Islamization and Democratization in Indonesia." In R. Hefner and P. Horvatich, eds., *Islam in an Era of Nation-States: Politics and Religious Renewal in Muslim Southeast Asia*, pp. 72–97. Honolulu: University of Hawaii Press.

Hill, Hal. 1988. *Foreign Investment and Industrialization in Indonesia*. Singapore: Oxford University Press.

———. 1992. "Manufacturing Industry." In Anne Booth, ed., *The Oil Boom and After: Indonesian Economic Policy and Performance in the Soeharto Era*, pp. 204–257. Singapore: Oxford University Press.

———. 1996. *The Indonesian Economy Since 1966: Southeast Asia's Emerging Giant*. Cambridge: Cambridge University Press.

Hodgson, Marshall. 1974. *The Venture of Islam: Conscience and History in a World Civilization*. Chicago: University of Chicago Press.

Kwik Kian Gie and B.N. Marbun. 1991. *Konglomerat Indonesia: Permasalahan dan Sepak Terjangnya* (Indonesian conglomerates: Problems and behavior). Jakarta: Sinar Harapan.

Labrousse, Pierre, and Farida Soemargono. 1985. "De l'Islam comme morale du développement: L'action des bureaux de propagation de la foi (Lembaga Dakwah) vue de Surabaya." *Archipel* 30:219–228.

Liddle, R. William. 1973. "Modernizing Indonesian Politics." In Liddle, ed., *Political Participation in Modern Indonesia*, pp. 177–206. Yale University Southeast Asia Studies Monograph Series, no. 19. New Haven: Southeast Asian Studies.

Lombard, Denys. 1990. *Le carrefour javanais: Essai d'histoire globale*. Vol. 2, *Les reseaux asiatique*. Paris: Éditions de l'École des Hautes Études en Sciences Sociales.

MacDougall, John James. 1975. "Technocrats as Modernizers: The Economists of Indonesia's New Order." Ph.D. dissertation, Department of Political Science, University of Michigan.

MacIntyre, Andrew J. 1990. *Business and Politics in Indonesia.* Sydney: Allen & Unwin.

_____. 1992. "Politics and the Reorientation of Economic Policy in Indonesia." In MacIntyre and K. Jayasuriya, eds., *The Dynamics of Economic Policy Reform in South-East Asia and the South-West Pacific,* pp. 138–157. Singapore: Oxford University Press.

_____. 1993. "The Politics of Finance in Indonesia: Command, Confusion, and Competition." In S. Haggard, C.H. Lee, and Sylvia Maxfield, eds., *The Politics of Finance in Developing Countries,* pp. 123–164. Ithaca: Cornell University Press.

MacIntyre, Andrew J., and Kanishka Jayasuriya. 1992. "The Politics and Economics of Economic Policy Reform in South-east Asia and the South-west Pacific." In MacIntyre and Jayasuriya, eds., *The Dynamics of Economic Policy Reform in South-east Asia and the South-west Pacific,* pp. 1–9. Singapore: Oxford University Press.

Mackie, Jamie. 1992. "Changing Patterns of Chinese Big Business in Southeast Asia." In Ruth McVey, ed., *Southeast Asian Capitalists,* pp. 161–190. Ithaca: Southeast Asia Program, Cornell University.

Mahasin, Aswab. 1990. "The Santri Middle Class: An Insider's View." In Richard Tanter and Kenneth Young, eds., *The Politics of Middle Class Indonesia,* pp. 138–144. Clayton, Australia: Centre of Southeast Asian Studies, Monash University.

McVey, Ruth. 1992. "The Materialization of the Southeast Asian Entrepreneur." In McVey, ed., *Southeast Asian Capitalists,* pp. 7–33. Ithaca: Southeast Asia Program, Cornell University.

Parkin, Frank. 1979. *Marxism and Class Theory: A Bourgeois Critique.* New York: Columbia University Press.

Pranowo, Bambang. 1991. "Creating Islamic Tradition in Rural Java." Ph.D. dissertation, Department of Anthropology and Sociology, Monash University, Clayton, Australia.

Prospek. 1990. "Protes umat pada bisnis NU dan Muhammadiyah" (The Muslim community's protest of NU and Muhammadiyah business). December 1, 84–87.

_____. 1991. "Kapan menjadi tuan?" (When to become boss?) May 18, 84–97.

Putnam, Robert D. 1993. *Making Democracy Work: Civic Traditions in Modern Italy.* Princeton: Princeton University Press.

Rachbini, Didik. 1990. "Assalmu alaikum, kyai masuk bank" (God bless, religious leaders enter banks). *Infobank* 124:6–11.

Redding, S. Gordon. 1990. *The Spirit of Chinese Capitalism.* New York: Walter de Gruyter.

Reeve, David. 1985. *Golkar of Indonesia: An Alernative to the Party System.* Singapore and New York: Oxford University Press.

Reid, Anthony. 1993. *Southeast Asia in the Age of Commerce, 1450–1680.* Vol. 2, *Expansion and Crisis.* New Haven: Yale University Press.

Robison, Richard. 1986. *Indonesia: The Rise of Capital.* Sydney: Allen & Unwin.

_____. 1992. "Industrialization and the Economic and Political Development of Capital: The Case of Indonesia." In Ruth McVey, ed., *Southeast Asian Capitalists,* pp. 65–88. Ithaca: Southeast Asia Program, Cornell University.

Rodinson, Maxime. 1974. *Islam and Capitalism*. Austin: University of Texas Press.

Sjahrir. 1992a. *Refleksi pembangunan: Ekonomi Indonesia, 1968–1992* (Development reflections: The Indonesian economy, 1968–1992). Jakarta: Gramedia.

Sjahrir, with Colin Brown. 1992b. "Indonesian Financial and Trade Policy Deregulation: Reform and Response." In Andrew MacIntyre and K. Jayasuriya, eds., *The Dynamics of Economic Policy Reform in South-East Asia and the South-West Pacific*, pp. 124–137. Singapore: Oxford University Press.

Syamsuddin, M. Sirajuddin. 1991. "Religion and Politics in Islam: The Case of Muhammadiyah in Indonesia's New Order." Ph.D. dissertation, Program in Islamic Studies, University of California–Los Angeles.

Tempo 1992. "Terobang-ambing di tengah negosiasi" (About-face in the midst of negotiations). July 4, 62–67.

Ward, Ken. 1974. *The 1971 Election in Indonesia: An East Java Case Study*. Monash Papers on Southeast Asia, no. 2. Clayton, Australia: Centre of Southeast Asian Studies, Monash University.

Winters, Jeffrey A. 1996. *Power in Motion: Capital Mobility and the Indonesian State*. Ithaca and London: Cornell University Press.

World Bank. 1989. *Indonesia: Strategy for Growth and Structural Change*. Washington, D.C.: World Bank.

_____. 1990. *World Development Report, 1990*. New York: Oxford University Press.

Yoshihara Kunio. 1988. *The Rise of Ersatz Capitalism in South-east Asia*. Singapore: Oxford University Press.

nine

✦

Contingent Moralities

Social and Economic Investment in a Philippine Fishing Town

DAVID L. SZANTON

Sociologist Mark Granovetter (1985, 1992) has elaborated the concept of "embeddedness" as a middle ground between a view of economic action as determined by cultural norms and rational choice analyses of economic behavior. Recognizing some value but also the limitations of both approaches, Granovetter focuses on the interpenetration of the two in the structure of social relationships. His insistence on the importance of social relations and interpersonal trust seems to me on target. It is also flattering in that to make his case he has often drawn on the anthropological research my former wife and I conducted in the Philippines in the late 1960s (Szanton 1971, 1981; Szanton 1972).

There is, however, a problem: "Embeddedness" suggests something fixed in something else. One imagines a figure, a process, or a system set in some unchanging social or cultural bedrock. "Embeddedness" neither conveys nor encourages the idea that systems and processes may be interacting, interpenetrating, even mutually redefining. Nor does it encourage consideration that multiple, even contradictory, systems may be operating alongside each other or the dynamics of change over time.

This is unfortunate because my experience and research suggests that even small social worlds turn out to be multiple, unstable, malleable over time, and characterized by constant internally and externally generated perturbations. If economic action is in any sense "embedded," both the actors and the bed are often tossing about. Various people and institutions—some close by, others at some distance—are almost always fighting over who and how many should have a traditional feather bed or the "modern" water bed and who and how many will have to make do with a straw pallet. Even in small, seemingly homogeneous communities there are usually many very different kinds of beds—and many people in beds not of their own choosing.

Unfortunately, a sense of embeddedness, of the immobile insertion of economic action within a structure of social relations, a "tradition," is easy to find in the anthropological literature. Granovetter has read this literature, but I fear it has betrayed him. Historically, most anthropologists have invested a great deal of their time and energy simply trying to figure out how "their" community operated, the characteristic structure of relations that gave it its shape and continuity. The historic tilt in the discipline to the isolated village, to unearthing its structures and traditions, has left a powerful intellectual residue even now when anthropologists work in urban neighborhoods, factories, and offices. This is not hard to understand. Trying to describe holistically and in detail a complex interactive system at one point in time is difficult enough. Trying to discover and articulate its internal variations and conflicts, how it is evolving, even transforming, over extended periods of time is genuinely daunting. Until recently, many anthropologists have attempted to evade the issue by claiming to be writing in a standard, and thus legitimate, genre, "the ethnographic present," an "as if" world of timeless and enduring "tradition."

But clearly this stabilizing, homogenizing, and objectifying approach—aside from denying the postmodern problems of personal intellectual perspective and political stance—falsifies both human experience and on-the-ground social processes. People live, construct, and constantly reconstruct and understand their lives, actions, and relationships through *time*, not simply as atemporal points in a current and fixed social structural space. One's sense of self and one's surroundings is filled with continuities and discontinuities along a *time* dimension, marked, at least in part, by the shifting, context-sensitive salience of particular identities among the large repertoire of identities we all carry with us. Even in so-called simple and seemingly isolated societies, social institutions and value systems are quite differentiated and constantly evolving from internal dynamics and interactions with others.

Fortunately, the use of the stabilizing fiction of the "ethnographic present" is now declining; many anthropologists have taken up historical projects and approaches, are looking at the multiple voices within societies or the interaction of some so-called traditional society with an impinging outside world. Unfortunately, Granovetter has not yet incorporated these more nuanced accounts of the mutually constitutive and historically dynamic relations of culture and economic action.

Let me try to make plain the value of this more historical dynamic approach to internal differentiation from my continuing research in Estancia, Iloilo, "my" community to which Granovetter often refers. Estancia is a lively fishing, marketing, and port town near the northeast tip of Panay Island in the central Philippines. It faces onto the Visayan Sea, and its deep water pier, providing easy access to Manila and other urban markets, makes it a classic "central place" for thousands of families in municipalities up to fifty to seventy miles away. I did my dissertation research there in 1966–1968 and have been able to visit again eleven times since then.

Estancia does not represent the Philippines; it is neither a classic village nor a major urban center. It is in the lowlands, not the uplands, and its population is almost entirely Christian (with a few "freethinkers") in a country with significant Muslim and other minority ethnic groups. These differences make a difference. Nevertheless, there are scores of towns more or less like Estancia throughout the Philippines, and the major patterns of economic behavior and accumulation observable in Estancia are also found, with modifications, in the nation's villages and major cities as well. And because it has long been a rapidly growing, economically dynamic, and relatively prosperous community, it is a particularly good site for examining the historical interaction of social and cultural institutions and economic behavior. The processes of growth and change are close to the surface.

As an active fishing and marketing town, Estancia has large, highly productive and profitable enterprises that have produced high levels of inmigration as well as social and economic differentiation. Because the fishing industry is at the core, I will focus on its historical development to provide a concrete sense of the dynamic interaction of cultural forms and economic behavior in enterprise formation. More specifically, I will focus on the relationship of locally defined morality as an expression of and kind of surrogate for culture and on entrepreneurship as a concrete and highly visible local manifestation of economic behavior.

The use of local moral discourse as a surrogate for local "culture" derives from the simple observation that townspeople are constantly articulating moral judgments about the economic behavior of their townmates and themselves. For them, the production, distribution, accumulation, and use of economic assets are important moral issues. Indeed, much of the meaning of life as locally defined—that is, people's identity, status, and their strategies for maintaining and enhancing their personal and familial well-being, central issues for any culture—is directly tied to how they mobilize and utilize economic resources. These issues are a constant and quite public subject of attention, approbation, and critique. People are always talking, gossiping, or protesting righteously about how somebody is or is not wisely, foolishly, or cruelly using his or her resources (and as I will stress later, a "his" or a "her" makes a great difference) or else explaining ∩r justifying their own resource-allocation decisions.

It is crucial to understand, however, that different people have and are measured against different moral standards and expectations. There is no seamless "Philippine culture" or tightly fixed social structure operating here. Morals, meanings, and the resources one trades in are quite different if one is male or female, rich or poor, young or old, Filipino or Chinese, Roman Catholic or Protestant, locally born or a migrant, elite, middle class, or working class. And these differentiations, the conflicts and negotiations they give rise to, and their dynamics over time make a difference for individuals and families in the larger social and political life of a community, in the sources and incidence of entrepreneurship, and in the organization of economic enterprises.

Sources and Forms of Entrepreneurship

Estancia was founded in the late 1890s with the discovery of extremely rich fishing grounds just offshore of the then sparsely populated area. A well-protected harbor and the growing markets of Panay's two largest urban centers, Roxas City (65 km to the west) and Iloilo City (125 km to the south) justified establishing permanent fishing operations at what soon became a rapidly growing townsite. A deep-water channel close to shore and a large pier constructed in 1931 enabled interisland steamers to dock at the town, giving direct twenty-four-hour access to the huge Manila market several times a week. The local and regional fishing industry flourished. Marine supplies, consumption goods, and cash funneled through the town, providing an expanding economic base for other trades and businesses, schools and government agencies, and a local cadre of professionals as well as for subsistence farming, fishing, and marketing.

From its inception, however, the town's fishing industry, the primary source of its economic growth, has been split into two complementary halves. The fishing outfit operators, their master fishermen, and their crews have always been Filipinos.[1] In contrast, on-shore processing, transport to the urban markets, and wholesaling of the fish was organized entirely by town-based Chinese merchants linked to other Chinese merchants in still larger urban areas.

Both the Filipino outfit operators and the Chinese commercial fish dealers have long been classic Schumpeterian entrepreneurs (Schumpeter 1947). They both mobilized the factors of production and as quickly and continually as possible reinvested their profits, innovated technologically, and expanded their enterprises. The Chinese can be readily defined as merchant capitalists. Their Filipino outfit-operating counterparts might best be termed extractive capitalists, as they are in effect mining the sea.

Individually and, most significant, *collaboratively*, these Chinese and Filipino capitalists were from the beginning and remain today the generators of the town's economic growth. Their large and expanding enterprises contrast sharply with the economic activities of the town's subsistence and petty commodity producers, its professionals, and the private and government employees who eventually settled there. By the 1920s, thanks to the burgeoning fishing industry, Estancia was nationally known as the Alaska of the Philippines. That the town has grown twice as fast as the surrounding communities—and that its income-distribution curve is somewhat flatter—is testimony to the complementary successes of the local merchant and extractive capitalists.[2]

Yet here comes the initial puzzle. With all the now-nearly-century-long economic, social, and political elaboration fostered by this rapid growth and despite increasingly high levels of education, retail trade nationalization legislation, numerous national "development" programs, and the increasing influences of globalization, still today *the initial separation and complementarity of the merchants and outfit operators has both evolved and remained intact.* Fishing technology and marketing are now vastly more sophisticated and efficient. Townspeople now travel and are settled all over the world. Nevertheless, the town's outfit operators and its merchants *still* come from different segments of the population and run different kinds of businesses. *Nor do they ever trade places.*

Given the uncertainties of almost any economic venture in the Philippines and their own personal ambitions, the town's entrepreneurial merchants and outfit operators constantly work to enlarge, but also to diversify, their enterprises. The merchants, however, never expand into the operation of fishing outfits. Even when they have foreclosed on a fishing boat they helped to capitalize, they seek another Filipino to put it back into operation. Merchants instead diversify into other forms of retail or wholesale trade or set up subsidiary wholesale or retail businesses in some nearby location. Likewise, successful fishing outfit operators do not expand into commerce. Fishing outfit operators diversify into other local extractive, production-oriented, or labor-intensive enterprises; rice farming, coconut or sugar plantations, salt beds, small-scale mining, lumber yards, stevedoring, and so on. Despite the passage of five generations and intimate knowledge of the operation and organization of each other's businesses, the division of entrepreneurial labor between the town's merchant and extractive capitalists has not faded.

Local explanations for this continuing division of entrepreneurial labor cast it in moral terms, as rooted in the appropriate relationships among different categories of townspeople. This moral discourse is directly linked to the local definition of a good, secure, or meaningful life, community, and larger society in a setting of limited and highly differentiated control over resources. From an analytical perspective, morality, meaning, and exchange relationships are mutually constitutive and dynamically interactive. How does this work in practice?

The initial Chinese merchants at the turn of the century came from Roxas City, sixty-five bumpy kilometers or a two-day sail away. Still earlier, they themselves or their fathers had come from Amoy or Canton, China.[3] They helped found the town but from the beginning were nevertheless regarded by the equally recent migrant Filipino townspeople as outsiders to local society. Today, their counterparts, and in some cases their actual descendants in the town, are still regarded as outsiders. Concretely, this has meant they were not to be held to or expected to follow local norms of reciprocity or to engage in the larger social and political life of the community. It meant that despite their often considerable wealth, they were not asked and could not expect to play major public roles in the town.

Still, as "outsiders," the Chinese could legitimately establish narrow contractual relationships with local people. They could comfortably capitalize a Filipino outfit operator, providing funds for his boats or equipment, in exchange for all or a large share of the catch for 10–20 percent below market price. No matter how evidently wealthy or crammed with consumption goods and maritime supplies their shops might be, they could expect and obtain immediate payment for purchases. They might offer limited credit to government employees with regular salaries, but they could also demand and generally obtain on-time repayment. Local Filipinos justified this *maimut* (stingy) behavior on the grounds that as Chinese their primary and legitimate concern was doing business and making money. In effect, they were exempted from engaging in the moral obligations, the general social life, and certainly the personal needs of the local Filipino residents. Indeed, it was widely asserted by local Filipinos that the Chinese had no choice but to operate in these narrowly defined cash terms in order to maintain the flow of goods and their own credit and networks with their distant wholesale compatriot suppliers in Iloilo City, Manila, and beyond. At the same time, their considerable distance from their urban suppliers meant that Estancia's Chinese could limit their spending on the food and drink that seems so central to maintaining the dense *guanxi* networks among the Chinese merchants in the big cities.[4]

Being defined as outsiders brought Estancia's Chinese merchants distinct economic advantages. Although their shops might be in competition with each other, as a small minority (usually from 5–10 families) they formed a relatively wealthy subcommunity within the town. As such they exchanged among themselves credit information about Filipino customers, thereby reducing the frequency of bad debts. By paying their own suppliers in cash and on time, they could get their goods at the lowest possible prices, in turn keeping their own prices low, maximizing their turnover, and undercutting any eventual Filipino competition. One consequence was that local Filipinos often noted that although they might prefer to buy from Filipino merchants, in fact they made most of their purchases with the Chinese because their prices were lower. Furthermore, being outside all the local factions, the Chinese could not be pressed to make major financial contributions to local political campaigns, though they might make nominal gifts to *all* the contenders to ensure a good relationship with whoever won the next election. As uncertain Catholics (most identified themselves as Christian but also had a Chinese altar visible in their shop), they were hard to engage in the popular and wide-ranging obligations of *compadrazgo*—the Philippine variant of the

Spanish-introduced Roman Catholic ritual of coparenthood. And because they played *mahjongg* by their own Chinese rules, it was difficult to entice them into the local social networks that formed around that game.

In effect, being defined as outsiders, nearly classic cases of a "marginal trading minority" (Hagen 1962), meant the Chinese could escape the broader social obligations of membership in the local community. Secured by their linkages to wide-ranging national, and to some degree international, economic networks defined as part of "Chinese culture"—which I suspect most felt was superior to "Philippine culture" (few learned to speak the local language well)—they could limit their relationships to local Filipinos to a fairly tight cash nexus. In this domain they clearly had greater autonomy of action than their Filipino townmates.

But being marginal outsiders also had one major economic disadvantage; they could not discipline Filipino labor, or more precisely, large groups of male Filipino workers. Most of the labor in their enterprises came from their immediate or extended families. They might employ one or two Filipinos on a fixed wage for heavy work in a shop or warehouse or as a driver. But when they needed extra store clerks they hired young Filipinas. For the various types of fish processing they used, always on a piecework basis, older married Filipinas (and their small children). It was beyond the physical, social, and political capacity of a male Chinese to deal with large groups of Filipino men, precisely the kinds of workers needed to operate any sizable form of fishing outfit or other large-scale, labor-intensive enterprises. Filipino males, even the most unskilled, found it an affront to their dignity, to their definition of what it meant to be a man, to be ordered about by a Chinese boss, especially in front of their companions. Fishing requires backbreaking labor: in the early years, rowing long distances in the open sea and now, in the precise setting and hauling of the nets. Chinese outsiders could not make these demands on local Filipino men.[5]

But other Filipino men could. Locally born Roman Catholic Filipino men, members of the region's characteristically large bilateral extended families, were well positioned and often willing to take on the culturally familiar and valorized role of patron. They could organize, mobilize, and discipline over several years, even decades, scores and sometimes hundreds of local men, women, and children in their fishing and other similar enterprises. They could do so because although residing in the same town as the Chinese, they lived in another social and moral world.

Rural Philippine society is laced with morally charged expectations of reciprocity: support, favors, gifts. People view themselves and each other as part of a constantly evolving but ultimately and ideally mutually supportive system of relationships created and maintained by the exchange of valued goods. This holds most powerfully among kin (including kin through *compadrazgo*) but also simply among people born, raised, and socialized in the same community. In Estancia, as elsewhere in the Philippines, much of social life and one's personal identity is made meaningful in terms of the nature, dynamics, and balance of the personalized exchanges in which one is engaged. A standard greeting on meeting an old acquaintance is not "What do you do?" but "Who are you with?"

Exactly what is exchanged, by whom, and over what kind of time frame varies a great deal. Most often it is quite significantly not the same item but something else of roughly comparable value. The idea is to *maintain* the relationship of exchange. An exact repayment might suggest a possibly insulting desire to terminate relations. Numerically, most such exchanges are quite small, short term, and relatively "horizontal," for example, a neighbor borrows some salt or kerosene and within a day or two returns to give a small fish or a piece of fruit. Such exchanges are the stuff of ordinary life, the daily markers of mutual respect, acceptance, and interdependency.

But by far the most powerfully meaningful exchanges, those that are most subject to intense moral pride, debate, critique, and analysis, are "vertical," that is, between men (and here we are largely talking about relations among males) of significantly different levels of resources exchanging very different kinds of goods and often over long periods of time. Their social status and self-imagery, and the differentiation both within and between their families, are based on both the levels of resources under their control or to which they have access and the ways that they utilize them. People and families with resources—economic, political, or social—are morally enjoined to use them, at least partly, in ways that will benefit others and in the same process both secure the relationship and raise or confirm their own status.

It is well understood that different men and families have different kinds of resources they might share: The rich and powerful have money and connections; the poor have labor, votes, and subsistence goods. These largely incommensurable, asymmetrical, not necessarily monetized but highly valued vertical exchanges are often, as noted, spread over long time periods. They include, for example, jobs for votes; loans for errands; a bunch of coconuts for an emergency ride to the hospital; credit for consumption goods in lean times for labor when there is work to be done; medicine for a sick wife or child for a chicken; money for a school uniform for a plate of cooked fish; getting a son out of jail for helping in the kitchen at the next fiesta. These exchanges can be initiated by either party and by either the offer of a gift or a request for assistance, which, if granted, will bring forth an appropriate response in kind. They are also, of course, both the moral and economic bases for and manifestations of the classic patron-client systems that pervade much of lowland Philippine society.

Such asymmetrical exchanges have also long provided the simultaneously moral *and* economic base for a wide range of labor-intensive productive activities, including Estancia's large-scale fishing outfit operations. A local man willing and able to play the role of patron could readily organize but also legitimately discipline a set of Filipino crewmen as clients on board his fishing outfits. It was well understood that a patronal outfit operator, through the manipulation of the complex share system for dividing the catch, would retain the vast bulk of the profits for himself. Yet if not carried too far, this was considered legitimate by the fishermen and townspeople alike, as it would enable the outfit operator to accumulate the wealth necessary to be able to provide full and long-term security for the fishermen and their families.

In a relatively, if not absolutely, poor country, having a wealthy and well-connected patron willing and able to meet his obligations by assisting in times of emergency or calamity was (and remains) deeply valued and desired by most individuals and families. They were assured of a relatively secure livelihood, medical and educational assistance, protection from the police, and so on. In exchange, the fishermen and their families were expected to provide broad-ranging social and *political* support, particularly important in Estancia because the outfit operators were also often the leaders of the local political factions. Failure to respond appropriately by either party opened them to the demeaning charge of being *walang hiya* (without shame), that is, unwilling to meet their social and moral obligations.

These asymmetrical but complementary and continuing obligations between the entrepreneurial outfit operators and their crewmen and families have been central components of the fishing industry and crucial to its continuing growth ever since its inception. "Outsider" Chinese with their, by definition, minimal local obligations could not and would not be expected to play these roles. (Nor could local Protestants or members of the Philippine Independent Church, small in number and socially separated from the bulk of the community.) In contrast, both the patron and the client roles, modeled and idealized (even in the breach) in numerous relationships throughout the lowland Philippines, came relatively easily to the majority Roman Catholic Filipino men born and raised in the town; they had preestablished, wide-ranging, local bilateral extended family kinship and friendship networks.[6]

The role and possibilities of the patronal entrepreneur, however, also had their limitations. Despite, or perhaps because of, the obvious differences in resources, the local discourse of patronage was cast in moral terms of reciprocity, mutuality, sharing, generosity, and redistribution—giving what one had when one had it in the expectation of receiving what one needed when one was in need. The fact of differential wealth and power, although readily visible, was frequently phrased (disguised? glossed over?) by participants in a "we are all in this together" rhetoric that was at once egalitarian and communal. Thus even the largest fishing outfit's catch was referred to as the *cumon* (the "common"), theoretically owned by all and in which each fisherman, the owner, and "the boat" all had legitimate, if unequal, shares.

According to this conception of the *cumon*, the crew also had the right to bring home to their families for consumption or sale a daily string of fish from the catch. They could also sell small quantities of fish to local dealers who might approach the boat at sea and who, simply as townmates seeking a modest living, also had a moral "right to share" in the local catch. The proceeds of such sales at sea went directly into the pockets of the fishermen and were unreported to the outfit owner. Owners with an informant on board or simply generally aware of what was happening might complain about this piecemeal dissipation of the catch. But there was little they could do or were willing to do about it, as actions to stop it would affront the socially accepted and morally legitimate rights of their client-crewmen and fellow townsmen. Obviously, large sales at sea could bankrupt an outfit, much as too tight manipulation of the share system by the owner could impoverish and drive off the crew. It was thus in everybody's interest to find a simultaneously economic and moral balance—about which all might mutter a bit—that was generally acceptable and that would continue to tie everyone together. To seal these deals and to demonstrate that they were really just "one of the boys," several of the outfit operators got very publicly drunk with the crew once a month, when the shares were distributed.

More broadly problematic for the patronal outfit operator, his evident wealth would put him under continuous moral pressure to share more of whatever he had with his clients and kinsmen. And the pressure to expand his number of kinsmen and friends through *compadrazgo* or other devices could be enormous. An obviously well-endowed patron could scarcely deny a seemingly legitimate claim or request from a legitimate client or kinsman without fear of destroying the relationship, insulting the *amor proprio* of the client, and possibly provoking a violent response. And if the patron had any ambitions for local elective office, a publicized failure to meet his patronal obligations could lose him large numbers of votes.

The moral power of such sentiments also *prevented* patronally entrepreneurial Filipinos from going into commerce. A Chinese merchant could have a shop full of goods and insist on cash payments. No one would expect otherwise. A Filipino with the same shop could hardly deny requests from needy kinsmen, friends, and townmates for goods on credit. Not only might debts thus generated never be repaid, thus edging him toward bankruptcy, but he could not even request repayment without fear of insulting his debtor with the implied suggestion that he might not be willing or able to meet his obligation. Nor would Filipinos in trade give each other informal credit ratings, that is, information about customers who did not pay their debts, for fear of exposing to others that they themselves had been successfully taken advantage of. None of this was a problem for the Chinese merchants.

Gender Matters

But even for outfit operators without obvious consumption goods on a shelf, pressures on their resources from their fishermen, other clients, townmates, and kinsmen could be fierce. Probably their most frequent, indeed classic, line of socially legitimate defense against such claims rested on a key differentiation in local gender definitions. Whereas local men were morally enjoined to be generous and thicken their social and political networks, local women were praised for their complementary skills in controlling, directing, and ensuring a family's or an enterprise's economic well-being. As in most rural Visayan homes, most men in Estancia bring their wives their earnings, retaining only a small amount for drinks with their companions. Drawing on this socially validated model, it was relatively easy for an outfit operator to offer sympathy to a client seeking a loan but simultaneously speak in complaining tones of having a tightfisted wife who kept the outfit's accounts and who would insist that profits were down, expenses were up, and their savings were essential for new equipment or immediate family expenses. She did not have to say so publicly; he needed only to be able to say that she *would* say so in order to deflect a claim or request. Much as a client, potential client, or the patron himself might jointly grouse and commiserate, the patron's wife could usually legitimately veto a proposed claim. She might even garner begrudging respect for it, even from the disappointed claimant.

As this might suggest, the moral approbation for narrowly economic calculation as a central component in the definition of appropriate *female* behavior, combined with actual experience in keeping a family's or an enterprise's accounts, created commercial entrepreneurial opportunities for women that were denied their own husbands and sons. Indeed, starting in the 1930s, local women began opening a variety of small shops, restaurants, drugstores, and dressmaking establishments, that is, specialized commercial enterprises, often with a strong service component and only indirectly competing with the local Chinese merchants. During World War II, Estancia's Chinese merchant families fled the town in fear of local Japanese and Korean occupation troops. Fishing and business flagged during the war, but a number of women (and some recent male migrants) stepped in and gained further commercial experience. Thus by peacetime (1945–1948), when most of the Chinese merchants returned, they faced commercial competition from a number of local women who had added consumption goods and production supplies sold at competitive prices. By the 1960s, several of the most successful businesspeople in the town were women. Most of the town's private moneylenders were also women, lending to other women with whom they could establish contractual payment regimes.

The periods immediately before and after World War II had also seen a small influx of Filipino Protestants (mostly Southern Baptists) into Estancia. They too, as outsiders with limited and intentionally constrained relations with others in the community, began to enter commercial roles. Like some of the local women and a few other recent migrants, several have become major commercial entrepreneurs competing with, if rarely outcompeting, the local Chinese merchants. As might be expected, none of these newcomers have become fishing outfit operators or political leaders; the constraints on their local social relationships that enabled them to engage in commerce also precluded their entering into the patronally organized fishing industry or playing a major role in local politics.

Dynamics of Change

The patterned and stable male entrepreneurial roles might seem instances of "embedded" forms of economic action. But the differentiated and evolving roles of women, migrants, and Protestants in commerce begins to suggest more interactive and dynamic processes at work. Indeed, the mutually constitutive relationship between local moral norms and the uses of local resource endowments was most dramatically underscored in the period following the imposition of martial law by President Ferdinand Marcos in 1972 and the OPEC fuel-price increases of 1973 and 1974. Under martial law, there was a strict enforcement of a ban on using explosives in fishing, which reduced the catch of the two largest and most popular types of commercial fishing gear. The OPEC price increases quadrupled the cost of running the large on-board marine engines and the generators of these night-fishing outfits. The price of fish also rose, but not enough to compensate for the increased cost of production, with the result that these large outfits were either beached or sold, often at heavy losses. Yet the fish were still there, and a new type of much smaller, fuel efficient, day-fishing gill-net outfit quickly proliferated until there were several hundred of these small outfits operating from Estancia and nearby communities. The effect on income distribution was startling. The previously wealthy patronal fishing outfit operators lost a great deal of money, and some 100 fishermen, fish dealers, teachers, and local professionals invested in these relatively cheap new outfits. Comparable numbers of men were fishing at sea, but the dispersed ownership of the fishing boats produced a much wider distribution of income, clearly visible in house repairs and new construction. For many it also produced a buoyant spirit of autonomy, and there was a widespread sense in the town of people being out from under the domination of the local patrons. As for the former patrons, although they complained bitterly about their losses, they no longer had large crews to support, and thanks to martial law, they no longer needed votes because there would no longer be elections.

The new local morality, placing much greater emphasis on personal autonomy, lasted for about two and a half years. At that point the proliferating inexpensive gill-net outfits had overfished the local grounds for the species they could catch. At the same time, a number of the old outfit operators and a few new ones obtained major bank financing in Manila; purchased much larger, more efficient, flexible, and capital-intensive purse seiners; and quickly took over the fishing industry again. Wealth reconcentrated in their families, elections were promised and begun again, and the old patron-client system with all its moral justifications quickly reemerged. Mutually constitutive, the moral and economic systems had in three years gone full cycle and were back where they started.

Today, commerce in Estancia is dominated (in this order) by the Chinese, local women, recent migrants, and Protestants. The production-oriented fishing industry remains the nearly exclusive domain of local Roman Catholic men with widely ramifying patronal and political roles in town. Over time new categories of people have been able to enter and succeed in commerce. However, the town's Roman Catholic men are still blocked from it. Nearly a century after it began, the complementarity of large-scale commercial and productive roles and enterprises that has made Estancia relatively prosperous continues—and continues to be shaped by malleable moral notions concerning the appropriate utilization of economic resources by specific categories of people within the local society.

Occupational Continuities and Discontinuities Across Generations

Another instance of the mutually interactive moral, political, and economic dynamics of the town is evident in local intergenerational occupational continuities and investments. Parents' expectations for their children and the investments they make in their children's futures are not determinative, but they can have a profound effect on the shape of an economy.

In Estancia, local Chinese and Filipinos have long had strikingly different expectations of and investments in their children. The local Chinese families, cut off from high social status or local political careers but linked to national and international trade networks, clearly viewed commerce as a valued occupation for themselves and their children. Some children were pressed into higher education and the professions, but most were systematically trained in the family business(es). From an early age these children—sons or daughters—were required to work long hours in the family enterprise to learn business techniques (pricing, purchasing, bookkeeping, credit practices, customer relations, inventory control) and to establish personal contacts with suppliers and customers. Some might also be apprenticed for several years to a close relative in a related business. Next they were either incorporated into the family's enterprises or provided with capital to start a business of their own under a parent's watchful eye, either in Estancia or a nearby community. As a result of this conscious attention to the commercial training, support, and supervision of children designated to carry on the family businesses, local Chinese merchant families often were able to maintain and enhance their entrepreneurial skills and clientele, accumulate capital, and expand their businesses over several generations.

The pattern among Filipino families engaged in commerce contrasted sharply, tilting heavily toward pressing their children to enter the professions, government, or private-sector, white-collar employment. It might be acceptable for a migrant or local woman or a Protestant to engage in commerce, but for local Filipino children, enmeshed in the large array of local kinship and friendship networks and obligations, socially isolating careers in commerce were much less desirable. Instead, these children were strongly encouraged to obtain as much education as possible and move as rapidly as possible away from commerce and entrepreneurial roles. The children of the local Filipino merchants were thus likely to leave Estancia for professional or technical government or private white-collar employment in large-scale patronal enterprises elsewhere in the country or overseas. In the process, whatever accumulated business skills, capital, and contacts that a local Filipino merchant had developed almost invariably dissipated in the next generation.

These differences between local Chinese and Filipino attitudes and intergenerational investments in commerce were deeply consequential. Filipinos who entered commerce had to begin at the bottom and work their way up against strong and experienced local competition, and their business died with them. The Chinese merchant families operated on much longer multigenerational time horizons. Having been socialized into the value of commerce and trained in a family business with access to capital and goods from enduring extra-local networks, they could pass their businesses on to their children. These differences in intergenerational occupational continuity directly affected their ability to accumulate both wealth and status within their own community. As one local Filipino noted, "Filipinos enter trade to make money, Chinese enter trade as a way of life." They also made much more money at it.

At the same time, there were numerous examples of intergenerational continuity among Estancia's Filipino production-oriented fishing outfit operator families. The widely esteemed patronal role demanded by these enterprises was readily learned and passed on to at least some members of the next generation. In these relatively wealthy families most of the children had access to higher education and could enter the professions. However, one or two would generally inherit, maintain, and quite possibly expand the clientalistic network of crewmen or workers established by their parents. In several cases, all of the children began professional careers in Manila or elsewhere, but one or two returned to Estancia within a few years to take over an aging father's fishing operations.

Most recently, a small but visible middle class has begun to emerge in Estancia. It is composed of the new generation among the town's commercial- and production-oriented and professional families and derives from a combination of improved access (for the relatively wealthy) to English-language technical and professional education along with media-encouraged cultural globalization and opportunities for work, residence, and travel abroad. The ambitious children of this new middle class identify with a globalized consumer culture and increasingly seek opportunities overseas in larger and more economically stable settings than the Philippines. While still in Estancia, they distance themselves as much as possible from traditional social obligations. Transplanted abroad, they spread their families' risks but take with them human resources and the locally generated capital that was invested in their education.

For the poorer families in town the new middle class often generates deep resentment. Individuals and families wealthy enough and willing to play the patronal roles are still in high demand. By refusing to play these roles, members of the new middle class are viewed by the poor as failing in their obligations to their townsmen and limiting the opportunities of the poor to gain some stability in their own lives. By going abroad, the new middle class totally removes talent and resources that might otherwise have gone into new local employment and income-generating enterprises. So far, enough entrepreneurially inclined people have remained in or migrated to Estancia to maintain its economic vitality, but there are signs that the local (though internationally oriented) middle class is beginning to drain the economy. It has increased demand for high-end consumer goods (TVs, VCRs, telephones, express photo-developing services), but its major purchases and investments are made outside the town. This new middle class shows few signs of transforming the older patterns of entrepreneurial formation and differentiation.

A Brief Conclusion

Returning to the original concern with the relationship of cultural systems and economic action, I believe it is clear that at least in this small-town Philippine setting, the locally defined morality of various types of economic behavior directly shape entry into and local forms of economic organization and entrepreneurship as well as prospects for economic growth or transformation. But that morality must be understood as highly differentiated and capable of evolving reciprocally and dynamically with local, national, and global economic and political forces. Cultural norms, as they differentially apply to different segments of the population, do not determine economic action. Not all Roman Catholic men born in Estancia become patrons; nor do all migrants enter commerce. Economic and political resources (as well as more personal or psychological factors not discussed here) interacting with these norms shape the specific roles people come to play. Nonetheless, specific local norms do seem well adapted or preadapted for particular kinds of large-scale economic enterprises. It also seems worthwhile to emphasize that Estancia suggests the positive value of a differentiated population for rapid economic growth. Dynamic economies are rarely homogeneous; they do not operate on a single principle, and different types of enterprises seem to call for people with different backgrounds, goals, and moral codes. Insiders have certain advantages and skills, but outsiders to the dominant moral and social norms can often perceive and build upon economic opportunities that insiders cannot see or act upon. Migration to urban areas, where nearly everyone is "marginal," is often said to enable people to innovate culturally, socially, and economically in ways they could not at home. In Estancia it took the complementarity of Filipino insiders and Chinese (and eventually other) outsiders drawing on their separate networks and distinctive relationships to the local moral and social system to create the town's dynamic fishing industry.

More broadly, Estancia's evolution casts an ominous light on two of the currently fashionable sources of social transformation in much of the development literature: more education, and economic and cultural globalization. At least for the rural areas and small towns of the Philippines, though education and globalization create opportunities for some and can lead to the formation of a new middle class, they may also prove a serious drain on local growth and innovation. And from the point of view of the poor, and most people still are poor, the growth of a self-centered, internationally oriented, and consumerist middle class that is withdrawing its resources from local social obligations represents both a moral decline and a deepening insecurity.

NOTES

1. Since the beginning, Estancia's fishing industry has been marked by continuous technological change. Generally, every eight to twelve years, there has been a complete turnover in the dominant fishing gear. Gear found to be profitable is quickly copied and used so intensively that it eventually depletes the local stocks of the particular fish it captures. At the same time, outfit operators are constantly modifying and experimenting with new gear until a system is discovered or developed that is more profitable than the one currently in use. The cycle then repeats itself. For a description of the specific types of gear and their transformation over time, see Szanton 1981.

2. See Szanton 1981, chapter 2.

3. On the origins of the Chinese commercial population in the Philippines, see Wickberg 1965.

4. The complex array of Chinese merchant networks and organizations in Iloilo City, including financial institutions, chambers of commerce, business clubs, family associations, and so on, are described in Omohundro 1981, chapter 4. Estancia's Chinese merchant families were linked to some of these networks, but given the distance to Iloilo they participated only irregularly in their activities.

5. The difficulties of Chinese businessmen in Iloilo City—the provincial capital and much larger than Estancia—in dealing with Filipino labor are suggested in Omohundro 1981, 66–69.

6. The legitimacy of hierarchical relationships is pervasive, even among siblings. Brothers are rarely able to maintain partnerships or joint corporate activities, and in the few instances they have succeeded, their roles have been defined and clearly differentiated by an older dominant sister. Most partnerships among men quickly fracture on recriminations or suspicions that one is taking advantage of the other.

REFERENCES

Granovetter, Mark. 1985. "Economic Action and Social Structure: The Problem of Embeddedness." *American Journal of Sociology* 91:481–510.

_____. 1992 "The Nature of Economic Relations." In S. Ortiz and S. Lees, eds., *Understanding Economic Process*, pp. 21–37. Lanham, Md.: University Press of America.

Hagen, Everett E. 1962. *On the Theory of Social Change: How Economic Growth Begins.* Homewood, Ill.: Dorsey Press.

Omohundro, John T. 1981. *Chinese Merchant Families in Iloilo: Commerce and Kin in a Central Philippine City.* Manila: Ateneo de Manila University Press; and Athens, Ohio: Ohio University Press.

Schumpeter, Joseph A. 1947. "The Creative Response in Economic History." *Journal of Economic History* 7:149–159.

Szanton, David L. 1971. *Estancia in Transition: Economic Growth in a Rural Philippine Community.* Manila: Ateneo de Manila University Press.

_____. 1981. *Estancia in Transition: Economic Growth in a Rural Philippine Community.* Rev. and enl. Manila: Ateneo de Manila University Press.

Szanton, Maria C.B. 1972. *A Right to Survive: Subsistence Marketing in a Lowland Philippine Town.* University Park: Penn State University Press.

Wickberg, Edgar. 1965. *The Chinese in Philippine Life 1850–1898.* New Haven: Yale University Press.

ten

State Stigma,
Family Prestige, and the
Development of Commerce
in the Red River Delta
of Vietnam

SHAUN KINGSLEY MALARNEY

One of the distinctive features of modern capitalism, in its most minimal formulation, is the systematic investment of wealth into "productive activities
that are directly productive of additional wealth" (Hefner introduction, this
volume). Instead of channeling resources into activities that produce immediate social ends, such as the obligatory acts of generosity by patrons in the
Philippines (described by Szanton, this volume) or the prestige-enhancing
trips to Mecca by Negeri Sembilan men (described by Peletz, this volume),
individuals reinvest their wealth and profits into productive enterprises to
ensure their continued growth and productive capacity. The transition to the
systematic reinvestment of wealth frequently involves a significant reorientation of cultural values. Alan MacFarlane notes that the initial transition to
capitalism requires the development of an ethos in which "saving and profit-
seeking ... become ethically and emotionally attractive" (MacFarlane
1987:226). Ruth McVey elaborates on this cultural aspect when she argues

that the development of a capitalist economy also requires the recognition of business and commerce as legitimate occupations for the local elite (McVey 1992:24). McVey's position echoes Johannes Hirschmeier's earlier argument that the abandonment of the traditional stigmatization of commerce and its replacement by an ethic that glorified business to build a strong nation greatly facilitated the transformation of Japan's economy during the Meiji period (Hirschmeier 1964).

In this chapter I examine the history of commerce in the Red River Delta of northern Vietnam. I look at the cultural factors that have supported or obstructed economic development, such as the stigmatization of commerce, and also attempt to place these cultural factors in their sociopolitical context, particularly as regards the regressive economic policies promulgated by successive governments.[1] I do not assert that Vietnamese culture is anticommercial. To the contrary, elements of Vietnamese culture, such as the acceptability of wealth creation for family advancement, are conducive to the accumulation of capital and economic growth. Thus I focus on the process by which particular cultural values and pursuits have been selectively valorized or stigmatized, the linkage between these values and their sociopolitical context, and their consequences for economic life (see also McVey 1992). Cultural values have played an important role in Vietnam's economic history, but their consequences can be accurately understood only with reference to the context in which they were transmitted and transformed.

State Policy and the Stigma of Commerce in Precolonial Vietnam

Agriculture has long dominated the Red River Delta's economy. Researchers estimate that before the 1950s, over 90 percent of the delta's population lived in rural areas (Nguyen Kien Giang 1959:22) and that over 80 percent of peasant income was derived from agriculture (Gourou 1936:350).[2] During the colonial period, less than 7 percent of the delta's working-age population engaged full time in the second largest sector of the delta's economy, handicraft production (Gourou 1936:453), and an even smaller percentage of individuals engaged in the third most prominent pursuit, trading (Gourou 1936:539). With the exception of Hanoi, the delta had no major trading entrepôts (Tran Van Giau 1973:38), and large-scale trading was dominated by Chinese immigrants (Nguyen The Anh 1968:147). The majority of families practiced a mixed economy in which agriculture was supplemented with small-scale handicraft production during slack periods of the agricultural cycle (cf. Gourou 1936; Nguyen The Anh 1968), and small-scale trading by women was carried out year-round (Dao Duy Anh 1938:69). Apart from the Chinese and a small number of artisans, trading and handicraft production were only sidelines to agriculture.

A number of factors contributed to the limited development of nonagricultural pursuits in the delta. Foremost at the macrolevel was the "closed-door policy" *(be quan toa cang)* enforced by the vast majority of Vietnamese emperors from the tenth to the twentieth centuries. The monarchy viewed foreign traders, particularly those from Western countries, as possible spies and sources of heterodox ideas and therefore restricted their trading opportunities. When allowed to trade, they had to cope with stifling tariffs and bureaucratic procedures, the forced sale of their goods to Vietnamese authorities at below-market prices, and confinement to trading centers where their activities could be observed and limited (Tran Van Giau 1973:40; Tran Quoc Vuong and Ha Van Tan 1963:225). Some Chinese traders received permission to reside in Vietnam, generally serving as middlemen between foreign traders and the local market. No indigenous class, however, emerged to engage in foreign trade (Nguyen The Anh 1968:147).

Domestic trade also suffered from regressive government policies and actions. At a basic level, poor infrastructure constrained the development of trade throughout the delta (Nguyen The Anh 1968:140). More significant yet were excessive bureaucratic restrictions and heavy taxes. Under the Nguyen dynasty, for example, rice trading between provinces required the permission of officials in all of the involved regions (Nguyen The Anh 1968:138), and transit taxes had to be paid to every bailiwick. The movement of rice from the province of Nam Dinh to Nghe An, a distance of 150 kilometers, required the payment of taxes nine different times (Phan Huy Le et al. 1965:421). Government tax policies had other deleterious consequences for handicraft industries. Taxes were heavier on artisans than farmers, discouraging the formation and growth of guilds (Dao Duy Anh 1938:61). Artisans or individuals who casually produced handicrafts also sometimes abandoned production altogether because of excessive taxes or levies on their products (Dao Duy Anh 1938:63). Government interference in production could take on even a more extreme form: In 1481, local officials attempted to expel all traders from the city of Thang Long (predecessor of Hanoi; see Phan Huy Le 1962:136); in 1779, the government prohibited trade between the highlands and the lowlands (Tran Quoc Vuong and Ha Van Tan 1963:224); and in 1834, Emperor Minh Mang issued a decree closing all markets in Vietnam (Phan Huy Le et al. 1965:421). The monarchy's most effective means of impeding the development of handicraft production was its practice of conscripting talented artisans to work under grueling conditions for minimum wages on government work projects (Nguyen The Anh 1968:110; Dao Duy Anh 1938:62). This practice discouraged artisans from large-scale production and also encouraged the placement of bogus Chinese labels on local wares to avoid impressment (Nguyen The Anh 1968:110).

Beyond these basic features of political economy, there was in Vietnam a cultural stigmatization of commerce, trading, and entrepreneurship. Captured in the popular adage "Respect agriculture, disdain commerce" *(Trong nong, uc thuong)*, the Vietnamese mandarinate articulated a reified Confucian vision of the proper social organization that valorized agriculture as a virtuous pursuit and stigmatized trading and commerce (Tran Van Giau 1973:39). According to this model, society consisted of a four-tiered prestige-stigma hierarchy *(tu dan)*. At the apex were the educated scholar-officials *(si)*; below them were the agriculturalists *(nong)*; lower yet were the artisans and handicraft specialists *(cong)*; and at bottom were the traders *(thuong)*.[3] In practice, the distinctions between the bottom levels of this hierarchy were often blurred (Nguyen The Anh 1968:33), yet the overall prestige-stigma hierarchy remained salient. As one Vietnamese historian noted, "Trading was held in the public eye to be an occupation of cheating and lying, of hoarding until the time came to slit the people's throats" (Tran Van Giau 1973:42). Traders, artisans, and agriculturalists accrued further stigma because they engaged in manual labor. As Hy van Luong notes, precolonial Vietnamese society was marked by a "rigid distinction between mental and menial labor" (Luong 1992:68). The most prestigious lifestyle was that of the educated scholar-official, who when not serving the commonweal, led a life of quiet contemplation, reading the Chinese classics and writing poetry. Finally, trading was also considered to be something of a female occupation, discouraging the large-scale participation of men (see Luong, this volume). For all these reasons, the practice of trade and commerce was heavily stigmatized, and in conjunction with regressive government policies, this stigmatization inhibited the development of commerce and entrepreneurship in the delta region.

The Precolonial Economy: Competition and the Limits of Cooperation

Economic life in the precolonial Red River Delta was characterized by a discrete range of independent productive units engaged in competition with each other. The most basic unit of production was the family or household *(gia dinh)*, constituted by either nuclear, joint, or stem families. The definitive characteristics of the family economy were coresidence, a common budget with the pooling of members' incomes and resources, and coproduction. Independent residence generally entailed the formation of an independent family economy. Agricultural production, and to a large extent handicraft production, were organized exclusively by independent families. The second major unit of economic production was the guild *(phuong* or *ty)*. Located primarily in urban areas, guilds were the largest of the delta's social units of economic production. They had exclusive memberships and devoted themselves to the manufacture of a single item or commodity. Both family economies and guilds were inwardly focused in their devotion to maintaining a competitive advantage, and both mobilized patrilineal kinship relations as organizing structures for their enterprises. These qualities established the boundaries for economic competition and limited cooperation among different units of production.

Family economic independence had a number of features. In agriculture, families worked private plots (whether owned or rented) individually. The unique structure of land tenure in precolonial Vietnam has led some scholars to erroneously attribute a communal character to agricultural and economic production in delta communities.[4] Prior to 1954, approximately 25 percent of the cultivable land in the Red River Delta was classified as "communal land" *(cong dien* or *dat cong),* held by villages or local social groups. The remaining 75 percent was held privately (Tran Phuong 1968:30).[5] In practice, however, communal land was similar to private land inasmuch as it was rented out exclusively to individual villagers or families for cultivation (Gourou 1936:368). Villages did not have communal teams that worked the plots. Instead, as Martin Murray accurately notes, "the traditional village was actually an aggregation of small-scale owner-occupiers engaged in isolated family-type subsistence cultivation" (Murray 1980:385; see also Popkin 1979). This "isolation" had other features as well. Land constituted each individual family's patrimony and passed between the generations according to a partible inheritance rule in which each son received a portion. There was little mutual assistance and cooperation among families during the agricultural cycle. Families did not rely heavily on distant kin for agricultural labor (Gourou 1945:284; Malarney 1993:173). And unlike other peasant societies in Southeast Asia, such as in Malaysia or Bali, Red River Delta families did not form expansive labor-exchange groups composed of kin, friends, and neighbors during peak phases of the agricultural cycle (see Carsten 1989; Geertz 1959). In the 1930s, Pierre Gourou commented that among peasant families, "mutual help is possible only for tasks whose urgency is not absolute" (Gourou 1945:284). Farmers might exchange labor under very strict terms of equivalent reciprocity for less pressing tasks such as transplanting rice, but with such urgent tasks as harvesting, they hired labor (Gourou 1945:284).[6] Kinship was also not a basis for forming trade relations. Handicraft producers outside Hanoi and traders in Bac Ninh Province commented that the Vietnamese have long been wary of mixing economic activities with kinship because it can "damag[e] 'sentimental' *(tinh cam)* relations" among kin. They instead preferred to build up contacts with trusted nonkin. Dealing with them was easier and, as one elderly man noted, "less taxing" *(do phien;* cf. Peletz and Li, this volume).

Guilds and families engaged in handicraft production demonstrated a similar concern for economic independence. Guilds had existed in the Red River Delta since the fifteenth century, most notably in the capital and trading center of Thang Long (Phan Huy Le 1962:132). Similar to their European counterparts, guilds restricted their memberships to practitioners of the same trade. Entrance into a guild was difficult, as members feared jeopardizing their trade secrets. With the exception of a few outsiders, guilds admitted only male patrilineal relations of existing guild members. After admission, a member began a lengthy apprenticeship, and only after he had demonstrated his loyalty and trustworthiness did he learn the most important trade secrets (Phan Huy Le et al. 1965:133). This secretiveness inhibited the transmission of a guild's technical knowledge to competing groups who might gain a competitive advantage. The teaching of trades only to men also illustrates the importance of protecting the guild's knowledge. Vietnamese brides take up residence with their husbands after marriage, creating the possibility for the illicit transfer of technical knowledge to the husband or others (Nguyen The Anh 1968:104). Women therefore never learned the trades.

Handicraft production exhibited a similar concern with secrecy and competition. Gourou spoke of the "spirit of monopoly" associated with handicraft production at the village level (Gourou 1936:528). Across the Red River Delta, different villages were centers for the production of different trade items. Well known among such villages were Bát Tràng in Bac Ninh Province for pottery production (see Luong 1992), Giap Nhi in Ha Dong Province for paper votive items for the dead *(hang ma)*, and Dong Ho in Bac Ninh Province for traditional ink-block prints. Again, so as to maintain their competitive advantage, these centers discouraged the dissemination of knowledge to outsiders through such practices as confining the transmission of handicraft knowledge to males, prohibiting local women from marrying out of the village, or allowing outmarrying women familiar with manufacturing techniques to engage in production only in their natal villages (Gourou 1936:528). Local families employed similar strategies. Among the producers of votive objects in Giap Nhi and traditional prints in Dong Ho, technical knowledge for production was transmitted almost exclusively through men in the patriline. The most important component for ink-block production was the knowledge of the proper raw materials and the proportions needed to mix the colors. This was taught exclusively to senior men. The intricate procedures required to assemble complex votive items such as horses or household items were also taught only to sons, sons-in-law, and patrilineal descendants. Innovations were well-guarded secrets within the family. One exasperated French official who attempted to organize the cooperative production of handicrafts in Ha Dong Province in the 1930s concluded that perhaps the greatest obstacle facing any reform agenda was "as they say (i.e., the artisans), their atavistic mistrust which all too frequently prevents them from submitting to a common will as they dread seeing their neighbor gain a superior advantage" (quoted in Malarney 1993:171). Communist officials echoed this sentiment in *The Peasant Question (1937–1938)*: "Peasants also have the *mentality of private ownership*. They are accustomed to living and working separately. They are suspicious of talk of collective

work. Most of them do not like contributing money for common goals.
. . . We have yet to see peasants spontaneously organize societies that have a
common usefulness" (quoted in Truong Chinh and Vo Nguyen Giap
1974:21; emphasis in original).

In short, competition was a prominent feature of economic life in the precolonial Red River Delta. Families, villages, and guilds competed aggressively with each other, and few if any cooperative enterprises existed. The reluctance to share knowledge or collaborate in joint ventures inhibited the
formation of large-scale productive units and the accumulation of capital.
Guilds were the largest unit of production, but the number of guilds was still
quite small. And even at the family level, families were ambivalent about organizing relations with others. Agriculturalists avoided mobilizing kin during the production cycle, and handicraft producers relied on networks of
trusted nonkin for distribution. Moral obligations to assist kin during weddings and funerals or during the construction of a house were recognized
but did not extend beyond these spheres into the broader organization of
economic life (see Nguyen Danh Phiet 1979:265). This moral disjuncture lay
at the heart of cultural attitudes on economic activity.

Familism and the Legitimacy of Money
and Self-Advancement

Scholars studying Chinese business organization have emphasized the importance of the family-centric ethic and its role in facilitating economic activity. S. Gordon Redding notes that Chinese families "are essentially competing with each other for survival" (Redding 1991:34); Stevan Harrell adds
that Chinese family members share a "quest for material gain and the security of one's family" (Harrell 1985:218). The broader consequence of this
ideology, as Wong Siu-lun has noted in his study of Hong Kong business
families, is the utilization of all resources, both human and material, to
achieve the "collective advancement" of the family (Wong Siu-lun 1991:21).
The situation in the Red River Delta was markedly similar. Family advancement was a critical goal, and most families dedicated themselves to that end.
As a result, families valorized wealth creation because it created circumstances conducive to family advancement.

Like the Chinese, the Vietnamese are from birth "socialized to work hard
for the long-term benefit of the family" (Harrell 1985:224). Parents regularly
school their children in their singular responsibilities to their families. Children must not only fulfill such fundamental obligations as caring for their elderly parents or contributing part of their income to the family purse but
should also strive to excel in all of their activities to improve the family's
name. They should study hard, work hard, and avoid activities that might
dishonor the family. Alternatively, they should also use advantages presented

to them to advance family interests. This disposition is well expressed in the precolonial adage "If a man becomes a mandarin, his whole lineage can ask favors of him" *(mot nguoi lam quan, ca ho duoc nho)*. Yet as Adam Fforde notes in his discussion of the causes of nepotism and corruption during the cooperative period (1959–1986), "historical behavior encouraged the use of formal positions of authority for family gain. It also supported a view of them as the proper object of struggles for status and as sources of authority" (Fforde 1989:42).

One of the most critical mediums for the advancement of the family was the creation of wealth. Families used all available opportunities to generate more wealth, such as the sidelines into handicrafts or trading by most agricultural families, mentioned previously. Creating wealth, however, not only improved the material circumstances of the family but was also a measure of fealty to parents or ancestors. Local attitudes toward money illustrate this. In a number of Asian societies, money is a profoundly immoral force that is a source of chaos, a threat to the social order, or potentially destructive of family relations (see Carsten 1989; Mueggler 1991; see also Parry and Bloch 1989). Among the Vietnamese, money did not carry the same negative valence. Instead, money provided a visible expression of the proper execution of one's filial obligations.[7] Obligations to the living were met by providing the best circumstances possible for family members; duties to the dead involved providing a respectable funeral and elaborate mortuary ceremonies that featured the burning of large quantities of paper representations of both gold and coinage for the deceased's use in the afterlife. With money, both real and symbolic, one properly carried out one's most fundamental responsibilities in life. Far from being a polluting substance, money and the wealth it represented were highly prized.

Accumulating money for one's family, parents, or ancestors did not place one in a position of moral ambivalence and ambiguity. On the contrary, generating wealth in monetary form brought distinction to the family. Wealthy families in the colonial village, for example, garnered a level of social respect and esteem as a result of their wealth (Malarney 1993:104). Particularly among agriculturalists, the wealthy were seen to possess admirable qualities such as discipline, industriousness, and a sound knowledge of how to produce. Being wealthy and advancing one's family interests were therefore more than an improvement in one's material circumstances. They exemplified the proper execution of one's obligations and brought a measure of esteem to one's family. Nevertheless, as Peletz notes in this volume, the definition of success varies cross-culturally, and people strive to "succeed in culturally appropriate ways." Although families in the Red River valley esteemed wealth as a vehicle of social advancement, the uses to which such wealth were put were more varied than simple reinvestment in enterprise productive of further wealth.

The Economic Consequences of Stigma

During the precolonial period, most Red River Delta families engaged in small-scale commercial activities without reluctance. Dedicated to the general enrichment of the family, people entered into a wide range of economic activities beyond agriculture, such as handicraft production, petty trade, and perhaps wage labor, in order to supplement their agricultural incomes. However, as Gourou notes with regard to handicraft production, once families succeeded in their agricultural pursuits, they abandoned handicraft production (Gourou 1936:521). Once a family accumulated sufficient wealth, it usually converted it not into productive capital but into prestige and status through its children's education (Malarney 1993:104).

The abandonment of handicraft production and investment in education reveals the force of the stigma from which commerce suffered. As a method for accumulating wealth, commerce was acceptable, but it could not earn one the highest levels of status or prestige in the village social hierarchy (see also Luong 1992); these were the domain of the educated scholar-officials. Thus instead of reinvesting profits into productive enterprises, families often chose to commit their resources to activities that generated prestige. A number of historical examples illustrate this. Traders in the city of Thang Long often purchased land in the countryside to become members of the rural elite instead of reinvesting their funds in their enterprises (Phan Huy Le 1962:140). Many families had women who were successful traders, but instead of investing their profits back into their businesses, they used the money to advance the educational efforts of male family members (see Luong 1997). Prior to the revolution, newly wealthy families often invested their money in educations for their sons so that they could pass the examinations to become scholar-officials or ascend the village hierarchy (Malarney 1993:104). And virtually all families pooled their resources to educate at least one of their members (Nguyen Khac Vien 1974:25). Beyond prestige, it should be noted, becoming a scholar-official had other perquisites that encouraged people to join this higher rank. Passing an examination and earning an official title gave one access to tax exemptions, land, and administrative positions through which one could enrich oneself. Even if one failed the examinations and did not obtain an administrative post, one could still work in "the most honored profession" of village schoolteacher (Nguyen Khac Vien 1974:24). In this and other ways, investment in education brought greater prestige than commerce.

The twentieth-century Vietnamese intellectual Dao Duy Anh has commented, "People in our country in the past were industrious in their agricultural or academic pursuits while the trading was given over to the Chinese" (Dao Duy Anh 1938:72). Commerce was not a legitimate "elite occupation" (McVey 1992:24), and as a result, upwardly mobile families converted their accumulated wealth into prestige through education. The economic consequences of this prestige-stigma hierarchy were critical. Commerce flourished at a crude level due to its utility in creating wealth, but its stigmatization as not being a prestigious, elite occupation hampered its further development.

Colonialism, Revolution, and the Changing Structures of Stigma

The French seizure of northern Vietnam in the 1880s and the establishment of the colonial economy initiated a process that challenged the prior stigmatization of commerce and entrepreneurship. The consolidation of French control over Indochina opened up new points of access to social status, most notably through the accumulation of wealth or collaboration with the French. Fforde notes that the increased monetization of the Vietnamese economy during the colonial period and lenient French attitudes toward land accumulation facilitated the expansion of economic pursuits being utilized for social advancement (Fforde 1989:10). Becoming a wealthy comprador capitalist or a rich local trader generated a level of social esteem previously denied to Vietnamese entrepreneurs. Many Vietnamese intellectuals also questioned whether Vietnam could become a powerful and independent nation if commerce continued to be stigmatized. As early as the 1860s, the Vietnamese Catholic intellectual Nguyen Truong To (1828–1871) suggested that the Vietnamese elite needed to pay serious attention to business and commerce for Vietnam to advance (Marr 1981:121–123; Tran Van Giau 1973:394). During the 1920s, more intellectuals endorsed entrepreneurial activities as legitimate pursuits, arguing that without commerce Vietnam would remain poor and dependent.[8] Given the humiliation of Vietnam's elite because of the French conquest, the prestige traditionally associated with the scholar-official's life also diminished at this time, and that of trade and commerce increased.

The attainment of power by the Vietnamese Communists in 1954 entailed, among other things, an attempt to reconstitute the structures of prestige and stigma associated with economic activity. The Communists rejected the stigmatization of production and manual labor. Slogans such as "everything serves production," the elaboration of the "worker-peasant alliance" *(lien minh cong nong)*, exhortations for industry and self-sacrifice, and the glorification of work itself—these and other developments served to elevate labor and economic production to new levels of social respectability. Under the new cultural regime, productive labor, even of the manual variety, was glorious. But this valorization occurred only with labor deployed to specific social goals. Individuals were to be productive so that they could help build the nation and revolution. As former general secretary of the Vietnamese Communist Party Le Duan declared, "Each family, each person must work for the whole society, the whole nation" (Le Duan 1977:509). Working for oneself or working to increase one's profits remained stigmatized.

The new, official conceptions of stigma and prestige applied to a wide range of activities. At the broadest and most obvious level, the government condemned all forms of "capitalist" production because of their divisive, inegalitarian, and exploitive nature. According to official ideology, capitalism involved people "enriching themselves by exploitation" (Le Duan 1965b:vol. 1, 20). Economic activities that involved the pursuit of profit at someone else's expense, including tenant farming, moneylending, and petty trading, were seen as exploitative and were therefore to be "liquidated" (Le Duan 1965b:vol. 1, 86). Official ideology extolled communal, egalitarian production while simultaneously denouncing "individualism" *(ca nhan chu nghia)* and "the ideology of looking out for oneself" *(tu tuong tu tu tu loi;* see Vietnam National Peasant Liaison Committee 1957:35).

The government also marked family-based, "small-peasant production" *(san xuat tieu nong)* for elimination for a number of reasons. Economically, officials considered small-peasant production to be inefficient. As Le Duan commented, "Individual production will lead only to deadlock, poverty, and no advancement" (Le Duan 1965b:vol. 3, 42). During the colonial period, land in the Red River Delta had become extremely parcelized (Gourou 1936:352) due largely to the partible inheritance rule. Communist officials wanted to expand the units of production in agriculture so as to achieve economies of scale through which they could support the expansion of the industrial sector (see Vickerman 1986). Officials also vilified smallholder production because they saw it as a fertile incubus for capitalism. "Small production by itself," declared Le Duan, "begets capitalism daily and hourly" (Le Duan 1977:522). It not only produced exploitation but also invigorated anticommunal attitudes "because working for one-self, everyone only thinks about their own interests, everyone only worries about their own production" (Vietnam National Peasant Liaison Committee 1957:7). If Vietnam was to successfully build a collective socialist economy, it needed to "eradicate small-producer mentality and habits" (Le Duan 1970:96).

Socialism and the Family Economy

The creation of the socialist economy radically transformed Red River Delta economic life. The Land Reform Campaign from 1953 to 1956 effected the redistribution of the land to the peasantry, and the formation of agricultural cooperatives from 1959 to 1963 succeeded in establishing the foundation for collectivized agriculture. Throughout these years, the government also launched campaigns to either close down businesses or appropriate them as state enterprises (see Luong 1992). The commercial sphere, from large businesses to the small, local, periodic markets, underwent a rapid reduction in size as the government monitored, eliminated, or drove underground potentially "capitalist" activities. Despite official pressures to achieve the widespread acceptance of the newly defined prestige of producing for the commonweal, indigenous ideas regarding the importance of producing for the family remained strong.[9]

The land reform had redistributed land to farmers with the objective of eliminating the inequities of the prerevolutionary order, but party officials were troubled with the direction of change that soon followed. "The Land Reform," as one Vietnamese scholar commented, "had only eliminated the feudal land tenure regime, while the regime of individual private property in productive implements—the foundation of class differentiation and class oppression—still existed as before" (Dinh Thu Cuc 1976:37). As a result, "exploitation" in its various forms soon reemerged (Dinh Thu Cuc 1976:37; Vietnam National Peasant Liaison Committee 1957:7). From 1954 to 1960, rice yields in the Red River Delta were among the highest ever achieved, in some areas even double those before World War II (Vu Huy Phuc 1993:19). Nonetheless, many peasants struggled and ended up selling land to pay debts or becoming tenant farmers for more successful families. A number of local markets also remained vibrant, and some of the more entrepreneurial peasants, after receiving their land, sold it to use as start-up capital for trading enterprises (Tran Thanh 1958:7).

The advent of the cooperative period in 1959 saw no end to the problem of families following their own economic agendas. This trend was most evident in the problem of the "subsidiary family economy" *(kinh te phu gia dinh)*. Although regulations dictated that members devote the bulk of their labor to the cooperative, 5 percent of the cooperative's land was to be set aside for individual families to work as they wished so long as their efforts "did not interfere with the cooperative's management of labor" (Fforde 1989:32). Families could also freely dispose of the products of the "five percent land" and family economy. Fforde comments that the products of the 5 percent land "were often of great value to cooperators because they could generate cash incomes and protein sources" (Fforde 1989:33). Much to the chagrin of Communist cadres, cooperators worked harder on the 5 percent land than the regular cooperative lands. As early as August 1962, Le Duan noted that 55.5 percent of the average cooperative member's income was derived from the subsidiary household economy *(kinh te phu gia dinh)* and related sources, whereas only 44.5 percent came from the collective economy (Le Duan 1965a:283). Moreover, the estimated value of the 5 percent land's output was in the range of 60–70 percent of the output of the cooperative sector, which utilized 95 percent of cultivated land (Le Duan 1965a:284).[10]

The productivity of the 5 percent lands also helped maintain illicit economies with their own structures of value, as many peasants used the produce of the 5 percent land in ways that contradicted official regulations. One Vietnamese historian described this as the "problem of 'feasting going first, the interests of the nation going after'" *(an co di truoc, loi nuoc di sau;*

see Dinh Thu Cuc 1976:35). One secondary use for the 5 percent land was to provide food for pigs for sale to the government as part of each family's "responsibility to the nation" *(nghia vu nha nuoc)*. Many families used the land to provide pig fodder, but instead of selling the pigs to the government, they slaughtered them for ceremonial consumption. The 5 percent land also helped maintain small-scale marketing, as many families sold their produce at local markets to generate cash income. Although officially discouraged, small markets were nevertheless tolerated. For most peasant families, such market activity generally consisted of female members selling small quantities of basic necessities like fruits and vegetables. But this activity indicated that there was yet "a highly profitable free market" (Fforde 1989:86) outside of the cooperative economy that provided a market for goods produced on the 5 percent land.

The disproportionate effort put into the subsidiary family economy and the 5 percent land was a constant irritant to government and party officials. Officials criticized farmers for "the habit of working more actively for oneself than for the cooperative" (Le Duan 1977:489). "The ideology of looking out for one's family," one Vietnamese intellectual asserted in the prominent historical journal *Nghien Cuu Lich Su*, is "in the psychology of the peasant" (Dinh Thu Cuc 1976:37). In spite of an active propaganda campaign, agriculturalists never internalized the ideology of producing for the collective first and the family second. Furthermore, the state never completely convinced the people that petty commerce was truly exploitive and therefore deserving of stigma and elimination. On the contrary, many people remained actively involved in commercial activities to help provide for their families. As the chairman of a cooperative that had been recognized for outstanding production in 1982 matter-of-factly stated, "The responsibilities to the collective were never greater than those to the family."

"Renovation" and the Emerging Morality of the Market

The Vietnamese economy entered a period of severe stagnation after the unification of North and South Vietnam in 1975 (see Fforde 1989). This economic crisis forced the government to make "certain concessions to grassroots pressure for a reduction in the extent of the collective economy" (Fforde 1989:205). The primary response was a shift toward a household contracting system in which the administrative structure of the cooperatives remained in place but tasks were contracted out to households instead of carried out by production brigades. The initial phase of this program ended in 1981 with the legalization of household contracting in Directive 100.[11] The final phase began with the Communist Party's introduction of the "Renovation" *(Doi Moi)* policy during the Sixth Party Congress in December 1986 and concluded with the Central Committee's passage of Resolution 10 in April 1988. This latter resolution authorized the return of agricultural land to farming households and for all intents and purposes dissolved the agricultural cooperatives. The passage of Resolution 10 was a watershed in the economic history of the Socialist Republic of Vietnam. It allowed for "the long term cession of land to the peasantry, the primary reliance on individual labor as the mainstay of the economy, the appropriation of the household as the fundamental economic unit, independent management in production and trade, and diversification of the forms of property and cooperation in a multi-component economic structure" (Nguyen Sinh Cuc 1991:7). The government at last recognized the family economy as "a fitting component of the socialist economy" (Huu Tho 1987:85). The results in agricultural production were immediately evident. By 1989 the average annual rice yield increased from the 1978 low of 1,792 kilograms per hectare to a high of 3,230 (Vu Nong Nghiepet al. 1991:89).

The Renovation policy also opened the door for an expansion of commercial activities. The dissolution of the collective economy entailed an end to the state's control over sales and distribution. With businesspeople and traders to serve them, markets rapidly expanded to provide for the population. As in agriculture, the family has served as the core for the majority of new enterprises (see also Luong, this volume). In Thinh Liet commune, virtually all trading and commercial ventures are family run. Such enterprises most commonly involve the operation of a stall in front of the home, where small items are sold, or the pursuit of horticultural activities, petty trading, or petty handicraft production for sale in local markets. A recent study of small businesses in Hanoi indicates a similar appropriation of the family as the unit of enterprise organization (see Le Ngoc Hung and Rondinelli 1993). Based on official figures, the authors estimate that out of approximately 459,158 state and nonstate industrial and commercial establishments in 1992, a remarkable 446,771 (97.3 percent) were private household enterprises (Le Ngoc Hung and Rondinelli 1993:8). Officially such enterprises employed only 55 percent of the labor force (Le Ngoc Hung and Rondinelli 1993:9). But official figures probably do not adequately reflect the widespread phenomenon of people holding a state-sector job while simultaneously holding other jobs *(lam them)*. The authors note that small enterprises provide "a large number of jobs" and "generate a significant part of Vietnamese income" (Le Ngoc Hung and Rondinelli 1993:10).

The recent expansion of commerce and the emergence of entrepreneurship as a common occupation have generated a number of ideological debates. The move to unfettered independent family production has caused some Vietnamese to question its social consequences. Le Ngoc Hung and Dennis Rondinelli note that in Hanoi the majority of those engaged in trade or entrepreneurial pursuits are young and literate (Le Ngoc Hung and

Rondinelli 1993:10), a trend similar to the situation in Thinh Liet commune and Dong Ho village, where almost all entrepreneurs are under fifty years old. As the young move to take advantage of contemporary opportunities, some of their elders question whether the disadvantages of the recent changes outweigh the benefits. Common objections are that the endorsement of individual production has led to an emergent division between rich and poor; that wealth distinctions have created new structures of social inequality; and that greater disposable income has produced ever more egregious displays of status and conspicuous consumption in such venues as weddings and funerals. Criticism of the latter variety is common among the older and more committed Communist Party members, although it should be well noted that many people from the party's ranks have enthusiastically adapted to the recent changes. Three of the most prosperous and entrepreneurial families in Thinh Liet commune have fathers who were party members and former high-ranking officials in the agricultural cooperative. With the help of their sons, they branched out into such activities as transporting bricks, raising fish fingerlings and pigs for sale in the regions around Hanoi, or growing flowers—all of which generate significant profits. Many critics, however, feel that economic changes are fueling the atomization of society and its bifurcation into groups of haves and have-nots. These people argue that unlike the storied unity of the Vietnamese during the war years, contemporary society is disintegrating into a collection of selfish individuals who have no concern for the larger community.

Recent economic changes have also highlighted the continued ambivalence of Red River Delta residents regarding the virtues or liabilities of involving close kin in business enterprises. On the one hand, kin are considered more trustworthy than nonkin and therefore less likely to abscond with profits and capital. On the other, as kin they have a right to ask for assistance from their wealthier relations, frequently without the obligation of repayment. Even the most upright and honest family member can become an unexpected drain on resources. People also regard kin as more difficult to manage, a problem apparent in the formation of fishing teams after Thinh Liet commune dissolved its cooperatives in 1992. Thinh Liet's fishing brigades had been the most lucrative segment of the cooperative economy, but they required the flooding of large areas of land in which the fish could mature. To realize similar profits, families needed to combine their landholdings to create the needed area. Instead of mobilizing kin relations to create such holdings, families with contiguous plots or former comembers of the fishing brigades banded together to form small companies of approximately fifteen families. Utilizing contracts that detail each member's responsibilities and entitlements, these families jointly tend the ponds and split the profits. When asked about the desirability of organizing a company or large-scale enterprise with kin, members uniformly agreed that it introduced more problems than it solved because criticizing or giving orders to kin was difficult and unpleasant. These sentiments were echoed in discussions with entrepreneurs in Hanoi. Organizing small-scale production through a circle of very close family relations is possible and desirable. Le Ngoc Hung and Rondinelli note that in Hanoi "the average size of a small-enterprise is two or three family members and sometimes one or two full- or part-time employees" (Le Ngoc Hung and Rondinelli 1993:10). Many Vietnamese remain nonetheless ambivalent about organizing larger enterprises on the basis of kinship because of the many problems it creates.

Attitudes toward entrepreneurship and wealth accumulation also remain complicated. Officially, the state has ended its stigmatization of private commerce. Whereas before collective effort was the idealized foundation of the economy, family enterprise has now emerged as the main engine for the nation's growth. State propaganda extols the virtues of a "rich people, strong nation" *(dan giau, nuoc manh)*; one party member whom I knew observed that such a slogan would have been unthinkable only a decade ago. Despite official statements, however, some Vietnamese remain deeply ambivalent about entrepreneurship and the family economy. After surveying Hanoi residents, Le Ngoc Hung and Rondinelli found "lingering negative attitudes toward capitalism and entrepreneurs" (Le Ngoc Hung and Rondinelli 1993:17). "Both Confucian culture and a long period of central planning," they concluded, "has left many people with a distrust of small business owners and capitalists in general" (Le Ngoc Hung and Rondinelli 1993:17). Other factors have reinforced these attitudes: reports in the national press about swindlers and cheats who break contracts and steal profits; the maintenance among some elite segments of government and the intelligentsia of attitudes that value artistic or literary production over moneymaking and menial labor (see Woodside 1983:411); and the success in the market of women, a development that has confirmed some male impressions that commerce is really women's work.

The extraordinary commercial boom in Hanoi and the countryside, however, points to the emergence or reemergence of a different set of values. Both Thinh Liet commune and Dong Ho village feature large numbers of individuals and families actively pursuing market opportunities. A number of local families have made names for themselves in both locales by producing votive paper objects for mortuary ceremonies or by engaging in other profitable pursuits. In Hanoi, many successful entrepreneurs are highly respected. Business acumen and wealth accumulation are definite sources of prestige and respect in certain segments of society. Indeed, the most prestigious man in Thinh Liet commune was the chairman of the agricultural cooperative. Part of his prestige is due to his remarkable social skills, but his discipline, industriousness, and entrepreneurial flair have earned him greater adulation. Le Ngoc Hung and Rondinelli capture the socially prized qualities of many contemporary entrepreneurs when they comment that "the image of small business owners is beginning to change because small-shop owners, women shop-owners, and sellers of sundry goods are quietly striving to feed their families and improve Vietnam's economy" (Le Ngoc Hung and Rondinelli 1993:17). For many, commerce is no longer an occupation of "cheating and lying" but a respectable profession with clear social benefits.

Conclusion

The development of a capitalist economy depends on a number of factors beyond policies conducive to economic development. Supracontractual trust, the social acceptability of profit seeking, and attitudes amenable to saving and the reinvestment of profits all inform the broader sociocultural framework in which capitalism develops. As Vietnam moves toward capitalism, it is too early to predict the ultimate outcome, particularly as several of the early indicators appear quite negative. The first issue is the attitude of the government toward the growth of capitalism. Despite official endorsement of "market socialism," many factions within the government and party oppose this trajectory and seek a return to a more conventional socialist economy. This attitude has resulted in the issuing of a number of nebulous, contradictory, or regressive economic policies that neither protect entrepreneurs nor increase their confidence in the government (Le Ngoc Hung and Rondinelli 1993:16). Businesspeople also suffer from interference and harassment by local authorities. Bribes to underpaid officials are a source of great frustration and sour the business environment. Combined with government indecisiveness, they constitute a serious disincentive to entrepreneurship and commercial growth.

A second problem relates to the question of supracontractual trust. Scholars working in East Asia have emphasized the importance of trust between business partners in the development of the region's commercial enterprises (Chen and Hamilton 1991; Hamilton 1991; Redding 1991; Wong Siu-lun 1991). Gary Hamilton (this volume) has compellingly illustrated the manner in which trust and reciprocity create favorable conditions for business growth in the absence of state intervention and credit. Recent commercial expansion indicates that some businesspeople have begun building an ethic of business trust, but many Red River Delta entrepreneurs remain wary of entering into broadly collaborative business relations. The systemic atrophy of the Vietnamese legal system magnifies this problem, since it makes legal settlement of business disputes virtually impossible. Given that in Hanoi over three-quarters of the small enterprises in 1992 were service enterprises and less than a quarter were production enterprises (Le Ngoc Hung and Rondinelli 1993:9), it is difficult to predict how the issue of trust will affect the establishment of large-scale enterprises. But it is clear that effective measures for engendering trust and extending interfirm collaboration have yet to emerge.

A final consideration for the development of capitalism is the relative prestige or stigma of commerce and wealthmaking. As we have seen, commerce has long suffered from severe stigmatization in the Red River Delta, and as with most stigmatized social statuses, it was not something to which most people aspired (cf. Kelly 1993:17). This stigmatization, however, was the product of elite and official ideologies and the institutional structure they supported. With the declining prestige of both party membership and government office and in the absence of institutional stigmatization of commerce, a public reevaluation of these anticommercial values has begun. The effects of this reevaluation can be seen in declining university enrollments as young people choose business careers over a higher education that leads only to low-paying government jobs. The scale of this change is still quite tentative. Vietnam has yet to see the emergence of individuals similar to Meiji Japan's Fukuzawa Yukichi or Shibusawa Eiichi (Hirschmeier 1964:164–175) or Singapore's Lee Kuan Yeuh, who publicly affirm the virtues of commerce and capitalism, but a shift has begun nonetheless. As Vietnam's economy grows, its benefits in the form of consumer goods, changing lifestyles, and access to services are becoming more visible. So too are the inequities of the new capitalist economy, as seen in rising unemployment and a growing gap between rich and poor. All this is leading people to debate the new "capitalist" values and the system of which they are part. The results of these discussions and their interplay with government policy will play a decisive role in determining the fate of commercial development in the Red River Delta.

NOTES

Research in the Socialist Republic of Vietnam was carried out in the Thinh Liet commune of Thanh Tri District on the southern outskirts of Hanoi and in Dong Ho village, Thuan Thanh District, Bac Ninh Province, from March 1990 to August 1992 and December 1993 to February 1994. I am grateful to Le Van Sinh for his assistance in the field and John Coatsworth, Robert Hefner, and Hue Tam Ho-Tai for their comments on earlier drafts.

1. My approach to prestige and stigma owes a great debt to Raymond Kelly; see Kelly 1993.
2. For purposes of clarity, I divide the Vietnamese history into the following periods: the precolonial period extends up to the French conquest of Vietnam in the mid-nineteenth century; the colonial period from roughly the 1860s to 1954; the revolutionary period from 1954 to 1986; and the postrevolutionary, or reforming-socialist, period from 1986 to the present.
3. This prestige-stigma hierarchy was similar to that of China (see Hamilton 1991:55).
4. For a critique of this approach, see Murray 1980:348–349.

5. The Vietnamese monarchy originally created communal land to assist returning soldiers, widows, orphans, and village unfortunates. The actual amount of communal land in the delta is open to dispute; thus the figures provided are rough estimates; see Malarney 1993.

6. It is interesting that transplanting is a task performed primarily by women, whereas harvesting involves both men and women (Malarney 1993:173).

7. Oxfeld notes that the Hakka Chinese in Calcutta also consider wealth accumulation as filial behavior (Oxfeld 1993:106).

8. See Marr (1981:121–127) for a discussion of the moral controversies raised by the endorsement of business and profit seeking during the colonial period.

9. See Luong, this volume, for a discussion of the history of the ceramics industry in Bát Tràng and the pressures and tensions that existed during this period.

10. The most remarkable quality of the 5 percent land was its extraordinary productivity. During the 1970s, annual yields on some plots of 5 percent land planted with rice reached 9,000 kilograms per hectare (Tran Duc 1991:9). Party officials considered an annual yield of 10,000 kilograms per hectare to be the ideal, yet cooperative production during the same decade averaged only 2,096 kilograms per hectare (Vu Nong Nghiep et al. 1991:89). The productivity of the 5 percent land was so high that some farmers referred to it as the "miraculous land" (see Tran Duc 1991:9). Given this fact, some cooperatives ceded more than 5 percent of their land for family use.

11. Household contracting had a number of advocates in the late 1960s. The government opposed such moves and in 1968 declared household contracting for production illegal (White 1988:114).

REFERENCES

Carsten, Janet. 1989. "Cooking Money: Gender and the Symbolic Transformation of Means of Exchange in a Malay Fishing Community." In Jonathan Parry and Maurice Bloch, eds., *Money and the Morality of Exchange,* pp. 117–141. Cambridge: Cambridge University Press.

Chen, Edward, and Gary G. Hamilton. 1991. "Introduction: Business Groups and Economic Development." In Gary G. Hamilton, ed., *Business Networks and Economic Development in East and Southeast Asia,* pp. 3–10. Hong Kong: University of Hong Kong.

Dao Duy Anh. 1938. *Viet Nam van hoa su cuong* (History of Vietnamese culture). Hanoi: Nha Xuat Ban Bon Phuong.

Dinh Thu Cuc. 1976. "Buoc dau tim hieu ve qua trinh hinh thanh va phat trien tu tuong lam chu tap the cua nguoi nong dan Viet Nam" (First steps for understanding the process of realizing and developing collectivist ideology among the Vietnamese peasantry). *Nghien Cuu Lich Su* 2:34–45.

Fforde, Adam. 1989. *The Agrarian Question in North Vietnam, 1974–1979.* Armonk, N.Y.: M.E. Sharpe.

Gates, Hill. 1987. "Money for the Gods." *Modern China* 13, 3:259–277.

Geertz, Clifford. 1959. "Form and Variation in Balinese Village Structure." *American Anthropologist* 61:991–1012.

Gourou, Pierre. 1936. *Les paysans du delta tonkinois: Étude de géographie humaine.* Paris: l'École Française d'Extrême-Orient.

———. 1945. *Land Utilization in French Indochina.* Washington, D.C.: Institute of Pacific Relations.

Hamilton, Gary. 1991. "The Organizational Foundations of Western and Chinese Commerce: A Historical and Comparative Analysis." In Gary G. Hamilton, ed., *Business Networks and Economic Development in East and Southeast Asia,* pp. 48–65. Hong Kong: University of Hong Kong.

Harrell, Stevan. 1985. "Why Do the Chinese Work So Hard? Reflections on an Entrepreneurial Ethic." *Modern China* 11, 2:203–226.

Hirschmeier, Johannes. 1964. *The Origins of Entrepreneurship in Meiji Japan.* Cambridge: Harvard University Press.

Huu Tho. 1987. *Doi moi tu duy—nong nghiep: Phai thuc su la mat tran kinh te hang dau* (Renovating thinking—agriculture: It must truly be foremost on the economic front line). Hanoi: Nha Xuat Ban Su That.

Kelly, Raymond C. 1993. *Constructing Inequality: The Fabrication of a Hierarchy of Virtue Among the Etoro.* Ann Arbor: University of Michigan Press.

Le Duan. 1965a. *Giai cap vo san voi van de nong dan trong cach mang Viet-Nam* (The proletarian class and the problem of the peasantry in the Vietnamese revolution). Hanoi: Nha Xuat Ban Su That.

———. 1965b. *On the Socialist Revolution in Vietnam,* vols. 1, 2, 3. Hanoi: Foreign Languages Publishing House.

———. 1970. *The Vietnamese Revolution: Fundamental Problems, Essential Tasks.* Hanoi: Foreign Languages Publishing House.

———. 1977. *Le Duan: Selected Writings.* Hanoi: Foreign Languages Publishing House.

Le Ngoc Hung and Dennis A. Rondinelli. 1993. "Small Business Development and Economic Transformation in Vietnam." *Journal of Asian Business* 9, 4:1–23.

Luong, Hy van. 1992. *The Revolution in the Village.* Honolulu: University of Hawaii Press.

MacFarlane, Alan. 1987. *The Culture of Capitalism.* Oxford: Basil Blackwell.

Malarney, Shaun Kingsley. 1993. "Ritual and Revolution in Viet Nam." Ph.D. dissertation, University of Michigan.

Marr, David G. 1981. *Vietnamese Tradition on Trial, 1920–1945.* Berkeley: University of California Press.

McVey, Ruth. 1992. "The Materialization of the Southeast Asian Entrepreneur." In McVey, ed., *Southeast Asian Capitalists,* pp. 7–33. Ithaca: Southeast Asia Program, Cornell University.

Mueggler, Erik. 1991. "Money, the Mountain, and State Power in a Naxi Village." *Modern China* 17, 2:188–226.

Murray, Martin J. 1980. *The Development of Capitalism in Colonial Indochina (1870–1940).* Berkeley: University of California Press.

Nguyen Danh Phiet. 1979. "Giao duc lao dong trong cong dong lang xa" (Education on labor in the village community). In Vien Su Hoc, ed., *Nong thon Viet Nam trong lich su,* pp. 258–275. Hanoi: Nha Xuat Ban Khoa Hoc Xa Hoi.

Nguyen Khac Vien. 1974. *Tradition and Revolution in Viet Nam.* Berkeley: Indochina Research Center.

Nguyen Kien Giang. 1959. *Phac qua tinh hinh ruong dat va doi song nong dan truoc cach mang thang tam* (An outline of the situation of land and the life of the peasantry before the August revolution). Hanoi: Nha Xuat Ban Su That.

Nguyen Sinh Cuc. 1991. *Thuc trang nong nghiep, nong thon va nong dan Viet Nam, 1976–1990* (The situation of agriculture, the countryside, and the peasantry in Vietnam, 1976–1990). Hanoi: Nha Xuat Ban Thong Ke.

Nguyen The Anh. 1968. *Kinh te va xa hoi Viet-Nam duoi cac vua trieu Nguyen* (Vietnamese economy and society under the emperors of the Nguyen dynasty). Saigon: Nha Xuat Ban Trinh Bay.

Oxfeld, Ellen. 1993. *Blood, Sweat, and Mahjong: Family and Enterprise in an Overseas Chinese Community*. Ithaca: Cornell University Press.

Parry, J., and M. Bloch, eds. 1989. *Money and the Morality of Exchange*. Cambridge: Cambridge University Press.

Phan Huy Le. 1962. *Lich su che do phong kien Viet-Nam, tap II* (History of the Vietnamese feudal regime, volume 2). Hanoi: Nha Xuat Ban Giao Duc.

Phan Huy Le, Chu Thien, Vuong Hoang Tuyen, and Dinh Xuan Lam. 1965. *Lich su che do phong kien Viet-Nam, tap III* (History of the Vietnamese feudal regime, volume 3). Hanoi: Nha Xuat Ban Giao Duc.

Popkin, Samuel. 1979. *The Rational Peasant: The Political Economy of Rural Society in Vietnam*. Berkeley: University of California Press.

Redding, S. Gordon. 1991. "Weak Organizations and Strong Linkages: Managerial Ideology and Chinese Family Business Networks." In Gary G. Hamilton, ed., *Business Networks and Economic Development in East and Southeast Asia*, pp. 30–47. Hong Kong: University of Hong Kong.

Tran Duc. 1991. *Hop tac xa va thoi vang son cua kinh te gia dinh* (Cooperatives and the golden age of the family economy). Hanoi: Nha Xuat Ban Tu Tuong–Van Hoa.

Tran Phuong. 1968. *Cach mang ruong dat o Viet-Nam* (Land reform in Vietnam). Hanoi: Nha Xuat Ban Khoa Hoc Xa Hoi.

Tran Quoc Vuong and Ha Van Tan. 1963. *Lich su che do phong kien Viet-Nam, tap I* (History of the Vietnamese feudal regime, volume 1). Hanoi: Nha Xuat Ban Giao Duc.

Tran Thanh. 1958. *Lam the nao de cung co va phat trien phong trao doi cong hop tac* (How to strengthen and develop the cooperative labor exchange movement). Hanoi: Nha Xuat Ban Su That.

Tran Van Giau. 1973. *Su phat trien cua tu tuong o Viet-Nam tu the ky XIX den cach mang thang tam, tap I* (The development of Vietnamese thought from the nineteenth century to the August revolution). Hanoi: Nha Xuat Ban Khoa Hoc Xa Hoi.

Truong Chinh and Vo Nguyen Giap. 1974. *The Peasant Question (1937–1938)*. Ithaca: Southeast Asia Program, Cornell University.

Vickerman, Andrew. 1986. *The Fate of the Peasantry: Premature "Transition to Socialism" in the Democratic Republic of Vietnam*. New Haven: Yale Center for International and Area Studies.

Vietnam National Peasant Liaison Committee. 1957. *Lay doi cong hop tac lam trung tam day manh san xuat nong nghiep (Tai lieu huan luyen doi cong cho can bo xa va to truong doi cong)* (Take cooperative labor exchange as a center to strengthen agriculture [Instructional materials on labor exchange for communal-level cadres and chiefs of labor exchange groups]). Hanoi: Nha Xuat Ban Nong Thon.

Vu Huy Phuc. 1993. "Vai nhan xet ve nang suat ruong dat o mien bac thoi ky 1954–1960" (A few observations on land productivity in northern Vietnam, 1954–1960). *Nghien Cuu Lich Su* 4:19–23.

Vu Nong Nghiep, Tong Cuc Thong Ke, Vien Quy Hoach va Thiet Ke, Bo Nong Nghiep va CNTP. 1991. *So lieu thong ke nong nghiep 35 nam (1956–1990)* (Thirty-five years of statistics on agriculture [1956–1990]). Hanoi: Nha Xuat Ban Thong Ke.

White, Christine Pelzer. 1988. "Alternative Approaches to the Socialist Transformation of Agriculture in Postwar Vietnam." In David G. Marr and Christine P. White, eds., *Postwar Vietnam: Dilemmas in Socialist Development*, pp. 133–146. Ithaca: Cornell Southeast Asia Program.

Wong Siu-lun. 1991. "Chinese Entrepreneurs and Business Trust." In Gary G. Hamilton, ed., *Business Networks and Economic Development in East and Southeast Asia*, pp. 13–29. Hong Kong: University of Hong Kong.

Woodside, Alexander. 1983. "The Triumphs and Failures of Mass Education in Vietnam." *Pacific Affairs* 3, 56:401–427.

eleven

el/

Engendered
Entrepreneurship

Ideologies and Political-Economic
Transformation in a Northern Vietnamese
Center of Ceramics Production

HY VAN LUONG

Since the 1970s the strength of many economies in East and Southeast Asia, first in Japan and later in many other parts of the region, has led to a sharpened focus on whether, notwithstanding the Weberian thesis on the Protestant ethic and the spirit of capitalism, native ideologies might have facilitated the process of economic development through their impact on the relation among the state, society, and business as well as through entrepreneurship—the investment of material resources with a reasonable element of risk for capital accumulation (see Redding 1990). In general, however, this debate has not paid sufficient attention to the gender structuring of entrepreneurial activities. Nor has it attended sufficiently to the multiplicity of ideological voices at work in the historical interplay between gender structuring and the political framework and how this interplay has in turn transformed the relation between gender and entrepreneurship. In this chapter I seek to illuminate the gender dimension of entrepreneurship in the village of Bát Tràng, a northern Vietnamese center of ceramics production, in its historically embedded ideological and political-economic contexts.

Entrepreneurship in Vietnam has long been highly engendered. At least from the seventeenth century onward, foreign observers have consistently remarked on the dominance of women in Vietnamese commerce. I suggest that women have also played a major role in manufacturing activities, at least in the leading handicraft firms of pre-twentieth-century Vietnam. However, statistical data also indicate that the role of women in industrial entrepreneurship has suffered a decline in the twentieth century, including in the socialist era—despite the Marxist state's emphasis on gender equality. The available data suggest that in Vietnam, both the prominent role of women in entrepreneurial activities in the pre-twentieth-century era and the shift since then are strongly embedded in the Vietnamese ideological formation, which contains contradictory currents. However, these developments cannot be strictly reduced to ideological frameworks because the resolution of ideological contradictions involves the exercise of power in specific historical conditions.

Engendered Entrepreneurship: A Historical Overview

Located approximately fifteen kilometers from Hanoi, the village of Bát Tràng has long been renowned for the entrepreneurship of its members both in commerce and in small industrial production. Bát Tràng had little agricultural land before its merger with the neighboring and predominantly agricultural village of Giang Cao in the 1950s. In 1928, for a population of 2,377, the village owned only 70–80 *mâu* (62.3 to 71.2 acres) of alluvial fields besides the densely populated 38 *mâu* (33.8 acres) of residential land.[1] In 1988, out of the total of 101 hectares (249.6 acres), the combined village of Bát Tràng and Giang Cao had only 54 hectares of cultivable land (133.4 acres) for a population of 4,334.[2]

In fact, entrepreneurial activities have been so strong in Bát Tràng that few villagers have directly engaged in agricultural production even when land was available. In the French colonial period, villagers rented out their shares of alluvial fields to sharecroppers in the neighboring villages of Kim Quang and Xuan Quang for corn and soybean cultivation (Phan Huu Dat 1977:335–336, 343; Do thi Hao et al. 1989:16, 25, 27). Even in 1988, the households receiving agricultural land in the combined villages of Bát Tràng and Giang Cao hired laborers from surrounding communities to cultivate their crops and devoted their time to handicraft production.

In commercial entrepreneurship before 1954, many villagers in Bát Tràng engaged in wholesale delivery of fish sauce (from Thanh Hoa and Nghe An), areca nuts, and ceramic bowls; some others were petty traders. The thriving commerce in Bát Tràng at least from the seventeenth century to 1954 was reported regularly over centuries (see Nguyen Thua Hy 1983:35; and Vietnam Quoc su quan trieu Nguyen 1992:97–98). During my field visits to Bát Tràng, despite the overwhelming shift to ceramics production, a number of villagers were still engaged in the supply of raw materials and in the distribution of final products. In fact, they ranked among the wealthiest in the community. The Bát Tràng market still met daily for the whole day.

The development of a relatively important market in Bát Tràng and the specialization of many Bát Tràng natives in trade are inextricably linked to the position of the village as a major center of ceramics production in Vietnam since the fifteenth century (see Nguyen Trai 1966:69; Chu Quang Chu and Nguyen Du Chi 1991:259). The archaeological and historical data indicate that Bát Tràng was an important part of the pre-1954 golden age of Vietnamese ceramic production, a period that lasted from the fourteenth to the seventeenth century; during this time, a considerable amount of wares was exported to the rest of Southeast Asia. In a twenty-year period from 1663 to 1682, as documented in the archives of the Dutch East India Company (Volker 1954:193–222), the Dutch alone exported 1,450,000 pieces of porcelain (an average of 72,500 pieces a year) from Tonkin (North Vietnam) to other parts of Southeast Asia (184). Those figures compare favorably with the average of 63,300 pieces a year exported from Japan from 1653 to 1683 (a total of 1.9 million) and 114,700 pieces a year from China for the years 1608–1682 (a total of 8.6 million pieces; 193–222), although Tonkinese porcelain did not fare as well beyond Southeast Asia as the products from China and Japan. The export was obviously neither monopolized by the Dutch nor restricted to that period.[3]

Given the large quantity of exported products and our general knowledge about the technological conditions of ceramics production at the time, it is not far-fetched to hypothesize that the construction and operation of a kiln required a sizable capital investment, that the production was for market exchanges, and that it involved an assembly-line method in at least six stages: moulding, shape polishing, painting, glazing, loading, and firing. In other words, from an early period, ceramics production in Bát Tràng had been for profit and probably involved a clear differentiation of labor and capital. This was indeed the case at the turn of the century. In 1907, there were only 17 kilns in Bát Tràng that produced approximately 350,000 products a month, mostly inexpensive and coarse earthenware bowls (bat dan) for the entire northern market (Nguyen Cong Binh 1959:56).[4]

The high concentration of capital in Bát Tràng resulted from the large investments required both for the construction of the kiln and for the initial risk-laden kiln operation. This is amply illustrated in the narrative of a grandson of the first Bát Tràng entrepreneur, who adopted the Mong Cay chamber-kiln design in the late 1920s in order to increase the competitive edge of Bát Tràng products in the high-price categories:

When I was a child, my family was poor. At the turn of the century, my paternal grandfather worked in a kiln himself. At that time, the kilns here, also called

Tieochiu kilns, produced only coarse earthenware bowls *[bat dan]*. . . . My paternal grandfather, Tran van Tan, went to work in Mong Cay. He returned to the area in 1920, and built a kiln for a Vietnamese entrepreneur in Da Phuc [province of Phuc Yen]. He also built a family kiln at the end of the village. . . . But we lost everything. The chamber kilns of Mong Cay had steep slopes at 13 degrees. The fire was strong [as a result]. In Bát Tràng, we used red clay [at the time]. The wares cracked because of the high heat. He laboured again as a worker until 1930 when he constructed another kiln, an 8-chamber kiln, and found a white clay in Truc Thon [district of Dong Trieu, Hai Duong Province].[5] He was the first person to introduce the chamber kiln to Bát Tràng. We manufactured vases *[loc binh]* and bowls, although the quality of bowls initially did not match that of Mong Cay products. . . . At the beginning, we were not completely confident of a profit. We used a lot of family labor. We had only a few workers. My grandfather had to mould things himself on a potter's wheel. This was before the wooden mould was developed. He also moulded *don* and *thong* [ceramic stools] with his hands only, using a specially mixed clay. . . . Our kiln was known as the kiln of *cu* [the elderly] De.

As a result of a native son's experiment, the chamber-kiln design was gradually adopted by other Bát Tràng industrialists in the 1930s and 1940s. Also partly thanks to the discovery of a new source of clay in the neighboring Hai Duong Province, the ceramics firms of Bát Tràng began upgrading their basic-line bowls to coarse porcelain ones. They also diversified their product lines to include more decorative items (including statues and miniature animals) as well as electric porcelain devices among utilitarian ceramics. The ceramics industry was probably among the very first in the Vietnamese social formation where the capitalist mode of production and market orientation developed. To the extent that commercial and industrial entrepreneurship existed in rural northern Vietnam before the nineteenth century and during the French colonial period (1884–1954), Bát Tràng was a prominent center of entrepreneurial activities.

The entrepreneurship of Bát Tràng villagers continued well into the socialist reform period and into the present era despite the Vietnamese Marxist state's efforts to collectivize industrial production and commercial distribution from 1954 onward. In the ceramics industry of Bát Tràng, during the industrial reform in 1959, private firms were de facto abolished; a bureaucratic hierarchy was instituted within the state enterprise and adopted by handicraft cooperatives (their differences from state enterprises to be shortly explained); and the state's tight control of production and trade under soft-budget constraints reduced market pressure on state and cooperative firms because their survival and growth depend not on efficiency as much as on bureaucratic decisions for resource allocation (Kornai 1989; de Vylder and Fforde 1988; see also Luong 1993). The state firm of Bát Tràng was established that year, nominally as a joint state-private firm, from the merger of fourteen private enterprises. A pottery cooperative was established three years later, in 1962, and four others were formed in the 1976–1985 period. Under the control of the provincial government, the Bát Tràng state enterprise received capital, labor, and materials from the state and produced for the state commercial network according to administrative guidelines. The cooperative was established on the basis of members' capital and labor contributions. Although the state commercial network purchased most of the cooperative's products, it did not have monopoly rights over them. The state firm offered retirement incomes, paid holidays (17 days in 1988), health benefits and paid maternity leaves, greater employment security, upward mobility opportunities, limited housing facilities for single workers from other localities, and such fringe benefits as a work-study program up to the university level for qualified employees—a program with two months of paid educational leave each year (Vu Qúy Vy 1980:148). Under the close supervision of a state-organized union of ceramics cooperatives *(lien hiep xa)*, the labor relations in the cooperatives of Bát Tràng closely resembled those in state firms, although in 1988, cooperative members' retirement incomes averaged only 25 percent of state workers' and their rice subsidy was only at 30 percent, in contrast to 90 percent among state employees.[6] Encouraging the establishment of state firms and cooperatives, the state sought to construct a socialist formation in which large-scale production under state guidance would serve the collective interests of the workers and society at large. The socialist-oriented economy was centrally planned with the goal of rapid industrialization through state control of key resources (raw materials, labor, and capital) and marketing of output (through the state's trading network) (de Vylder and Fforde 1988:10, 26, 61; Fforde and Paine 1987:1).[7]

Notwithstanding the efforts of the state to collectivize industrial production and distribution and to stamp out private entrepreneurship, in Bát Tràng entrepreneurial activities persisted in the underground economy and contributed to undermining the state and cooperative sectors. As early as 1967, a few households in the village constructed small household kilns and manufactured earthenwares (teapots, cups) for the open market, using clay from paddy fields and lead paint (illegally stripped from the landmark Long Bien [Paul Doumer] bridge) for coloring the wares. Technically illegal, these family enterprises operated in an underground market in raw materials and ceramic products. The underground economy in ceramics developed in the context of the decline in the purchasing power of state workers' incomes due to an inflationary monetary policy.[8] In order to meet both workers' needs for higher incomes and the state's production targets, the state firm also implemented in 1969 a contract system *(gia cong)* with its workers that indirectly strengthened the underground economy and eventually undermined the state and collective sectors. Although the contract system initially involved only two specific tasks (moulding and trimming) and 100 workers and their families, by 1971, the contract system had expanded to 302 households and to include two additional tasks (painting and glazing).[9] By 1977, it had evolved to the point that the firm delivered raw materials, provided materials for the construction of household kilns, received final products, and paid the contractors for their labor (see Luong 1993:124–125). The number of contracted products increased steadily from 200,000 semiproducts in 1969 to 8.5 million products in 1978, and the number of family kilns increased to at least 218 by the latter year (Vu Qúy Vy 1980:145). Although the Vietnamese state remained indifferent toward, if not hostile to, private enterprises relying primarily on nonhousehold labor, it tolerated family firms using household labor in symbiotic relation with the state sector. In Bát Tràng, family firms were allowed as long as they operated within the orbit of the state enterprise.

However, the family enterprises of Bát Tràng did not merely function as contractors to the state firm. Many also produced for the open market. Surplus raw materials and "defective" products were reportedly not delivered to the state enterprise (P.T.V. 1972:52). A number of family enterprises were also established not as contractors to the state enterprise but as independent manufacturers, circumventing the state's efforts to prevent the growth of a private or capitalist sector. As one worker reported, "Initially, if a worker had a box-shaped kiln, the firm or village authorities would demand to see the contract agreement [with the state firm]. If it could not be produced, the owner would be arrested by the firm if s/he was a worker, or by village authorities if somebody else. But whatever the penalty, people would continue doing it."

In Bát Tràng, from a microscopic viewpoint, the contract system and villagers' entrepreneurship led to increased worker absenteeism in the state enterprise. In one enterprise unit with only 11 percent of its members on household contract, labor input in the workplace increased, but in two others with 66 percent and 75 percent of members on contract, labor input declined (P.T.V. 1972:50). From a macroscopic perspective, the growing informal economy and private entrepreneurial activities undermined the state's control of final product distribution.

In 1978–1980, the Vietnamese economy faced a serious crisis with serious shortages of food and consumer products (de Vylder and Fforde 1988:60–62). As a result, the state began accommodating private entrepreneurship with a number of piecemeal measures and concessions that had cumulative and far-reaching effects on the economy. In 1979, the state officially sanctioned the development of *independent* family enterprises among retired state employees as a supplementary income source for these workers. In other words, family enterprises could operate not only as contractors to state firms but also as independent units. On the one hand, the legalization of independent family firms sanctioned an existing practice; in Bát Tràng, many firms had long produced for the open market. On the other, it further encouraged their development, which potentially challenged state and cooperative enterprises. As a result of the legalization of independent family enterprises and the collapse of the contract system, the production level at the Bát Tràng state firm declined precipitously in the late 1970s and early 1980s (see Luong 1993:127–129).[10]

Certain reforms within the system notwithstanding, the state did not fundamentally change its overall vision of the economy. It still attached the utmost importance to the role of large-scale state enterprises and emphasized the superiority of state and cooperative firms in the process of economic development. The state reaffirmed its policy that only a state or cooperative unit had the legal status *(tu cach phap li)* to enter into contracts with another unit and to maintain a bank account. The legal status was particularly important because in the 1978–1987 period, the state controlled both the provision of many raw materials and the distribution of most finished products. In Bát Tràng, in 1983, the state confiscated a newly built two-story house of the son of a former kiln owner in the French colonial period because his income, derived mainly from the supply of raw materials to household producers, was considered illegal. In this context, in the 1977–1985 period, four new large cooperatives were created in order to facilitate the procurement of raw materials and the distribution of final products for independent family enterprises. However, at least one of these cooperative firms was de facto a private enterprise. This private firm with a nominal cooperative status initially served as an organizational umbrella and broker for many family enterprises; although legal at this time, family enterprises could not enter into contracts with the state for the purchase of subsidized raw materials and the distribution of products.

In December 1986, the Sixth Congress of the Vietnamese Communist Party officially sanctioned the emergence of a multiple-sector economy. The state accepted the coexistence of five sectors: state, joint state-private, cooperative, private or capitalist, and family. Family enterprises were distinguished from private ones in that the former employed mostly family labor and the latter relied mainly on labor hired from outside the family. In the last quarter of 1987, the state allowed an open market in most raw materials and products, thereby relinquishing its trading monopolies. A 1988 directive further sanctioned the removal of state-imposed wage-ceiling restrictions, the remaining subsidies (e.g., low-interest capital and low-priced foods and raw materials), and many administrative controls (e.g., over the labor force; see Lê Trang 1990:168).

Economic reforms since 1987 have further spurred private entrepreneurship. By 1988, the workforce at the state enterprise had declined from its peak of approximately 1,800 workers in 1977 to 1,272. By 1996, the state enterprise was only an empty shell: it had leased or sold most of its properties to private entrepreneurs. Even the five cooperatives that had employed as many as 700 workers in 1988 had de facto collapsed by 1994. The only units functioning in reality as state enterprises were the two firms operated by the armed forces. They played an insignificant part in village production. Prospering were approximately 1,000 household enterprises and 14 private firms that served as brokers between household producers and major domestic and foreign clients and that provided high-quality raw materials to the former. The household enterprises were set up in the 1980s when the state allowed family handicraft production independent from the state and cooperative sectors. They originally operated with small box-shaped kilns for which construction costs ranged from U.S.$200 to U.S.$500 and more recently switched to larger kilns of the same design that cost about U.S.$3,000. They have also shifted away from the production of bowls for the domestic market to that of decorative items for foreign markets. The firms of Bát Tràng daily employ about 2,000 workers from surrounding communities.

Engendered Entrepreneurship

Village entrepreneurship in Bát Tràng was highly engendered from the beginning. Women played a dominant role both in commerce and in industrial production in the pre-1954 period. In fact, trade was nearly the exclusive domain of women. Because Bát Tràng women could not move beyond their specialized moulding tasks in ceramics production during this period, trade was the only venue of upward mobility (Luong 1997). Female petty traders with limited capital served the needs of the Bát Tràng population by purchasing commodities from major regional markets for daily retail in the Bát Tràng market.[11] They sold foods and other commodities (paper, combs, etc.) to villagers as well as to the long-distance sampan traders. At any point, at least five to seven sampans reportedly cast their anchors at the Bát Tràng dock on the way to or from Hanoi and other Red River ports. At times the number might increase to forty or fifty. They stopped in Bát Tràng to pick up ceramic wares or to unload two other products—areca nuts and fish sauce from Nghe An and Thanh Hoa in north-central Vietnam—for redistribution in the periodic marketing system of northern Vietnam at the time. Female wholesalers from Bát Tràng purchased large quantities of these products for resale in major nearby markets. They hired laborers from surrounding villagers on a daily basis to carry the goods for them. A few also opened ceramics retail outlets in Earthware Bowl Street (Pho Bat Dan) of Hanoi and in other towns. Female villagers who considered themselves fortunate started trading in their youth and never engaged in ceramics production:

> I worked as a petty trader, selling fruits and vegetables. My husband prescribed native medicine. . . . Wealthy female villagers engaged in wholesale trade. Poorer people like myself were petty traders. The poorest people worked for capitalist

firms. The lives of workers were hard. About two thirds of village women engaged in trade. No men. [At what age did you begin to engage in trade?] I began at the age of 13 or 14, helping my mother who had earlier worked in a kiln. I operated independently after marriage, in my late 20s. [Did you carry the goods?] No, we had carriers, people from other villages who worked for us during slack agricultural seasons. A smaller trader usually had one laborer, and bigger ones had 2 or 3. It was impossible for us to carry the goods for a distance of 15–20 kilometers. . . . [Did you pay bowl manufacturers up front, or after selling the wares?] After. [How many were carried each time?] 300 to 500 bowls. [How much profit did you make?] About 10% after expenses and the damage to the wares during transportation.

The trade was not without risks, especially during wartime. An elderly woman in her eighties who started working in ceramics kilns in her youth reported on the trading risks during the Franco-Vietminh War:

During the French occupation period [after 1946], I also sold bowls from the Ly Ba kiln. . . . Because many of the kilns had ceased production, I switched to trade. We regularly crossed both the French and Vietminh areas. I carried two identity cards with different names, one issued by the French, and the other, our [Vietminh] identity card. . . . If our troops detained me for questions, I could talk to them, saying that I was only hired to carry things for other merchants. The troops would let me go with the merchandise. But the French troops would not. They seized everything. Merchandise worth 500 piasters in a sampan was seized at one point. 2,000 piasters were lost at another as a trader had to bury them in the fields to hide them from the French. At one point, the French detained us for one night. I thought that if they saw my [Vietminh] money, I would be beaten to death. I buried it in a field that had been already plowed. I told a female passer-by: "Senior aunt, I have left my money in the plowed field. Please hold it for me." I thought that when released, I would be able to get back half of the money. But the woman did not return any to me. It was a lot of hardships.

The mercantile activities of women were facilitated by the child-care assistance of other female relatives within an extended household structure. These activities seldom involved nighttime work.

Some merchants accumulated sufficient wealth to move into ceramics production, as in the case of a Mrs. Lien who was a first patrilateral cousin of the largest kiln owner, Tran Quang Khai. This female owner of one of the first five chamber kilns in Bát Tràng elaborated on her entrepreneurial career path:

I did not have a cannon kiln, because only extremely wealthy people could own one. I actually started out moulding *bat dan* [earthenware bowls] for Mrs. Ly Ba, a patrilateral first cousin of mine. I started working early because my parents had passed away when I was only 6 or 7. Each day, I moulded about 450 bowls. But I switched to trade because of the higher earning potential and the less arduous work. . . . I sold bowls, fish sauce, and areca nuts at local markets. . . . I later bought bowls from female kiln owners, who were all sisters and cousins. I had them transported by waterways and sold them wholesale to shops in Nam Dinh, Hanoi, and Hai Phong. Because I knew the boat owners, I entrusted the cargo to them and took a ship to those cities. When I reached those cities, I just took pedicabs to the shops. Many of the store owners in those places were Bát Tràng natives. [Did you deliver always on request?] No. Whatever I took from the kilns, I could sell them because the bowls were in demand. The shops took a few *mo* [tens of thousands of bowls] at a time. If the price of rice there was reasonable, I also bought a large quantity and had it transported by boat back to Bát Tràng. I even travelled to Thanh Hoa on one occasion, because a junior relative lived in Cau Bo. . . . I was a trader for a long time before we began ceramics production. Initially, we sold unfired wares to other people. Or if they could not be sold, we rented kiln space. We hired only a few workers: clay processors, moulders, and loaders. . . . I still engaged in trade at the time. Later on, we owned a chamber kiln, of which we used only four chambers, and which we fired only once a month. [Did you sell the wares of your own kiln too?] No. The wares were of high quality. The wholesalers had to come here to buy them. Our wares were either bought by traders from other places or by village traders who brought them to Hanoi or Nam Dinh.

The successful career path of Mrs. Lien, from ceramics worker to trader and to kiln ownership, reinforced a long-existing model for many female villagers.[12] The oral histories of Bát Tràng indicate that women were prominent in the ownership and management of ceramics firms, especially in the cannon-kiln era. Toward the end of the nineteenth century and at the beginning of the twentieth century, two of the three largest industrialists in the ceramics industry were women (Mme. Nhieu Huyen and Mme. Pho Tu). In the next generation, two of the three largest kiln owners were also women (Mme. Cuu Boi and Mme. Ly Ba).

The grandson of Mme. Nhieu Huyen related the family legend about the latter:

Over one hundred years ago [toward the end of the nineteenth century], my maternal grandparents' firm [Nhieu Huyen firm] was already a big one, making up about half the production in this village. She had 3–4 kilns, each producing 40–50,000 bowls with each firing. My maternal grandfather was a Confucian scholar, leaving the management of hundreds of workers to his wife. . . . Although my maternal grandmother was illiterate, she did not make mistakes. When 1000 products were received, she put a cross on a piece of clay.

In the chamber-kiln period, of the eleven kiln owners by 1954, four were women who directly managed their firms. Of the four other producers who were classified as small capitalists (entrepreneurs without kilns) during the Marxist-initiated industrial reform in 1959, three were women.

Even when a kiln was owned by a male entrepreneur, his wife or sister usually played an important managerial role. Legends abound about the tight-fisted female owners and managers. In a chamber kiln owned by a Mr. Cuu Huynh, his sister as the firm's manager normally accepted only 70 percent of the semiproducts; thus because of the piece-rate system, workers were deprived of 30 percent of their incomes. Her practice stood in contrast to the management style of Mr. Cuu Khai, the biggest kiln owner in Bát Tràng in the same period, who accepted virtually all products but who paid lower piece rates. A moulder from the neighboring village of Kim Lan reported on the management styles of the female kiln owners for whom she worked:

[How do you compare the three kiln owners, Mme. Cuu Boi, Mme. Ly Ba, and Mr. Cuu Khai?] Only the son of Mrs. Ly Ba and Mrs. Cuu Khai treated me well. Mr. Cuu Khai, who calculated the wages, was firm. I was scared of him, both of his appearance and his firm decision. He did not say much of anything, but he did not change his mind. It was impossible to plead with him. Uncle Khanh, the son of Mrs. Ly Ba, was impulsively generous *[xoi]*. If the mother went into the kitchen, he lowered the debt figure, and even burnt the piece of debt paper. When the mother asked: "How much did she *[chi]* owe?" he answered: "She *[chi]* owed 10 piasters," when I actually owed more. Mr. Cuu Khai and Mme. Ly Ba were tight-fisted. As to Mme. Cuu Boi, she yelled a lot, using obscene language *[nói tuc]*. She would fire people right away. The family was all addicted to opium.

In Bát Tràng and numerous other northern Vietnamese communities, the wealth from women's commercial and industrial activities played a critical role in providing for the needs of household members and nurturing men's bureaucratic careers. As mentioned in a narrative excerpt above, the husband of Mrs. Nhieu Huyen, a major ceramics producer in Bát Tràng at the turn of the century, was a Confucian scholar. Some of these scholars achieved scholarly or bureaucratic fame: Nine native sons of Bát Tràng succeeded in Confucian court examinations from the seventeenth to the nineteenth century; five others served in major positions in the mandarinate in the same period (Do thi Hao et al. 1989:38–50). Although most of these scholars were not successful in their examinations to gain access to the mandarinate, their entrepreneur wives usually provided strong support for their aspirations.[13] The vital role of women in the entrepreneurial activities of Bát Tràng and the privileged position of Bát Tràng men are reflected in two frequently quoted local proverbs:

Song lam trai Bát Tràng
Chet lam thanh hoanh Kieu Ky
Most fortunate when alive are the men of Bát Tràng
Most privileged when deceased is the tutelary god of Kieu Ky[14]

Be thi com me com cha
Nhung nhung com vo, ve gia com con
When a child, it is the mother's and the father's rice,
In adulthood, it is the wife's foods; and in old age, they come from the children.

The dominant role of Vietnamese women in entrepreneurship was not restricted to Bát Tràng. It has been observed by numerous foreign visitors throughout the country at least since the seventeenth century. A Chinese traveler to Hanoi in 1688 remarked: "Trade was the domain of women. Even the wives of high-ranking mandarins were not concerned about losing face [with their trading activities]" (Thanh The Vy 1961:91). The British traveler Dampier made a similar point: "Money-changing is a great Profession here. it is managed by Women, who are very dextrous and ripe in this Employment. They hold their Cabals in the Night, and know how to raise their Cash as well as the cunningest Stock-jobber in London" (Dampier 1906:608. See also Thanh The Vy 1961:92–93; Crawfurd 1970:270; and Barrow 1975:303–304).[15]

If the role of women in the ceramics firms of Bát Tràng at the turn of the century is any indication, female entrepreneurs also played a dominant role in Vietnamese market-oriented manufacturing activities in northern Vietnam before and during the initial period of French colonialism. The role of women in industrial entrepreneurship, however, has steadily declined since the turn of the century. In Bát Tràng, it was male entrepreneurs who spearheaded the wave of technological changes in the 1920s and 1930s through the adoption of the chamber kiln. Before 1945, four of the five new chamber-kiln owners were male. As mentioned earlier, by 1954, of the eleven kiln owners, only four were women who directly managed their firms. This development seems to have paralleled a larger trend in northern Vietnam in the French colonial era. The wealthiest northern Vietnamese entrepreneurs of the post–World War I era were all male: Bach Thai Buoi in transportation, Tran Van Thanh in brick production in Yen Vien (Bac Ninh), Nguyen van Tan and Nguyen Ba Chinh in ceramics production, respectively in Hai Phong and Thanh Tri (Ha Dong) (Nguyen Cong Binh 1959:92, 98, 116, 120; Anonymous 1924; Bonifacy 1924).

In the socialist era, in the entire ceramics industry of Bát Tràng by the end of the 1980s, among the six major firms only one woman reached the top management position. Even during the Vietnam War in the 1960s and early 1970s, no women reached the top managerial ranks in the two state and cooperative firms of this period. It was not until 1985 and only for three years that a woman achieved the position of the president of a handicraft cooperative. She served during a difficult period when the cooperative could offer few incentives to keep its best members because of a booming household economy. The only female top executive of a major ceramics firm in Bát Tràng faced numerous challenges, as she elaborated:

I served as the president of Hop Thanh cooperative for three years, from 1985 to 1988. It was a demanding job. . . . I did not look for this president's job. I had been elected in my absence during my recovery from an appendectomy in February 1985. When informed [of the election], I was reluctant to assume the position. I asked them [fellow members of the cooperative]: "Can I decline?" My husband and I discussed the matter. He said: "A declination would mean not accepting the responsibility. [That makes it not a viable option.] But an acceptance would demand a total devotion to the job." To be frank, it was a challenging and complicated job at that time. The cooperative had prospered in the 1970s. But it encountered a number of problems in the early 1980s. It had lost many skilled workers because some moved to the state enterprise due to the more generous benefits and incomes there, and because many others took early retirements to concentrate on their household enterprises. We lost big fish. The rate of absenteeism was also high. Many members did not show up for work because they had small children and because household enterprises yielded higher incomes. The management did not fire anybody although in principle, if a member violated the cooperative regulations many times, the membership would be terminated. In four years in a row, the cooperative had not been able to fulfill its contract with the state's commercial firms. The cooperative had slipped from its excellent standing to the verge of bankruptcy in 1984. The district government evaluated that the cooperative was on the verge of collapse that year. [What do you mean by "the verge of collapse" in 1984?] That was the judgment of the district government. The cooperative had run out of raw materials, capital, and operating funds. Even many pieces of broken equipment remained unfixed. When I became president in April 1985, members had not received any payment for three months. I had to ask them to accept IOUs from the cooperative.

If we include cooperative vice presidents, only 2 out of 14 senior cooperative managers (14.3 percent) were women at the time of my in-depth field research in 1988, although female workers composed 52.5 percent of the labor force in the five cooperatives of Bát Tràng at the time. In 1996, of the seventeen major raw materials, production, and marketing firms, only one was headed by a woman.

The conditions in Bát Tràng during the period of socialist reforms were far from unique. According to the 1989 census, women made up only 17.32 percent of top enterprise managers in the state and cooperative firms in the urban areas of the North (Hanoi and Haiphong) and 9.02 percent of those in three predominantly rural northern provinces (Vinh Phu, Quang Ninh, and Ha Son Binh). Female workers composed 29.39 percent of the industrial workforce in the former areas and 43.23 percent in the latter (Vietnam Census 1991:vol. 5, 29, 33, 41, 45, 89, 101, 105, 107, 111, 312, 316, 324, 328, 372, 376, 384, 388, 390, 394). Even when we include small- and medium-sized firms, including many private ones, and trading enterprises where women might have played more prominent roles than in industrial firms, only 23 percent of the owners or top managers of the 256 small urban enterprises surveyed in

1991 in the North were female, in comparison to 10 percent among the 255 small rural ones (Vietnam Institute of Labour 1993:42, 95, 116). Women composed 34.9 percent and 37.8 percent, respectively, of the labor force in these enterprises (201, 227, 240). Women remained well represented in commerce at 70.8 percent, including 52.5 percent of the personnel in the state trading organizations, 63.6 percent in sales cooperatives, 78.8 percent of the officially registered private traders, and 70 percent of the discovered unregistered ones (Vietnam Centre for Women's Studies 1991:68, 154). However, there is no indication that women in commerce fared considerably better at the senior level than their counterparts in manufacturing firms.

Ideology and Political Economy

On one level, the entrepreneurship of Vietnamese women, especially in the pre-French era, was inextricably linked to the dominant ideological premises of pre-twentieth-century Vietnam on gender and the sociocultural universe. In the dominant Confucian conception of social order at the time, hierarchy was constructed on the basis of both gender and moral cultivation. Scholars were ranked at the top because they were supposed to transcend narrow self-interests and to maintain exemplary moral behavior in larger social causes. Merchants were at the bottom among the four social categories because mercantile activities, unless on behalf of the state, were considered essentially self-interested and amoral. The dominant Confucian tradition also engendered subordination as female. In this context, the Confucian emphasis on moral self-cultivation for public causes in pre-twentieth-century Vietnam did not constrain women's behavior as much as men's because of the former's ideologically constructed inferiority. Within the dominant Confucian framework of that era, the ethical dilemma faced by men in commercial and industrial activities was not the same as that faced by women (cf. Alexander, this volume).

However, the active participation of women in precolonial commerce and entrepreneurial activities was shaped not only by the male-centered Confucian ideology but also by the alternative bilateral and non-Confucian model of kinship and gender relations. As I have discussed elsewhere (Luong 1989), the bilateral model emphasized the unity of men and women, not their segregation and formal hierarchy as postulated by Confucianism. This model centered on the household, the social unit of greatest significance to women, over whose budgets women had considerable control. As a result, women did not simply participate in the labor force as a last resort but actively pursued household-strengthening economic activities. Constrained by the Confucian ideological framework, these activities of Bát Tràng women were restricted to commercial and industrial entrepreneurship, activities at the lower rungs of the Confucian status ladder (these lower rungs being agriculture, handicrafts, and especially commerce). I would like to suggest that the prominent positions of women in the labor force and in the management of the ceramics industry in Bát Tràng involved a modus vivendi between the dominant Confucianism-structured female subordination and their enhanced responsibility within an alternative household-centered framework (cf. Weller and Malarney, this volume).

The dominant Confucian ideology of pre-twentieth-century Vietnam also directly structured the local *institutional framework* that further reinforced the emphasis on male superiority and moral education. The public sphere of power both excluded women and honored education and public services more than wealth in and of itself. Only men could fully participate in the rituals at the village communal house. In Bát Tràng, like in other Vietnamese communities at the time, women had to worship at the two Buddhist pagodas, both of which were (re)constructed in the eighteenth century.[16] At the Bát Tràng communal house itself, artisans and merchants, if any, were ranked at the bottom of the social hierarchy. According to a literary piece on the communal house written in 1725, the male village participants in communal feasts were divided into three classes: (1) mandarins, literati, notables, and the wealthy; (2) ceramics artisans; and (3) petty traders and other artisans (Phan Huu Dat 1977:333; Do thi Hao et al. 1989:26–27). The inner seats, the most honored in the communal house, were reserved for the ritual master (the highest-degree holder or the highest-ranked mandarin) and the village president *(tien chi)*, who had to be either a Confucian doctorate-degree holder or a military mandarin with the duke status *(quan cong)* (Bát Tràng 1931:30–31).[17] At the biggest ceremony, from the fifteenth to the twenty-second of the second lunar month, only the degree holders could participate in the ritual in the communal house; village officials had to wait outside. Even the honor bestowed on the male benefactor who had given the most to the village reflected the belief in the importance not of wealth but of public causes. Women who had no access to education had no formal positions in the communal house system.[18] The apparent wealth from industrial and commercial capitalist enterprises in and of itself did not necessarily yield power and status in either in Bát Tràng or the larger society.

In the pre-French era, the state rarely, if ever, created favorable conditions for the growth of private enterprises in the commercial and handicraft sectors. In the seventeenth and eighteenth centuries, for example, the Vietnamese court established state factories not only in defense- and treasury-related fields (shipyards, armament factories, and mints) but also for the provision of luxury goods to the royal household (Nguyen Thanh Nha 1970:143–144; Nguyen The Anh 1971:187, 190, 191; Chu Thien 1961:47–48). The Vietnamese state regularly drafted many of the most successful artisans into state services with low pay in order to meet the needs of the state and the royal household. It was not a policy conducive to industrial growth.

Wealthy merchants and industrialists were also subject to arbitrary demands by the bureaucracy. Samuel Baron, who provided an excellent description of northern Vietnam in the seventeenth century, commented on the impositions on and extortions of native merchants by the mandarinate, a situation lasting to various degrees to the end of the nineteenth century:

> [Hanoi] merchants, though they live in the city, are rated in the aldeas or villages of their ancestors and parents, and are liable besides to the vecquun [*ve quan*], or lords service of the city, at their own expences, and are obliged to work and drudge themselves, or hire another in their room, to perform what the governor orders, whether it be to mend the broken walls, repair the banks and ways of the city, dragging timber for the King's palaces, and other public buildings, &c.
> . . . Since it is one of the policies of the court not to make the subjects rich, lest they should be proud and ambitious, and aspire to greater matters, the King connives at those disorders, and oppresses them with heavy taxes and impositions; and should he know that any persons were to exceed the ordinary means of a private subject, they would incur the danger of losing all on some pretence or other; which is a great discouragement to the industrious, and necessitates them to bury their wealth, having no means to improve it. (Baron 1812: 663–667)

The institutional constraints on entrepreneurship directly reflected the ideological view that agriculture constitutes the foundation and center of the economy, whereas commerce is simply peripheral. They reinforced the ideological devaluation of craftsmanship and commerce and, within the framework of gender inequality, further predisposed the male elite toward bureaucratic and scholarly careers. It is not surprising that in the Vietnamese institutional and ideological context before the French conquest, wealth was at least partly rechanneled into agricultural land (Nguyen Quang Ngoc 1984: 42–43, Nguyen Quang Ngoc and Phan Dai Doan 1985:31–32) and into public careers either through investments in sons' study for Confucian examinations or through the purchase of bureaucratic titles (Nguyen Thanh Nha 1970:135; Tran Trong Kim 1964:308–309; see also Malarney, this volume). The successful accumulation of wealth did not necessarily intensify entrepreneurial activities. It led neither to the emergence of large firms in ceramics nor to a capitalist transformation of the economy in the pre-French era.

In the French colonial period, the greater and more prominent participation of indigenous entrepreneurs (including men) in the pursuit of wealth can be similarly explained with reference to the transformation of the ideological field and the institutional framework. Although the Confucian framework retained a strong influence in northern Vietnam, the self-interested pursuit of wealth carried no stigma within the capitalist ideology of the French metropolis or of colonial Indochina. The institutional constraints on both domestic commerce and manufacturing activities were formally removed. The state itself disbanded state manufacturing enterprises and ended the conscription of the more successful artisans into state services. Indigenous entrepreneurship increased significantly in this period, although in Bát Tràng, due to the impact of the century-old sociocultural formation as well as to the destabilizing effects of Chinese competition and technological changes, no local firms emerged as industrial leaders (Nguyen Cong Binh 1959:92, 98, 116, 120). A major transformation, however, took place with the increasingly visible role of male entrepreneurs in local manufacturing activities. This process was ideologically facilitated by the lack of stigma on the self-interested pursuit of wealth by either men or women, as evidenced by the role of many Frenchmen in the commercial and industrial sectors of the colony (see also Marr 1981:122–126, 199). Concurrently, in terms of institutional processes, the more complex and modern bureaucratic system under French colonialism required a higher level of literacy on the part of major entrepreneurs, thus indirectly favoring native men who, under the Confucian influence, had a privileged access to modern education.

In the postcolonial era, despite the ideological emphasis of the Marxist-Leninist state on gender equality and women's liberation, male dominance in the management of ceramics manufacturing accelerated due to the institutional trend toward greater bureaucratization both within the microcosm of an enterprise and within the larger economic system. As reported earlier, within the state and cooperative enterprises themselves, bureaucratization took place through standardizing rules and regulations within a national framework and encompassing production within a command economy. Careers within these enterprises were defined within the state bureaucracy and in terms of the national cause of industrial development. High managerial positions thus required a certain level of education and officially involved *public* service, rendering them more attractive to the male and educated elite (cf. McVey 1992:26). Even in the private firms whose legitimacy was partly restored beginning in the late 1980s and that, at least medium and small ones, are far from bureaucratized, the modern and at times contradictory bureaucratic regulations require a higher level of literacy on the part of enterprise managers, thus slightly favoring men with their greater access to education. The highly complex bureaucratic system has also indirectly led to the increasing importance of informal contacts, frequently developed through extensive travel, as a problem-solving mechanism and for the circumvention of rules and regulations. In my opinion, the importance of informal contact gives an advantage to male managers; many of them know one another through armed services or party channels, and their domestic division of labor is in general more conducive to the extensive travel. The highest-ranked female manager in Bát Tràng, the president of a ceramics cooperative from 1985 to 1988, elaborated some of the difficulties of a female manager:

The job of the president of Hop Thanh cooperative . . . was a demanding job, requiring frequent travel and extensive contact throughout the district and in Hanoi city. Although other people could represent me, or normally accompanied me whenever it was necessary to travel to other provinces, I still had to show up on the more important occasions. Upon returning home, I had to take a rest. I did not look for this president's job. They [district leaders] had tried to enlist my help, actually as early as 1983. I told the vice-chairman of the district government: "If I accept your suggestion, my children would go hungry." He asked: "Why?" I explained: "The job requires a total commitment and a close attention to reality to manage over 100 people. It demands considerable energy, making it impossible to work at home, while the salary is insufficient to feed the children." [At the time of my election in 1985,] I was also worried because I was a woman. . . .

The job demanded a strong will and quick decisions, not all of which yielded positive results. I was fortunate in that during my terms, no decision led to major negative consequences. If the decision of a cooperative president did not yield a positive result, rumors spread. The rumors would spread especially because I was a woman, and because some cooperative members coveted the president position. I was fortunate in that I had had fairly extensive contact with other managers and the district leadership in my years as the chief accountant of the cooperative. A number of enterprise accountants whom I had known had moved up to more influential positions and were in positions of assistance to me. My contact was also extensive from other activities. I had been a member of the executive committee of the party in the village. At one point, I had been in charge of youth activities for the cooperative. I had been the head of the women's association branch at the cooperative since 1967, and had served on the executive committee of the village's women's association. Members [of those units] just elected me to these positions. What could I do? But these positions helped to extend my contact. From the provincial level down, authorities tried to help the cooperative. They followed the situation of the cooperative on a monthly basis. The party secretary of the district kept a close watch on every step [in order to be of help]. The Vietnamese have the proverb: "If the child does not cry, the mother does not know when to breast-feed." As a result, I had to travel all over. The travel was exhausting. Furthermore, the time was also irregular. At times, I was still at work at 10 at night. At 2 o'clock in the morning, if a cooperative member came back with raw materials, I had to mobilize members to work to move them to the right areas in the cooperative. On occasions, I was so sick that I could not eat much, but I still had to go. Nobody demanded it, but without me, without orders from above, cooperative members would be reluctant to proceed with tasks.

[How did you handle domestic chores during your terms as the cooperative president?] I was not good at all in domestic work. A cooperative president had no time left for domestic chores. I relied on my husband. [Did your husband take care of domestic chores?] My children did. My daughter was already 16 in 1985. She did well in her school and attended a school close to our home. She could therefore help with the work at home. But at times, the entire family lost sleep because at mid-night, I was called by a cooperative guard.

In this woman's case, even her supportive husband contributed little to domestic chores. She could assume the position partly because of the help of a teenager daughter at home and partly because, despite her gender, she had developed informal contacts over the years in order to obtain credit and other forms of assistance. Without the help of elder daughters, other female members of their extended families, or, in urban areas, domestic servants, female managers encountered the problem of making arrangements to cover both daily domestic chores and other domestic responsibilities when they were traveling, a problem not faced by their male counterparts.

Despite the shift to the market economy, the male-dominated bureaucracy still played an important role in the success and failure even of private enterprises through its control of licenses and taxation. I would like to suggest that the bureaucratization of the economy in the twentieth century accounted for the greater prominence of men in managerial positions in both the French colonial period and the socialist era (see also Luong 1997; cf. Walder 1986). To the casual observer, Vietnamese women still played a visible role in the economic arena, but if the data on the historical transformation of ceramics firms in Bát Tràng are indicative of a larger trend in Vietnam, women's leading role in the manufacturing and large-scale entrepreneurial activities of the earlier period has diminished.

Needless to say, the institutional frameworks of different eras in Vietnamese political economy were strongly embedded in their ideological contexts. The difficulties encountered by female managers in reaching the top positions in the bureaucratic hierarchy or in spearheading entrepreneurial activities in the modern era can be traced to the widely accepted and persisting native ideology that justifies the domestic orientation of women, their primary responsibilities for domestic chores, and their minimal access to educational opportunities. Increasing bureaucratization at the microscopic level within state and cooperative firms has multiple genealogies (Foucault 1986:81)—the pre-French state-centered ideology of the economy and the Marxist-Leninist conceptual framework that sanctions both a command economy with soft budget constraints and the privileged position of labor within the economic system. Bureaucratization at the national level is rooted in the Western belief in rational control and, in the socialist era, in the Marxist-Leninist command economy ideology. Practice and institutions themselves are strongly embedded within ideological frameworks.

Embedded as practices and institutions are in their ideological contexts and in their multiple genealogies, they cannot be reduced to the latter because in numerous contexts, the ideological field contains contradictions within itself (cf. Janelli and Kim 1997). For example, the ideology of gender equality of the Marxist state directly conflicts with the century-old ideology in Vietnam that justifies the household division of domestic labor The resolution of these ideological conflicts is embedded in the power-laden and historically specific negotiations in concrete contexts with a certain degree of indeterminacy The role of Vietnamese women in entrepreneurial activities and a certain measure of decline in their participation in these activities in the twentieth century, both in Bát Tràng and throughout northern Vietnam, can be understood only in terms of the interplay of ideologies and the political economic framework.

NOTES

1. Village residential surface was reduced from 45 *mâu* (40 acres) in 1889 to 38 *mâu* (33.8 acres) in 1903 because of a landslide (Phan Gia Ben 1957:79). A significant part of Bát Tràng's alluvial fields were not obtained until the early part of the twentieth century. Colonial archival records contained a 1912 letter to the cadastral services in Tonkin regarding the conflict among the three villages of Bát Tràng, Dong Du, and Giang Cao concerning newly formed alluvial fields (Archives of Vietnam, Residence Supérieur du Tonkin M3–66266). According to a village folk ballad, a Bát Tràng notable successfully recruited fellow community members and manufactured arms for a battle with members of the neighboring Giang Cao over new alluvial fields (Phan Huu Dat 1977:336). The village of Bát Tràng divided these fields among its male members from the ages of eighteen to sixty once every few years through their patrilineages (Phan Huu Dat 1977:335–336, 343; Do thi Hao et al. 1989:16, 25, 27).

2. The amount of cultivable land averaged only 124.6 square meters per person in 1988, well below the figure of 1,496.7 square meters at the same point in time for the Red River Delta (Vietnam General Statistical Office 1991:46, 102).

3. It was in the fourteenth century that Vietnamese ceramics began its sizable entry into the Asian trade network, according to archaeological findings in insular Southeast Asia (Guy 1986a:260, and 1986b:45. See also Nguyen Trai 1966:71, 73, 123; and Do Van Ninh 1989:155–157).

4. According to elderly villagers, rural landowners preferred to purchase the inexpensive bowls of Bát Tràng to feed their laborers during the harvest season because of their low cost of replacement if broken. In the pre-1930s period, Bát Tràng also manufactured other utilitarian pottery items as well as decorative ceramics. The former included a more expensive line of bowls (*bat yeu* or *bat chiet yeu*), different kinds of cups and saucers, teapots, steamed-rice containers, lime pots, wine decanters, water pipes for smoking, and floor tiles. Among decorative ceramic products were incense burners, ceramic stools, and vases and pots of different sizes (Barbotin 1912:675, 831–833). These products were fired in partially partitioned cannon kilns with a fish shape and a slightly curving floor (called *lo ca sop* or *lo bat dan*). Barbotin (1912:681) describes a typical fish-shaped kiln whose singular inner chamber is 12 meters long, 2.6 meters high, and 3.6 meters wide and whose total structure is 16.44 meters long, 4 meters high, and 6.8 meters wide (see also Nguyen Viet 1962:32–33). The coarse earthenwares of Bát Tràng were contrasted with the higher-priced *bat su* (porcelain bowls) or *bat ngo* (Chinese bowls), coarse porcelain bowls that were manufactured in the Chinese-owned kilns set up at the turn of the century in Mong Cay (Vedrenne 1939).

5. A 7-chamber kiln is approximately 17 meters long, 1.6 meters high, and 4 meters wide. These kilns had steep slopes from 12 to 20 degrees.

6. The union was supposed to represent the production units in their relations with the state, but it played such a large role in enforcing state guidelines on labor and finances that even the expansion of a cooperative's labor force required union authorization.

7. Fforde and Paine have referred to this model in Vietnam as the Democratic Republic of Vietnam model (Fforde and Paine 1987). It should be added that private rural markets remained open, although the transaction volumes in those markets seem to have significantly declined with the competition from the state's trading network, wherein state firms could sell their products only to the state.

8. According to one estimate, the real wages of state employees declined by 25 percent from 1960 to 1975 (Fforde and Paine 1987:93–95). No data are available for Bát Tràng.

9. State employees contributed 30 percent of the labor time input in household production; their children, 50 percent; and the elderly, 20 percent (P.T.V. 1972:47).

10. The state firm's contract system collapsed due to the considerable delay in the payment for contracted labor. The state bank sometimes delayed payments by as much as a year..

11. An elderly and former petty trader reported that before 1945, approximately 100 traders could be found daily in the market of Bát Tràng. The overwhelming majority came from other communities. Most were women, although a few male traders also came from other villages.

12. Career opportunities within a firm were virtually nonexistent for ceramics workers from Bát Tràng, since owners or their family members directly supervised the production and since there was no organizational hierarchy among moulders and polishers. Workers who desired upward mobility typically left their firms. However, in contrast to female workers' departure from the industry, in the French colonial period, male polishers of coarse earthenware bowls might leave for financially more rewarding positions in a new firm that manufactured electrical porcelain devices.

13. It appears that the combination of a man's bureaucratic-scholarly career or aspirations and his wife's entrepreneurship was a widespread pattern in northern Vietnam at least until the turn of the century, if not until 1954. In the well-known trading village of Phu Luu (district of Tien Son, Bac Ninh), the commercial wealth from female entrepreneurial activities sustained male villagers' educations and bureaucratic careers (Nguyen Quang Ngoc 1993:127, 135). In contrast, in Da Nguu and Bao Dap, where men dominated commercial activities, few succeeded in higher Confucian examinations for the court's consideration of mandarin appointments (1993:94, 113).

14. The nearby village of Kieu Ky was known for its wealth and its silversmith tradition. Villagers made generous offerings to their tutelary deity.

15. It should be added that although women played a salient role in commercial entrepreneurship, men also engaged in trade in a small number of cases. For example, in the specialized trading villages of Da Nguu and Bao Dap, respectively in Bac Ninh and Nam Dinh Provinces, trade was conducted mostly by men (Nguyen Quang Ngoc 1993:83, 105). However, Da Nguu specialized in herbal medicine, and the knowledge and role of herbal pharmacists were traditionally reserved to men.

16. Before the 1931 departure from the long-existing tradition, the only exception was the village festival in the second lunar month, when the two wealthiest female villagers each sponsored sixteen young villagers (one male team and one female team) for approximately one month in preparation for the human chess performance: Chess masters directed the moves of the nicely dressed human chess pieces (males in purple and females in red) at the festival, and the chess pieces and their sponsors were allowed to enter the communal house for the feast. However, they entered more as entertainers than as full-fledged participants.

17. Other honored positions in the communal house were reserved for the elderly above the age of 100 and the most important village benefactor *(trum)*, a wealthy man who had given a large donation to village causes.

18. In the 1931-modified village regulations, communal house seats, but not official titles, were bestowed on *female* villagers who donated funds to village coffers (Bát Tràng 1931:32).

REFERENCES

Anonymous. 1924. "L'industrie de la porcelaine au Tonkin: L'usine de MM. Nguyen-Ba-Chinh et Cie a Thanh Tri, pres de Hanoi." *L'Éveil Économique de l'Indochine* 391:5–6.

Baron, Samuel. 1812. *A Description of the Kingdom of Tonqueen.* Reprinted in John Pinkerton, ed., *Voyages and Travels*, vol. 9, pp. 656–707. London: Cass.

Barbotin, A. 1912. "La poterie indigene au Tonkin." *Bulletin Économique de l'Indochine* 15:659–685, 815–841.

Barrow, John. [1806] 1975. *A Voyage to Cochinchina.* Oxford: Oxford University Press.

Bát Tràng. 1931. "Huong voc lang Bát Tràng" (Regulations of Bát Tràng village). Unpublished manuscript.

Berger, Peter, and Hsin-Huang M. Hsiao, eds. 1988. *In Search of an East Asian Development Model.* New Brunswick: Transaction Books.

Bonifacy. 1924. "La fabrique de porcelaine de Monsieur Nguyen-van-Tan a Haiphong." *L'Éveil Économique de l'Indochine* 387:5–6.

Chu Quang Chu and Nguyen Du Chi. 1991. "Cac nghe thu cong my nghe dan gian" (Folk art handicrafts). In Dinh Gia Khanh and Tran Tien, eds., *Dia chi van hoa dan gian Thang Long-Dong Do-Ha Noi* (Hanoi folk culture geography), pp. 249–274. Hanoi: So Van Hoa Thong Tin Ha Noi.

Chu Thien. 1961. "Vai net ve cong thuong nghiep trieu Nguyen" (A sketch on commerce and industry in the Nguyen dynasty). *Nghien Cuu Lich Su* 33:47–62.

Cole, Robert. 1979. *Work, Mobility, and Participation: A Comparative Study of American and Japanese Industry.* Berkeley: University of California Press.

Crawfurd, John. [1823] 1970. "Report on the State of the Annamese Empire." Reprinted in A. Lamb, *The Mandarin Road to Old Hue: Narratives of Anglo-Vietnamese Diplomacy from the 17th Century to the Eve of the French Conquest*, pp. 255–277. London: Chatto & Windus.

Dampier, William. 1906. *Dampier's Voyages.* Ed. John Masefield. London: E. Grant Richards.

de Vylder, Stefan, and Adam Fforde. 1988. *Vietnam: An Economy in Transition.* Stockholm: Swedish International Development Authority.

Do van Ninh. 1989. "Van Don." In Le van Lan et al., eds., *Do thi co Viet Nam* (Ancient towns in Vietnam), pp. 150–167. Hanoi: Khoa Hoc Xa Hoi.

Do thi Hao et al. 1989. *Que gom Bát Tràng* (The home of ceramics: Bát Tràng). Hanoi: Hanoi Publishing House.

Fforde, Adam, and Susan Paine. 1987. *The Limits of National Liberation.* London: Croom Helm.

Foucault, Michel. 1986. "Nietzsche, Genealogy, and History." In Paul Rabinow, ed., *The Foucault Reader,* pp. 76–100. New York: Pantheon.

Guy, John S. 1986a. "Vietnamese Ceramics and Cultural Identity: Evidence from the Ly and Tran Dynasties." In David G. Marr and A.C. Milner, eds., *Southeast Asia in the 9th to 14th Centuries,* pp. 255–270. Singapore: Institute of Southeast Asian Studies.

_____. 1986b. *Oriental Trade Ceramics in Southeast Asia: Ninth to Sixteenth Centuries.* Oxford: Oxford University Press.

Hicks. G.L., and S. Gordon Redding. 1983. *Industrial East Asia and the Post-Confucian Hypothesis: A Challenge to Economics.* Hong Kong: University of Hong Kong Centre of Asian Studies.

Janelli, Roger, and Dawnhee Kim. 1997. "The Mutual Constitution of Confucianism and Capitalism in South Korea." In Timothy Brook and Hy van Luong, eds., *Culture and Economy: The Shaping of Capitalism in Eastern Asia,* pp. 107–124. Ann Arbor: University of Michigan.

Kornai, Janos. 1989. "The Hungarian Reform Process: Visions, Hopes, and Reality." In David Stark and Victor Nee, eds., *Remaking the Economic Institutions of China and Eastern Europe,* pp. 32–94. Stanford: Stanford University Press.

Lê Trang. 1990. "Renewal of Industrial Management Policy and Organisation." In Per Ronnas and Orjan Sjöberg, eds., *Doi Moi: Economic Reforms and Development Policies in Vietnam,* pp. 153–181. Stockholm: Swedish International Development Authority.

Luong, Hy van. 1989. "Vietnamese Kinship: Structural Principles and the Socialist Transformation in Twentieth-Century Northern Vietnam." *Journal of Asian Studies* 38:741–756.

_____. 1993. "The Political Economy of Vietnamese Reforms: A Microscopic Perspective from Two Ceramics-Manufacturing Centers." In William Turley and Mark Selden, eds., *Reinventing Vietnamese Socialism: Doi Moi in Comparative Perspectives,* pp. 119–148. Boulder: Westview Press.

_____. 1997. "Capitalism and Noncapitalist Ideologies in the Structure of Northern Vietnamese Ceramics Enterprises." In Timothy Brook and Hy van Luong, eds., *Culture and Economy: The Shaping of Capitalism in Eastern Asia,* pp. 187–206. Ann Arbor: University of Michigan Press.

McVey, Ruth. 1992. "The Materialization of the Southeast Asian Entrepreneur." In Ruth McVey, ed., *Southeast Asian Capitalists,* pp. 7–34. Ithaca: Southeast Asia Program, Cornell University.

Marr, David. 1981. *Vietnamese Tradition on Trial, 1920–1945.* Berkeley: University of California Press.

Nguyen Cong Binh. 1959. *Tim hieu giai cap tu san Viet Nam thoi Phap thuoc* (Understanding the Vietnamese capitalist class in the French colonial period). Hanoi: Van Su Dia.

Nguyen Quang Ngoc. 1984-1985. "May nhan xet ve ket cau kinh te cua mot so lang thuong nghiep o vung dong bang Bac bo the ky XVIII, XIX" (Some observations on the economic structures of a few trading villages in the northern delta in the eighteenth and nineteenth centuries). *Nghien Cuu Lich Su*, pp. 37–43, 77.

———. 1993. *Ve mot so lang buon o dong bang bac bo the ky XVIII-XIX* (On a number of [specialized] trading villages in the northern delta in the eighteenth and nineteenth centuries). Hanoi: Vietnamese Historical Association.

Nguyen Quang Ngoc and Phan Dai Doan. 1985. "Hoat dong thuong nghiep nong thon dong bang Bac bo the ky XVIII–XIX" (Rural trade in the northern delta in the eighteenth and nineteenth centuries). *Nghien Cuu Lich Su* 5:26–34.

Nguyen Thanh Nha. 1970. *Tableau économique du Vietnam aux XVIIe et XVIIIe siècles*. Paris: Cujas.

Nguyen The Anh. 1971. *Kinh te va xa hoi Viet Nam duoi cac vua trieu Nguyen* (Vietnamese economy and society under the kings of the Nguyen dynasty). Saigon: Lua Thieng.

Nguyen Thua Hy. 1983. "Mang luoi cho o Thang Long: Ha Noi trong nhung the ky XVII–XVIII–XIX" (The market network in Thang Long: Hanoi in the seventeenth, eighteenth, and nineteenth centuries). *Nghien Cuu Lich Su* 1:33–43.

Nguyen Trai. 1966. *Uc Trai Tuong cong di tap: Du dia chi* (The book of Uc Trai Tuong cong: Geography). Translated into modern Vietnamese by Tran Tuan Khai. Saigon: Nha Van Hoa.

Nguyen Viet. 1962. "Ban ve mam mong tu ban chu nghia o Viet Nam duoi thoi phong kien" (On the origin of Vietnamese capitalism in the feudal period). *Nghien Cuu Lich Su* 35:21–34 and 36:28–37.

P.T.V. 1972. "Mot hinh thuc kêt hop giua xi nghiep cong nghiep dia phuong va gia dinh" (A form of cooperation between a local industrial enterprise and households). *Nghien Cuu Kinh Te* 60:45–52.

Phan Gia Ben. 1957. *So thao lich su phat trien tieu thu cong nghiep Viet Nam* (A brief history of handicraft and small industrial development in Vietnam). Hanoi: Van Su Dia.

Phan Huu Dat. 1977. "Vai tai lieu ve lang gom Bát Tràng truoc cach mang thang tam" (Certain documents on the pottery craft village of Bát Tràng before the August revolution). In Vien Su Hoc, *Nong thon Viet Nam trong lich su* (Rural Vietnam from a historical perspective), pp. 332–344. Hanoi: Khoa Hoc Xa Hoi.

Redding, S. Gordon. 1990. *The Spirit of Chinese Capitalism*. Berlin: Walter de Gruyter.

Rohlen, Thomas. 1974. *For Harmony and Strength: Japanese White-Collar Organization in Anthropological Perspective*. Berkeley: University of California Press.

Thanh The Vy. 1961. *Ngoai thuong Viet Nam hoi the ky XVII, XVII va dau XIX* (The external trade of Vietnam in the seventeenth, eighteenth, and early nineteenth centuries). Hanoi: Nha Xuat Ban Su Hoc.

Tran Trong Kim. 1964. *Viet Nam su luoc* (A brief history of Vietnam). Saigon: Khai Tri.

Vedrenne, Bernard. 1939. "Les poteries de Mon-cay." *Bulletin Économique de l'In-dochine* 37:939–960.

Vietnam Centre for Women's Studies. 1991. *So lieu chon loc ve phu nu Viet Nam* (Selected indicators on women's status in Vietnam). Hanoi: Nha Xuat Ban Thong Ke.

Vietnam General Office of Statistics and Ministry of Agriculture Institute of Planning. 1991. *So lieu nong nghiep Viet Nam 35 nam (1956–1990)* (Vietnamese agricultural data for thirty-five years [1956–1990]). Hanoi: Thong Ke.

Vietnam Institute of Labour and Social Affairs. 1993. *Doanh nghiep nho o Viet Nam* (Small enterprises in Vietnam). Hanoi: Nha Xuat Ban Khoa Hoc Va Ky Thuat.

Vietnam 1989 Population Census. 1991. *Ket qua dieu tra toan dien* (Completed census results). Hanoi: Central Census Steering Committee.

Vietnam Quoc su quan trieu Nguyen. 1992. *Dai Nam nhat thong chi* (The general geography of Dai Nam), vol. 4. Translated into modern Vietnamese by Pham Trong Diem and edited by Dao Duy Anh. Hue: Thuan Hoa.

Volker, T. 1954. *Porcelain and the Dutch East India Company.* Leiden: E.J. Brill.

Vu Qúy Vy. 1980. "La fabrique de céramique de Bát Tràng." *Études Vietnamiennes* 62:136–150.

Walder, Andrew. 1986. *Communist Neo-traditionalism: Work and Authority in Chinese Industry.* Berkeley: University of California Press.

Weber, Max. 1958. *Religion of China.* New York: Macmillan.

About the Book and Editor

One of the most remarkable developments of our time has been the growth of capitalist enterprise among overseas Chinese and Southeast Asians. *Market Cultures* examines this event not in terms of formal models and faceless abstractions but in light of the institutions through which local people give meaning and moral value to business enterprise. The chapters show that some Chinese and Southeast Asians have welcomed new forms of enterprise and consumption, but others regard both with strong ethical reservations. Eschewing talk of a uniform Asian "miracle," the authors argue that Chinese and Southeast Asian societies had cultural precedents for and against market capitalism, reflecting subcultural heritages of religion, ethnicity, gender, and class.

The case studies illustrate the deeply embedded nature of market institutions and reveal a moral and organizational variety unacknowledged in most analyses of modern capitalism. Rather than a unitary Confucian perspective on capitalism, contributors show that modern Chinese tradition has been interpreted in strikingly different ways by men and women, elites and masses, the wealthy and the poor. Avoiding stereotypes of "Asian values," the volume's chapters on China, Taiwan, Vietnam, the Philippines, Malaysia, Indonesia, and Singapore portray local worlds deeply—but differentially—engaged with market capitalism.

Addressing one of the great social transformations of our time, *Market Cultures* will be of interest to anthropologists, sociologists, political economists, and students of Asian history and culture as well as those concerned with the economic ascent of modern Asia and its implications for our world.

Robert W. Hefner is professor of anthropology and associate director at the Institute for the Study of Economic Culture at Boston University.

About the Contributors

Jennifer Alexander is an Australian Research Council fellow based in the Department of Anthropology at the University of Sydney. She is the author of *Trade, Traders, and Trading in Java* and has written extensively on the political economy of Java and Sarawak.

Dru C. Gladney is senior research fellow at the East-West Center and Professor of Asian Studies at the University of Hawaii at Manoa. His recent publications include *Muslim Chinese: Ethnic Nationalism in the People's Republic* and *Dislocating China: Muslims, Minorities, and Other Subaltern Subjects.*

Gary G. Hamilton is professor of sociology at the Jackson School of International Relations, the University of Washington, and the author of numerous works on society and business in East Asia, including *Business Networks and Economic Development in East and Southeast Asia.*

Hy van Luong is professor of anthropology at the University of Toronto. He is the author of *Discursive Practices and Linguistic Meanings: The Vietnamese System of Person Reference, Revolution in the Village: Tradition and Transformation in North Vietnam, 1925–1988*, and numerous articles on language, social structure, and political economy in modern Vietnam.

Jamie Mackie is professor emeritus in the Department of Economics, Research School of Pacific and Asian Studies, the Australian National University, and the author of numerous books and articles on politics, economics, and the Chinese in Southeast Asia.

Shaun Kingsley Malarney is assistant professor of cultural anthropology at the International Christian University in Tokyo. He is currently completing a book entitled *In Socialism's Wake: Reconstructing Culture and Ritual in Northern Viet Nam.*

Tania Murray Li is associate professor in the Department of Sociology and Social Anthropology at Dalhousie University in Halifax, Nova Scotia. She writes on issues of culture, economy, and development in Southeast Asia and is the author of, among other works, *Malays in Singapore.*

Michael G. Peletz is professor of anthropology and W.S. Schupf Professor of Far Eastern Studies at Colgate College. His most recent books include *Reason and Passion: Representations of Gender in a Malay Society* and (with A. Ong) *Bewitching Women, Pious Men: Gender and Body Politics in Southeast Asia.*

David L. Szanton is executive director of the Program in International and Area Studies, University of California–Berkeley. He is currently completing a book on the social transformation of the town briefly described in his chapter in this volume.

Robert P. Weller is senior research associate at the Institute for the Study of Economic Culture and associate professor in the Department of Anthropology, Boston University. His works include *Resistance, Chaos, and Control in China: Taiping Rebels, Taiwanese Ghosts, and Tiananmen* and *Unities and Diversities in Chinese Religion.*

Index